AICT 2018

The Fourteenth Advanced International Conference on Telecommunications

July 22 - 26, 2018

Barcelona, Spain

AICT 2018 Editors

Ustijana Rechkoska-Shikoska, Uversity for Information Science & Technology "St. Paul the Apostle", Republic of Macedonia

Manal Assaad, Scientific Research Associate, The University of Applied Sciences Emden-Leer, Emden, Germany

Printed from e-media with permission by:

Curran Associates, Inc.
57 Morehouse Lane
Red Hook, NY 12571

Some format issues inherent in the e-media version may also appear in this print version.

Printed by Curran Associates, Inc. (2018)

International Academy, Research, and Industry Association (IARIA)
412 Derby Way
Wilmington, DE 19810

Phone: (408) 893-6407
Fax: (408) 527-6351

petre@iaria.org

Additional copies of this publication are available from:

Curran Associates, Inc.
57 Morehouse Lane
Red Hook, NY 12571 USA
Phone: 845-758-0400
Fax: 845-758-2633
Email: curran@proceedings.com
Web: www.proceedings.com

Table of Contents

AICT 2018

Foreword

The Fourteenth Advanced International Conference on Telecommunications (AICT 2018), held between July 22 - 26, 2018- Barcelona, Spain, covered a variety of challenging telecommunication topics ranging from background fields like signals, traffic, coding, communication basics up to large communication systems and networks, fixed, mobile and integrated, etc. Applications, services, system and network management issues also received significant attention.

The spectrum of 21st Century telecommunications is marked by the arrival of new business models, new platforms, new architectures and new customer profiles. Next generation networks, IP multimedia systems, IPTV, and converging network and services are new telecommunications paradigms. Technology achievements in terms of co-existence of IPv4 and IPv6, multiple access technologies, IP-MPLS network design driven methods, multicast and high speed require innovative approaches to design and develop large scale telecommunications networks.

Mobile and wireless communications add profit to large spectrum of technologies and services. We witness the evolution 2G, 2.5G, 3G and beyond, personal communications, cellular and ad hoc networks, as well as multimedia communications.

Web Services add a new dimension to telecommunications, where aspects of speed, security, trust, performance, resilience, and robustness are particularly salient. This requires new service delivery platforms, intelligent network theory, new telecommunications software tools, new communications protocols and standards.

We are witnessing many technological paradigm shifts imposed by the complexity induced by the notions of fully shared resources, cooperative work, and resource availability. P2P, GRID, Clusters, Web Services, Delay Tolerant Networks, Service/Resource identification and localization illustrate aspects where some components and/or services expose features that are neither stable nor fully guaranteed. Examples of technologies exposing similar behavior are WiFi, WiMax, WideBand, UWB, ZigBee, MBWA and others.

Management aspects related to autonomic and adaptive management includes the entire arsenal of self-ilities. Autonomic Computing, On-Demand Networks and Utility Computing together with Adaptive Management and Self-Management Applications collocating with classical networks management represent other categories of behavior dealing with the paradigm of partial and intermittent resources.

We take here the opportunity to warmly thank all the members of the AICT 2018 Technical Program Committee, as well as the numerous reviewers. The creation of such a broad and high quality conference program would not have been possible without their involvement. We also kindly thank all the authors who dedicated much of their time and efforts to contribute to AICT 2018. We truly believe that, thanks to all these efforts, the final conference program consisted of top quality contributions.

Also, this event could not have been a reality without the support of many individuals, organizations, and sponsors. We are grateful to the members of the AICT 2018 organizing committee for their help in handling the logistics and for their work to make this professional meeting a success.

We hope that AICT 2018 was a successful international forum for the exchange of ideas and results between academia and industry and for the promotion of progress in the field of telecommunications.

We are convinced that the participants found the event useful and communications very open. We hope that Barcelona provided a pleasant environment during the conference and everyone saved some time to enjoy the charm of the city.

AICT 2018 Chairs:

AICT Steering Committee
Kevin Daimi, University of Detroit Mercy, USA
Eugen Borcoci, University "Politehnica" of Bucharest (UPB), Romania
Carlos Becker Westphall, Federal University of Santa Catarina, Brazil
Tulin Atmaca, Telecom SudParis, France
Mariusz Głąbowski, Poznan University of Technology, Poland
Mario Freire, University of Beira Interior, Portugal
Ioannis Moscholios, University of Peloponnese, Greece
Masayuki Murata, Osaka University Suita, Japan
Wenzhong Li, Nanjing University, China
Ali Houssein Harmouch, Lebanese University, Lebanon

AICT Publicity Chair
Ustijana Rechkoska-Shikoska, University for Information Science and Technology "St. Paul the Apostle" - Ohrid, Republic of Macedonia

AICT Industry/Research Advisory Committee
Mayank Raj, IBM, USA
Sergei Semenov, Huawei Technologies, Lund, Sweden
Dragana Krstic, University of Niš, Serbia
György Kalman, Norwegian University of Science and Technology, Norway
Seema Garg, Nokia, India
Runxin Wang, Vmware, Ireland
Sungsoo Choi, Korea Electrotechnology Research Institute (KERI), South Korea
Motoyoshi Sekiya, Fujitsu Laboratories Limited, Japan

AICT 2018

COMMITTEE

AICT Steering Committee

Kevin Daimi, University of Detroit Mercy, USA
Eugen Borcoci, University "Politehnica" of Bucharest (UPB), Romania
Carlos Becker Westphall, Federal University of Santa Catarina, Brazil
Tulin Atmaca, Telecom SudParis, France
Mariusz Głąbowski, Poznan University of Technology, Poland
Mario Freire, University of Beira Interior, Portugal
Ioannis Moscholios, University of Peloponnese, Greece
Masayuki Murata, Osaka University Suita, Japan
Wenzhong Li, Nanjing University, China
Ali Houssein Harmouch, Lebanese University, Lebanon

AICT Publicity Chair

Ustijana Rechkoska-Shikoska, University for Information Science and Technology "St. Paul the Apostle" - Ohrid, Republic of Macedonia

AICT Industry/Research Advisory Committee

Mayank Raj, IBM, USA
Sergei Semenov, Huawei Technologies, Lund, Sweden
Dragana Krstic, University of Niš, Serbia
György Kalman, Norwegian University of Science and Technology, Norway
Seema Garg, Nokia, India
Runxin Wang, Vmware, Ireland
Sungsoo Choi, Korea Electrotechnology Research Institute (KERI), South Korea
Motoyoshi Sekiya, Fujitsu Laboratories Limited, Japan

AICT 2018 Technical Program Committee

Ghulam Abbas, GIK Institute of Engineering Sciences and Technology, Pakistan
Iwan Adhicandra, University of Sydney, Australia
Michele Albano, University of Pisa, Italy
Petre Anghelescu, University of Pitesti, Romania
Kamran Arshad, Ajman University, UAE
Manal Assaad, University of Applied Sciences Emden/Leer, Germany
Tulin Atmaca, Telecom SudParis, France
Ilija Basicevic, University of Novi Sad, Serbia
Carlos Becker Westphall, Federal University of Santa Catarina, Brazil
Dhafer Ben Arbia, Qatar Mobility Innovations Center, Qatar
Ilham Benyahia, Université du Québec en Outaouais (UQO), Canada
Stefano Berretti, University of Firenze, Italy

Josip Juraj Strossmayer University in Osijek, Croatia
Mariusz Zal, Poznan University of Technology, Poland
Martin Zimmermann, Lucerne University of Applied Sciences and Arts, Switzerland
Piotr Zwierzykowski, Poznan University of Technology, Poland

Copyright Information

A Modeling Suggestion for Predicting Damage of Complex Disasters About Vector-born Disease

Byung-Hoon Lee
Chung-buk national university
Cheongju, South Korea
Email: qud7942@naver.com

Byung-Jin Lee
Chung-buk national university
Email: byung2487@naver.com

Seung-Hee Oh
Electronics and Telecommunications Research Institute
Email: seunghee@etri.re.kr

Yong-Tea Lee
Electronics and Telecommunications Research Institute
Email: ytlee@etri.re.kr

Kyung-Seok Kim
Chung-buk national university
Email: kseokkim@cbnu.ac.kr

***Abstract*— This paper proposes to model the damage estimates for complex hazards caused by natural disasters. Although a single disaster system is currently in place for both natural and social disasters, the system for complex disasters is still in development. Complex disasters can be classified into different types, depending on the type of disaster. A study was conducted on the diseases caused by floods among complex disasters. Research methods were examined to suggest a complex disaster prediction model in conjunction with the existing natural disaster prediction model developed, and appropriate modeling methods were proposed estimating the infection rate of the disease. This paper will help build a complex disaster prediction system.**

Keywords-Natural disaster; Social disaster; Complex disaster; Prediction; vector-borne disease; Modeling.

I. INTRODUCTION

Property damage and casualties caused by natural disasters such as flood and earthquake have been an issue for a very long time. Several countries carried out studies to minimize the damage caused by disasters and have developed methods to calculate the expected damage and extent of occurrence.

However, this natural disaster can lead to complex disasters where various kinds of disasters occur at the same time. A single disaster means that only one disaster occurs, such as a flood or earthquake. A complex disaster is a disaster made out of single disasters that occur one after the other. In order to solve these complex disaster problems, we selected a flood and vector- borne disease disaster that can predict the extent of the damage by each single disaster calculation model.

In this paper, we calculated the possibility of infection of vector-borne diseases depending on the magnitude of the flood, which represents the spread of vector diseases. It also showed the extent of the damage expected as a result of the occurrence of the vector-borne disease.

II. ANALYSIS OF EXISTING DISASTER PREDICTION SYSTEM

We analyzed the flood damage prediction system and the vector diffusion prediction system to understand the information of the existing system related to the prevention and prediction of disaster damage. The Extreme Programming-Stormwater & Wastewater Management Model (XP-SWMM) system was selected as the flood damage prediction system and the Spatio-Temporal Epidemiological Modeler (STEM) system was selected as the vector diffusion prediction system. Each system is primarily used to identify the spread of floods and disease.

In order to run XP-SWMM and STEM systems, data must be entered directly by the user. In XP-SWMM system, the user must directly input the location information of the area and the rainfall data of the corresponding area [1]. In STEM system, disease information and data on local populations and transport systems should be entered in advance. When a disease occurs, the user must enter data about the location and information about the disease. [2].

III. COMPLEX DISASTER LINKAGE PLAN THROUGH VECTOR-BORNE DISEASE

XP-SWMM and STEM can be analyzed for floods and diseases, but they cannot be utilized in the event of a disaster in which both occur in combination. Therefore, a linkage plan about complex disasters is needed.

A. A modeling plan for complex disaster damage prediction

The rate of disease incidence caused by disasters is applied to the prediction model of social disaster, which indicates the extent of damage to the final complex disaster. To apply infection rate data of vector-borne disease to the STEM, a social disaster prediction model, the McDonald-Ross method should be applied, which is a method for analyzing the spread of the disease. The McDonald-Ross method is structured as shown in Figure 1.

h is the total population, h_s is the susceptible person, h_i is the infected person, h_r the recovered person, h_u the death rate, m_s the susceptible mosquito, m_i the infected mosquito, m_u the proportion of the dead mosquito, b the bite rate, h_b is the probability of infection from mosquitoes to humans, m_b is the probability of mosquito infection in humans, and b_y is the rate of recovery [3].

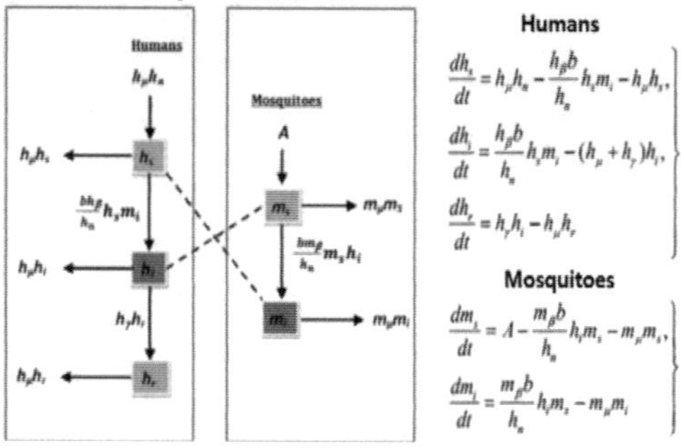

Figure 1. Structure of McDonald-Ross method

B. *Calculation method of infectious disease rate*

In order to calculate the infection rate to be applied to the McDonald-Ross method, the probability of mosquito occurrence in the floodplain when the flood occurred was calculated and then the disease infection rate was calculated.

First, if a flood occurred and a certain amount of time passed, we check for the existence of mosquitoes in the floodplain and calculate the number of bites per person according to the number of mosquitoes in the area. Next, we need to calculate the rate of infection of the disease in unit area using the number of bites per person.

The probability of mosquito occurrence is calculated by the number of mosquito species and the number of occurrences according to the flooded area. To determine if mosquitoes are present in the flooded area, a mosquito existence discrimination formula based on the Indices of Local Wetness (ILW) is applied. ILW represents a wetting index according to a water level threshold within a certain range. To represent the ILW value, the area to be measured is divided into the number of areas to be calculated.

The procedure for calculating ILW values is as follows. Divide the area of 10 square meters into 576 squares and set the flood threshold to 0.5 m. Calculate a value of 1 if the value of inundation in the flooded area is greater than the flood threshold value. Otherwise, calculate a value of zero. Then, add up the calculated values for each block to calculate the ILW value. Based on the calculated ILW value, the probability of occurrence of mosquitoes in the area to be measured is calculated [4].

The number of bites per unit area can be calculated from the mosquito incidence calculated and the number of mosquito populations when the mosquito occurs. The number of bites per person is calculated by dividing the number of mosquitoes per unit area by the number of people per unit area as shown in (1), then multiplying Human Blood Index (HBI) which is the probability of a person being bitten by a mosquito. The probability of HBI in this paper is 0.008% [5].

$$\text{Bites per person} = \frac{\textit{Mosquitoes per unit area}}{\textit{People per unit area}} \times HBI. \quad (1)$$

The number of bites per person can be used to calculate the infection rate of the vectors. The rate of infection can be calculated at (2) and the rate of infection can be calculated using the number of m of mosquito bites per person and the rate of transmission of mosquitoes r [6]. In case of mosquito transmission rate, the statistical value specified by each country can be applied. For example, in the United States, it is assumed that the disease occurred when the transmission rate of mosquitoes was more than 0.1 percent.

$$\mathrm{P} = 1 - e^{-mr}. \quad (2)$$

IV. SIMULATION RESULT AND CONCLUSION

In the results of the natural disaster module XP-SWMM, the flood range and the inundation data are transferred to the input data from the disease connection module. Connection modules calculate the rate of infection, according to the amount of mosquitoes generated by the input data and provide it as input data for social disasters.

The output data of the link module are input to the social disaster module STEM to calculate the main diffusion path according to the type of the disease type, and finally, the spread range of the disease is calculated. Assuming that sufficient time has elapsed since the flood, we calculate ILW data and mosquitoes occurrence in Region A. If mosquito existence is detected, the infection rate of the disease can be calculated and the disease spread path can be confirmed as shown in Figure 2.

Figure 2. Examples of spread of Vector-borne disease by mosquitoes

In this paper, a study was conducted to integrate each analysis model of flood and disease. We proposed a connection method to integrate existing analytical models into a single model. We derived the expected diffusion result, according to the data value calculation. If we continue this study, it will be easier to identify and respond to the extent of damage about various complex disasters. If the research continues, we will eventually be able to integrate the various disaster analysis models into one.

ACKNOWLEDGMENT

This research was supported by a grant (2017-MOIS31-001) from Fundamental Technology Development Program for Extreme Disaster Response funded by Korean Ministry of Interior and Safety (MOIS).

REFERENCES

[1] Phillips, B. C., Yu, S., Thompson, G. R., and De Silva, N. "1D and 2D modelling of urban drainage systems using XP-SWMM and TUFLOW." 10th International Conference on Urban Drainage. Denmark Copenhagen, 2005.

[2] Ford, D.A., Kaufman, J.H., and Eiron, I. "An extensible spatial and temporal epidemiological modelling system." International Journal of Health Geographics 5.1 , 2006.

[3] Phaijoo, G. R., and Gurung, D. B. "Mathematical study of biting rates of mosquitoes in transmission of dengue disease." Journal of Science. Engineering and Technology 11, 2015, pp.25-33.

[4] Shaman, J., Stieglitz, M., Stark, C., Le Blancq, S., and Cane, M. "Using a dynamic hydrology model to predict mosquito abundances in flood and swamp water." Emerging infectious diseases 8.1, 2002.

[5] Lee, H. I., Lee, J. S., Shin, E. H., Lee, W. J., Kim, Y. Y., and Lee, K. R.. "Malaria transmission potential by anopheles sinensis in the republic of korea", The Korean Journal of Parasitology Vol. 39, No. 2, 1-10, June 2001.

[6] Gu, W., Unnasch, T. R., Katholi, C. R., Lampman, R., and Novak, R. J. "Fundamental issues in mosquito surveillance for arboviral transmission." Transactions of the Royal Society of Tropical Medicine and Hygiene 102.8, 2008, pp.817-822.

Teaching Workbench for Channel Emulation Attenuation

Debora Meyhofer Ferreira
Decom - Unicamp Campinas, Brazil
De.ferreira@gmail.com
Pedro Chaves - Dsif - Unicamp Campinas, Brazil
pchaves@dsif.fee.unicamp.br
Eduardo Lima - Instituto Eldorado
eduardo.lima@eldorado.org.br

Omar Carvalho Branquinho
Leonardo Delforno
Engenharia Elétrica
PUCCamp
Campinas, Brazil
Omar.branquinho@gmail.com
l_delforno@hotmail.com

***Abstract* — With the increasing use of the Internet of Things, wireless solutions like Low Power Wide Area Networks will be in demand. The behavior of the radio link constitutes a major challenge for these solutions. It dictates the quality of the service and is dependent on the communication channel that in turn is correlated to the environmental conditions where the network is to be installed. Professionals in this area need to understand the propagation mechanisms to plan, implement and manage these networks. The learning of these principles can be arduous if using real radio links in open areas, due to the impossibility to control the propagation mechanisms. This paper presents the first results of a low-cost channel emulation workbench to be used in classrooms for the learning of propagation principles in different scenarios. The proposal is to emulate flat fading channel behaviors and thus facilitating the learning of propagation principles and the effects in link quality with different channel models, like Friis and Log-Distance. The testing and benchmarking of the workbench was done with the use of an open source wireless sensor network to measure the radio signal intensity and thus verify the reproduction of the flat fading model by the workbench. The initial results demonstrate the usefulness of this workbench as it incorporates an automatic setup that permits the execution of different propagation experiments in the classroom.**

Keywords* – *LPWAN; IoT; Network; WSN; channel emulation.

I. INTRODUCTION

The number of devices connected to the Internet is growing with the perspective of yearly increases [1]. This will generate a large amount of data that will need to be processed in order to control industrial processes or simply assure more comfort or safety, such as residential automation and applications in smart cities.

The Low Power Wide Area Networks (LPWAN) technologies are a solution. Several technologies have been proposed to meet different Internet of Things (IoT) scenarios such as Lora [2] and SigFox [3]. The knowledge of how LPWAN works is fundamental for the effective implementation of IoT, especially the communication channel since there is no point in focusing on the storage of data if there is no guarantee of communication between nodes.

To assure connectivity, it is necessary to invest in the operation of LPWAN, monitoring the behavior of the channel.

There are many studies about channel effects focusing on the higher layers of the protocol as in [4], where there is a concern regarding the teaching of LPWAN, focusing on network configuration, data set and software engineering. In [5] solutions are proposed only for routing and medium access through a simulation model.

There is also some use of LPWAN to teach other subjects [6] and [7] despite IoT and data communication and there are some authors who use simulation to explain the communication channel, as in [8] and [9].

The teaching of wireless networks stumble on the complexity of assembling experiments that allow the reproduction of the phenomena found in radio frequency (RF) connections. In laboratory it would be difficult, for example, to create free space attenuation scenarios or environment effects by varying the loss with physical obstacles. There are some commercial channel emulators like Propsim Channel Emulator from Keysigth [10], however these are quite complex to operate and expensive to acquire, rendering them unsuitable for use in undergraduate classes.

This article presents a low-cost strategy for teaching the particularities of wireless communications, simulating the disturbances suffered by the RF signal, as it is essential to understand how the system reacts to the channel. To create the conditions for the learning and understanding of these processes, a radio channel emulator is proposed. With this strategy, it is possible to imprint, on the radio signal, the characteristic signal fluctuations while generating statistical representations. The emulator reproduces propagation phenomena, such as free space attenuation, log-normal, Rayleigh, etc. With this capability, it is possible to present communication concepts in real conditions, with experiments that can be evaluated in laboratory.

The emulation is accomplished using software-controlled attenuators, connected to real wired networks using a shielded camera, so that it is possible to evaluate the channel effect in the communication with regard to the wireless network physical layer [11]. Parameters, such as modulation, data rate, power, frequency offset, etc. can then be controlled and explored.

Section II presents a review of the literature on propagation in Free Space and Log Distance models. Section III presents the emulation table, while Section IV presents the materials used. Section V shows the test methods and emulations with the results in Section VI and conclusions in Section VII.

II. FREE SPACE AND LOG DISTANCE MODELS

The Received Signal Strength Indication (RSSI) decreases over the distance on any transmission medium. In wireless systems this attenuation can be quite strong due to large distances and types of environment in which the system is operating.

Considering a simple network with two nodes, for the monitoring of IoT devices, as shown in Figure 1. It is necessary to think about the channel effect over the system to appropriately ensure the communication's quality between the nodes.

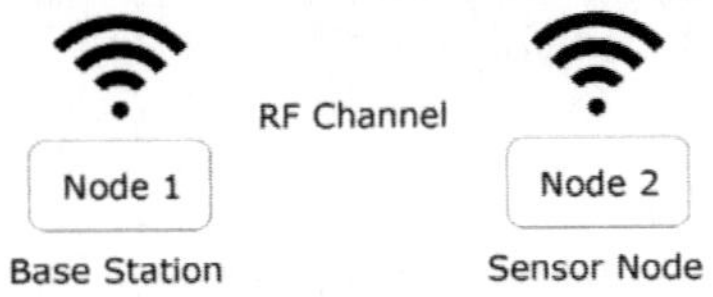

Fig 1: Nodes connectivity

The models used to plan the communication channels, which are still the subject of research, are usually deterministic or statistical [12]. Regarding the deterministic models, it is important to consider the exact physical characteristics of the propagation medium. In this paper we will consider the Free Space and the Log Distance models.

The Free Space model considers the transmission power (PTX), the gains on the transmission (GTX) and the reception (GRX) antennas, the distance between nodes and the operating frequency [3]:

$$P_{rx} = P_{tx} + G_{tx} + G_{rx} - 10\log(\frac{4\pi d}{\lambda})^2 \quad (1)$$

This expression considers as attenuation only the distance between nodes and the frequency of operation, which can be observed in Figure 2:

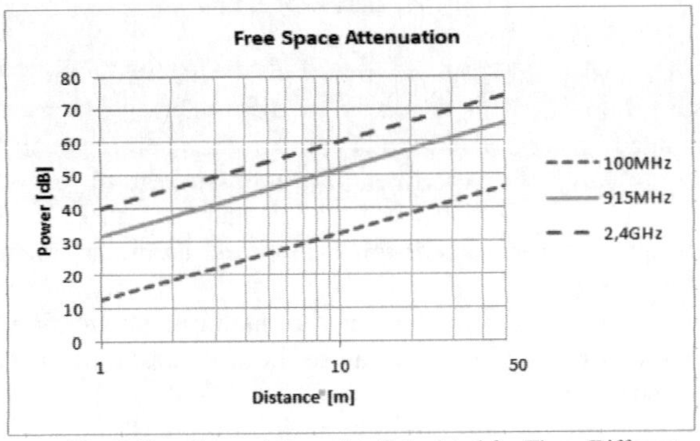

Fig. 2: Free Space Attenuation Calculated for Three Different Frequencies

The Log Distance model considers the Path Loss Attenuation factor (β) that characterizes the different types of environments, according to Table 1:

TABLE I: Path loss β [12]

Environment	Path Loss β
Free Space	2
Rural (plane)	3
Suburban (plane)	4
Urban (high buildings)	4.5

This model assumes that the $P_{RX(d)}$, at a distance d, can be calculated by considering β and a reference $P_{RX(d0)}$ at a point close to the transmitter (with Free Space attenuation), according to Figure 3 [13].

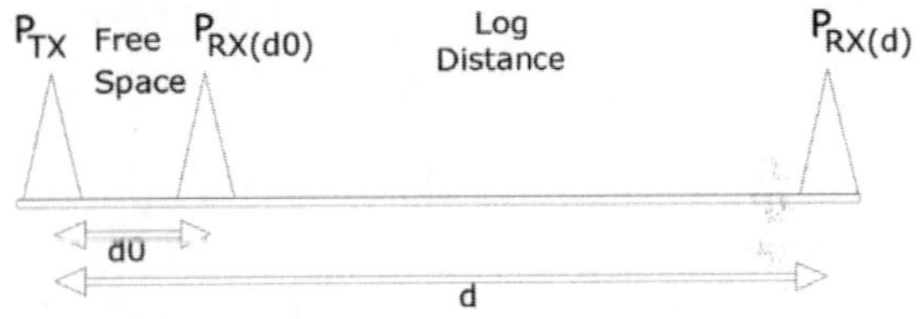

Fig. 3: Log Distance Model

$$P_{RX}(d) = P_{RX}(d_0) - 10\beta\log\left(\frac{d}{d_0}\right) \quad (2)$$

The calculations based on the Log Distance model, for 3 different values of β (Figure 4), consider that to know the total attenuation of the system, it is necessary to add the attenuation of the Free Space, according to (2):

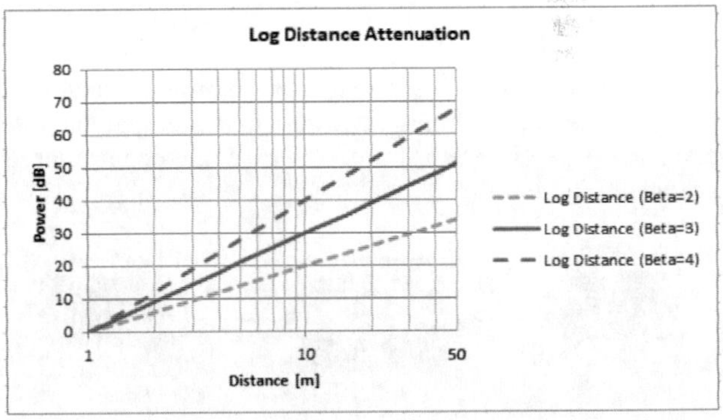

Fig. 4: Log Distance Attenuation Calculated

The Free Space Model predicts that the received power decays as the negative square root of the distance and the Log Distance increases the decay according to the propagation environment. Although they are simple and deterministic models, they are the base for the characterization of the workbench and the development of other statistical models.

III. EMULATION WORKBENCH

According to [14], both simulated experiments (virtual laboratories) and real remotely operated plants (remote laboratories), have recently been used more often. The advantage of remote laboratories resides in the fact that students can use real equipment that exist in several areas of engineering [15] [16].

The emulating workbench replicates a two-node LPWAN, showing what would happen to the propagation signal if those nodes were transmitting information through a RF channel (Figure 5), where the nodes are interconnected by an emulated RF channel.

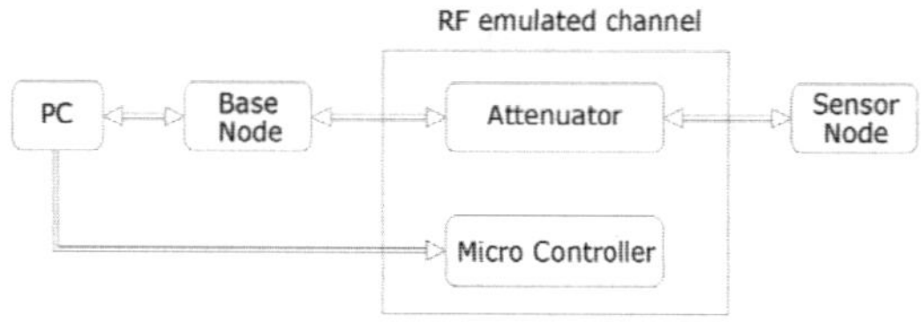

Fig. 5: Emulation Workbench Diagram

Only two nodes were used to demonstrate the workbench in this work, but the system allows the use of several nodes to emulate characteristics like routing techniques, for example.

IV. MATERIALS

Currently, there are many LPWAN technologies. Among these technologies, Radiuino [17] was chosen mainly because it is an open platform created specifically for LPWAN. It is based on the Arduino development environment (IDE).

i. Hardware

For the RF channel emulation, the base and the sensor were interconnected through a Mini-Circuits digital variable attenuator (ZSAT -31R5+) operated by a microcontroller as shown in Figure 6:

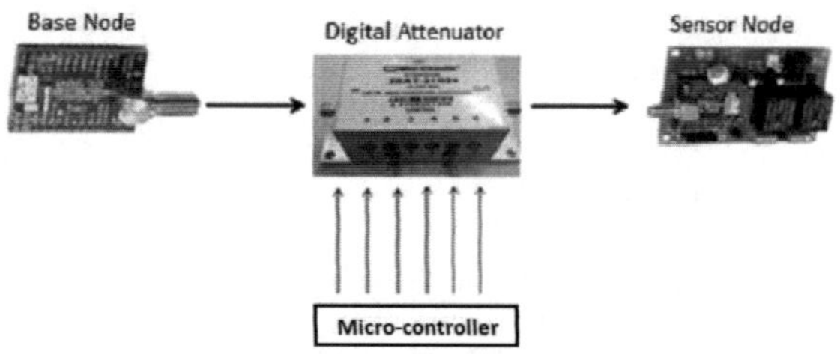

Fig. 6: Emulation Workbench Materials

ii. Firmware

The base and sensor node programming was done with the Arduino's Integrated Development Environment (IDE), the firmware was developed in C ++ and Radiuino-specific libraries [17].

iii. Software

The programs used to control the base node, as well as the sensor node and the digital attenuator were developed in Python.

V. METHODS AND RESULTS

The final test configuration included a PC-Base and a PC-Microcontroller connection made via a USB cable. The Base-Attenuator-Sensor connection was made through a coaxial cable, eliminating the antennas. The digital attenuator created the attenuation effect on the channel.

The computer sent the Arduino's 52-byte packet to the base via the USB, the base incremented the address identification (ID) and transmitted via emulated RF with the power previously programmed into the base firmware. For each packet sent, the attenuation value was changed. The sensor node received the packet from the base, measured the RSSI, verified the instructions regarding what should be done and returned the information to the base to be processed by the computer.

The digital variable attenuator of 31.5 dB was controlled by an Arduino. For each received packet, the attenuation was incremented to represent the attenuation in Free Space and Log Normal models with several values of β.

Figure 7 shows the graph for the RSSI on the primary vertical axis against the attenuation on the secondary vertical axis.

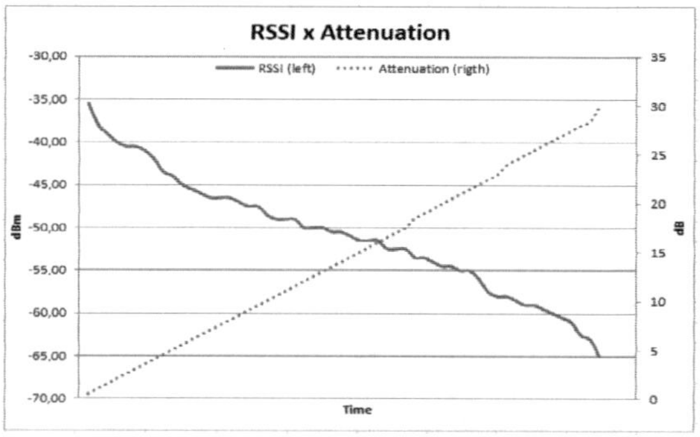

Fig. 7: Emulation Results

The attenuation ranged from 0 to 31.5dB, while the RSSI went from -35 dBm to nearly -67dBm. The time was also emulated to vary. The graphs confirm the usefulness of this setup to carry out experiments. It is possible to observe the expected inverse correlation between attenuation and intensity of the emulated signal, representing the attenuation in free space.

Figure 8 shows the emulated of path loss attenuation for different values of β according to the attenuation in the Log Distance model.

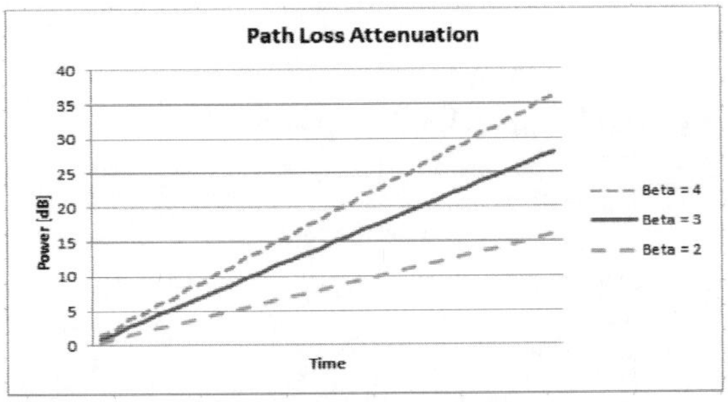

Fig. 8: Log Distance Emulation Results

The graph highlights the versatility the workbench lends to the task of varying the attenuation curve to reflect different environments.

Figure 9 presents the comparison between the emulated workbench and the calculated Free Space model, with the power on the primary vertical axis against the attenuation on the secondary vertical axis.

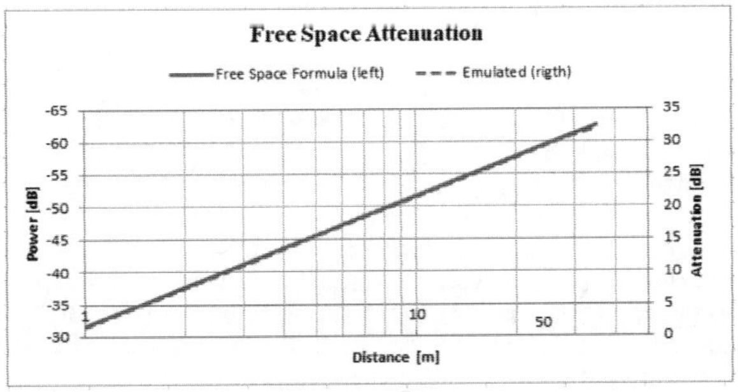

Fig 9: Emulated x Calculated Comparison

It is possible to verify that as the attenuation of the emulated system (continuous line) grows, the RSSI proportionally degrades, coinciding with the calculated values (dashed line), demonstrating the efficiency and accuracy of the workbench.

VI. CONCLUSION AND FUTURE WORKS

This paper presented an emulation workbench that can be used for testing LPWAN technologies and for the demonstration of how these technologies behave in an unstable and non-repeatable environment such as RF communication, using the Free Space and Log Distance models as examples.

Results from the workbench using Radiuino LPWAN technology demonstrate that a set up consisting of two interconnected nodes and a digital attenuator can emulate the characteristics of a real environment.

Teaching RF channel becomes much more effective with an emulated system that uses real IoT components. The workbench also allows the testing and comparison of other technologies for predetermined scenarios, making it easier to define the technologies to be used, since IoT technologies must be customized per application.

The great advantage of this type of emulation is the control over the attenuation imprinted on the channel. It can be used for the emulation of models like the propagation in free space, Log Distance or any other type of probabilistic distribution. As a future work, we propose to extend the emulation bench to cater for probabilistic models of channel propagation, such as Log Normal, Rayleigh and Rice. In addition, we also intend to use other LPWAN technologies to compare performance and efficiency, as well as to enable the emulation bench to be accessible remotely.

REFERENCES

[1] U. Raza, P. Kulkarni, and M. Sooriyabandara, "Low Power Wide Area Networks: An Overview," IEEE Commun. Surv. Tutorials, vol. 19, no. 2, pp. 855–873, 2017.

[2] Lora Alliance. [Online]. Available: https':/lora-alliance.org [Accessed: 03-Apr-2018]

[3] Sigfox [Online]. Available: https://www.sigfox.com/en [Accessed: 03-Apr-2018]

[4] E. Tanin, "Teaching Wireless Sensor Networks at the University of Melbourne," IEEE Distrib. Syst. Online, vol. 8, no. 6, pp. 3–3, Jun. 2007.

[5] G. Zhou, T. He, S. Krishnamurthy, and J. A. Stankovic, "Impact of radio irregularity on wireless sensor networks," in Proceedings of the 2nd international conference on Mobile systems, applications, and services - MobiSYS '04, 2004, p. 125.

[6] A. Lei, C.-U. Lei, N. Wong, and K. Lok Man, "Integration of a Wireless Sensor Network Project for Introductory Circuits and Systems Teaching," pp. 19–23, 2013.

[7] P. Lin, V. Provenzano, G. Palumbo, T. Gabb, and J. Telesman, "A Weblab For A Level And Temperature Control Plant ," Symp. A Q. J. Mod. Foreign Lit., pp. 243–253, 2010.

[8] A. Martinez-Sala, et al, "An accurate radio channel model for wireless sensor networks simulation," J. Commun. Networks, vol. 7, no. 4, pp. 401–407, Dec. 2005.

[9] R. G. [UNESP] Nespolo, "Sensor Deployment 3D para Redes de Sensores Sem Fio (RSSF)," Aug. 2016.

[10] Keysigth - Propsim Channel Emulator. [Online]. Available: http://www.mrc-gigacomp.com/pdfs/Keysight-Propsim-F8-Datasheet.pdf [Accessed: 03-Apr-2018]

[11] K. Pentikousis, "TCP in wired-cum-wireless environments," IEEE Commun. Surv. Tutorials, vol. 3, no. 4, pp. 2–14, 2000.

[12] S. Haykin and M. Moher, Modern Communication Systems. Porto Alegre, Brasil.: Bookman, 2008.

[13] T. S. Rappaport, Comunicações Sem Fio: Principios e Prática, 2nd ed. Pearson, 2009.

[14] J. Uhomoibhi, F. Ubwa, and I. Ibhuiyan, "Virtual and remote laboratory implementation in engineering education and research" in 2014 International Conference on Interactive Collaborative Learning (ICL), 2014, pp. 1095–1099.

[15] S. Lopez, A. Carpeno, and J. Arriaga, "Remote Laboratory eLab3D: A Complementary Resource in Engineering Education," IEEE Rev. Iberoam. Tecnol. del Aprendiz., vol. 10, no. 3, pp. 160–167, Aug. 2015.

[16] D. A. Miele, B. Potsaid, and J. T. Wen, "An Internet-based remote laboratory for control education," in Proceedings of the 2001 American Control Conference. (Cat. No.01CH37148), 2001, pp. 1151–1152 vol.2.

[17] "Radiuino." [Online]. Available: radiuino.cc. [Accessed: 03-Apr-2018].

SEC and Survival RSA Problem on EONs with Time-Varying Traffic

Der-Rong Din
Computer Science & Information Engineering
National Changhua University of Education
Changhua City, Taiwan, R. O. C.
deron@cc.ncue.edu.tw

***Abstract*—For serving *time-varying traffic* on an Elastic Optical Network (EON), the spectrum allocated for the connection request can be expanded or contracted to meet the traffic requirement. For the survival connection, both the primary and the backup lightpaths should be expanded/contracted at the same time. In this paper, the *Spectrum Expansion/ Contraction* (SEC) and Survival Routing and Spectrum Allocation (SRSA) problems on EONs with time-varying traffic for the dynamic case are studied. For each protecting scheme, two survival routing algorithms and the respective SEC operation are developed to solve it. These algorithms are examined through simulations and the results show that the proposed algorithms can achieve good results.**

Keywords- spectrum expansion/contraction; survival routing; routing and spectrum allocation; time-varying traffic.

I. INTRODUCTION

Elastic Optical Networks (EONs), which employs *Optical-Orthogonal Frequency Division Multiplexing* (O-OFDM) technology, have been proposed to increase the flexibility of optical networks. The spectrum of a link in EONs is divided into *Frequency Slots* (FSs) and the necessary amount of consecutive FSs are assigned to support the connection request. Besides, more efficient spectrum allocation is achieved in these networks [1]. Specifically, a BW-variable O-OFDM transponder can assign an appropriate number of FSs to serve a lightpath [1].

In an optical network, each connection can be transmitted by an optical channel, which consists of a *central frequency* (CF) and a *size*. The size of the channel is determined by the requested bit-rate, the modulation technique applied, the (fixed) slice width, and the Guard Band (GB) introduced to separate two spectrum adjacent connections, among others. Due to the *spectrum continuity constraint* [1], the *Routing and Spectrum Assignment* (RSA) problem has emerged as the essential problem for spectrum management on EONs. For a given connection request, the goal of the RSA problem is to find a lightpath on the network and assign the required FSs.

A. Time-Varying Traffic

Several *Spectrum Allocation* (SA) schemes that change the bandwidth dynamically have been studied in [2][3]. A general policy to allocate FSs to time-varying traffic was presented in [3]. For time-varying traffic demands on EONs, there are three SA schemes of different levels of elasticity [3]. The *elastic* scheme [3], both the assigned central frequency and the size can be subject to change by performing Spectrum Expansion/Contraction (SEC) in each time interval, is the most efficient method [2]. Recently, several SEC schemes have been considered and the EONs enable to expand/contract slot width of the channel [4]. Furthermore, future EONs will change slot width according to time-varying traffic by changing the number of FSs flexibility. Din et al., [5] studied the SEC problem for the multipath routing scheme for Routing, Modulation, and Spectrum Assignment (RMSA) on EONs was studied.

B. Survivable EONs

In the traditional *Wavelength Division Multiplexing* (WDM) networks, network survivability has been extensively studied; several various network protection techniques were proposed in [6]. The protection techniques can be divided into the categories of *Dedicated Path Protection* (DPP) and *Shared Backup Path Protection* (SBPP) [6]. Dedicated path protection means that there is dedicated backup capacity to protect primary capacity. In contrast, shared protection means that the protection capacity can be shared among multiple protection lightpaths as long as their corresponding primary lightpaths do not fail simultaneously. Because of capacity sharing, the shared protection scheme are generally more capacity efficient than the dedicated protection scheme [6].

For the case of static traffic demand on the EON, Klinkowski et al. [7] focused on the problem of RSA with DPP. Shen et al. [8] developed Integer Linear Programming (ILP) models for the SBPP on EONs. For the case of dynamic traffic demand, Shao et al. [9] studied the shared-path protection on EONs for RSA model. A heuristic algorithm was proposed to solve this problem. N. G. Anoh et al. [10] studied a hybrid protection scheme with shared and dedicated backup paths resources for the RMSA model.

C. Studied Problem

In this paper, the *Spectrum Expansion/Contraction* (SEC) and Survival Routing and Spectrum Allocation (SRSA) problem with time-varying traffic on EONs is studied. For a given EON and a sequence of survival connection requests, the goal is to add/delete/expand/contract (primary and backup) lightpaths and assigned suitable channels to the lightpaths to meet the traffic requirement of the survivable connection request such that the performance measure can be optimized. The RSA model is considered in this paper, that is, the transparent network only with single modulation format.

Two protecting schemes DPP and SBPP are considered in this article. When a new connection request arrived, the *Survival Path Routing Algorithm* (SPRA) is performed to find a pair of link-disjoint primary and backup lightpaths. If the required bandwidth cannot be allocated, then the connection request is blocked. Otherwise, these lightpaths are established, the required FSs of lightpaths are allocated. If the connection request is an adjusted request (that is, there exists a pair of primary and backup lightpaths with the same source and destination nodes), based on the selected SEC policy, the allocated FSs of the existing lightpath are adjusted.

In this article, the elastic allocation scheme is used, that is, both the CF and the size of the lightpath can be adjusted (expanded or contracted). If the bandwidth variation can be accommodated, then the adjusted connection is updated. Otherwise, the SPRA is performed to route the new connection (after the old lightpaths are torn down). According to literature analysis by the author, only the SEC problems for single path [3] and multipath [5] were studied. Based on the survey, there is no article considered the SEC problem for survivable routing.

II. Problem Definition

In the following, the assumptions, constraints, notations and the definitions of the studied problem are given.

A. Notations

- $G = (V, E)$: The physical topology of the network, where $V = \{v_1, v_2, ..., v_n\}$ and $E = \{e_1, e_2, ..., e_m\}$ is the set of nodes and links, respectively.
- $r = (s, d, B_{sd}, q)$: The connection request, where $s \in V$ and $d \in V$ is the source and destination node of the request, respectively. B_{sd} is the required bandwidth (Gb/s) of the lightpaths between nodes s and d, q ($0 \le q \le 1$) is the *protection level requirement* of the connection [11].
- B: The number of FSs provided with each link of the network. Assume that each spectrum slot occupies C_f GHz bandwidth.
- K: The number of shortest paths for each node-pair are pre-computed for finding routing path.
- P_{sd}: The set of candidate routing paths for node pair s-d.
- $b_l(j)$: The bit-mask $b_l(j)$ of the link $e_l \in E$ ($j = 1, 2, ..., B = 100$), is the status of the jth FS of the link e_l.
- If the jth FS of link e_l is occupied, then $b_l(j) = 1$; otherwise, $b_l(j)=0$.

When the link failure occurs on the primary path, the backup path can provide at least $q \times B_{sd}$ bandwidth. If $q = 0$, then there is no protection; $q = 1$ is *full protection* and 0< <1 is *partial protection*. If the request is supported by a single lightpath, the minimal required number of FSs of the primary lightpath (denoted as N_{sd}) can be computed by $N_{sd} = \lceil B_{sd}/C_f \rceil$ + GB, where C_f is the bandwidth (Gb/s) provided by each FS. The minimal required number of FSs of the backup lightpath (denoted as BN_{sd}) can be computed by $BN_{sd} = \lceil (q \times B_{sd})/C_f \rceil +$ GB.

B. Assumptions

The assumptions of the SEC problem for survivable routing on EONs are given as follows.

- For each link, there is a fiber connecting the end-nodes and signal can be transmitted bidirectional.
- All nodes in the network are equipped with *Bandwidth Variable Wavelength Cross-Connects* (BV-WXC) and *Bandwidth Variable Transceiver* (BVT).
- For simplicity, the numbers of FSs provided by links are all equal.
- A GB or guard subcarrier should be allocated between two lightpaths.
- The network is a 2-connected graph, only the single-edge failure case is considered.
- If the expansion is not possible, the current primary and backup paths are expanded as many numbers of FSs as possible.

Three constraints are considered in this paper, they are *spectrum continuity constraint, subcarrier consecutiveness constraint*, and *non-overlapping spectrum constraint.* Due to space limitation, the definition of these constraints can be found in [5].

III. Survival Routing and SEC for DPP Scheme

In DPP scheme, for each connection request $r = (s, d, B_{sd}, q)$, a pair of link-disjoint primary and backup paths is found. Where the bandwidth provided by the primary path and backup path is greater than or equal to B_{sd} and $q \times B_{sd}$ Gb/s, respectively. In this section, two algorithms are proposed to solve the DPP routing problem and then the SEC operations are developed to perform traffic updating.

A. Survival Path Routing Algorithm - DPP

In this subsection, the survival path routing algorithm for a new connection request for DPP scheme is developed. To find the routing paths of the request, two algorithms are proposed, they are *Dynamic Survival Path Routing Algorithm* (DSPRA) and *Semi-Dynamic Survival Path Routing Algorithm* (SDSPRA).

1) Dynamic Survival Path Routing Algorithm (DSPRA): In this subsection, the DSPRA is described. In DSPRA, for finding the primary path with N_{sd} FSs, the layered graphs LG^i, i= 1, 2, ..., B-N_{sd}+1 of the network are constructed according to the current status of the network and connection request. The i-th layer graph is denoted as LG^i (V^i, E^i), where $V^i = V$, $E^i = \{e_l | \Sigma_{j=i}^{i+Nsd-1} b_l(j)=0, e_l \in E\}$. On layered graph LG^i, if a path from s to d can be found, then there exists a path with N_{sd} FSs on G and it can serve as the primary path of the request. The K-shortest paths on LG^i are found as the candidate paths of the primary lightpaths. If the primary path can be found on LG^i, then the resources of primary lightpath are temporarily allocated and the Backup Path Finding Algorithm (BPFA) is performed to find the backup path of the request. If both the primary and backup lightpaths can be found, then the resources are allocated. Otherwise, another possible primary path on the same layered graph or on the different layered graph is selected, and then the backup lightpath is examined again. In the BPFA, first, the links passed by the primary lightpath are removed. Then, the layered graph approach is applied again to find the backup path. The details of the DSPRA and the BPFA are described in Figure 1 and Figure 2, respectively.

Algorithm 1 DSPRA

```
Input : G(V, E), request r = (s, d, B_sd, q);
Output : primary path and backup path of the request;
i = 1, P^i_sd = ∅
while (i ≤ B − N_sd + 1) do
    Construct the layered graph LG^i(V^i, E^i) of the network according
    to status of the network.
    Find the set P^i_sd of K-shortest paths on LG^i from s to d.
    if (P^i_sd ≠ ∅) then
        j = 1;
        while (j ≤ |P^i_sd|) do
            Select the j–th path in P^i_sd as the primary path p1.
            Temporarily allocate FSs for the path p1.
            Perform BPFA to find the backup path p2 of the request.
            if (p2 can be found) then
                Allocate FSs for the path p1 and p2, and return p1 and p2.
            end if
            Release all FSs allocated to p1.
            j = j + 1;
        end while
    end if
    i = i + 1;
end while
return BLOCK.
```

Figure 1. DSPRA.

Algorithm 2 Backup Path Finding Algorithm (BPFA)

```
Input : G(V, E), request r = (s, d, B_sd, q), primary path p1;
Output : backup path p2 of the request;

Remove links on primary path p1 from G to form a new graph
G'(V', E').
i = 1, BN_sd = ⌈(q × B_sd) / C_f⌉;
while (i ≤ B − BN_sd + 1) do
    {
    Construct the layered graph BLG^i(V^i, E^i) of the
    network G' according to status. Where V^i = V',
    E^i = {e_l | Σ_{j=i}^{i+BN_sd−1} b_l(j) = 0, e_l ∈ E'}.
    Find the shortest path p2 on BLG^i from s to d.
    if (p2 can be found) then
        return backup path p2.
    end if
    i = i + 1;
    }
end while
return false.
```

Figure 2. BPFA.

2) Semi-Dynamic Survival Path Routing Algorithm (SDSPRA): In this subsection, the SDSPRA was proposed. First, a set P_{sd} of candidate paths on $G(V, E)$ is found and paths in the P_{sd} are sorted increasingly according to the length of the path. Path in P_{sd} are examined in order. If the examined path can be allocated on the current network, then the primary lightpath is temporarily allocated and removed from the network, and then the BPFA (by using the layered graph approach) is performed to find the backup path of the request. The details of the Semi-Dynamic Survival Path Routing Algorithm are described in Figure 3.

B. SEC operation for DPP

For the survivable connection request, if the connection changed to $r = (s, d, B_{sd}^{new}, q^{new})$, the currently deployed (primary and backup) lightpaths should be adjusted to meet the bandwidth requirement. If B_{sd}^{new} is zero, the primary and backup lightpaths are deleted and the possessed resources are released. If q^{new} is zero, the backup lightpath can be deleted and the possessed resources can be released.

If $B_{sd}^{new} > (N_{sd}-1)\times C_f$ and $q^{new}\times B_{sd}^{new} > C_f\times(BN_{sd}-1)$, the bandwidth of primary and backup lightpaths should be increased, respectively. Two lightpaths can be expanded separately. Several cases should be considered and described as follows.

- Case 1: If both primary and backup lightpaths can be expanded successfully, then the expansion operation is performed to meet the requirement.
- Case 2: If the primary lightpath can be expanded but the backup lightpath cannot, then the primary lightpath is expanded in the first step, and then, the original backup path is removed and the BPFA is performed to find a new backup lightpath.
- Case 3: If the backup lightpath can be expanded but the primary lightpath cannot, then the backup lightpath is expanded in the first step. Then, the primary path is removed and a new primary lightpath, which is link-disjoint to the backup lightpath, is found by performing the BPFA.
- Case 4: If both primary and backup lightpaths cannot be expanded, then the primary and backup lightpaths are removed. Then, the SPRA is performed to find a pair of new primary and backup lightpaths.
- Case 5: If the backup (or primary) lightpath cannot be found in the previous Cases 2 and 3, then the primary (or backup) lightpath is removed in the first step. Then, the respective SPRA (SSPRA, DSPRA, and SDSPRA) is performed to find a pair of new primary and backup lightpaths for the request. If failed to find the pair of lightpaths, then the request would be blocked.

For the case with $B_{sd}^{new} > (N_{sd}-1)\times C_f$ or $q^{new}\times B_{sd}^{new} > C_f \times (BN_{sd}-1)$, the bandwidth of primary lightpath or backup lightpath should be increased separately. The expansion action is expanded first, and then the respective lightpath is re-found. If these two actions cannot be done, then the old lightpaths are deleted and then a pair of new lightpaths are found by performing the respective SPRA to route the request. In the contraction, it is worth noting that the actually provided bandwidth $N_{sd}\times C_f$ may be greater than the newly required bandwidth B_{sd}^{new}. The similar situation can be applied to the backup path. If $B_{sd}^{new}\leq(N_{sd}-1)\times C_f$ and $q^{new}\times B_{sd}^{new}<(BN_{sd}-1)\times C_f$, then the bandwidth of the primary and backup path should be contracted, respectively. In the contraction, the higher-index FS allocated to the selected path will be contracted first.

Algorithm 3 SDSPRA

```
Input : G(V, E), request r = (s, d, B_sd, q), P_sd: candidate set of
paths;
Output : primary path and backup path of the request;
while (P_sd ≠ ∅) do
    Select and remove a path p1 from P_sd.
    if (p1 can be allocate on network with required N_sd FSs) then
        Temporarily allocate FSs for the path p1.
        Perform BPFA to find the backup path p2 of the request.
        if (p2 can be found) then
            Allocate FSs for the path p1 and p2, and return p1 and p2.
        end if
        Release all FSs allocated to p1.
    end if
end while
return BLOCK.
```

Figure 3. SDSPRA.

IV. SURVIVAL ROUTING AND SEC FOR SBPP SCHEME

In this section, the SBPP scheme is used. In SBPP scheme, two backup lightpaths, which pass through same fiber (or path), can share the spectrum resource on it, if their primary lightpaths are link-disjoint. In this section, two survival path routing algorithms and the SEC operations are developed to solve the problem.

A. SSPRA-SBPP

In this subsection, for SBPP scheme, two algorithms static-SPRA-SBPP (SSPRA-SBPP) and dynamic-SPRA-SBPP (DSPRA-SBPP) are proposed to solve this problem. It is worth noting that these algorithms used the same algorithm to find the backup path of the primary lightpath.

1) SSPRA-SBPP: In SSPRA-SBPP, a set P_{sd} of pre-computed paths are found as the candidate set of primary paths. All paths are sorted in increasing order according to the length of the paths. Then, a path in P_{sd} is selected and examined sequentially as the primary path. If the selected path can be successful allocated, then the *Shared Backup Path Protecting Algorithm* (SBPPA) is performed to find the backup path. The details of the SSPRA-SBPP are described in Figure 4.

To describe the backup path-finding process, several notations used in the algorithm are listed as follows. The number of required FSs of the backup path is equal to $BN_{sd} = \lceil q \times B_{sd}/C_f \rceil$. Let c_l be the basic cost of link $e_l \in E$, which is set to 1 initially. The value of c'_l is determined by the current network state. Let P_b be the set of existing backup paths whose respective primary paths are link-disjoint to the primary path p_1. It is worth noting that the primary and backup paths can use different starting indices of FSs.

To find the backup path with the great resource sharing of the primary path on layered graph BLG^i, the cost of links is dynamically adjusted according to the formula (1), and then the Dijkstra's algorithm is used to find a link-disjoint backup path with the minimum cost on BLG^i.

$$c'_l = \begin{cases} +\infty, & \text{if } e_l \in p_1 \\ c_l - \frac{B_{li}}{BN_{sd}}, & \text{if } ((e_l \notin p_1) \cap (e_l \in P_b)) \\ c_l, & \text{otherwise.} \end{cases} \qquad (1)$$

On the layered graph BLG^i, the links having the same link with the primary path cannot be used, the cost of links is set to $+\infty$. If the link e_l has not been used by any primary or backup path on BLG^i, the cost of e_l is set to c_l. If the link e_l is not passed by the primary path and there are some FSs used by other backup lightpaths whose respective primary path is link-disjoint to the path p_1, then the cost of link e_l is set to $c_l - B_{li}/BN_{sd}$. Where $B_{li} = \Sigma_{z=i}^{i+BNsd-1} b^*_l(z)$ is the number of frequency slots of the link $e_l \in BLG^i$ used by some backup lightpaths. Moreover, $b^*_l(z)=1$ represents that the z-th FS of link e_l is only used by backup paths; otherwise, $b^*_l(z)=0$. The cost of link e_l is set to $c_l - B_{li}/BN_{sd}$ for increasing the resource-sharing ratio. In addition, the links that have reserved enough shared backup frequent slots have less link cost. If the backup path traverses these links, then there is no need to reserve new frequency-slots and the frequency sharing can be enhanced. The details of the SBPPA are described in Figure 5.

Algorithm 4 SSPRA-SBPP

Input: $G(V, E)$, request $r = (s, d, B_{sd}, q)$;
Output : primary path and backup path of the request;
Pre-computed the set K paths between the nodes s and d and stored in P_{sd}. Paths are sorted in increasing order according to the length of the paths.
while ($P_{sd} \neq \emptyset$) **do**
  Select and remove a path p_1 from P_{sd} and check whether the required bandwidth B_{sd} can be allocated alone the path p_1 on network G.
  if (success) **then**
    Temporarily allocate required number of FSs to the path p_1.
    Perform the **SBPFA** to find the backup path p_2 of the request.
    if (p_2 can be found) **then**
      return p_1 and p_2.
    end if
    Release all FSs allocated to p_1.
  end if
end while
return BLOCK.

Figure 4. SSPRA-SBPP.

Algorithm 5 SBPPA

Input : $G(V, E)$, connection request $r = (s, d, B_{sd}, q)$, primary path p_1;
Output : backup path of the request;
Remove links on primary path p_1 from G to form a new graph $G'(V', E')$.
$i = 1$, $BN_{sd} = \lceil \frac{q \times B_{sd}}{C_f} \rceil$;
while ($i \leq B - BN_{sd} + 1$) **do**
  Construct the layered graph BLG^i of the network G' according to status. Where $V^i = V'$, $E^i = \{e_l | \sum_{j=i}^{i+NB_{sd}-1} b^*_l(j) = 0, e_l \in E'\}$.
  Set up the cost c'_l of link $e_l \in E^i$ according to the formula (1).
  Perform Dijkstra algorithm on graph G' to find the backup path p_2.
  if (backup path can be found) **then**
    Allocate resources for the backup path and **return** p_2.
  end if
  $i = i + 1$;
end while
return false.

Figure 5. SBPPA.

2) DSPRA-SBPP: In this subsection, the details of the DSPRA-SBPP is described. In the DSPRA-SBPP, the layered graph approach is applied. The main algorithm is the same as the proposed DSPRA described in Section III.A.1, except for the backup path-finding algorithm. The backup path-finding algorithm is changed to the SBPPA described in Figure 5.

B. SEC operation for SBPP

The SEC operation for the SBPP scheme is more complex than that of the DPP scheme. In SBPP, the backup resources are shared by several backup lightpaths. If the bandwidth of a connection decreases, the backup resources cannot decrease directly. Since releasing the shared resources of a backup path directly may cause other primary paths unprotected. Moreover, for the SEC operation, the spectrum-sharing feature should be considered in designing the expansion and contraction algorithms to improve the spectrum sharing.

1) Expansion: For a bandwidth increasing connection, if both primary and backup paths can be expanded directly, then the resources of these paths are expanded and the paths are unchanged. When the backup path expansion is performed, the sharing status of FSs should be taken into consideration. To expanse a frequency slot for the allocated lightpath, if the FS of an edge to be expanded is free (not been allocated to any primary or backup lightpath), then the FS can be expanded directly. If the FS of an edge to be expanded is allocated to a primary lightpath, then the FS cannot be selected to expand.

If the FS of an edge to be expanded is allocated to several backup lightpaths, then the FS should be examined further. Assume p_I and b_I be the primary and backup lightpath to be expanded, respectively. For the edge $e_i \in b_I$ and the jth selected FS, let $PS=\{p^1{}_{ij}, p^2{}_{ij}, ..., p^z{}_{ij}\}$ be the set of primary lightpaths whose backup lightpaths pass through the edge e_i and use the selected FS. If the selected FS of an edge to be expanded have the property that p_I is link-disjoint to all paths in *PS*, then the FS can be expanded. For a selected FS to be expanded, if all edges of the backup path can be expanded, then the selected FS can be expanded. The cost of the selected FS to be expanded is defined as the resource sharing value. For the expandable j^{th} FS of an edge ei, the weight (denoted as w_{ij}) of the FS is defined as the number of shared backup paths on it. For the expandable j^{th} FS of a path *p*, the weight (denoted as w_{jp}) of the FS is defined as the total number of shared backup paths on all edges of the path. That is, $w_{jp}=\Sigma_{\forall e_i \in p} w_{ij}$. For the backup path, the expandable method is selected by checking and selecting the expandable (immediate upper or lower index) FS with maximal weight repeatedly, until it meets the bandwidth requirement.

If the backup path cannot be expanded directly, then the currently allocated resources for the backup are temporarily contracted (by the method described later) as the first step. Then a new backup path is found by performing the SBPPA.

If the primary path cannot be expanded, then this is a new situation should be considered further. Since the sharing status of the backup path is determined based on the primary lightpath, once the primary path changes, the backup path should be changed accordingly. In this case, the current primary lightpath is removed and backup path is contracted (by the method described later). Then, the respective Survival Path Routing Algorithm for SBPP scheme (SSPRA-SBPP or DSPRA-SBPP) is performed to find a pair of new primary and backup lightpaths for the request. If failed to find the pair of lightpaths, then the request would be blocked.

2) Deletion or Contraction: If the demand of the new request is 0, then the primary path can be deleted and resources can be released directly. But the resources allocated to the backup lightpath should be considered further. If the selected FS of an edge is not shared by other lightpaths (used by the affected backup path only), then the resource can be released directly. If the selected FS of an edge is shared by other lightpaths, then the resource cannot be released directly. For each FS of an edge, a set of *path-allocating records* is used to store the sharing backup lightpaths and the respective primary lightpaths. The record of the released FS of an edge should be updated by deleting the affected backup path. For the contraction operation, the path-allocating record should be updated after releasing the selected FSs of the affected backup lightpath.

Consider the example shown in Figure 6, Figure 6(a) shows the primary and backup lightpaths of four requests and Figure 6(b) shows the allocated FSs and sharing status of the edges on the backup path b_1: $1 \rightarrow 4 \rightarrow 5 \rightarrow 7 \rightarrow 8$. The number of allocated FSs for the backup lightpaths b_1, b_2, b_3, and b_4 are 18, 3, 3 and 10, respectively. The FS allocation for the primary lightpaths is not shown here. The backup lightpaths near to the right of the FSs allocation of lightpaths denoted as the path-allocating of the FS of the edge. For example, the first and second FSs are used by b_2 and 1-3 FSs of edges (1, 4) and (4, 5) are shared by the lightpaths b_1 and b_2. If backup lightpath b_1 is deleted, the FS allocation is shown in Figure 6(c) and 5 free FSs are released. If six FSs are contracted from the backup lightpath b_1, the best contraction method will be determined and selected, that is, the region of the allocated FSs will within 5-16 (as shown in Figure 6(d)).

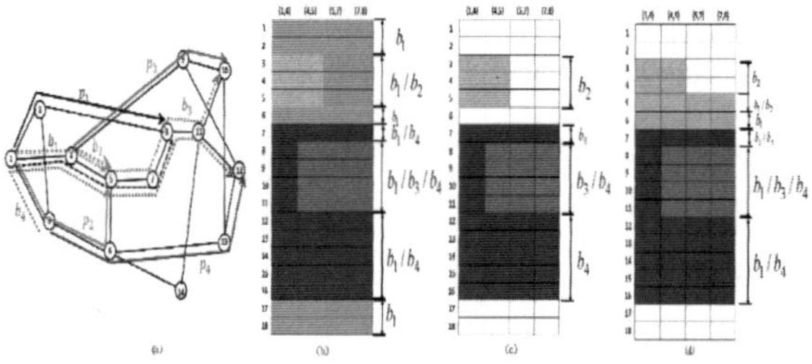

Figure 6. Examples of SEC for SBPP: (a) primary and backup lightpaths, (b) before deleting backup path b_1, (c) after deleting backup path b_1, (d) after contracting backup path b_1.

V. SIMULATION RESULTS

The proposed algorithms were coded by using C++ programming language. All simulations were run on a notebook computer with Intel Core i7-4710 HQ CPU 2.5GHz, 16.0 GB RAM and with Windows 10 pro 64-bit operating system. Two topologies (COST239 and NSFNET showed in Figure 7) were used for simulations.

In the simulation, the arrival of request to the network follows the Poisson distribution with λ=20 connection requests per unit time and the connection-holding time obeys negative exponential distribution with a mean value of $1/\mu$=4 and 4000 connection requests are randomly generated. The updated traffic is randomly generated uniformly for different pairs of nodes. The expansion/contraction operations are performed according to the updated traffic comparing to the currently provided bandwidth. The value of *q* is randomly generated uniformly with [0, 1]. These connections are simulated for each algorithm for six different network loads.

For each proposed SEC method, a respective algorithm is also implemented for comparison. The method is denoted as

"*Release and Add* (RA)". That is, for each updated traffic, the established lightpaths and allocated FSs for original traffic demand are released and then the new primary and backup lightpaths are re-established. Several performance criteria are considered in this paper, they are (1) Blocking Ratio (BR), (2) Resource Utilization Ratio (RUR) which is the ratio of protecting resources to that of the primary resources and (3) total number of allocated FSs.

First, for the COST239 network, the simulation results are shown in Figure 8. Figure 8(a) shows that the BR of the algorithm with RA is worse than that of the respective SEC method, thus the SEC operation can get better performance than RA operation. For the proposed algorithms with DPP protection, the SDSPRA-DPP can get the lower BR than that of the DSPRA-DPP. For the proposed algorithms with SBPP protection, the DSPRA-SBPP can get the lower BR than that of the SSPRA-SBPP. Survival routing with SBPP scheme can get better BR performance than that of the method with DPP scheme. The BR increases as the network load increases. Figure 8(b) shows that the RUR of the algorithm with RA is lower than that of the algorithm since remove and re find the primary and backup lightpaths can help to find better RUR paths. Survival routing with SBPP scheme can get better RUR performance than that of the DPP scheme. Figure 8(c) shows that the total FSs of the algorithm with RA is higher than that of the respective SEC algorithm. First, for the NSFNET network, similar simulation results can be obtained and not shown here.

VI. Conclusions

In this paper, the spectrum expansion/contraction and survival routing problems with time-varying traffic on EONs have been studied. For a given EON and a set of connection requests, the goal is to design a spectrum expansion and contraction method to update the CF and the channel size of the lightpath so as to fit the required of the request. In the studied problem, the DPP and SBPP protecting schemes have been are considered and several routing algorithms and SEC operations have been proposed to solve this problem. Simulations were conducted to evaluate the performance of the proposed algorithms.

The proposed algorithms are heuristic algorithms and can be executed in a reasonable polynomial time. This work can be extended in the future to hand other failure cases, such as node-failure, two or more links (or nodes) failure.

Acknowledgment

This work was supported in part by the MOST projects under Grant 105-2221-E-018-018 and 106-2221-E-018-002.

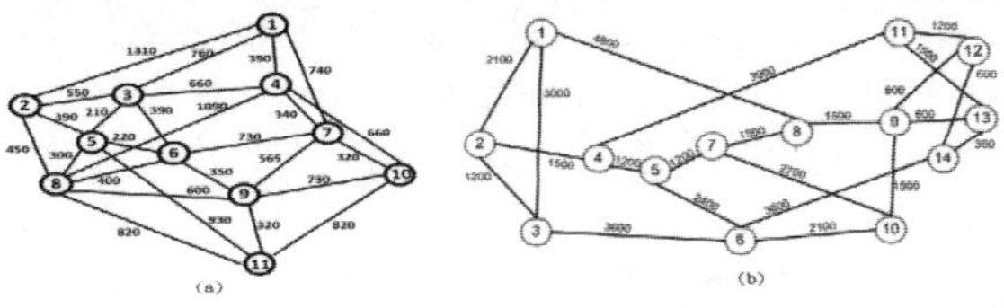

Figure 7. (a) COST239 network, (b) NSFNET

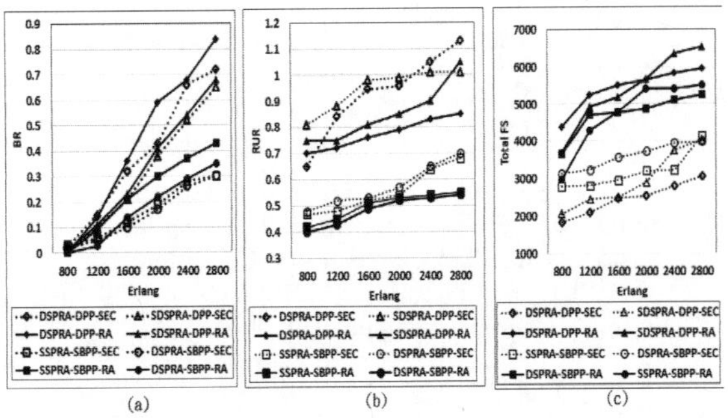

Figure 8. Simulation results on the COST239 network (a) BR, (b)RUR, (c) total number of FSs.

References

[1] G. Zhang, M. D. Leenheer, and A. Morea, "A survey on OFDM-based elastic core optical networking," IEEE Commun. Surv. & Tut. vol. 15, First Quarter 2013, pp. 65-87, doi: 10.1109/SURV.2012.010912.00123.

[2] G. Shen, Q. Yang, S. You, and W. Shao, "Maximizing time-dependent spectrum sharing between neighbouring channels in CO-OFDM optical networks," Proc. IEEE Symp. Transparent Optical Networks (ICTON 2011), IEEE Press, Jun. 2011, doi: 10.1109/ICTON.2011.5970769.

[3] M. Klinkowski, et al., "Elastic spectrum allocation for time-varying traffic in flexgrid optical networks," IEEE JSAC, vol. 31, Jan. 2013. pp. 26-38, doi:10.1109/JSAC.2013.130104.

[4] M. Chino, et al., "Adaptive elastic spectrum allocation based on traffic fluctuation estimate under time-varying traffic in flexible OFDM-based optical networks," IEICE Trans. on Commun., vol. E100.B, June 2017, pp. 962-973, doi: 10.1587/transcom.2016EBP3300.

[5] D. R. Din, Y. F. Wu, B. J. Guo, C. Chen, and P. J. Wu, "Spectrum expansion/contraction problem for multipath routing with time-varying traffic on elastic optical networks," Proc. Int. Conf. on Internet of Things, Data and Cloud Computing (ICC'17), March 2017.

[6] G. Shen, H. Guo, and S. K. Bose, "Survivable elastic optical networks: survey and perspective," Photon. Netw. Commun., vol. 31, Feb. 2016. pp. 71-87, doi:10.1007/s11107-015-0532-0.

[7] M. Klinkowski and K. Walkowiak, "Offline RSA algorithms for elastic optical networks with dedicated path protection consideration," Proc. IEEE Symp. Ultra-Modern Telecommunications and Control Systems and Workshops (ICUMT, 2012), IEEE Press, Oct. 2012, doi:10.1109/ICUMT.2012.6459751.

[8] G. Shen, Y. Wei, S. K. Bose, "Optimal design for shared backup path protected elastic optical networks under single-link failure," IEEE/OSA J. Opt. Commun. Netw., vol. 6, July 2014, pp. 649-659, doi:10.1109/JOCN.2014.6850206.

[9] X. Shao, Y. K. Yeo, Z. Xu, X. Cheng, L. Zhou, "Shared-path protection in OFDM-based optical networks with elastic bandwidth allocation," Proc. IEEE Symp. Optical Fiber Communication Conference and Exposition (OFC/NFOEC), IEEE Press, March 2012.

[10] N. G. Anoh, st al., "An efficient hybrid protection scheme with shared/dedicated backup paths on elastic optical networks," Digital Commun. and Netw., vol. 3, pp. 11-18, 2017, page OTh4B.4, doi:10.1364/OFC.2012.OTh4B.4.

[11] L. Ruan, N. Xiao, "Survivable multipath routing and spectrum allocation in OFDM-based flexible optical networks," J. Opt. Commun. Netw., vol. 5, Mar. 2013, pp. 172-182, doi:10.1364/JOCN.5.000172.

The RBCMLSA Problem on EONs with Flexible Transceivers

Der-Rong Din
Computer Science & Information Engineering
National Changhua University of Education
Changhua City, Taiwan, R. O. C.
deron@cc.ncue.edu.tw

Meng-Xun Zhan
Computer Science & Information Engineering
National Changhua University of Education
Changhua City, Taiwan, R. O. C
moncky2000@gmail.com

***Abstract*—Benefiting from the development of coherent detection and digital signal processing, innovative optical transceivers enable the dynamic adaptation of the baud rate, modulation level and Forward Error Correction (FEC) coding to the optical transmission properties. Next generation optical networks will require high levels of flexibility, being able to fit rate, bandwidth, FEC coding and optical reach requirements of different connections. For serving transmission on an Elastic Optical Network (EON), the flexible lightpath routing and the spectrum allocated for the connection request should be developed to meet the traffic requirement. In this paper, the Routing, Baud rate, FEC Coding, Modulation Level, Spectrum Allocation (RBCMLSA) problem is defined and studied. A heuristic algorithm, which integrates single/multiple path routing schemes, is proposed. The proposed algorithm is examined through simulations and the results show that the proposed algorithms can achieve good results.**

Keywords-routing; baud rate; FEC code; modulation level; spectrum allocation (RBCMLSA); flexible transceiver; elastic optical network (EON).

I. INTRODUCTION

Recently, the *Elastic Optical Network* (EON) has attracted intensive research because of employing *Optical-Orthogonal Frequency Division Multiplexing* (O-OFDM) technology, which has been used to scale the demands by efficiently utilizing the spectrum. A key feature of EON is that the modulation format and the spectrum can be adaptively adjusted and allocated according to the distance and capacity requirements [1] [2]. Based on variable bandwidth devices (such as Bandwidth-Variable Transponders (BVTs) and Bandwidth-Variable Wavelength Cross-Connects (BV-WXCs)), EONs require more sophisticated bandwidth allocation mechanisms. The spectrum of a fiber on an EON is divided into *Frequency Slots* (FSs) and the necessary amount of consecutive FSs are assigned to support the connection request [1] [2]. The number of required FSs is determined by the requested bandwidth, the modulation format, the (fixed) slice width and the Guard Band (GB) introduced to separate two spectrum adjacent connections, among others. The controller should find Routing, Modulation Level and Spectrum Assignment (RMLSA) for the connection request.

In EONs, the transmitting rate of the transmitter ranges from 2.5 Gb/s to 400 Gb/s. Benefiting from the development of coherent detection and digital signal processing, innovative optical transceivers enables the dynamic adaptation of the baud rate, modulation level and Forward Error Correction (FEC) coding to the optical transmission properties.

Sambo et al. [3] proposed a programmable controller on the Software Definition Network (SDN)-EONs. Several parameters (such as channel types, number of carries, transmitting rate, modulation format, central frequency, channel wide, FEC types, and number of FSs) can be dynamically determined to meet the connection request on the network. Cugini et al. [4] proposed the idea of the plug and play auto-configuring transmitters of the optical network. In the proposed environment, the control plane should be capable of performing effective routing and spectrum assignment as well as proper selection of the transmission parameters (e.g., baud rate, modulation format, coding type) depending on the required *Transmission Reach* (TR) or maximum transmission distance.

A. Multipath Routing

For online provisioning, it is difficult to serve certain large *bandwidth* (BW) requests with single-path routing due to the BW or TR limitation. Thus, it results in high request blocking probability [17] [18]. Lu et al. [18] suggested that a connection's traffic could be split over multiple paths without causing significant bandwidth waste. They proposed a dynamic multi-path algorithm, which considers the differential delay constraint. Zhu et al. [17] proposed two dynamic algorithms that incorporate a Hybrid Single-/Multi-path Routing (HSMR) scheme on the RMLSA model (denoted as RMLSA-HSMR). They considered dynamic RMLSA problem with various path selection policies for multipath provisioning in EONs [17]. The simulating results showed that the proposed hybrid single-/multi-path routing scheme could effectively reduce the blocking probability, by comparing to the single-path routing scheme.

B. Studied Problem

In the future, the next generation optical networks will require high levels of flexibility. Based on the new provided capabilities of the transponders, the controller will be able to adjust baud rate, bandwidth, FEC coding, modulation format and optical reach requirements of different connections. In this paper, the dynamic routing problem on EONs with flexible transceivers is studied. In the given EONs, the parameters of transceivers (including baud rate, modulation format, and FEC type) can be determined and selected by the network controllers. For a given EON and a sequence of connection requests, the goal is to find lightpaths and assigned suitable channels to lightpaths and meet the traffic and TR requirement such that the performance measure can be optimized. Since for each request, the baud rate, modulation format, and FEC type should be determined and find suitable spectrum, this problem is denoted as the **Routing, Baud rate, Code, Modulation Level, and Spectrum Allocation (RBCMLSA) problem**. Unlike previous works in RCMLSA and RMLSA, the proposed algorithm selects not only the route and the spectrum but also the baud rate, FEC type, and modulation format best suited to establish an optical connection.

In the paper, the hybrid single-/multi-path routing scheme is considered. The blocking performance of the proposed algorithm is evaluated in comparison to the RCMLSA and RMLSA approaches. Based on the survey, there is no article that considered the RBCMLSA problem with flexible transceivers for multipath routing. In this paper, a heuristic algorithm is proposed to solve the RBCMLSA problem with dynamic traffic. The proposed algorithm is examined through simulations and the results show that the proposed algorithm can achieve good results.

The remainder of this paper is as follows: Section 2 describes the related works; Section 3 defines the new RBCMLSA problem; Section 4 presents the details of the proposed algorithm; Section 5 gives performance evaluation by means of simulation; Section 6 concludes the paper.

II. RELATED WORKS

In this section, several studies related to the RBCMLSA problem will be stated.

A. FEC

In an optical network, the Optical Signal to Noise Ratio (OSNR) of a high data rate optical signal would degrade significantly over long transmission distances. This degradation can be compensated by using the FEC coding techniques [5]. FEC technologies were first proposed for fiber-optic communications, before signal modulation and transmission. In FEC coding, redundant *overhead* (OH) bits are added to the information bits [6]. FEC techniques with different error correcting capabilities were studied to evaluate both the performance of different FEC types and corresponding tradeoffs between their Net Coding Gains (NCGs) and their coding overheads. The future trends expected for FECs to combat even higher transmission impairments were presented in [7]. The evolution of FEC technologies can be classified into three generations [7] [8]. The first generation used block codes. A typical example is Reed-Solomon (RS)[255, 239]. The second generation used concatenated codes. An example is RS[255, 239]+Bose-Chaudhuri-Hocquenghem (BCH)[1023, 963]. The third generation used the more powerful soft decision decoding technique. The Block Turbo Code (BTC) and Low Density Parity Check (LDPC) code are two representatives of this generation. The OH, NCG, data rate and OSNR values are summarized in Table 1 [6]. Guo et al. [6] considered Shared Backup Path Protection (SBPP)-based EONs with the adaptive FEC allocation strategy. They developed an Integer Linear Programming (ILP) optimization model as well as a Spectrum Window Planes (SWPs)-based heuristic algorithm. The results showed that the adaptive FEC allocation strategy is very effective in significantly increasing the network capacity of an EON [6].

TABLE I. FEC TYPES OF OPTICAL NETWORK

FEC type	OH(%)	NCG(dB)@10^{-13}	Data Rate (Gb/s)	OSNR limit
RS[255, 239]	6.69	5.8	106.69	14.5
RS[255, 239] + BCH[1023, 963]	13.34	7.3	113.34	12.6
LDPC[4161, 3431, 0.825]	21.2	11.27	121.2	9.1

TABLE II. PARAMETERS OF TRANSCEIVER

Parameter	value	Modulation	SNR_{min}
P_S	1 mW	QPSK	2.031 dB
L_{span}	100 km	8 QAM	3.367 dB
h	6.626×10^{-34} m² kg/s	16 QAM	4.955 dB
fs	1.935×10^{14} Hz	32 QAM	6.722 dB
AG	20 dB QPSK	64 QAM	9.020 dB
NF	5.5 dB		
R_S	1.0×10^{9}		

B. RCSA vs. RCMLSA

Sambo et al. [9] [10] studied the Routing, Code, and Spectrum Assignment (RCSA) problem. For a given connection request and fixed modulation format, a set of candidate paths is constructed and the coding scheme with minimal extra information is selected, and then the required spectrum is allocated. Sambo et al. [9] [10] considered the *Time Frequency Packing* (TFP) [11] as the coding scheme.

Garrido et al. [12] considered the Routing, Code, Modulation Level, and Spectrum Allocation (RCMLSA) problem. In RCMLSA, not only the route and spectrum but also the pair FEC code-modulation format best suited are selected to establish an optical connection in EONs. In [12], the provided data rates (10, 40, 100, 400, 1000 Gb/s), modulation formats (Binary Phase Shift Keying (BPSK)/ Quadrature Phase Shift Keying (QPSK)) /8 Quadrature Amplitude Modulation (QAM)/16QAM/32QAM/64QAM) and different FEC codes (non-FEC/type 1 FEC/type 2 FEC/type 3 FEC) are considered. They proposed an algorithm to determine the route/modulation level/FEC type to minimize the number of required FSs for the connection request. Simulating results showed that the blocking probability of the RCMLSA model is lower than that of the RMLSA and RCSA models. However, in [12], the baud rate of the transceiver was fixed and cannot be selected by the network controller. In this paper, we use the RCMLSA problem as a base and extend it by considering the baud rate selection. The TR of a transmitting parameter may change if the baud rate change, thus this results in a new and more practical routing problem.

Alvarado et al. [13] found that joint optimization of the constellation and FEC OHs can yield large gains in terms of overall network throughput. They also studied the performance of the EON whose transmitters with two baud rates and a single constellation. The result in [13] suggested that one low baud rate could be used for the worst performing connection, while the other rate is used to increase the overall network throughput. Moreover, the results are quite close to the optimal baud rate of the corresponding one-rate scheme [14].

C. *Transmission Reach*

The TR or maximum distance of a single-core optical-amplified fiber is determined by several factors. The major impairments are Amplified Spontaneous Emission (ASE) noise and fiber nonlinearities [15]. The TR of a fiber-optic link can be estimated by the following formula [15]:

$$TR = P_S \times L_{span} / (SNR_{min} \times h \times fs \times AG \times NF \times R_S), \quad (1)$$

where P_S is the optical power at the transmitter. L_{span} is the distance between amplifiers. SNR_{min} is the required *Signal to Noise Ratio* (*SNR*) at the receiver side, which is related to the selected modulation format and Bit Error Ratio (BER) rate. For example, QPSK is 2.031dB, 8 QAM is 3.367 dB at BER 10^{-3}, etc. (shown in Table II)) [15]. *AG* is the gain of the amplifiers, *h* is Planck's constant, *fs* is the optical signal frequency, *NF* is the noise factor of the amplifiers, and R_S the symbol rate including the coding overhead (optimum Nyquist pulses are assumed).

Gho et al. [16] proposed a rate-adaptive transmission scheme using variable-rate FEC codes (concatenated RSs) with a fixed signal constellation and a fixed symbol rate. They studied the problem that how achievable bitrates vary with distance in a long-haul fiber system. They found that, with zero margins, an information bitrate could be realized up to 2000 km, with the achievable rate decreasing by approximately 40% for every additional 1000 km.

III. PROBLEM DEFINITION

In the following, the assumptions, constraints, notations and the definitions of the studied problem are given.

A. *Assumption*

- For each link, there is a fiber connecting the end-nodes and signal can be transmitted bidirectional.
- All nodes in the network are equipped with BV-WXC and BVT.
- For simplicity, the numbers of FSs provided by links are all equal.
- A GB should be allocated between two lightpaths.
- The bandwidth requirement between nodes can be transmitted by using multiple lightpaths with the same or different routes and numbers of FSs [18].

B. *Constraints*

Three constraints are considered in this paper, they are *spectrum continuity constraint*, *subcarrier consecutiveness constraint*, and *non-overlapping spectrum constraint*. Due to space limitation, the definition of these constraints can be found in [1]. To avoid a request from being split over too many lightpaths and causing too many guard bands, a *BW allocation granularity* (denoted as *g* FSs) is included [17]. Specifically, when the request is provisioned over more than one routing path, the minimum number of the FSs, which can be allocated on each path, is *g* [17].

C. *Notations*

- $G=(V, E, l)$: The physical topology of the network, where $V=\{v_1, v_2, ..., v_n\}$ is the set of nodes ($|V| = n$), $E=\{e_1, e_2, ..., e_m\}$ is the set of links ($|E| = m$), and $l(e)$ is the distance (kilometers) of the link e in E.
- $r=(s, d, BW_{sd})$: The connection request, where *s* in *V* and *d* in *V* is the source and destination node of the request, respectively. BW_{sd} is the required bandwidth (Gb/s) of the lightpaths between nodes *s* and *d*.
- *B*: the set of baud rates.
- *M*: the set of modulation formats {PM-QPSK, PM-8QAM, PM-16QAM, PM-32QAM, PM-64QAM} in the network.
- *F*: the set of FEC types, and *F*={no-FEC, Type 1 with RS[255, 235], type 2 with RS[255, 239]-BCH[1023, 963], type 3 with LDPC[416, 3431, 0.825], type 4 rate-adaptive code}.
- $R_{sd} = \{R^1_{sd}, R^2_{sd}, ..., R^k_{sd}\}$: The set of *k* routing paths between *s* and *d*. This set can be computed by performing the Eppstein algorithm [19] in $O(|E|+k|V|+|V|\log|V|)$.
- $OH[b, f, m]$: A 3-dimensional matrix, where the element $OH[b, f, m]$ represents the required overhead when the baud rate $b \in B$, the modulation format $m \in M$ and the FEC scheme $f \in F$ are used.
- $D[b, f, m]$: A 3-dimensional matrix, where the element $D[b, f, m]$ represents the TR when $b \in B$, $m \in M$ and $f \in F$.
- $FM(R^i_{sd}, BW_{sd})$: A priority queue, which contains all the triples (b, f, m) whose transmission reach is equal to or higher than the length of routing path. That is, $FM(R^i_{sd}, BW_{sd})=\{(b, f, m) | \text{dist}(R^i_{sd}) \le D[b, f, m]\}$ for $b \in B$, $m \in M$ and $f \in F$ and $\text{dist}(R^i_{sd})$ is the distance of the path R^i_{sd}.
- P^{new}: The set of routing paths, $P^{new} = \{(p^i_{sd} (b_i, f_i, m_i, N_i), i = 1, 2, ..., z\}\}$, where $b_i \in B$, $f_i \in F$, $m_i \in M$ and N_i is the number of allocated FSs of the ith lightpath.

The values of $OH[b, f, m]$ can be obtained from Table I, which are assumed independent with the *b* and *m*. Moreover, for the type 4 rate-adaptive FEC coding, the overhead is set to 66.66% for extending the TR to 1000 km from non-FEC coding [16]. The values of $OH[b, f, m]$ can be calculated by using the formula (1) for the non-FEC type and estimated by using linear interpolation based on the observation in [16] and shown in Table IV. Each flexible transceiver was assumed capable of operating with five modulation formats and five FEC coding levels and several possible baud rates (shown in Table IV). For some baud rates, several modulation formats and some data rates are not supported. For example, consider Table IV, for baud rates 28, 30, 32, only the PM-QPSK and PM-16QAM and data rates (10, 40, 100) are supported.

After selecting the routing path $R^i_{sd} \in R_{sd}$ the number of required FSs for different bandwidth (10, 40, 100, 400, 1000) of the request can be determined by using *b*, *f*, *m*. If the request is supported by a single lightpath, the minimal number of required FSs of the lightpath (denoted as N_{sd}) can be computed by

$$N_{sd} = \left\lceil \frac{BW_{sd} \times (1 + OH[b, f, m])}{C_f \times m} \right\rceil + GB, \quad (2)$$

where C_f is the bandwidth (Gb/s) provided by each FS. If the connection request is supported by z (>1) multiple lightpaths and the set of routing paths are $path_1$, $path_2$, ..., $path_z$, then the minimal number of required FSs for the demand BW_{sd} by using the multipath routing can be computed by the formula:

$$N_{sd} = \sum_{i=1}^{z} \left(\left\lceil \frac{BW_{sd}^{i} \times (1 + OH[b_i, f_i, m_i])}{C_f \times m_i} \right\rceil \right) + z \times GB, \quad (3)$$

where b_i, f_i and m_i are the selected parameters of the $path_i$, and subjects to constraints $\Sigma^{z}_{i=1} BW^{i}_{sd} \geq BW_{sd}$ and $\lceil BW^{i}_{sd} \times (1+OH[b_i, f_i, m_i])/(C_f \times m_i) \rceil \geq g$, $\forall i = 1, 2, ..., z$.

IV. PROPOSED ALGORITHM

In this section, the details of the proposed RBCMLSA-HSMR algorithm are described. For a new connection request $r = (s, d, BW_{sd})$, the set $P^{new} = \{p^{i}_{sd} | \ i = 1, 2, ..., z\}$ of lightpaths should be established to route the request.

A. RBCMLSA-HSMR

For the connection request $r = (s, d, BW_{sd})$, the k-shortest paths algorithm is performed on the network $G(V, E, l)$ to find a set of candidate paths $R = \{R^{i}_{sd}, i=1, 2, ..., k\}$. Paths in P are sorted in ascending order according to the distances of the paths $dist(R^{i}_{sd})$ on the network $G(V, E, l)$. The shortest path is selected first because more efficient modulation format and better FEC type can be selected such that the number of required FSs can be reduced. For the selected path R^{i}_{sd}, $1 \leq i \leq z$ the following steps are performed.

- The priority queue $FM(R^{i}_{sd}, BW_{sd})$, which contains all possible triples (b, f, m) is obtained. All triples in list $FM(R^{i}_{sd}, BW_{sd})$ are sorted increasingly according to the number of required FSs (if there is a tie, the order is determined by the smaller $OH[b, f, m]$ and larger m).
- If the list $FM(R^{i}_{sd}, BW_{sd})$ is empty, the next candidate path $(i=i+1)$ in P is selected and analyzed.
- If the list $FM(R^{i}_{sd}, BW_{sd})$ has at least one element, the pair (b, f, m) corresponding to the minimum value in $OH[b, f, m]$ is selected. That is, those parameters (the baud rate, modulation format, and FEC type) requiring the lowest OH for the given bit ate BW_{sd} is selected.
- Next, a spectrum allocation algorithm (first-fit method) is executed to allocate the selected number of FSs along the route if possible.
- If the spectrum allocation algorithm succeeds, the found resources will be allocated. Otherwise, a new route is analyzed $(i=i+1)$. Since it is impossible to find available resources on the same path for more required resources.
- If no more candidate paths are available in R, i.e., all paths in R are examined and there is no single-path can be allocated to the lightpath, and then the multipath routing scheme will be applied if possible.
- If multipath routing paths cannot be found, the request will be rejected.
- In multipath routing scheme, the path with the best parameter (b, f, m) is selected and maximal available number of FSs is selected and allocated.
- The remaining unsupported bandwidth is selected from the same path first (with the same parameter or different parameters) if possible.
- Otherwise, other paths in R are examined repeatedly until the required bandwidth is satisfied.

The request is first routed by a single path, if possible. After checking all possible paths for single-path routing and the request cannot be routed by a single path, then the multi-path routing scheme is applied. It is worth noting that the same candidate path can be selected as the routing path more than once but with different FS index. The bandwidth BW^{i}_{sd} allocated to the selected path $p^{i}_{sd} \in P^{new}$ is determined based on the network status and should satisfy the constraint $BW_{sd} \leq \sum_{\forall p^{i}_{sd} \in P^{new}} BW^{i}_{sd}$.

When the connection request is routed by multiple paths, more FSs will be used for the guard band. In the context of this study, we assume that $GB = 1$ and this guard band is inserted as the highest indexed slot in the spectrum assignment of each connection. The request $r = (s, d, BW_{sd})$ is blocked, if a feasible set of routing paths $P^{new} = \{p^{i}_{s,d} (b_i, f_i, m_i, N_i), i = 1, 2, ..., z\}$ cannot be found. The details of the RBCMLSA-HSMR algorithm are shown in Algorithm 1.

V. SIMULATION RESULTS

The proposed algorithms were coded by using C++ programming language. All simulations were run on a notebook computer with Intel Core i7-4710 HQ CPU 2.5 GHz, 16.0 GB RAM and with Windows 10 pro 64-bit operating system. The COST239 network (showed in Figure 2), which is a famous and widely used network topology, was used for simulations. The distance between nodes in COST239 can fit the parameters provided in Table IV. Other well-known network topologies will be examined in the future study. In Figure 2, the number nears the link is the length (km.) of the fiber.

In the simulation, the static traffic is simulated for different sets with different numbers (50, 100, 150, and 200) of requests. The number of candidate paths for a request is $k = 20$. The connection request is randomly generated uniformly for different pairs of nodes, the number of required bandwidth (Gb/s) is within [10, 2000]. For each fiber of the network, 320 FSs are provided and $C_f = 12.5$ Gb/s. Two algorithms for different models are implemented for comparison; they are RCMLSA model [12] and RMLSA model [17].

Algorithm 1 RBCMLSA-HSMR Algorithm

Input: $G(V, E, l)$, $r = (s, d, BW_{sd})$;
Output: the set of lightpaths $P^{new} = \{(p^i_{s,d}(b_i, f_i, m_i, N_i), i = 1, 2, ..., z\}$, subject to $\sum_{i=1}^{z} BW^i_{sd} \geq BW_{sd}$ and $N_i \geq g$.
$P^{new} = \emptyset$, $B = BW_{sd}$;
sort the paths in R in ascending order based on the distances $dist(R^i_{sd})$, $\forall R^i_{sd} \in R$, $R' = R$;
//single-path routing
while (($R \neq \emptyset$) and (found == **false**)) **do**
{
select and remove a path R^i_{sd} from R;
construct the list $FM(R^i_{sd}, BW_{sd})$;
select a triple $(b, f, m) \in FM(R^i_{sd}, BW_{sd})$ with the minimum number of required FSs which is computed by $N_{sd} = \left\lceil \frac{BW_{sd} \times (1+OH[b,f,m])}{C_f \times m} \right\rceil + GB$, for the selected modulation level m, baud rate b and FEC type f;
if (the required resources of the path R^i_{sd} can be allocated on the network) **then**
allocate resources and add path $p^i_{sd} = R^i_{sd}$ with parameters (b, f, m) to P^{new};
found = **true**, **return success** and P^{new};
end if
}
end while

//multi-path routing
$BW = 0$; //currently allocated bandwidth of the request
while (($R' \neq \emptyset$) and ($BW < BW_{sd}$)) **do**
{
select and remove a path R^i_{sd} from R';
construct the list $FM(R^i_{sd}, BW_{sd} - BW)$, which is implemented by the priority queue according to the number of required FSs of the selected parameter (b, f, m) increasingly;
while (($FM(R^i_{sd}, BW_{sd} - BW) \neq \emptyset$) and ($BW < BW_{sd}$)) **do**
{
select the first triple (b, f, m) from the list $FM(R^i_{sd}, BW_{sd} - BW)$;
determine the number of required FSs (N^i_{sd}) to route the required bandwidth $(BW_{sd} - BW)$ with parameters (b, f, m);
if ($N^i_{sd} < g$) **then**
$N^i_{sd} = g$; //check for constraint
end if
check the maximum number of allocatable FSs N^i of the path R^i_{sd} on the network;
if ($N^i \geq N^i_{sd}$) **then**
temporarily allocate N^i_{sd} FSs on the network and add path $p^i_{sd} = R^i_{sd}$ with parameters (b, f, m, N^i_{sd}) to P^{new};
$BW = BW + \frac{1}{1+OH[b,f,m]} \times N^i_{sd} \times m \times C_f$;
else if ($N^i_{sd} > N^i \geq g$) **then**
temporarily allocate N^i FSs on the network and add path $p^i_{sd} = R^i_{sd}$ with parameters (b, f, m, N^i) to P^{new};
$BW = BW + \frac{1}{1+OH[b,f,m]} \times N^i \times m \times C_f$;
else
break; //current path cannot be used
end if
}
end while
}
end while
if ($BW \geq BW_{sd}$) **then**
allocate spectrum, **return success** and P^{new};
else
recovery all the spectrum allocations for paths in P^{new};
remove all paths from P^{new}, mark the request as block and **return false**;
end if

Figure 1. RBCMLSA-HSMR

For each algorithm, both the single-path routing and the hybrid simple-/multi-path routing schemes are implemented. The parameters for RMLSA model are shown in Table III, which are the same as the best parameters for RBCMLSA (shown in Table IV), but without FEC overhead. The maximum distance or TR limits by 1,292 km. The parameters for RCMLSA model are selected from the central part of Table IV, but the highest bandwidth limitation is released (i.e. it can support up to 1000 Gb/s).

Several performance criteria are considered in this paper, they are:

- Blocking Ratio (BR), which is defined as the ratio of the number of blocked requests versus the number of total requests.
- Multipath Ratio (MR), which is the ratio of the number of requests routed by multiple paths to that of the number of successful requests.
- The average number of allocated FSs per lightpath,
- the average hops per lightpath,
- the average number of lightpaths per request, and
- computation time.

In the COST239 network, the simulation results are shown in Figure 3. Figure 3(a) shows the average number of paths per request of the RCMLSA method is greater than that of the other methods. The average number of paths per request increases as the number of requests increases. Figure 3(b) shows the average number of FSs per lightpath of the RCMLSA single path routing method is greater than that of the other methods. The average number of FSs per lightpath decreases as the number of requests increases. The average number of FSs per lightpath for single-path routing scheme is higher than that of the multipath routing scheme. Figure 3(c) shows the average number of hops per lightpath of the RMCMLSA multipath routing method is greater than that of the other methods.

The average number of hops per lightpath decreases as the number of requests increases from 50 to 150. The average number of hops per lightpath for multipath routing scheme is higher than that of the single-path routing scheme. Figure 3(d) shows that the BR of the RBCMLSA multipath routing is lower than that of the other methods. For single-path routing, the BR of the RBCMLSA method is lower than that of the other methods. The result also shows that multipath routing scheme can reduce the BR about 40%. The BR increases as the number of requests increases. Figure 3(e) shows that the MR of the RCMLSA multipath routing is higher than that of the other methods. The MR increases as the number of requests increases. Figure 3(f) shows that the CPU time in seconds of the RCMLSA multipath routing is higher than that of the other methods. The RBCMLSA multipath is the second highest.

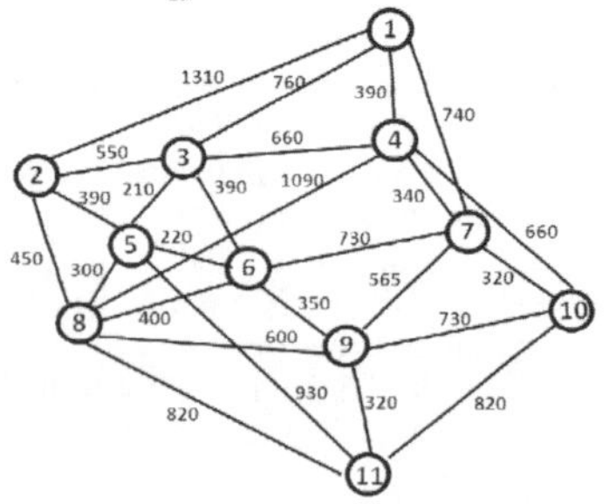

Figure 2. COST239 network.

VI. CONCLUSIONS AND FUTURE WORK

In this paper, the Routing, Baud rate, FEC Coding, Modulation Level, and Spectrum Allocation (RBCMLSA) problem has been defined and studied. For serving transmission on an EON, the goal is to design a routing and spectrum assignment algorithm to establish lightpaths. In the studied problem, the hybrid single/multipath routing scheme has developed to increase the spectrum efficiency. A heuristic algorithm denoted as RBCMLSA-HSMR, which integrates single/multiple paths routing scheme has been proposed. The proposed algorithm has been examined through simulations on the COST239 network and the results show that the proposed algorithms can reduce the blocking probability about 40%.

The results show that using flexible transmitters and adaptive transmitting parameters, the proposed algorithm can get lower blocking probability both in single-path and multiple-path routing schemes. Thus, the performance for routing in the RBCMLSA model is better than that of RMLSA and RCMLSA models. This is because of that controller can find a better routing path together with better parameters in RBCMLSA model, such that the required number of FSs can be reduced and the spectrum of the network can be used more efficiently. Simulation results also show that multipath-routing scheme does reduce the blocking probability whatever in RMLSA, RCMLSA, or RBCMLSA models.

In the future, the performance of the proposed algorithm on different networks will be simulated, and more feasible transmitting parameters of the flexible transceivers will be collected and examined. Moreover, the more problems in the RBCMLSA model that are important will be studied. For example, the survival routing problem, de-fragmentation problem on the single-fiber network or the multi-fiber network.

TABLE III. PARAMETERS OF RMLSA

Transmission Reach (km)	b	m	modulation format
1292	120	2	PM-QPSK
1147	1147	3	PM-8QAM
1031	64	4	PM-16QAM
937	51	5	PM-32QAM
840	43	6	PM-64QAM

ACKNOWLEDGMENT

This work was supported in part by the MOST project under Grant 106-2221-E-018-002.

REFERENCES

[1] G. Zhang, M. D. Leenheer, and A. Morea, "A survey on OFDM-based elastic core optical networking," IEEE Commun. Surv. & Tut. vol. 15, First Quarter 2013, pp. 65-87, doi: 10.1109/SURV.2012.010912.00123.

[2] M. Klinkowski and K. Walkowiak, "Routing and spectrum assignment in spectrum sliced elastic optical path network," IEEE Commun. Lett., vol. 15, Aug. 2011, pp. 884-886, doi: 10.1109/LCOMM.2011.060811.110281.

[3] N. Sambo, et al., "Programmable transponder, code and differentiated filter configuration in elastic optical networks," J. Lightw. Technol., vol. 32, June 2014, pp. 2079-2086, doi:10.1109/JLT.2014.2319859.

[4] F. Cugini, et al., "Toward plug-and-play software-defined elastic optical networks," J. Lightw. Technol., vol. 34, Mar. 2016, pp. 1494-1500, doi:10.1109/JLT.2015.2511802.

[5] W. D. Grover, "Forward error correction in dispersion-limited lightwave system," J. Lightw. Technol., vol. 6, May 1988, pp. 643-654, doi:10.1109/50.4049.

[6] H. Guo, et al., "OSA benefit of adaptive FEC in shared backup path protected elastic optical network," Optics Express, vol. 23, July 2015, pp. 20158-20175, doi:10.1364/OE.23.020158.

[7] T. Mizuochi, "Next generation FEC for optical transmission systems," Proc. IEEE Symp. Optical Fiber Communications Conference (OFC 2003), IEEE Press, Feb. 2004, paper ThN1, doi:10.1109/ OFC.2003.315927.

[8] T. Mizuochi, "Recent progress in forward error correction and its interplay with transmission impairments," IEEE J. Sel. Top. Quantum Electron. vol. 12, July, 2006, pp. 544-554, doi: 10.1109/JSTQE.2006.876597.

[9] N. Sambo et al., "Routing, code, and spectrum assignment (RCSA) in elastic optical networks," Proc. IEEE Symp. of Optical Fiber Communications Conference and Exhibition (OFC 2015), IEEE Press, Mar. 2015, page W1I.1, doi:10.1364/OFC.2015.W1I.1.

[10] N. Sambo et al., "Routing code and spectrum assignment (RCSA) in elastic optical networks," J. Lightw. Technol., vol. 33, Dec. 2015, pp. 5114-5121, doi:10.1109/JSTQE.2006.876597.

[11] M. Secondini, et al., "Optical time-frequency packing: principles, design, implementation, and experimental demonstration," J. Lightw. Technol., vol. 33, Sept. 2015, pp. 3558-3570, doi:10.1109/JLT.2015.2443876.

[12] D. Garrido, A. Leiva, A. Beghelli, R. Ahumada, and R. Olivares, "Routing, code, modulation level and spectrum assignment (RCMLSA) algorithm for elastic optical networks," Proc. IEEE Symp. Transparent Optical Networks (ICTON 2016), IEEE Press, Aug. 2016, pp.Tu. B3.4, doi:10.1109/ICTON.2016.7550388.

[13] A. Alvarado, D. J. Ives, S. J. Savory, and P. Bayvel, "On the impact of optimal modulation and FEC overhead on future optical networks," J. Lightw. Technol., vol. 34, May 2016, pp. 2339-2352, doi: 10.1109/JLT.2016.2517699.

[14] D. J. Ives, P. Wright, A. Load, and S. J. Savory, "Using 25GbE client rates to access the gains of adaptive bit- and code-rate networking," J. Opt. Commun. Netw., vol. 8, July 2016, pp. A86-A91, doi:10.1364/JOCN.8.000A86.

[15] R.-J. Essiambre, G. Kramer, P. J. Winzer, G. J. Foschini, and B. Goebel, "Capacity limits of optical fiber networks," J. Lightw. Technol., vol. 28, Feb. 2010, pp. 662-701, doi:10.1109/JLT.2009.2039464.

[16] G.-H. Gho, L. Klak, and J. M. Kahn, "Rate-adaptive coding for optical fiber transmission systems," J. Lightwave Technol., vol. 29, Jan. 2011, pp. 222-233, doi:10.1109/JLT.2010.2099208.

[17] Z. Zhu, W. Lu, L. Zhang, and N. Ansari, "Dynamic service Parameters of RMLSA provisioning in elastic optical networks with hybrid single-/multi-path routing," J. Lightw. Technol., vol. 31, Jan. 2013, pp. 15-22, doi: 10.1109/JLT.2012.2227683.

[18] W. Lu, X. Zhou, L. Gong, M. Zhang, and Z. Zhu, "Dynamic multi-path service provisioning under differential delay constraint in elastic optical networks," IEEE Commun. Lett., vol. 17, Jan. 2013, pp. 158-161, doi:10.1109/LCOMM.2012.120612.121343.

[19] D. Eppstein, ``Finding the k shortest paths," SIAM J. Comput., vol. 28, Apr. 1999, pp. 652-673, 1999, doi:10.1137/S0097539795290477.

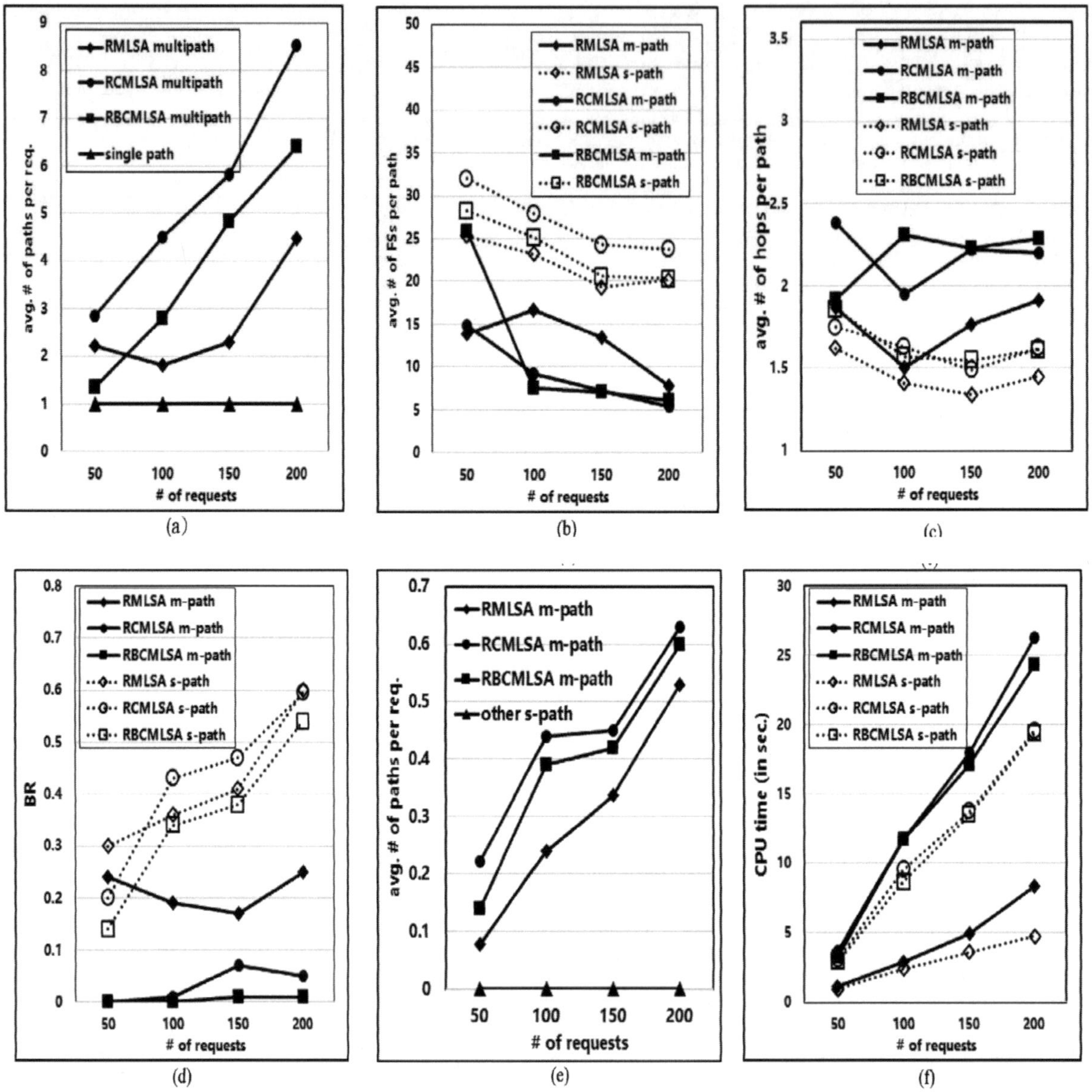

Figure 3. Simulation results on the COST239 network (a) the average number of path per request, (b) the average number of paths per request, (c) the average number of hop per path, (d) BR, (e) MR, (f) CPU time.

TABLE IV. THE NUMBER OF REQUIRED FSS FOR THE SELECTED PARAMETER, DATA RATES, AND TRANSMISSION REACH

m	b	FEC Type f Trans. reach (km)				
(10,40,100) $D[b, f, m]$		no-FEC	Type 1	Type 2	Type 3	Type 4
PM-QPSK	FSs	(1,2,4)	(1,2,5)	(1,2,5)	(1,2,5)	(1,3,7)
	28	1674	1774	1874	1992	2674
	30	1856	1956	2056	2174	2856
	32	2084	2184	2284	2402	3084
PM-16QAM	FSs	(1,1,2)	(1,1,3)	(1,1,3)	(1,1,3)	(1,2,4)
	28	1064	1164	1264	1382	2064
	30	1134	1234	1334	1452	2134
	32	1216	1316	1416	1534	2216
(10, 40, 100, 400) $D[b, f, m]$		no-FEC	Type 1	Type 2	Type 3	Type 4
PM-QPSK	FSs	(1,2,4,16)	(1,2,5,18)	(1,2,5,19)	(1,2,5,20)	(1,3,7,27)
	112	1122	1222	1322	1440	2122
	120	1201	1301	1401	1519	2201
	128	1292	1392	1492	1610	2292
PM-8QAM	FSs	(1,2,3,11)	(1,2,3,12)	(1,2,4,13)	(1,2,4,13)	(1,2,5,18)
	75	1011	1111	1211	1329	2011
	80	1075	1175	1275	1393	2075
	85	1147	1247	1347	1465	2147
16 QAM	FSs	(1,1,2,8)	(1,1,3,9)	(1,1,3,10)	(1,1,3,10)	(1,2,4,14)
	56	920	1020	1120	1238	1920
	60	972	1072	1172	1290	1972
	64	1031	1131	1231	1349	2031
PM-32QAM	FSs	(1,1,2,7)	(1,1,2,7)	(1,1,2,8)	(1,1,2,8)	(1,2,3,11)
	45	844	944	1044	1162	1844
	48	888	988	1088	1206	1888
	51	937	1037	1137	1255	1937
64 QAM	FSs	(1,1,2,6)	(1,1,2,6)	(1,1,2,7)	(1,1,2,7)	(1,1,3,9)
	37	765	865	965	1083	1765
	40	801	901	1001	1119	1801
	43	840	940	1040	1158	1840
(10, 40, 100, 400,1000)		no-FEC	Type 1	Type 2	Type 3	Type 4
PM-32QAM	FSs	(1,1,2,7,16)	(1,1,2,7,18)	(1,1,2,8,19)	(1,1,2,8,20)	(1,2,3,11,27)
	112	724	824	924	1042	1724
	120	756	856	956	1074	1756
	128	791	891	991	1109	1791
PM-64QAM	FSs	(1,1,2,6,14)	(1,1,2,6,15)	(1,1,2,7,16)	(1,1,2,7,17)	(1,1,3,9,23)
	93	665	765	865	983	1665
	105	692	792	892	1010	1692
	117	722	822	922	1040	1722

Routing and Spectrum Allocation Method to Avoid the Generation of Crosstalk and the Blocking of Lightpath Establishment in Multi-Core Fiber Networks

Tomotaka Kimura*, Keita Goto†, Kai Morita†, Kouji Hirata†, Yutaka Fukuchi‡, and Masahiro Muraguchi‡
* Faculty of Science and Engineering, Doshisha University, Kyoto 610-0321, Japan
Email: tomkimur@mail.doshisha.ac.jp
† Faculty of Engineering, Kansai University, Osaka 564-8680, Japan
Email: {k698542, k009696, hirata}@kansai-u.ac.jp
‡ Faculty of Engineering, Tokyo University of Science, Tokyo 125-8585, Japan
Email: {fukuchi, murag}@ee.kagu.tus.ac.jp

Abstract—**This paper proposes a dynamic routing and spectrum allocation method that avoids the generation of crosstalk and the blocking of lightpath establishment in elastic optical networks with multi-core fibers. In the elastic optical networks with multi-core fibers, crosstalk occurs when the same frequency band is used for signals of adjacent cores. The proposed method provides a routing and spectrum allocation strategy, which suppresses the generation of crosstalk by avoiding using the same frequency band in adjacent cores and blocking of lightpath establishment by selecting appropriate routes. Through simulation experiments, we show the effectiveness of the proposed method.**

Keywords–Elastic optical network; multi-core fiber; crosstalk; routing and spectrum allocation.

I. Introduction

Recently, elastic optical networks have attracted much attention because they can accommodate rapidly increasing network traffic by utilizing network resources flexibly [1][2]. In the elastic optical networks, frequency spectrum is divided into small pieces named frequency slots and data are transmitted on lightpaths, which are routes allocated frequency slots. Furthermore, the elastic optical networks use multilevel modulation such as Quadrature Phase Sift Keying (QPSK) and Quadrature Amplitude Modulation (QAM) according to the transmission distance, instead of using on-off pulses in conventional Wavelength Division Multiplexing (WDM) optical networks. By doing so, the elastic optical networks further enhance the utilization efficiency of frequency resources.

In order to design elastic optical networks, we should consider a Routing and Spectrum Allocation (RSA) problem [3][4][5], which is one of most important technical issues. The RSA problem determines a route and frequency slots for a lightpath to transmit data. The RSA problem is categorized into two problems: static and dynamic. The static RSA problem assumes that traffic demands of all sender and receiver pairs (i.e., traffic matrix) in a network are known in advance. Routes and frequency slots for established lightpaths are determined by solving optimization methods such as mathematical programming and meta-heuristic, based on the traffic matrix. On the other hand, the traffic matrix is not available for the dynamic RSA problem. In the dynamic RSA problem, lightpath-setup requests are stochastically generated with the time elapsed and the lightpaths are dynamically established accordingly. After the holding time of the lightpaths, they are released. This paper focuses on the dynamic RSA problem.

Generally, the performance metric of the dynamic RSA problem is the blocking probability of lightpath establishment. A lightpath must use successive frequency slots. Moreover, the lightpath must use common frequency slots in all links along its route. Lightpaths are established by RSA under these constraints. When there are no available frequency slots that meet these constraints on candidate routes for a lightpath to be established, the lightpath establishment is blocked. Therefore, the performance of elastic optical networks strongly depends on RSA.

In order to enhance the performance of elastic optical networks, multi-core fibers have been developed in the past [6][7]. The multi-core fibers have multiple cores and different optical signals can be simultaneously transmitted through the cores. By using multi-core fibers in elastic optical networks, we can reduce the blocking probability of lightpath establishment because multi-core fibers can relax the above-mentioned constraints. Specifically, multiple lightpaths can simultaneously use the same frequency slots in the same fiber when they pass through different cores. However, when the same frequency slots are used in neighboring cores, crosstalk occurs between them. The crosstalk generates noise in the neighboring cores and thus degrades the quality of the optical signals. Therefore, in order to design high-quality multi-core fiber networks, we need to consider the crosstalk in addition to the blocking of lightpath establishment.

In this paper, we propose a dynamic RSA method that aims at avoiding the blocking of lightpath establishment and the generation of crosstalk in elastic optical networks with multi-core fibers. The proposed method balances the usage of frequency slots by selecting a route and frequency slots for a newly established lightpath according to available frequency slots. By doing so, the proposed method avoids the blocking of lightpath establishment. Furthermore, the proposed method selects frequency slots and cores in such a way that the same frequency slots are not used in neighboring cores, which avoids the generation of crosstalk. Through simulation experiments, we show the effectiveness of the proposed method.

The rest of this paper is organized as follows. In Section II, we explain elastic optical networks with multi-core fibers. Section III discusses our proposed method. In Section IV, the performance of the proposed method is discussed with the results of the simulation experiments. Finally, we conclude the paper in Section V.

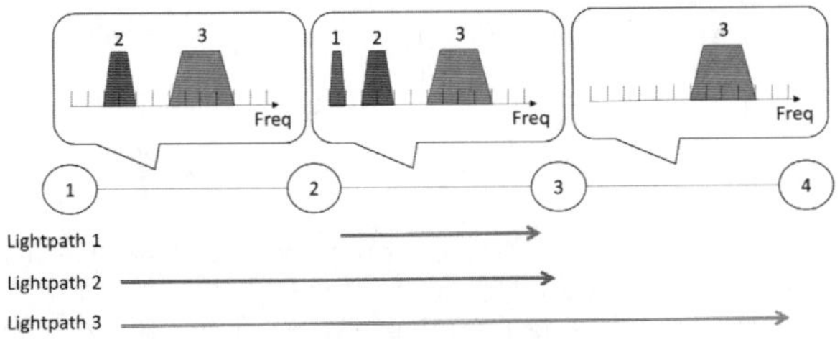

Figure 1. Elastic optical network.

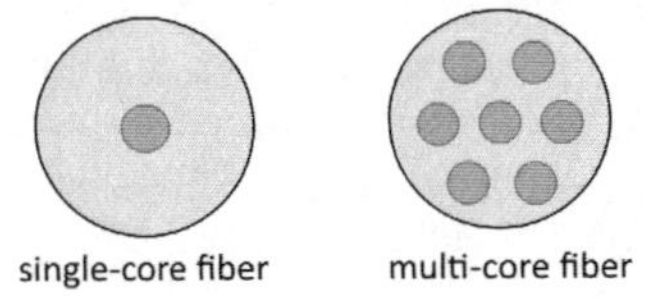

Figure 2. Single-core and multi-core fibers.

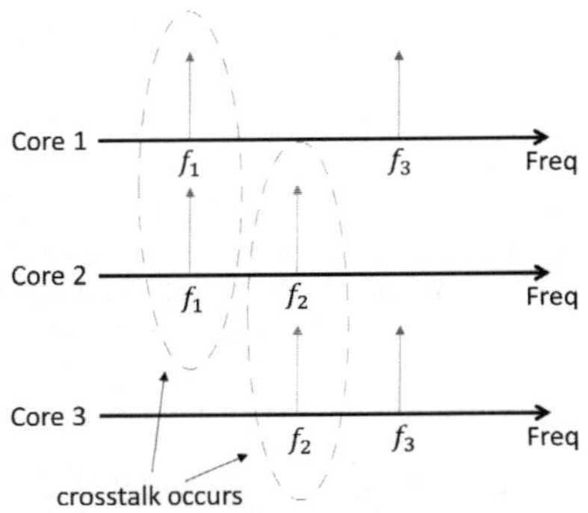

Figure 3. Crosstalk in a multi-core fiber.

II. Elastic Optical Networks with Multi-Core Fibers

In elastic optical networks, the unit of frequency slots is 12.5 [GHz] or less, which is smaller than that in conventional WDM networks. Lightpaths are established with multiple frequency slots and the number of frequency slots used for the lightpaths can be changed according to their traffic demands as shown in Figure 1. Thus, frequency resources are efficiently utilized. Furthermore, by using multilevel modulation according to the length of the lightpaths, the elastic optical networks enhance the utilization efficiency of frequency resources. For example, when the length of a lightpath is short, we can use modulation schemes such as 16-QAM and 64-QAM, whose frequency utilization efficiency is high, because of high Optical Signal-to-Noise Ratio (OSNR). On the other hand, for a lightpath whose length is large, modulation schemes with low frequency utilization efficiency, such as Binary Phase Sift Keying (BPSK) and QPSK are used because OSNR is low.

In order to communicate in elastic optical networks, lightpaths are established between senders and receivers by selecting routes and frequency slots. When we establish a lightpath, we should consider two constraints about frequency slots. The first constraint is that successive frequency slots must be assigned to the lightpath as shown in Figure 1. Frequency slots that are not adjacent to each other cannot be used for the lightpath. The second constraint is that common frequency slots must be assigned to all links used in the lightpath. We cannot use different frequency slots for different links through which the lightpath passes. We need to consider a RSA method to meet these constraints.

For multi-core environments, we should further consider the generation of crosstalk. In the multi-core fiber networks, a fiber consists of multiple cores as shown in Figure 2. Different lightpaths can be established in different cores in the same fiber, and thus the transmission capacity of elastic optical networks is enhanced according to the number of cores. However, crosstalk occurs when the same frequency slots are used in different cores in the same fiber as shown in Figure 3. The crosstalk degrades the quality of optical signals. The effect of the crosstalk exponentially decreases with the increase in the distance between cores. Therefore, the effect of the crosstalk becomes the strongest when the same frequency slots are used in adjacent cores. For simplicity, in this paper, we assume that the crosstalk occurs only when the same frequency slots are used in adjacent cores. We also assume that the impact of the crosstalk is the same for each frequency slot.

In the past, several RSA methods that aim at suppressing the generation of crosstalk and/or the blocking of lightpath establishment have been proposed. In [8], the authors proposed a RSA method that considers immediate reservation and advance reservation of network resources for elastic optical networks. This method allocates frequency slots to lightpaths according to the required number of frequency slots of the lightpaths, so that blocking probability of lightpath establishment is reduced. Furthermore, in [9] the authors have proposed a spectrum and core/mode assignment method that aims at reducing the blocking probability of lightpath establishment. This method prioritizes frequency slots and lightpaths are allocated to the frequency slots according to the number of frequency slots required by them. In [9], [10], the authors have proposed a dynamic spectrum allocation method that considers both the blocking of lightpath establishment and crosstalk. This method prioritizes cores in such a way that non-adjacent cores are preferentially used to avoid the generation of crosstalk. Furthermore, lightpaths are allocated to the cores according to the number of frequency slots required by them to avoid the blocking of lightpath establishment. Specifically, lightpaths with different number of frequency slots use different cores. By doing so, this method reduces the blocking probability of lightpath establishment and the number of crosstalk occurrences. However, this method cannot flexibly accommodate fluctuating traffic demand because it needs to determine cores to which lightpaths are allocated according to the required number of frequency slots in advance. Furthermore, this method does not consider routing. On the other hand, our proposed method adaptively selects routes, frequency slots, and cores for established lightpaths based on current network status, and thus it is expected to flexibly accommodate fluctuating traffic demand.

III. Proposed RSA Method

In this section, we first explain the overview of our proposed method in Section III-A, and then we detail the procedure in Section III-B.

A. Overview

Our proposed RSA method provides a route, frequency slot, and core selection strategy that considers not only the blocking of the lightpath establishment owing to the depletion of the frequency resources but also the generation of crosstalk due to multi-core fiber environments. In the proposed method, a route, frequency slots, and cores of each fiber along the route for a newly established lightpath is selected based on two policies. Note that the proposed method selects a route from the pre-defined candidate routes constructed by the K-shortest path algorithm because multilevel modulation schemes used for the lightpath are determined according to the length of the routes. The two policies a) and b) are described as follows:

a) In order to avoid the blocking of lightpath establishment, we should balance the usage of frequency slots in each link. A bottleneck link is generated when traffic concentrates in a certain link and there are no available frequency slots in all the cores of the link. In this case, new lightpaths cannot be established further in the link. In order to distribute the load and avoid the generation of bottleneck links, the proposed method selects a route, frequency slots, and cores according to the number of available frequency slots in each core of each link along candidate routes.

b) In order to avoid the generation of crosstalk, we should not use the same frequency slots in adjacent cores. The crosstalk decays the communication quality of lightpaths. The crosstalk generated in each link accumulates along a lightpath as noise at a receiver node. When the effect of crosstalk is large, it is highly possible that data transmission fails even if the lightpath is correctly established. In order to avoid this situation, the proposed method also selects a route, frequency slots, and cores according to the usage of frequency slots in adjacent cores.

B. Procedure of the proposed method

In what follows, we describe the detailed procedure of the proposed method. Note that we assume that the usage of frequency slots, which is needed for lightpath establishment, is known in advance by periodically collecting it.

1) Construction of candidate routes: The proposed method selects a route from a set of candidate routes. In this paper, we use the K-shortest path algorithm to make the set $\mathcal{P}_{i,j} = \{p_1^{[i,j]}, p_2^{[i,j]}, \ldots, p_K^{[i,j]}\}$ of candidate routes for each sender i and receiver j pair. Let $G = (\mathcal{V}, \mathcal{E})$ denote a directed graph, where $\mathcal{V}$ and $\mathcal{E}$ denote sets of nodes and links, respectively. The K-shortest path algorithm first finds the shortest path from $i \in \mathcal{V}$ to $j \in \mathcal{V}$ on G, where the cost of each link is set to be 1, using a general shortest path algorithm such as Dijkstra's algorithm. It then adopts the path as a candidate route and doubles the cost of each link along the route. We find the new shortest path on the resulting graph and the path is adopted as a new candidate route. The procedure is repeated until K candidate routes are found. Modulation schemes used for lightpath along routes are determined according to the length of the routes.

2) Lightpath establishment: Let $\mathcal{F} = \{1, 2, \ldots, |\mathcal{F}|\}$ denote a set of frequency slots supported by each fiber. In order to establish a lightpath for a pair of sender i and receiver j, we use the cost $C_{p,f}$ of each frequency slot $f \in \mathcal{F}$ along each route $p \in \mathcal{P}_{i,j}$, based on the current usage of frequency slots on each link l on the route. The cost $C_{p,f}$ is defined by

$$C_{p,f} = \sum_{l \in p} \left\{ \min_{m \in \mathcal{M}_l} \sum_{f'=f}^{f+B_p-1} U_{l,m,f'} \right\}, \tag{1}$$

where $\mathcal{M}_l$ denotes a set of cores in link l's fiber, $U_{l,m,f}$ denotes the cost of the frequency slot f of core m in link l, and B_p denotes the required number of frequency slots to establish the lightpath along the route. Note that $\sum_{f'=f}^{f+B_p-1} U_{l,m,f'}$ indicates the total cost when the frequency slots from f to $f + B_p - 1$ are used for the lightpath. Specifically, the starting frequency slot is f and the number of frequency slots for the lightpath is B_p, the value of which is determined according to modulation schemes and traffic demands. The proposed method uses the smallest $\sum_{f'=f}^{f+B_p-1} U_{l,m,f'}$ among cores in order to calculate $C_{p,f}$.

Let $u_{l,m,f}$ be 1 if frequency slot f of core m in link l is already used; otherwise, 0. If the frequency slot f of core m in link l is available (i.e., $u_{l,m,f} = 0$), the cost $U_{l,m,f}$ of frequency slot f of core m in link l is given by

$$U_{l,m,f} = \sum_{f' \in \mathcal{F}: f \neq f'} u_{l,m,f'} + \beta \sum_{m' \in \mathcal{M}_l: m \neq m'} a_{m,m'} u_{l,m',f}; \tag{2}$$

otherwise (i.e., $u_{l,m,f} = 1$),

$$U_{l,m,f} = \infty, \tag{3}$$

where β is a parameter ($\beta > 0$). $a_{m,m'}$ is a variable that is equal to 1 if core m is adjacent to core m'; otherwise, 0. In (2), the first term derives from policy a) described in Section III-A. Specifically, the cost $U_{l,m,f}$ increases as the number of used frequency slots in the same core increases. Also, the second term derives from policy b) and the cost $U_{l,m,f}$ increases with the number of frequency slots used in adjacent cores. We can adjust the impact of policies a) and b) with the parameter β. (3) means that the lightpath cannot be established with the frequency slot of the core in the link.

Whenever a new lightpath-setup request arrives, the proposed method calculates the cost $C_{p,f}$ with (1) for each frequency slot f along each route p. Then, the proposed method selects a combination of a route and frequency slots with the smallest cost $C_{p,f}$. If the cost $C_{p,f}$ is infinity for all the combinations, the lightpath-setup request is blocked. If there are two or more combinations with the minimum cost, the proposed method selects the combination with smaller number of hops. Furthermore, the proposed method selects one randomly if the numbers of hops among them are the same. After selecting a route and frequency slots, the proposed method selects a core in each link along the selected route. Specifically, the proposed method uses core m given by

$$\arg\min_{m \in \mathcal{M}_l} \sum_{f'=f}^{f+B_p-1} U_{l,m,f'},$$

the cost of which is used for $C_{p,f}$ in (1).

Figure 4 shows an example of the proposed method. In this figure, we assume that node 1 is a sender and node 3 is a receiver and there are two links 1 and 2 along a route between them. Each link consists of 3 cores and each core supports 6 frequency slots. Core 2 is adjacent to both core 1 and core 3.

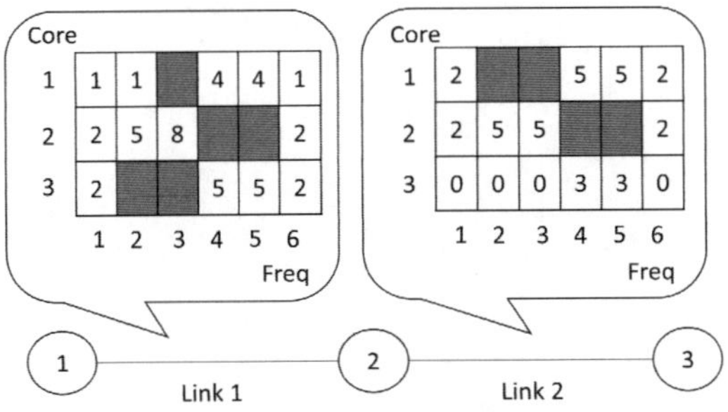

Figure 4. Example of the proposed method.

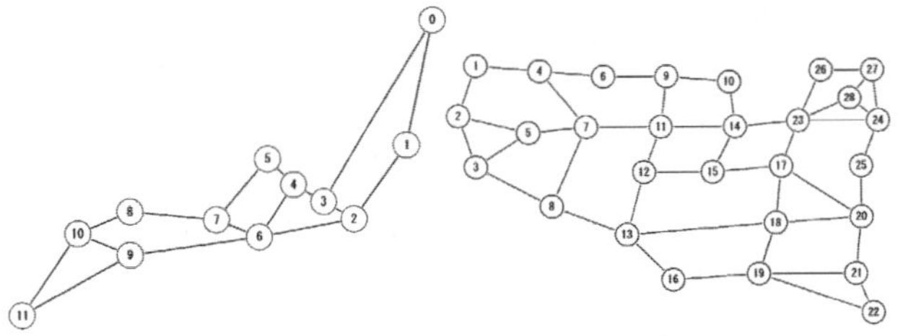
(a) JPN network (b) USA network

Figure 5. Network model.

Core 1 and core 3 are not adjacent to each other. Red cells (e.g., frequency slot 2 of core 3 in link 1) indicate that the cells are already used by other lightpaths. The number in each cell indicates the value of $U_{l,m,f}$, where β is set to be 3. For instance, the value for frequency slot 2 of core 2 of link 1 is 5 because two frequency slots 4 and 5 are already used in core 2 and frequency slot 2 of adjacent core 3 is already used (i.e., $U_{1,2,2} = 2 + 3 \times 1 = 5$). In this case, we calculate $C_{p,f}$ as follows, where $B_p = 2$. For frequency slot 1 in link 1, $\sum_{f'=1}^{2} U_{1,1,f'} = 2$, $\sum_{f'=1}^{2} U_{1,2,f'} = 7$, and $\sum_{f'=1}^{2} U_{1,3,f'} = \infty$, and thus $\min\{2, 7, \infty\} = 2$. Similarly, for frequency slot 1 in link 2, $\sum_{f'=1}^{2} U_{2,1,f'} = \infty$, $\sum_{f'=1}^{2} U_{2,2,f'} = 7$, and $\sum_{f'=1}^{2} U_{2,3,f'} = 0$, and thus $\min\{\infty, 7, 0\} = 0$. Therefore, the cost $C_{p,1}$ is $2 + 0 = 2$. We can also calculate $C_{p,f}$ for other frequency slots and other routes. After calculating $C_{p,f}$ for all the combinations, the proposed method selects a route and frequency slots with the smallest $C_{p,f}$.

IV. PERFORMANCE EVALUATION

We first describe the simulation model in Section IV-A, and then we show the results of the simulation experiments in Section IV-B.

A. Model

To evaluate the performance of the proposed method, we conduct simulation experiments with two network models: JPN network and USA network shown in Figures 5(a) and (b), respectively. In the networks, each link consists of a multi-core fiber. We assume that each node fills the role of an intermediate switch, a sender node, and a receiver node. We use three types of multi-core fibers that has 7, 12, and 19 cores shown in Figures 6(a), (b), and (c), respectively. The number $|\mathcal{F}|$ of frequency slots supported by each fiber is equal to 320.

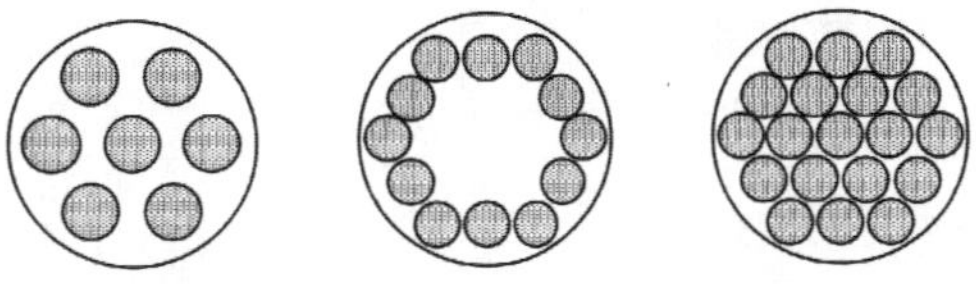
(a) Core 7 (b) Core 12 (c) Core 19

Figure 6. Three types of multi-core fibers

TABLE I. REQUIRED NUMBER OF FREQUENCY SLOTS (JPN NETWORK)

# of hops	required # of frequency slots
1 - 4	1
5 - 9	2
10 -	3

Lightpath-setup requests are generated according to a Poisson Process with rate λ [1/sec] at each node and the destination of each request is independently chosen equally likely among all the possible nodes. The holding time of each lightpath follows an exponential distribution with mean H [sec]. After the holding time, the lightpath is released. The parameter β in (2) is set to be 200. The number K of candidate routes constructed by the K-shortest path algorithm described in Section III-B1 is set to be 3. For simplicity, we assume that the length of each link is identical and the traffic demand of each lightpath-setup request is also identical. Therefore, the required number of frequency slots for each lightpath establishment is determined based on the number of hops of the lightpath as shown in Tables I and II. This means that the required number of frequency slots becomes small when a high-level modulation scheme is used for the established lightpath. We define ρ as the offered load per frequency slot in a core:

$$\rho = \frac{\lambda H}{|\mathcal{F}||\mathcal{M}|},$$

where $|\mathcal{M}|$ denotes the number of cores in each fiber. We obtain an average of 10 independent samples from each simulation experiment.

For the sake of comparison, we use a first-fit method. The first-fit method prepares K candidate routes as well as the proposed method. It preferentially selects the shortest path in terms of the number of hops from among the candidate routes with available frequency slots whenever a new lightpath-setup request arrives. Then, the first-fit method looks for available frequency slots on the selected route in a first-fit manner. If there are no available frequency slots meeting the requirement of the lightpath in the route, then the first-fit method looks for available frequency slots on the next route. If there are no available frequency slots on all the routes, the lightpath-setup request is blocked.

B. Results

Figure 7(a) shows the blocking probability of lightpath establishment as a function of the offered load ρ in the JPN network, where the number $|\mathcal{M}|$ of cores in each fiber is 7. We define the blocking probability of lightpath establishment

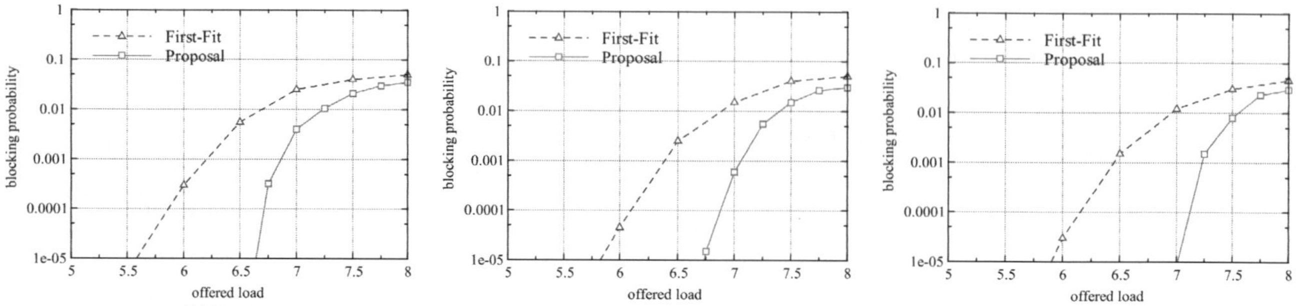

(a) $|\mathcal{M}| = 7$ (b) $|\mathcal{M}| = 12$ (c) $|\mathcal{M}| = 19$

Figure 7. Blocking probability of lightpath establishment in the JPN network.

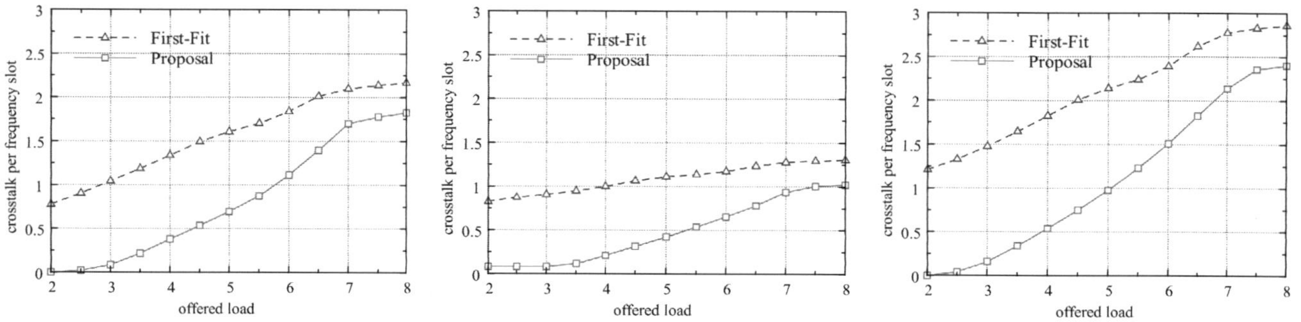

(a) $|\mathcal{M}| = 7$ (b) $|\mathcal{M}| = 12$ (c) $|\mathcal{M}| = 19$

Figure 8. Average number of crosstalk occurrences in the JPN network.

TABLE II. REQUIRED NUMBER OF FREQUENCY SLOTS (USA NETWORK)

#of hops	required # of frequency slots
1, 2	1
3 - 5	2
6 - 9	3
10 -	4

as follows:

$$\text{blocking probability of lightpath establishment} = \frac{\text{number of blocked lightpath-setup requests}}{\text{total number of lightpath-setup requests}}.$$

As we can see from Figure 7(a), the blocking probability of lightpath establishment in the first-fit method is very high. This is because the usage of frequency slots in each link is uneven in the first-fit method and bottleneck links are often generated. By contrast, our proposed method efficiently reduces the blocking probability of lightpath establishment because the proposed method considers wavelength availability in each link.

Figures 7(b) and (c) show the blocking probability of lightpath establishment as a function of the offered load ρ in the JPN network, where $|\mathcal{M}| = 12$ and 19, respectively. As we can see from these figures, the blocking probability of the proposed method is smaller than that of the first-fit method, similar to the result of $|\mathcal{M}| = 7$. From these figures, we also observe that the blocking probability of lightpath establishment decreases with the increase in the number $|\mathcal{M}|$ of cores because of the large-scale effect.

Figure 8(a) shows the average number of crosstalk occurrences per frequency slot as a function of the offered load ρ in the JPN network, where $|\mathcal{M}| = 7$. We count the number of crosstalk occurrences every time a new lightpath is established and the average number of crosstalk occurrences is defined by

$$\text{average number of crosstalk occurrences} = \frac{\text{total number of crosstalk occurrences}}{\text{number of established lightpaths}}.$$

As we can see from this figure, the proposed method greatly reduces the crosstalk effect in lightly loaded situations while the first-fit method is severely affected by crosstalk. The average number of crosstalk occurrences increases with the offered load ρ because it is highly possible that there are no available frequency slots that are not used in adjacent cores in heavily loaded situations.

Figures 8(b) and (c) show the average number of crosstalk occurrences per frequency slot as a function of the offered load ρ in the JPN network, where $|\mathcal{M}| = 12$ and 19. From these figures, we observe that the proposed method efficiently reduces the average number of crosstalk occurrences as well as the case of $|\mathcal{M}| = 7$. Note that values of the average number of crosstalk occurrences depend on the placement of cores shown in Figure 6, so that the average number of crosstalk occurrences in the case of $|\mathcal{M}| = 12$ is smaller than those in the other cases.

Figures 9(a)-(c) show the blocking probability of lightpath establishment as a function of the offered load ρ in the USA network, where $|\mathcal{M}| = 7$, 12, and 19, respectively. Also, Figures 10(a)-(c) show the average number of crosstalk

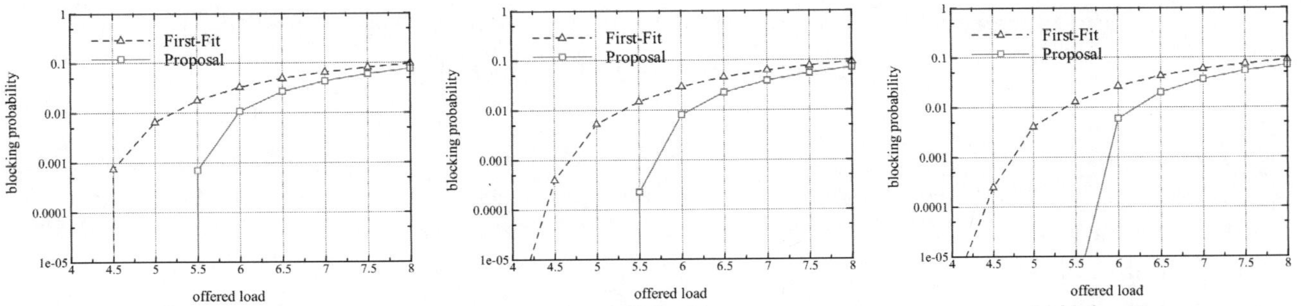

(a) $|\mathcal{M}| = 7$ (b) $|\mathcal{M}| = 12$ (c) $|\mathcal{M}| = 19$

Figure 9. Blocking probability of lightpath establishment in the USA network.

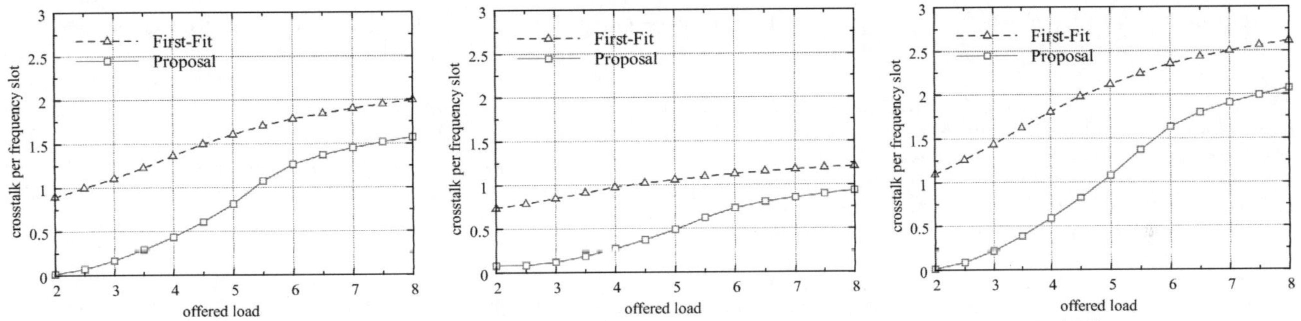

(a) $|\mathcal{M}| = 7$ (b) $|\mathcal{M}| = 12$ (c) $|\mathcal{M}| = 19$

Figure 10. Average number of crosstalk occurrences in the USA network.

occurrences per frequency slot as a function of the offered load ρ in the USA network, where $|\mathcal{M}| = 7$, 12, and 19, respectively. As we can see from these figures, the proposed method dramatically reduces both the blocking probability of lightpath establishment and the average number of crosstalk occurrences, regardless of the number $|\mathcal{M}|$ of cores in each fiber, similar to the results in the JPN network.

V. Conclusion

This paper proposed a dynamic RSA method that avoids the generation of crosstalk and the blocking of lightpath establishment in elastic optical networks with multi-core fibers. The proposed method provides a routing and spectrum allocation strategy, which suppresses both the generation of crosstalk and blocking of lightpath establishment. Through simulation experiments, we showed the effectiveness of the proposed method.

Acknowledgment

This work was partially supported by Grant-in-Aid for Scientific Research (C) of the Japan Society for the Promotion of Science under Grant No. 18K11282.

References

[1] M. Jinno, H. Takara, B. Kozicki, Y. Tsukishima, Y. Sone, and S. Matsuoka, "Spectrum-efficient and scalable elastic optical path network: Architecture, benefits, and enabling technologies," *IEEE Communications Magazine*, vol. 47, no. 11, pp. 66–73, 2009.

[2] M. Jinno, B. Kozicki, H. Takara, A. Watanabe, Y. Sone, T. Tanaka, and A. Hirano, "Distance-adaptive spectrum resource allocation in spectrum-sliced elastic optical path network," *IEEE Communications Magazine*, vol. 48, no. 8, pp. 138–145, 2010.

[3] K. Christodoulopoulos, I. Tomkos, and E. Varvarigos, "Elastic bandwidth allocation in flexible OFDM-based optical networks," *Journal of Lightwave Technology*, vol. 29, no. 9, pp. 1354–1366, 2011.

[4] Y. Wang, X. Cao, and Y. Pan, "A study of the routing and spectrum allocation in spectrum-sliced elastic optical path networks," in *Proc. IEEE INFOCOM'11*, pp. 1503–1511, Apr. 2011.

[5] Z. Zhu, W. Lu, L. Zhang, and N. Ansari, "Dynamic service provisioning in elastic optical networks with hybrid single-/multi-path routing," *Journal of Lightwave Thechnology*, vol. 31, no. 1, pp. 15–22, 2013.

[6] J. Sakaguchi, B. J. Puttnam, W. Klaus, Y. Awaji, N. Wada, A. Kanno, T. Kawanishi, K. Imamura, H. Inaba, K. Mukasa, R. Sugizaki, T. Kobayashi, and M. Watanabe, "19-core fiber transmission of 19 × 100 × 172-Gb/s SDM-WDM-PDM-QPSK signals at 305 Tb/s," in *Proc. OFC/NFOEC'12*, pp. 1–3, May 2012.

[7] D. Richardson, J. Fini, and L. Nelson, "Space-division multiplexing in optical fibers," *Nature Photonics*, vol. 7, no. 5, pp. 354–362, 2013.

[8] S. Sugihara, Y. Hirota, S. Fujii, H. Tode, and T. Watanabe, "Dynamic resource allocation for immediate and advance reservation in space-division-multiplexing-based elastic optical networks," *Journal of Optical Communications and Networking*, vol. 9, no. 3, pp. 183–197, 2017.

[9] H. Tode and Y. Hirota, "Routing, spectrum, and core and/or mode assignment on space-division multiplexing optical networks," *Journal of Optical Communications and Networking*, vol. 9, no. 1, pp. A99–A113, 2017.

[10] S. Fujii, Y. Hirota, H. Tode, and K. Murakami , "On-demand spectrum and core allocation for reducing crosstalk in multicore fibers in elastic optical networks," *IEEE/OSA Journal of Optical Communications and Networking*, vol. 6. no. 12, pp. 1059–1071, 2014.

Performance Improvement of Colored Optical Packet Switching Thanks to Time Slot Sharing

Amira Kamli
Tulin Atmaca
and Catherine Lepers

Samovar, Telecom SudParis,
CNRS, University of Paris-Saclay
Telephone: +33 (0)1 60 76 40 40

Artur Rataj

Institute of Theoretical and Applied
Informatics, Polish Academy of Sciences
Email: arturrataj@gmail.com

Djamel Amar

Institut Mines-Telecom, Atlantique
Bretagne-Pays de la Loire, Brest, France
Email: djamel.amar@imt-atlantique.fr

***Abstract*—N-GREEN is a cost attractive optical network which uses coloured optical packets. Its basic component is a ring of novel overdimensioned switch/router nodes, which promises low latency, making it interesting for applications with strict latency requirements like 5G. Nevertheless, it suffers from a low efficiency of resources usage, especially when it is used in the Unicast mode popular in the metro aggregation. Here, we try to ensure a better use of network resources by proposing an alternate packet management and transmission method referred to as Ssh-time which could be used in both the Unicast mode and the Broadcast-and-Select (B&S) one. We show by simulation that the proposed method improves not only the resources efficiency in case of a metro-aggregation network, but also decreases the mean access delay.**

Keywords–optical networks; coloured optical packets; N-GREEN; Time Slot Sharing; slotted ring.

I. Introduction

The optical packet switching technology has been identified as substantial for an improvement of data rate, transparency of a modulation format, fine switching granularity and efficient bandwidth utilization [1]. On the other hand, such optical interfaces are very expensive and power-hungry which limits their applications; this is why the N-GREEN [2] architecture is proposed. It provides streamlined, cost-optimised interfaces [3][4] which use 10 fixed wavelengths yet without the expensive add-ones like accordable lasers, a possibility of an independent assignment or routing of the wavelengths. In applications like the X-haul networks or 5G where the majority of traffic is real-time [5]; N-GREEN is typically overdimensioned. It can be even more simplified by removing any substantial buffer management as well as processing and thus guarantee a very low latency. This is possible, for example, if there are up to 10 Ethernet cards of 10 Gbit each connected to a single N-GREEN ring whenever the network operates in B&S mode.

Nonetheless, due to its reduced cost in terms of price and energy, N-GREEN seems to be attractive also in a number of other segments of network that are less demanding in latency where resource efficiency is important namely in metro aggregation network [6]. Some existing proposals of enhancements of N-GREEN node use input buffers which would improve its performance. Among them we find Ssh-wavelength [7] which proposes to take advantage of the network overdimensioning in order to reduce the latency and increase the network efficiency. The limit condition of this method is that it is restricted to the B&S mode. However, in some cases, we need to use the Unicast mode in order to not flood a whole ring by a local traffic (e.g., two neighbouring nodes in a machine-to-machine traffic). On the other hand, within this mode, different queues should be considered for each destination, which imply that grooming at the source node is not allowed and thus not only low efficiency of resources but also high latency is resulted [7].

For all these reasons and for a further improvement of the network, we propose a method of slot filling referred to as Ssh-time which could be used for both the Unicast and the B&S mode.

The article is organized as follows. Section II discusses basic traits of an N-GREEN ring. In Section III, Ssh-time is elaborated and our simulation setup is presented. Section IV and Section V show performance improvements thanks to Ssh-time in terms of container filling and insertion delay.

II. Architecture

In the metro and aggregation networks [8] and also small sized data centres, physical ring topology is often used. A single network consists of two parallel rings, one for each direction. It could be used both for data transmissions or which could be used both for data transmission or one ring for transmission and the other for protection. Let us assume that both rings are used for data transmissions. In each ring we dispose of x fixed size slot of size S = 12500 bytes each, 1250 bytes per a wavelength. A slot passes a node in 1 μs which gives a transfer rate of 100 Gbps. There is no arbitrariness in the choice of a carrier wavelength in a single node since we dispose of fixed lasers. A typically 10 Gbps Ethernet card emits or receives traffic which is converted to/from an optical form by a fixed shift register. Each 10 μs of packets in the electronic form can fit into 1μs of an optical signal of all 10 wavelengths, as illustrated in Figure 1. An additional wavelength is reserved for network control as data and control information are sent separately. This control channel is regenerated at each intermediate node to guarantee in particular a self synchronization of the network. A specificity of N-GREEN is that there is only a single semiconductor optical gate/amplifier (SOA) [9] for all wavelengths (see Figure 1), which stays in contrast to a separate SOA for every wavelength in the much more expensive POADM technology [10]. This means that a slot can only be cleared in its totality, when all the wavelengths are either transferred or suppressed.

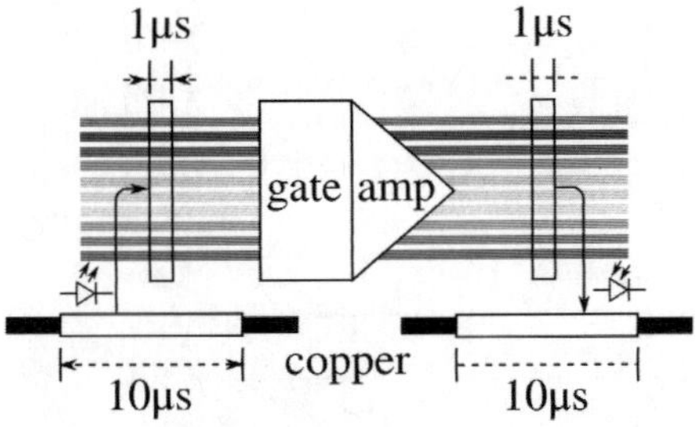

Figure 1: A symbolic presentation of an NGREEN node connected to a 10Gbps Ethernet.

An N-GREEN network includes two types of nodes: those on the ring termed *bridge nodes* and the node that closes the ring by an electrical bridge termed *optical switch node*. Transit traffic bypasses intermediate nodes in a transparent way, i.e., it does not need to be demodulated inside the nodes' electronic structures. Indeed an *optical switch node* connects the ring to other rings where Optical Electrical Optical(OEO) conversions occur at the level of this node. The architecture in question is shown in Figure2 We investigate the performance within the two distribution modes: Unicast, where slots are used by data packets sent to a single other node, and B&S where slots can be used by packets sent to a set of other nodes. In the former mode, a slot has a single destination and that receiver node extracts its corresponding packets and releases the slot. In the B&S mode, a slot may have parts with multiple destinations and as it can only be cleared in its entirety; it may carry an information which is no longer needed. Note that the traffic exchanged between two nodes uses the direction which does not pass by the switch node to avoid OEO conversions and reduce the energy consumption. As packets crossing the switch will be dropped, a special routing is needed where node I sends a packet to node J clockwise if $J \leq I$, or counter-clockwise if $J \geq I$ as shown in Figure 2.

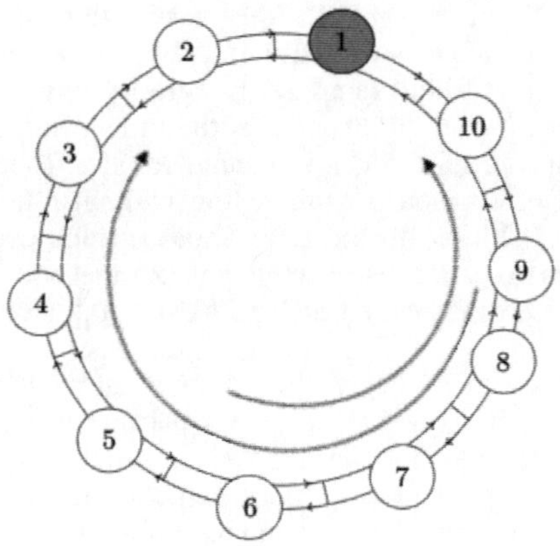

Figure 2: Optical ring topology.

III. SSH-TIME AND CONSIDERED SCENARIOS

In Ssh-time, each node always sends its packets in a sub slot over all the 10 wavelengths. A partially filled slot can be reused by another node which will place its packets over the 10 wavelengths but after the used part of the slot, yet a guard time must be added in between. This margin or gap is required for lasers and other electronic components to be re-adjusted, and to avoid collisions with the fragment already in the fiber. Technically, the guard time consists of zero bits of a minimal duration of 32.8 ns per sub slot. In our simulation, the slot is divided into 4 sub slots in order not to lose more than 18% of its capacity. Figure 3 presents an example of a shared slot encoding according to the two different methods: without and with Ssh-time. The traffic is assumed to be uniformly distributed: packets destinations are randomly chosen with the same probability. Packet size is fixed at 125 bytes which represents an average Ethernet packet size. Packets arrival to nodes are assumed to follow a Poisson process. Note that the packet Loss Rate (PLR) criterion is not considered since no packet loss is allowed in the overdimensioned network. We simulated time division multiplexing (TDM) [11] in which containers are sent upon a regular interval of time (e.g., 10μs) regardless of current network state and container filling level. As for the based-timer mechanism [12], container sending is delayed until the expiration of a previously fixed delay (timer value in T20=20μs, T30=30μs or T40=40μs), unless it is completely filled before timer expiration. In the following we set timer values between T20 and T40. These values were chosen for two reasons: firstly, to avoid an excessive latency since obviously increasing this very value increases subsequently the latency latency, and secondly, whenever a node has enough packets to fill the slot, Ssh-time has almost no interest. Adding to that, in our case timer values have been chosen according to the applied transmission mode respectively $20\mu s$, $40\mu s$ for the Unicast mode and $10\mu s$, $20\mu s$ for the B&S mode. Contrary to the B&S mode, the Unicast one requires more packets to fully fill the slot hence, we attribute it bigger timer value.

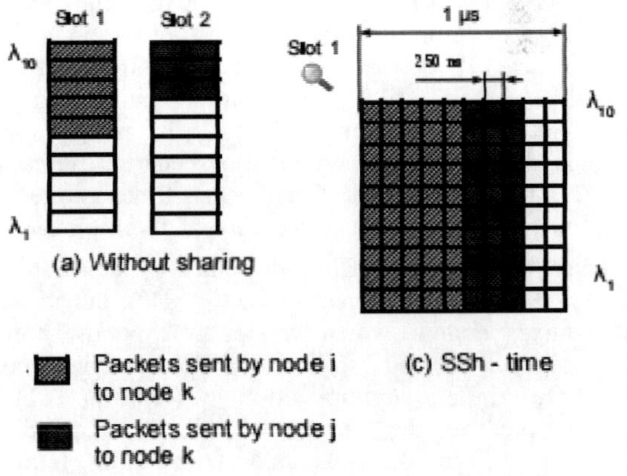

Figure 3: Packet insertion methods.

IV. RESULTS WITHIN UNICAST MODE

The results for Unicast are presented hereafter where Figure 4 and Figure 5 show network load as a function respectively of a mean access delay and the container filling for all scenarios. Note that SSh T20 and SSh T40 stand respectively for 20 and 40 μs timer based mechanism when applying Ssh-time. We pinpoint that the container filling ratio has a value between 0 (entirely empty) and 1 (entirely full) and it is equal to the ratio between the useful data (inserted packets) size and the container size which is in our study equal to 12500 bytes (10 μs at 10 Gbps). While the mean access delay represents the average waiting time of a packet before being inserted into the ring.

The access delay of the first inserted packet in the container is equal to 10 μs. Within TDM insertion method, the mean access delay has to be independent from the system load. When $\rho = 0.9$, the access delay of the inserted packets follows an arithmetic progression with common difference on packets' duration (100 ns). The sum of an arithmetic sequence is:

$$Sn = (n+1) \times \frac{(U_0 + U_n)}{2} \quad (1)$$

where n is the number of terms and U_0 and U_n are respectively the first and the last terms. Let $\overline{A}$ define the mean access delay at $\rho = 0.9$:

$$\overline{A} = \frac{101}{100} \times \frac{(100\,\mathrm{ns} + 10\mu s)}{2} = 5.2\mu s. \quad (2)$$

As expected, the mean access delay is almost constant for TDM insertion method, and has a value between 5.2 and 5.8 μs. Obviously, the TDM mode and one-aside timer 40 (i.e, T40) present respectively the biggest and lowest access delay. However, the slot filling rate remains too low mostly within the TDM mode. It is due to the fact that the packets generated during 10 μs will be put and transported in 9 different slots. Therefore, in order to increase the resources use efficiency by avoiding sending containers with very low occupancy rate; different values of timer has been considered (i.e, T20 and T40). As expected, increasing the timer value significantly improves the container filling yet at the expense of the access delay. This is due to packets clustering that engenders their waiting until the timer is elapsed. Therefore the timer duration should be carefully chosen to achieve a good trade-off between latency and container filling. As seen in Figures 4 and 5, the latency and container filling problems arise mostly when the system is not overloaded within the scenarios without Ssh-time. This is caused by the fact that the timer expires before the slot is fully filled even in the case of the high load.

Thanks to Ssh-time, each node sends its packets to one of the other 9 nodes (division by $(n_{nodes} - 1)$), but in addition to the primary node to which the slot corresponds, three other nodes can share the slot, so during a slot time, we may have up to three emitters (multiplication by $(n_{subslot} - 1)$ where $n_{subslot}$ represents the number of sub slots considered as represented in Figure3). Thus, as pointed out in Figure 4 and Figure 5, Ssh-time improves significantly the container filling and therefore the mean access delay, more particularly, for lower and medium load cases by 20% compared to scenarios without sharing.

It is also important to note that for Ssh-time , in the case of a low load, we does not improve too much the latency however we consider it a beneficial method since it improves the resources use efficiency by 30% as demonstrated in Figure 5. Applying Ssh-time using larger timer values, can improve the latency and slot filling rate for small load values but degrades its performance when the load is big compared with scenarios without Ssh-time. This is due to the guard time that causes a loss of resources.

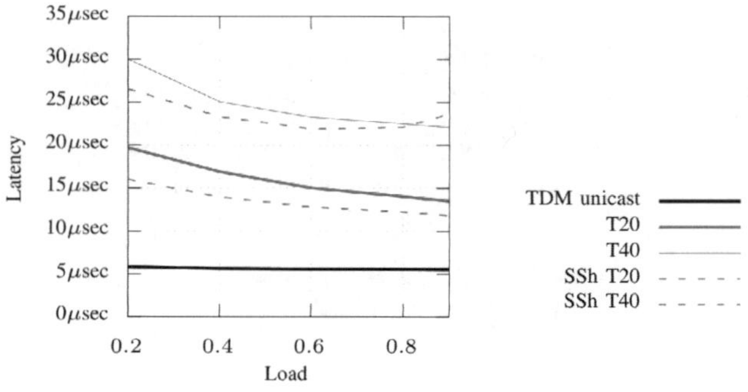

Figure 4: Mean Access delay within Unicast transmission mode for scenarios with and without Ssh-time

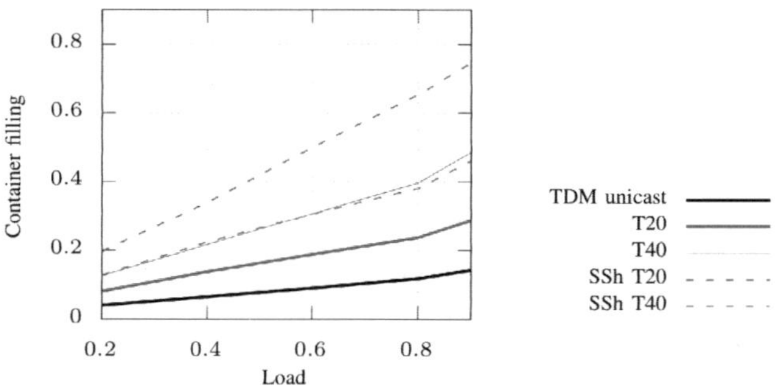

Figure 5: Container filling within Unicast transmission mode for scenarios with and without Ssh-time

V. RESULTS WITHIN B&S MODE

The results of the BS mode are presented below in Figure 6 and Figure 7 where SSh TDM and SSh T20 stands respectively for TDM and 20 μs timer based mechanism applying for both Ssh-time. Within TDM B&S, the packets gathered during $10\mu s$ will be put in the worst case into two different slots which makes the slot filling rate less than the system load, ρ. As for the Unicast mode, an increase in the timer value increases the slot filling ratio and does the same for the latency as shown in Figure 6. To increase this filling without affecting latency, we apply Ssh-time to the B&S mode, which causes the said bandwidth loss because of the guard time and thus the slot is considered fully filled at 0,8. At $\rho = 0.9$, we have almost not only the same filling rate as in the case without Ssh-time but also the same latency: the principal emitter node to which corresponds the slot has sufficient packets to entirely fill the container and the slot sharing does not occur. As ρ decreases, the filling rate increases. Indeed, the principal emitter node does not entirely fill the container, as such other nodes will be able to share the slot. A next sharing node will begin by sending its first buffered packets till filling the container. Since those packets were buffered at the same time or before, their access delay is the same compared to the mean delay of the principal emitter packets. As a result, the mean access delay of all the sent packets during a shared slot is a little less.

Regarding the slot filling rate, as seen in Figure 7, Ssh-time improves the slot filling rate but not as expected since we will have at most three nodes ($n_{subslot} - 1$) that can add their packets in the slot.

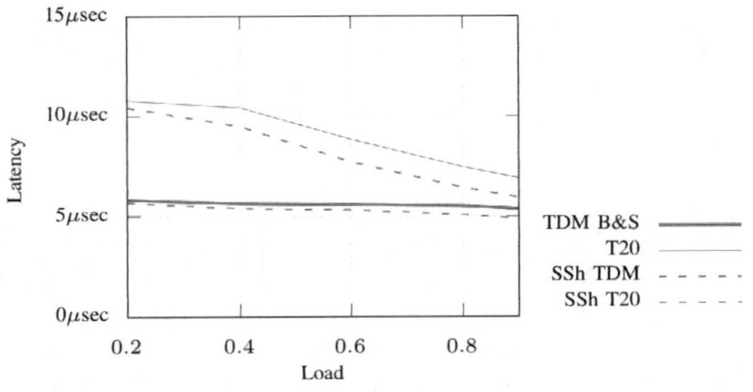

Figure 6: Mean Access delay within B&S mode for scenarios with and without Ssh-time.

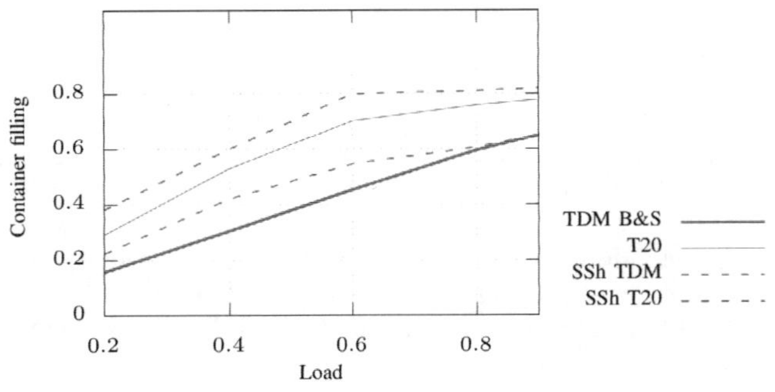

Figure 7: Container filling within B&S mode for scenarios with and without Ssh-time.

VI. Conclusions

In this paper, we have presented the specifities of the N-GREEN architecture compared to legacy existing solutions. We were interested in performance analysis of the metro part of the network. Within a slotted ring architecture, we have proposed and simulated Ssh-time approach for Unicast and B&S distribution modes. In conclusion, our approach Ssh-time improves the performance in terms of latency and the utilisation of resources especially for low and medium network loads reinforcing as such N-GREEN advantages in terms of cost and energy consumption reductions.

Acknowledgements

This work was supported by ANR through the N-GREEN project (ANR-15-CE25-0009). The authors also thank all the partners of the N-GREEN project for their fruitful discussions.

References

[1] C. Guillemot, M. Renaud, P. Gambini, C. Janz, I. Andonovic, R. Bauknecht, B. Bostica, M. Burzio, F. Callegati, M. Casoni et al., "Transparent optical packet switching: The european acts keops project approach," Journal of lightwave technology, vol. 16, no. 12, 1998, pp. 2117–2134.

[2] C. Ware and D. Chiaroni, "Towards WDM slot switching for aggregation access and metropolitan applications: the anr n-green project," in Transparent Optical Networks (ICTON), 2017 19th International Conference on. IEEE, 2017, pp. 1–4.

[3] A. Triki, A. Gravey, P. Gravey, and M. Morvan, "Long-term capex evolution for slotted optical packet switching in a metropolitan network," in Optical Network Design and Modeling (ONDM), 2017 International Conference on. IEEE, 2017, pp. 1–6.

[4] D. Chiaroni and B. Uscumlic, "Potential of wdm packets," in 2017 International Conference on Optical Network Design and Modeling (ONDM), May 2017, pp. 1–6.

[5] M. A. Lema, A. Laya, T. Mahmoodi, M. Cuevas, J. Sachs, J. Markendahl, and M. Dohler, "Business case and technology analysis for 5g low latency applications," IEEE Access, vol. 5, 2017, pp. 5917–5935.

[6] MEF, "Implementation Agreement, MEF 23.2 Carrier Ethernet Class of Service Phase 3," 2016.

[7] D. Amar, C. Lepers, F. Gillet, M. Lourdiane, C. Ware, and D. Chiaroni, "WDM slot sharing of colored optical packets for latency improvement and class of service differentiation," in Transparent Optical Networks (ICTON), 2017 19th International Conference on. IEEE, 2017, pp. 1–4.

[8] C. V. N. Index, "The zettabyte era–trends and analysis," Cisco white paper, 2017.

[9] M. Renaud, D. Keller, N. Sahri, S. Silvestre, D. Prieto, Dorgeuille et al., "SOA-based optical network components," in Electronic Components and Technology Conference, 2001. Proceedings., 51st. IEEE, 2001, pp. 433–438.

[10] I. Popescu, "Evaluation of transparent optical multiplexing techniques in transport networks," Theses, Télécom Bretagne ; Université de Bretagne Occidentale, Sep. 2015.

[11] D. M. Spirit, A. D. Ellis, and P. E. Barnsley, "Optical time division multiplexing: Systems and networks," IEEE Communications Magazine, vol. 32, no. 12, 1994, pp. 56–62.

[12] T. Eido, D. T. Nguyen, and T. Atmaca, "Packet filling optimization in multiservice slotted optical packet switching man networks," in Telecommunications, 2008. AICT'08. Fourth Advanced International Conference on. IEEE, 2008, pp. 221–226.

Securing Tire Pressure Monitoring System

Kevin Daimi
Computer Science and Software Engineering
University of Detroit Mercy
Detroit, USA
email: daimikj@udmercy.edu

Mustafa Saed
HATCI Electronic Systems Development
Hyundai-Kia America Technical Center
Superior Township, USA
email: msaed@hatci.com

***Abstract*—Potential security attacks on vehicular networks have been ceaselessly growing. All the known wireless security attacks in addition to vehicle network specific attacks can possibly be experienced. They can target the privacy of the driver and the integrity and confidentiality of messages sent and received within the vehicle and those messages travelling outside the vehicle. One of those possible attacks can be directed at the Tire Pressure Monitoring System (TPMS) sensor. The message broadcasted by the sensor is intended for the TPMS Electronic Control Unit (TPMS ECU). This message cannot be encrypted and authenticated due to the lack of processing capabilities at the sensor side, and therefore, it could be attacked. If the attack is successful, the ID of the sensor, which is unique and transmitted in all broadcasted messages, will be invested to track vehicles, and thus, violating drivers' privacy. Furthermore, the attacker can replace the original message with a malicious one that could possibly adversely impact other Electronic Control Units. This paper attempts to secure the TPMS by suggesting the inclusion of smart sensors to replace the current sensors. Since these smart sensors possess computing power, encryption and authentication will be made possible. The original ID is replaced with an anonymous one, and the whole message including the IDs are encrypted. An unsophisticated encryption approach is used. Both the key and the anonymous ID are replaced with fresh ones after each message is received.**

Keywords*—*TPMS Security; Cryptography; Smart Sensors; Vehicle Security; Security Protocol; Authentication

I. INTRODUCTION

With the constantly expanding vehicular wireless network, connected vehicles, and the increasing number of vehicle Electronic Control Units (ECUs), securing vehicle assets is turning out to be more problematic. With the increasing volume of interconnections between and within vehicles, the attack rate of internal vehicle networks is rising abruptly [1]. The vehicular ad-hoc networks are decentralized dynamic networks that demand effective and secure communication requirements as a result of the vehicles being constantly in motion. Such networks are more prone to various attacks, such as Worm Hole attacks, denial of service attacks, and Black Hole Attacks [2]. To sustain the enhancements in safe vehicle technologies, it is critical to create a robust vehicle network security system, which identifies security vulnerabilities, threats, and attacks facing vehicle network [3]. Security is indispensable to the vehicle-to-anything (V2X) technology, and privacy is an intact component of V2X security that can be safeguarded with privacy preserving/anonymous authentication [4]. A key development in the automotive industry is the need to adapt proven functional safety processes and techniques for security engineering to allow vehicles to be resilient against cyber-attacks [5]. Security issues in automotive systems are obfuscated by the demand for real-time mitigation against in-field threats, and the in-field configurability and extensibility of security aspects [6]. In connected vehicles, there are different types of attacks that can target the entities vehicle, infrastructure, cloud, and mobile phone individually and the communication between them [7]. Communications of connected vehicles are subject to various security issues and result in immense concerns with respect to privacy and data confidentiality [8].

Modern vehicles utilize several busses in their networks. Among these are the Local Interconnect Network (LIN), Controller Area Network (CAN), Media-Oriented System Transport (MOST), and FlexRay buses. Connected to these buses are various ECUs. These are embedded systems controlling one or more of the vehicle's functions. They play a central role in controlling many functions in vehicles [9] – [15]. Those ECUs are vulnerable to security attacks that could be fatal and can result in casualties. Hence, there is a critical need to protect the ECUs infrastructure [16]. By equipping vehicles with cutting-edge sensors and actuators, and the growing number of formidable network of ECUs, complexity and probability of defects and security vulnerabilities increase [17]. CAN is the dominating bus in the automotive realm due to its simplicity, low cost, and robustness [18]. There is some belief that the CAN bus, to which many ECUs are attached, can be hardly compromised. Pan et al [19] discussed viable scenarios where a vehicle is no longer safe after its CAN bus is compromised by analyzing potential attacks on CAN and their effect on the safety of the vehicle driver and passengers.

One of the ECUs, the Tire Pressure Monitoring System ECU (TPMS ECU) can be attacked as a result of compromising the measurement (Pressure/temperature) broadcasted by the TPMS sensor. The attack can spread over to other ECUs as ECUs share buses. The sensor used in this system is not a smart sensor. It is capable of sending messages (measurements) but not receiving messages. They also lack computing power and storage. A smart sensor is composed of a sensing part with processing resources provided by a microprocessor. In other words, smart sensors are principal sensing parts with embedded intelligence that can provide important data to the receiver with amplified reliability and integrity [20]. Smart sensors should incorporate the following features; self-identification, self-diagnosis, time and location aware, higher order functions, and conforming to communications and protocols standards [21]. A smart sensor may include a microprocessor, a flash memory of 16 KB (8 KB for firmware, and 8 KB for other uses), a 512 B RAM, and 64 parameter registers, and 8 MHz clock [22].

The rationale for having Tire Pressure Monitoring System (TPMS) in vehicles is to warn drivers that one or more tires are substantially under-inflated, possibly creating unsafe driving conditions. The TPMS sensor will forward the tire pressure value and possibly other values, such as temperature, to the TPMS ECU. The TPMS ECU causes the low tire pressure indicator (a yellow symbol) to illuminate on the dashboard instrument panel [23]. The TPMS allows drivers to promptly realize the current status of each tire's pressure. It is made up of TPMS sensors and a TPMS monitoring device (TPMS ECU). TPMS sensors measure the pressure and the temperature of tires and transmit them to the TPMS ECU [24]. The TPMS ECU analyzes the tire information received from the TPMS sensors and reveal the tire pressure status to the driver [25].

Messages broadcasted by the TPMS sensors can be attacked. Since the message includes the unique ID of the sensor, the vehicle could be tracked, and the privacy of the driver compromised [26]. The captured message could be modified by the attacker and then broadcasted. This could impact other ECUs connected to the Control Area Network (CAN) bus [27]. Roufa et al [28] presented a privacy and security evaluation approach of wireless Tire Pressure Monitoring Systems based on laboratory experiments with separated tire pressure sensor modules and other experiments using a complete vehicle system. They concluded that eavesdropping is certainly possible at a distance of approximately 40 meters from a moving vehicle. It was further concluded that reverse-engineering of the original protocols exposed the static 32-bit identifiers and the messages to be easily tracked remotely. This fact, together with the absence of authentication and validation of the messages, will raise concerns about privacy of drivers by tracking their vehicles and allow remote spoofing of sensor messages.

Kilcoyne, Bendelac, Ernst, and Michaels [29] analyzed the cybersecurity of the TPMS wireless communications interface and proposed adopting a more secure TPMS protocol that employs a simple linear feedback shift register (LFSR) based message encryption. They used an interesting experiment that involved a TPMS and various equipment apparently in a lab setting. They encrypted the sensor ID with LFSR but left the pressure and temperature untouched. Knowing that that current TPMS sensors are one-way sensors (they send but cannot receive), and with the lack of any processing power, it is not clear how the message sent by sensor can be encrypted while the TPMS is in the tire. Furthermore, leaving the readings of pressure and temperature as plain messages will make them prone to attacks. In other words, the approach works fine in a lab setting, but it cannot be implement in reality.

This paper suggests the deployment of smart sensors instead of the current sensors and introduces a security protocol that encrypts a message by a key simultaneously created by the smart sensor and the TPMS ECU. To protect the privacy of vehicle location, an anonymous ID for the sensor is used. The remaining of the paper is organized as follows: Section II briefly explains smart sensors. The TPMS security architecture is introduced in Section III. The proposed TPMS security approach is presented in Section IV, and the security analysis is performed in Section V. Finally, the paper is concluded in Section VI.

II. SMART SENSOR SYSTEM MODULES

The smart sensor modules are briefly explained in this Section. These modules are depicted in Figure 1 below. The system has a sensor for pressure and another sensor for temperature of the tire in question. It can also contain further sensors, such as motion sensor, acceleration sensor, and load detection sensor. The module, Other Sensors, refers to these sensors. Because all the measurements detected by the sensors are analog, an Analog-to-Digital Convertor is essential. The heart of the smart sensor system is the microcontroller. It is comprised of a microprocessor, a flash memory for firmware and possibly other uses, a RAM, a register, and a clock. Communications with the TPMS ECU is accomplished through the Communication Media of the smart sensor. The Microcontroller module will play a key role in securing the communication between the smart sensor and the TPMS ECU.

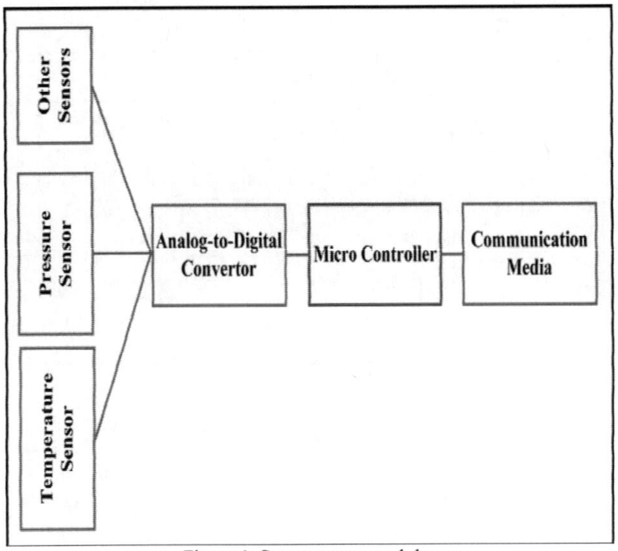

Figure 1. Smart sensor modules

III. TPMS Security Architecture

The current sensors of the TPMS are one-way (one-directional) devices. They can only transfer the readings to the TPMS ECU but cannot receive. They do not have any processing power. Therefore, the measurements forwarded to TPMS cannot be encrypted. This paper suggests replacing the currently installed sensors with smart sensors.

Each tire will be equipped with a smart sensor. All the smart sensors are connected to the TPMS ECU as with the current situation. The sensors can now send and receive data. Furthermore, their microcontroller will furnish them with the needed computing capabilities to implement the needed security functions to safeguard the broadcasted readings/measurements. The TPMS security architecture in Figure 2 reveals the following common subset of ECUs; Telematics Control Unit (TCU), Audio Control Module (ACM), Engine Control Module (ECM), Powertrain Control Module (PCM), and Body Control Module (BCM). Because different vehicle manufacturers use different ECUs, we labeled the rest as ECU1, ECU2, etc. The presented ECUs are selected to show that attacking the TPMS ECU through the non-smart tire sensors (current sensor) can impact other ECUs causing further problems and possibly casualties.

The TPMS security architecture will only try to ensure that ECUs attacks through the broadcasted messages (measurements) are prevented. Securing the ECUs against other attacks is beyond the scope of this paper. A security approach to protect the ECUs is presented in [9].

The smart sensors and the TPMS ECU agree on using Pseudo-IDs instead of the real IDs to protect privacy, cryptographic algorithms, techniques for creating and changing the key, and the order of the transferred messages. They further agree on nonce calculation to ensure the currency of the exchanged messages.

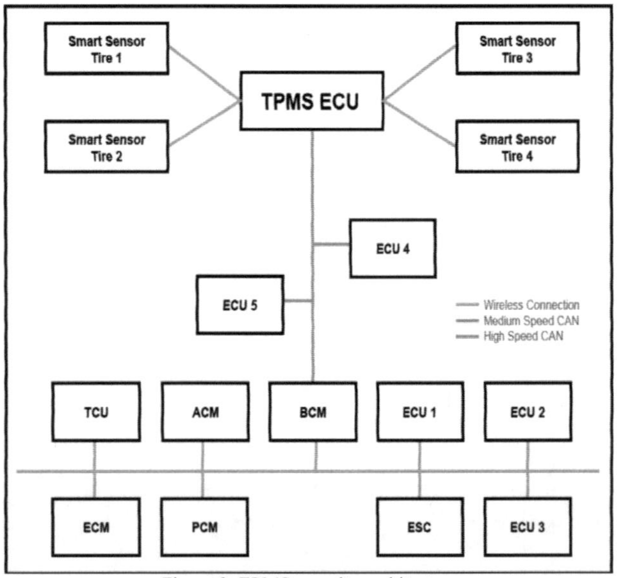

Figure 2. TPMS security architecture

IV. Proposed TPMS security approach

The proposed TPMS security approach is broken up into seven components. The purpose of this subdivision is to facilitate the comprehension of the suggested approach. The notations used in this approach are depicted in Table 1 below. In this security approach, a session is concluded when the messages in the security protocol below (Section F) are processed. Once the two messages are received, a new session starts.

A. Initialization

At manufacturing time, all the sensors should have their IDs ($ID_1 - ID_4$), 64-bit secret key, 64-bit secret value, nonce, and the ID of the TPMS ECU (ID_{TMPS}) preinstalled. The TPMS ECU will have $ID_1 - ID_4$, secret (symmetric) key, nonce, and secret value in addition to its ID_{TMPS} preinstalled. In addition, the MAC key, KM, is also taken care of for both the TPMS and the smart sensors at manufacturing time. For every session, the IDs will be replaced with anonymous IDs to maintain location privacy. The secret key, secret value, and the MAC key will also be replaced with freshly calculated values.

B. Secret Value Computation

The secret value, S, is deployed to further confuse the attacker. It is recalculated after each message as follows:

1. Expand A-ID to 64 bits to get S_1
2. Complement the bits of S_1
3. $S_2 = S_1 \oplus K$
4. Shift left the bits of S_2 16-bit position to get S_3
5. $S = S_3 \oplus$ A-ID

C. Counter

A 1-bit counter, *CTR-1* will be employed to control generating various values. It is initially set to zero. If it is 0, the tire pressure is used for generating the new symmetric key, secret value, MAC key, nonce, and anonymous ID. The counter is then incremented. If it is 1, the tire temperature is used instead, and the counter is incremented.

D. Keys and Anonymous IDs Generation

The subscripts n, p, and c indicate that new, previous, and current values will be used. The goal is to generate the new symmetric key (K), Mac key (KM), anonymous ID (A-ID), and nonce (N). Both the smart sensors and the TPMS ECU will perform these calculations after the measurements are sent by the sensors and received by TPMS ECU. In what follows, P/T indicates using either P or T depending on the value of CTR-1, and the addition is carried out with modulus 64.

$$K_n = (K_p \oplus K_c) + P/T$$

$$KM_n = (KM_p \oplus KM_c) + P/T$$
$$A\text{-}ID_n = (A\text{-}ID_p \oplus A\text{-}ID_c) + P/T$$

$$N_n = (N_p \oplus N_c) + P/T$$

Once the first message exchange is executed, both parties (sensors and TPMS ECU) have only one value for the variables above. In other words, they only have the current values K_c, KM_c, A-ID_c, N_c. Accordingly, the calculations above are modified as follows:

$$K_n = K_c \oplus P$$

$$KM_n = KM_c \oplus P$$

$$A\text{-}ID_n = A\text{-}ID_c \oplus P$$

$$N_n = N_c \oplus P$$

For all these calculations, A-IDs, P, T, and N need to be expanded to 64 bits. An A-ID is expanded by complementing its bits and inserting them as the leftmost 32 bits. For P, T, and N, the expansion is achieved by repeating their value (8-bit) three times to generate 32 bits, complementing them and inserting the complement as the leftmost 32 bits. Once the new values are obtained, only the right most 8 bits for N, P, and T will be used, and the right most 32 bits for A-ID will be valid.

E. *Cryptographic Algorithm*

Before stating the algorithm, it is essential to describe the contents of messages containing the measurements of tire pressure and temperature. This paper will rely on 64-bit messages. Larger messages can be used provided the registers' size at the smart sensors allows that. Vehicles manufacturers assign 32 bits for tire ID. Therefore, the bit distribution will be as follows:

ID	Nonce	Temperature	Pressure	MAC
32 bits	8 bits	8 bits	8 bits	8 bits

The encryption part of the proposed cryptographic algorithms XORs the message M with the key K, adds the ID of TPMS ECU to the result (modulus 64), and then XORs it with the ID of the smart sensor. This is represented symbolically as;

1. $X = M \oplus K$
2. $Y = X + A\text{-}ID_{TPMS}$
3. $C = Y \oplus A\text{-}ID_i$, $i = 1$ to 4

Note that C is the cipher text, and X, Y are just used to simplify the calculations.

The decryption part is the reverse of the above encryption because it is a symmetric algorithm. It is depicted below:

1. $Y = C \oplus A\text{-}ID_i$, $i = 1$ to 4
2. $X = Y - A\text{-}ID_{TPMS}$
3. $M = X \oplus K$

F. *Security Protocol*

Each smart sensor will concatenate the pressure, P, the temperature, T, and the rightmost 48 bits of the secret value, S. It then finds the MAC for them. Having done that, the ID, P, T, MAC, and N are concatenated, encrypted with the symmetric key, K, and forwarded to the TPMS ECU.

$$X = P \parallel T \parallel S$$

$$SS_i \rightarrow TPMS: E\ [K, A\text{-}ID_i \parallel P \parallel T \parallel N \parallel MAC\ (KM, X)]$$

Note that during the first message exchange, ID_i is used instead of A-ID_i. Upon receiving this message, the TPMS ECU decrypts it with K, ensures the message is current and not a replay by comparing it to its nonce, verifies the ID (A-ID_i) of the smart sensor, obtains the MAC of P || T || S and compares it to the MAC of the message. If they are equal, it retrieves the values of P and T and act accordingly.

Prior to every subsequent session, the new A-IDs are generated and exchanged. Before the encryption is applied, N || A-ID_i || MAC (A-ID_i), and N || A-ID_{TPMS} || MAC (A-ID_{TPMS}), are expanded to 64 bits by inserting 16 zeros on the right. The anonymous ID exchange is as follows:

$$SS_i \rightarrow TPMS: E\ [K, N \parallel A\text{-}ID_i \parallel MAC\ (KM, A\text{-}ID_i)]$$

$$TPMS \rightarrow SS_i: E\ [K, N \parallel A\text{-}ID_{TPMS} \parallel MAC\ (KM, A\text{-}ID_{TPMS})]$$

Both parties will decrypt the received message, make sure the message is not a replay by comparing it to their nonce, ensure the message is authentic by calculating the MAC of the ID and comparing it to the MAC in the message, and save the received IDs. All other values including the symmetric key, MAC key, nonce, and secret value need not be exchanged because they are calculated simultaneously by both parties.

G. *Replacing TPMS Smart Sensor/ECU*

It is possible that either the smart sensor or the TPMS ECU may malfunction and the dealership decides to replace them. In this case, the keys will not be symmetric, IDs are new and unknown to other parties, nonce cannot be verified, and secret values will not be the same. The suggested approach to deal with such a scenario is explained below.

If a TPMS smart sensor is replaced, the ID of the sensor is fed to the TPMS ECU either manually or automatically. The values ID_{TPMS}, K, KM, and N are copied from the TPMS to the new sensor. When communicating with this smart sensor, the approach of Section *D* for calculating the new K, KM, A-ID, and N when only the first message is exchanged is followed until current and previous values are available. This methodology also applies when replacing a tire with a spare tire if the TPMS does have the details of the spare tire.

When the TPMS malfunctions, the ID of the TPMS is entered into all the sensors either manually or automatically. The ID, symmetric key, MAC key, and nonce of each of the smart sensors is fed into the TPMS ECU. At this point, the communication will be treated as a fresh one for all parties.

It could be argued that those values are known by the technician at the dealership, and therefore they can be used for attacking the TPMS ECU and compromising other ECUs. This can never occur since these values will continue to change right after the vehicle is driven.

TABLE 1. NOTATIONS USED

Symbol	Meaning
P	Pressure
T	Temperature
K	Symmetric/Secret key
KM	MAC key
MAC	Message Authentication Code
S	Secret value
$ID_1 - ID_4$	ID of smart meters 1-4
SS_i	Smart sensor i, i= 1-4
ID_{TPMS}	ID of TPMS ECU
$A\text{-}ID_{TPMS}$	Anonymous ID of TPMS ECU
$A\text{-}ID_1$	Anonymous ID of ID_1
$A\text{-}ID_2$	Anonymous ID of ID_2
$A\text{-}ID_3$	Anonymous ID of ID_3
$A\text{-}ID_4$	Anonymous ID of ID_4
N	Nonce
E	Encryption
$\oplus$	Exclusive OR
$\|\|$	Concatenation
$\rightarrow$	Send to
C	Cipher text

V. SECURITY ANALYSIS

In the above protocol, only authenticated messages will be accepted. Authentication is achieved by appending the MAC of the messages; MAC (KM, (P || T || S), MAC (KM, $A\text{-}ID_i$), and MAC (KM, $A\text{-}ID_{TPMS}$) to their respective messages, calculating the MACs upon receiving the message and comparing the results. Furthermore, the confidentiality of messages is assured by encrypting the message and the MAC with the symmetric key, K. Only the party that holds K can decrypt the message.

The ID of the smart sensors and the TPMS ECU are replaced with anonymous IDs; $A\text{-}ID_i$ and $A\text{-}ID_{TPMS}$ respectively. This ensures the privacy of the vehicle location is preserved. Furthermore, the anonymous IDs are changed with every session to allow additional security with regards to the vehicle location.

The security approach above adopts the one-time pad. This is demonstrated by continuously replacing the key after each session. Each new message will retain a new key. This scheme is unbreakable.

The security value, S, is adopted to baffle the attacker by granting added security. S is also modified with every session to even further obscure the attacker.

Finally, a dynamic nonce, N, is implemented to verify the currency of the received message. The received N is compared to the N of the receiver to ensure currency. This nonce is vigorously updated using the algorithm above.

VI. CONCLUSION

Current vehicles encompass high data connectivity. There are various communication routes that have access to critical functionality of the vehicle. This obviously demands protecting vehicle infrastructure and functionalities through enforcing efficient methods, techniques, and processes to secure vehicle network. In an effort to contribute to securing vehicle network, this paper proposes a technique for protecting the communication between tire pressure/temperature sensors and the Tire Pressure Monitoring System ECU. The goal of this technique is to prevent locating the vehicle using its ID and thwart attacking other vehicle ECUs through eavesdropping on the message broadcasted by the sensors. This can occur because the receiving ECU, TPMS ECU, is connected to other ECUs through the CAN bus and other busses. If this attack succeeds, it can cause vital damage to the vehicle and the safety of drivers and passengers. For the security approach presented in this paper to work, smart sensors should replace regular sensors. The real IDs are not used after the first communication. They are replaced with anonymous IDs to prevent vehicle location attack. Security (symmetric) keys, Message Authentication Code key, nonce, secret value, and anonymous IDs are re-generated after each session. A session is made up of two communications: sending the measurements for pressure P, and temperature T by the smart sensors, and exchanging the new anonymous IDs.

Should other sensors, such motion sensor (MS), acceleration sensor (AS), and load detection sensor (LDS), be added, the approach could be easily scaled up by redistributing the bits among the measurements. If needed, the message containing the measurements could be divided into two or more messages of 64-bit each. T/P will be replaced with other measurements, such as T/P/MS/AS/LDS. The size of the counter CTR-1 need to be increased correspondingly.

REFERENCES

[1] P. Mundhenk, A. Paverd, A. Mrowca, S. Steinhorst, M. Lukasiewycz, S. A. Fahmy, and S. Chakraborty, "Security in Automotive Networks: Lightweight Authentication and Authorization," ACM Transactions on Design Automation of Electronic Systems, vol. 22, no. 2, pp. 1-27, 2017.

[2] P. Tyagi, and D. Dembla, "Performance Analysis and Implementation of Proposed Mechanism for Detection and Prevention of Security Attacks in Routing Protocols of Vehicular Ad-Hoc Network (VANET)," Egyptian Informatics Journal, vol. 18, pp. 133–139, 2017.

[3] S. Rizvi, J. Willet, D. Perino, S. Marasco, and C. Condo, "A Threat to Vehicular Cyber Security and the Urgency for Correction," in Proc. Complex Adaptive Systems (CAS 2017), Chicago, Illinois, USA, 2017, pp. 100-105.

[4] Y. Yang, Z. Wei, Y. Zhang, H. Lu, K. R. Choo, and H. Cai, "V2X Security: A Case Study of Anonymous Authentication," Pervasive and Mobile Computing, vol. 41, pp. 259–269, 2017.

[5] G. Machera, H. Sporer, E. Brenner, and C. Kreiner, "An Automotive Signal-Layer Security and Trust-Boundary Identification Approach," in Proc. The 8th International Conference on Ambient Systems, Networks and Technologies (ANT 2017), Madeira, Portugal, 2017, pp. 490-497.

[6] S. Ray, W. Chen, J. Bhadra, and M. A. Al Faruque, "Extensibility in Automotive Security: Current Practice and Challenges," in Proc. The 54th Annual Design Automation Conference (DAC'17), Austin, Texas, USA, 2017, pp. 1-6.

[7] E. G. AbdAllah, M. Zulkernine, Y. X. Gu, and C. Liem, "Towards Defending Connected Vehicles Against Attacks," in Proc. The Fifth European Conference on the Engineering of Computer-Based Systems (ECBS'17), Larnaca, Cyprus, 2017, pp. 1-9.

[8] S. Tbatou, A. Ramrami, and Y. Tabii, "Security of Communications in Connected Cars Modeling and Safety Assessment," in Proc. The 2nd International Conference on Big Data, Cloud and Applications (BDCA'17), Tetouan, Morocco, 2017, pp. 1-7.

[9] K. Daimi, M. Saed, S. Bone, and J. Robb, "Securing Vehicle's Electronic Control Units," in Proc. The Twelfth International Conference on Networking and Services (ICNS 2016), Lisbon, Portugal, 2016, pp. 29-34.

[10] M. Richter, "Understanding the ECU – What it Does and How it Works," MC^2 Magazine, 2006, http://www.fes-auto.com/upload/articles/Understanding%20the%20ECU.pdf, pp. 62-65, [retrieved: May 2018].

[11] ETAS GmbH, "Electronic Control Unit (ECU) – Basics of Automative ECU," 2014, http://www.scribd.com/doc/268828296/20140121-ETAS-Webinar-ECU-Basics#scribd, pp. 1-30, [retrieved: May 2018].

[12] Freescale, "Future advances in Body Electronics" https://cache.freescale.com/files/automotive/doc/white_paper/BODY DELECTRWP.pdf, 2013, pp. 1-18, [retrieved: May 2018].

[13] On Semiconductor, "Basics of In-Vehicle Neworking (INV) Protocols," http://www.onsemi.com/pub_link/Collateral/TND6015-D.PDF, pp. 1-27, [retrieved: May 2018].

[14] S. Seo, J. Kim, S. Hwang, K. Kwon, and J. Jeon, "A Reliable Gatway for In-Vehicle Networks Based on LIN, CAN, and FlexRay," ACM Transcation on Embedded Computing Systems, vol. 4, no. 1, pp. 1-24, 2012.

[15] B. Zou, M. Gao, and X. Cui, "Research on Information Security Framework of Intelligent Connected Vehicle," in Proc. The 2017 International Conference on Cryptography, Security and Privacy (ICCSP '17), Wuhan, China, 2017. pp. 91-95.

[16] M. Kang, and J. Kang, "Intrusion Detection System Using Deep Neural Network for In-Vehicle Network Security," PLOS ONE Journal, pp. 1-17, 2016.

[17] A. Lima, F. Rocha, M. Völp, and P. Esteves-Verissimo, "Towards Safe and Secure Autonomous and Cooperative Vehicle Ecosystems," in Proc. The 2nd ACM Workshop on Cyber-Physical Systems Security and Privacy (CPS-SPC'16), Vienna, Austria, 2016, pp. 59-70.

[18] M. Lukasiewycz, and P. Mundhenk, S. Steinhorst, "Security-Aware Obfuscated Priority Assignment for Automotive CAN Platforms," ACM Transactions on Design Automation of Electronic Systems, vol. 21, no. 2, pp. 1-27, 2016.

[19] L. Pan, X. Zheng, H. X. Chen, T. Luan, H. Bootwala, and L. Batten, "Cyber Security Attacks to Modern Vehicular Systems," Journal of Information Security and Applications, vol. 36, pp. 90–100, 2017.

[20] G. W. Hunter, J. R. Stetter, P. J. Hesketh, and C. Liu, "Smart Sensor System," The Electrochemical Society Interface, pp. 29-34, 2010.

[21] R. N. Johnson, "Applying Smart Sensor Technology to Existing Real-World (Legacy) Systems," Telemonitor Inc., pp. 1-10, 2002, http://telemonitor.com/wp-content/uploads/2015/06/Smart-real-world-legacy-system-SmLegManu.pdf, [retrieved: May 2018].

[22] A. Yang, "TPMS," Freescale, pp. 1-74, 2014, http://cache.freescale.com/files/training/doc/dwf/DWF14_TechDay_CN_Baoding_SEP_25_007.pdf, [retrieved: May 2018].

[23] Bridgestone Tires, "What is TPMS and How Does It Work," https://www.bridgestonetire.com/tread-and-trend/drivers-ed/tire-pressure-monitoring-system-how-tpms-works, [retrieved: May 2018].

[24] S. Kim, C. K. Bae, Y. M. Ko, and D. J. Kim, "Communication Protocol for Bidirectional TPMS," in Proc. The Ninth International Conference on Ubiquitous and Future Networks (ICUFN'17), Milan, Italy, 2017, pp. 791-793.

[25] H. W. Chun, "Technology and Service Trends of Smart Car," ETRI Electronics and Telecommunications Trends, vol. 27, no. 1, pp. 147-157, 2012.

[26] P. Bright, "Cars Hacked Through Wireless Tire Sensors," Arstechnica, https://arstechnica.com/information-technology/2010/08/cars-hacked-through-wireless-tyre-sensors, [retrieved: May 18].

[27] K. Koscher, A. Czeskis, F. Roesner, S. Patel, T. Kohno, S. Checkoway, D. McCoy, B. Kantor, H. Shacham, and S. Savage, "Experimental Security Analysis of a Modern Automobile," in Proc. The 2010 IEEE Symposium on Security and Privacy (SP), Berkeley/Oakland, CA, USA, 2010, pp. 447-462.

[28] I. Roufa, R. Millerb, H. Mustafaa, T. Taylora, S. Ohb, W. Xua, M. Gruteserb, W. Trappeb, and I. Seskarb, "Security and Privacy Vulnerabilities of In-Car Wireless Networks: A Tire Pressure Monitoring System Case Study," in Proc. The 19th USENIX conference on Security (USENIX Security'10), Washington, DC, USA, 2010, pp. 21-36.

[29] D. K. Kilcoyne, S. Bendelac, J. M. Ernst, and A. J. Michaels, "Tire Pressure Monitoring System Encryption to Improve Vehicular Security," in Proc. The 2016 IEEE Military Communications Conference (MILCOM 2016), Baltimore, MD, USA, 2016, pp. 34-44.

QBAIoT: QoS Based Access for IoT Environments

Ahmad Khalil, Nader Mbarek, Olivier Togni
University of Bourgogne Franche-Comté
Dijon – France
emails: Ahmad.Khalil@u-bourgogne.fr, Nader.Mbarek@u-bourgogne.fr, Olivier.Togni@u-bourgogne.fr

Abstract—**Providing users with a service level guarantee in the Internet of Things (IoT) is a challenging task in order to ensure a better user experience in such environment. We present in this paper an adaptation of the slotted Carrier-Sense Multiple Access with Collision Avoidance (CSMA/CA) method used in the Media Access Control (MAC layer) of the IEEE 802.15.4 standard in order to provide IoT smart objects with a differentiated wireless access according to the Quality of Service (QoS) class of their generated traffic (Real Time Mission Critical, Real Time Non Mission Critical and Non Real Time). The proposed method ensures a service level guarantee for a Low Rate Wireless Personal Area Network (LR-WPAN) in an IoT environment. Our adaptation consists in creating different Contention Access Periods (CAP); each will be specific for a traffic type and so for a specific QoS class. To do so, we propose firstly a QoS based wireless access method specified by an algorithm to be used by the coordinator, known as the gateway in the IoT architecture. Secondly, we propose an algorithm used by the IoT smart objects. This method enables the coordinator to configure different contention periods with a specific number of slots so that the nodes (i.e., IoT objects) of the same QoS class will access the channel only during their respective contention periods without collision with the nodes of other classes.**

Keywords-Internet of Things; IEEE 802.15.4; Slotted CSMA/CA; QBAIoT; IoT Gateway; IoT objects .

I. INTRODUCTION

The impact of the Internet of Things (IoT) on our everyday life is very important. It changes how people interact with connected objects in order to improve life's quality. Therefore, the enhancement of the corresponding IoT services is an important challenge enabling its expansion. In order to expand the usage of this environment, a better user experience is expected. Consequently, Quality of Service (QoS) mechanisms should be implemented within the IoT environment and especially the communication technologies used in the sensing layer of the IoT architecture such as IEEE 802.15.4 [1]. IEEE 802.15.4 standard specifies the physical (PHY) and the Media Access Control (MAC) layers to provide an important foundation for other standards. Indeed, it is used by 6LowPAN [2], ZigBee [3] for their lower layers implementation.

In this context, we specify a novel QoS based wireless access method for IoT environments called QBAIoT. It is an enhancement of the slotted Carrier-Sense Multiple Access with Collision Avoidance (CSMA/CA) technique, used by the IEEE 802.15.4 standard, to ensure a differentiation between traffics while using the wireless channel of the IoT sensing layer. QBAIoT allows serving different IoT generated traffics while respecting the requirements of each traffic type (i.e., reduced delay for Real Time traffic). In this paper, we aim to present the design details of our proposed QoS based access method, as well as the corresponding simulation results. The reminder of the paper is organized as follows. We present in Section 2 the state of the art concerning the IoT environment, as well as the related technologies and we introduce the important characteristics of the IEEE 802.15.4 technology. Section 3 describes the QoS motivations in the IoT and some related research works. Then, we specify in Section 4 our proposed method enabling QoS based access for IoT environments. Section 5 presents a detailed performance evaluation of our novel access method along with a comparison with the standard access method. Finally, we conclude the paper in Section 6 and present future works.

II. STATE OF THE ART

A. IoT environment

By 2020, 20 to 30 billion objects will be connected to the Internet inducing an important expansion of the IoT [4]. The IoT uses external resources such as cloud computing and fog computing for the processing and the storage of huge amount of data. Cloud computing functionalities enhance reliability and efficiency of IoT service provision [5]. On the other hand, fog computing decentralizes the computing capacities and distributes the operations on network extremities [6]. Based on definitions and concepts presented by different standardization organizations and international research projects, we can propose the following IoT definition: IoT is a system of systems interconnected via standard and interoperable communication technologies. This interconnection allows creating a considerable network of communicating objects, each addressed uniquely, in order to offer new services for improving the quality of human life. Also, self-management capabilities are essential in the IoT in order to offer autonomous self-managed objects.

Different application domains with a variety of services are used in the IoT environment. These application domains cover a wide variety of everyday services like health services, industry services, road services, city management services, etc. In order to offer these services, various communication technologies interconnect IoT objects and gateways within IoT environments. Each technology is suitable for a specific scenario based on different criteria such as energy consumption, CPU utilization, range of the technology, etc. We describe in the following section one of these technologies, which is the foundation of our proposed QoS based access method.

B. IEEE 802.15.4

The IEEE 802.15.4 standard is an IEEE proposed standard for Wirelsss Personal Area Networks with low data rate (LR-

WPAN). It defines the physical and the MAC layers to provide a basic format. This format will be used by other technologies and protocols by adding their own specificities through the specification of the higher layers. The IEEE 802.15.4 physical layer specifies different essential parameters: 250 Kbit/s of data rate for a 2.4 GHz band, control functions like the activation or deactivation of the radio module, the test of the channel occupation and the choice of the transmission channel. On the other hand, the MAC layer defines the data management format and specifies the usage of the slotted CSMA/CA. It provides also some management features, such as access to medium, frame exchanges, synchronization, etc. As for data encryption, the IEEE 802.15.4 standard uses AES-128 to ensure data confidentiality [7]. Different standards use IEEE 802.15.4 as a foundation for their lower layers. We can mention as an example the 6LowPAN standard that combines IPv6 with low power WPAN networks. Another example is ZigBee, a specification for a series of high-level, low-power communication.

IEEE 802.15.4 supports a beacon-enabled mode using a superframe structure. The superframe consists of an active part known as the Superframe Duration (*SD*) and can be followed by an inactive period. The active part is formed by 16 equally sized time slots partitioned into a Contention Access Period (*CAP*) where nodes compete to gain the access to the channel; and an optional Contention Free Period (*CFP*) where nodes are allocated guaranteed time slots. In beacon-enabled mode, the coordinator sends periodically a beacon frame on the network including all the superframe specifications. The beacon, sent at the Beacon Interval (*BI*) time, allows the coordinator to identify its WPAN and ensure that all the objects are synchronized. The Becon Order (*BO*) and Superframe Order parameters determine the Beacon Interval (*BI*) and *SD*, respectively as mentioned in (1) and (2). The Base Superframe Duration (*BSFD*) corresponds to the minimum duration of the superframe ($SO = 0$).

$$BI = BSFD * 2^{BO} \quad (1)$$

$$SD = BSFD * 2^{SO} \quad (2)$$

BSFD is fixed to 960 symbols of 4 bits or 15.36 ms assuming the data rate of 250 Kbit/s for the 2.4 GHz band. In addition, *BO* and SO should respect the inequality $0 \leq SO \leq BO \leq 14$ [7].

Three variable are used in the slotted CSMA/CA algorithm: the Backoff Exponent (*BE*), the Contention Window (*CW*) and the Number of Backoffs (*NB*). To compute the backoff delay, that an object has to observe before performing the Clear Channel Assessment (*CCA*), the algorithm chooses a random value for the backoff delay between 0 and ($2^{BE} - 1$). CW is the number of backoff periods during which the channel must be idle before accessing the channel. By default, the value of *CW* is fixed to 2. *NB* is the number of backoff executed for channel access. This value is initialized to 0 and is compared to a maximum value, *macMaxCSMABackoffs* by default equal to 5. In case the *NB* value is greater than this maximum value, a failure occurs.

- The slotted CSMA/CA algorithm is activated for each transmission of a new packet and is executed during the *CAP* as follows [7]: *NB* and *CW* are initialized
- If the battery life extension is true *BE* is initialized to the minimum between 2 and *macMinBE* (by default 3). If the battery life extension parameter is fixed to false, *BE* is initialized to 2
- The node using the algorithm waits the backoff delay, and then perform *CCA*
- If the channel is busy, *CW* is re-initialized to 2, *NB* and *BE* are incremented. *BE* must not exceed *aMaxBE* (by default 5). If *macMaxCSMABackoffs* is reached, the algorithm reports a failure to the higher layer. If $NB < macMaxCSMABackoffs$, the backoff operation is restarted and the *CCA* should be performed again
- If the channel is sensed idle and $CW > 0$, the *CCA* is repeated and *CW* decremented. Otherwise, the node attempts to transmit if the remaining time in the current *CAP* is sufficient to transmit the frame and receive the acknowledgement. If not, the process is deferred to the next superframe.

III. QoS GUARANTEE IN THE IoT

A. Motivations and challenges for QoS guarantee in IoT

The ITU T E.800 [8] has defined QoS as the totality of the characteristics of a telecommunication service to satisfy in order to meet the user requirements. In this context, a QoS requirement is expressed in terms of QoS parameters (Delay, Jitter, Packet Delivery Ratio, Effective Data Rate, etc.). QoS guarantee in the IoT environment requires an effective and optimized management of the corresponding resources to improve users' experience. In order to provide predictable services, QoS mechanisms in the IoT environment handle delays, jitter, bandwidth and packet loss ratio by classifying traffic. As the IoT environment is made of different technologies and heterogeneous networks, different types of data and streams exist on a single system. Hence, it is important to provide the IoT environment with QoS guarantee mechanisms to meet the requirements of each type of traffic [9]. QoS guarantee is a critical challenge in the IoT, as the number of connected objects increases considerably leading to a greater amount of created and transported data with different characteristics. Consequently, the performance of the IoT system will be affected and especially QoS constrained data traffic due to congestion periods. Deploying QoS mechanisms within IoT environment will enhance the performance by identifying traffic and differentiating it allowing a reduced cost and a better scalability [10]. The ITU-T describes the importance of QoS integration in the IoT through various documents such as Y.2066 [1] where it was mentioned that service priority is an important requirement. In addition, Y.2066 indicates that the prioritization functionality satisfies different service requirements of IoT users.

B. Related research work

Different international projects and research works had studied the Quality of Service in the IoT environment and its impact on the service provision. The European project OpenIoT [11] specified different QoS parameters and metrics for the IoT. These metrics include utility metrics related tosensors and other metrics related to the network and application. As an example of utility metrics, OpenIoT indicated the Quality of sensors that determines the accuracy of measurement, the energy consumption, data volume, and bandwidth. For the other metrics, system lifetime is taken into consideration. In addition, traditional QoS parameters are used such as latency, jitter, delay, throughput, etc. On the other hand, this project presented a high level architecture based on a QoS Manager that keeps track of the following parameters: quality of sensors, energy consumption, trustworthiness, bandwidth and data volume.

Furthermore, other research works had focused on the QoS in the lower layer of the IoT achitecture (sensor layer). For example, the research work conducted in [12], tried to use different queues and a scheduler to ensure a certain priority for QoS constrained flows. Moreover, different research work tried to adapt the slotted CSMA/CA algorithm to ensure QoS guarantee. Thus, the authors present in [13] a contribution that allows the delivery of critical data with a highest priority during the CFP. In [14], the authors describe the usage of different values for *CW*, *minBE* and *maxBE* to differentiate services thanks to three different priority levels. However, these research works did not take into consideration the existence of real time applications in the IoT environment requiring a reduced delay that does not exceed milliseconds range. For this matter, our proposed QoS based access method aims to provide a differentiation between IoT objects' flows based on different QoS classes' characteristics.

IV. QoS Based Access for IoT

We describe in the following our QoS based access method for IoT environments called QBAIoT. The specification of our novel access method is based on a new superframe structure, as well as algorithms implemented within the IoT Gateway and IoT objects enabling Class based Contention Free Periods.

A. *Class based Contention Free Period Access*

Our proposed access method consists in using an IEEE 802.15.4 superframe that respects the requirements of QoS constrained applications. We had taken into consideration four types of traffic corresponding to four QoS classes as specified in a previous work [15]: Real Time Mission Critical (RTMC), Real Time Non Mission Critical (RTNMC), Streaming and Non Real Time (NRT).

Our specified Real Time QoS classes are more sensitive to delay and jitter variation. The Streaming class is more sensitive to jitter variation while the Non Real Time class is a non-constrained QoS traffic class. In order to achieve our QoS guarantee according to the requirements of these different traffics, we adapt the structure of the IEEE 802.15.4 superframe in order to include a CAP (called QoS CAP) for each traffic corresponding to a specific QoS class. Moreover, there are no CFP and inactive periods in our adapted superframe.

We had removed the inactive period to reduce the delay of Real Time generated data. In this context, we can find up to four QoS CAPs in our superframe in case the IoT gateway (Coordinator) is configured with four QoS classes (see Fig. 1).

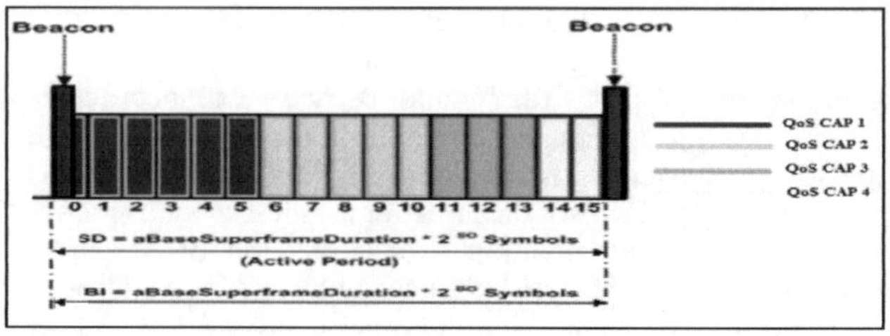

Figure 1. QBAIoT superframe structure

During each QoS CAP, only objects belonging to the corresponding QoS class can try to use the slots in order to send their data. The slots configuration and the number of QoS CAPs in the superframe is based on the number of QoS classes available in the IoT gateway environment. Different configurations for the superframe based on the existence of Real Time applications and the number of QoS classes in the considered IoT environement are possible. If the network includes one QoS class, a single CAP will exist in the superframe and the normal IEEE 802.15.4 slotted CSMA/CA algorithm is used. If there are multiple QoS classes with a minimum of one Real Time class in the network, *BO* and *SO* will be configured with the value 2 in order to minimize the latency of Real Time traffic thanks to a reduced Superframe Duration among others. Consequently, based on (1) and (2), *BI* and *SD* correspond to 61,44 ms with a slot time of 3,84 ms. If multiple QoS classes exist with no Real Time classes, *BO* and *SO* are set to 3 fixing BI and SD to 122,88 ms with a slot time of 7,68 ms. We specify for each QoS CAP a fixed number of slots. This configuration differs according to the number of existing QoS classes in the IoT Gateway environment. For example, in the case of 4 QoS classes the superframe slot configuration is as follows: RTMC class QoS CAP is allocated 6 slots, RTNMC class QoS CAP is allocated 5 slots, Streaming class QoS CAP is allocated 3 slots and NRT class QoS CAP is allocated 2 slots. So, slots configuration and the number of QoS CAP in the superframe is based on the number of existing QoS classes.

B. *IoT Gateway QoS based access method design*

For the coordinator part (i.e., IoT Gateway) of our proposed QBAIoT access method, we specify Algorithm 1 (see Fig. 2) among with the corresponding variables described in Table I.

Algorithm 1 Gateway QBAIoT Access Method Algorithm

```
Input: Nb_QoS_Classes, RT_Classes
N ← 1
if (Nb_QoS_Classes = 1) then
    BO, SO ← 14
    MAC ← Slotted_CSMA
    While true do
        Send_Bcn (BO, SO, CAP)
        Receive_Data ()
    end while
```

```
else
    if (RT_Classes = 0) then
        BO, SO ← 3
        MAC ← QBAIoT
        Initial_Slots_Configuration ()
        While true do
            Send_Bcn (BO, SO, QoS CAPs)
            While(N<=Nb_QoS_Classes) do
                Receive_Data (QoS CAP)
                N ← N + 1 // Next QoS CAP
            end while
        end while
    else
        BO, SO ← 2
        MAC ← QBAIoT
        Initial_Slots_Configuration ()
        While true do
            Send_Bcn (BO, SO, QoS CAPs)
            While(N<=Nb_QoS_Classes) do
                Receive_Data (QoS CAP)
                N ← N + 1 // Next QoS CAP
            end while
        end while
    end if
end if
```

Figure 2. Gateway QBAIoT Access Method Algorithm

TABLE I. VARIABLE SPECIFICATION OF ALGORITHM 1

Name of the variable	Description
Nb_QoS_Classes	Number of QoS classes
RT_Classes	Number of Real Time classes
N	Index of QoS classes
MAC	Channel access algorithm
QoS CAP; CAP	Configuration of the CAP (CAPStart and CAPEnd)
Initial_Slots_Configuration()	Algorithm that computes the slots configuration based on the Number of QoS classes and Number of Real Time classes.

The IoT Gateway using our QoS based access method (i.e., QBAIoT gateway) will receive data from objects during the corresponding QoS CAPs. At each Beacon Interval, the gateway sends the beacon including the information regarding the values of *BO*, *SO* and the first and final slot for each QoS CAP. These values are used by the IoT objects to calculate the slot time and to determine during which time they are allowed to compete for the channel. A QBAIoT gateway should include also self-management capabilities. A self-configuring capability enables the gateway to adapt the superframe slots configuration according to the existing number of QoS classes within its environment. A self-optimizing capability is performed in case of unused slots in a QoS CAP thanks to a slot reallocation mechanism covering the entire superframe. The self-management capabilities design is out of the scope of this paper.

C. Class based access for IoT objects

For the IoT object part of our proposed QBAIoT access method, we specify Algorithm 2 (see Fig. 3) among with the corresponding variables described in Table II.

Algorithm 2 Object QBAIoT Access Method Algorithm

```
Receive_Beacon (BO, SO, QoS CAPs)
Configuration (BO, SO, QoS CAPs)
while (Slot ∈ [CAPStart, CAPEnd] and Data = true) do
    if (Slotted_CSMA (Slot) = Success) then
        Send_Data (Success, PAN Coordinator)
// slotted CSMA/CA returns a success state
    else
        Send_Data (Failure, PAN Coordinator)
// slotted CSMA/CA returns a failure state
    end if
end while
if (Slot < CAPStart) then
    Wait_until (Slot ∈ [CAPStart, CAPEnd])
else
    Wait_Until (Beacon) // Wait until next superframe
end if
```

Figure 3. Object QBAIoT Access Method Algorithm

TABLE II. VARIABLE SPECIFICATION OF ALGORITHM 2

Name of the variable	Description
QoS CAP	Configuration of the CAP (CAPStart and CAPEnd)
CAP_Start_Slot	The first slot for the corresponding QoS CAP assigned to the object
CAP_End_Slot	The last slot for the corresponding QoS CAP assigned to the object

Any object in the IoT Gateway environment receives the beacon. According to the QoS class it belongs to, the object will determine during which QoS CAP it can compete to access the shared medium. When an IoT object generates data, it should test if it has the right to compete in order to send its traffic. If the corresponding QoS CAP of the object has not started, it waits until its CAP time and then competes to send the data according to our adapted slotted CSMA/CA algorithm. If the object QoS CAP had passed, it should wait until the corresponding QoS CAP in the next superframe.

V. Performance Evaluation and Results

A. *Simulation environment*

In order to evaluate our proposed QBAIoT access method, we conduct a simulation study using OMNeT++ based on the IEEE 802.15.4 model [16] including all the necessary features like the beacon, the superframe structure, etc. We had adapted this model to take into consideration our proposed QoS based access method thanks to a superframe with no CFP and different QoS CAPs. In our simulation scenario, we simulated four QoS classes (RTMC, RTNMC, Streaming, NRT). We used a star topology with a single coordinator (i.e., IoT Gateway) where all devices (i.e., IoT objects) are in each other's radio range. Each device transmits data to the coordinator. The data packets are generated periodically but are transmitted during the corresponding QoS CAP. Table III shows the used simulation parameters.

TABLE III. SIMULATION PARAMETERS

Parameter	Value
Carrier Frequency	2.4 GHz
Transmitter Power	1 mW
Bit rate	250 Kbps
Simulation Time	100 s
Max Frame Retries	3
Mac Payload Size	50 Bytes

In the considered simulation scenario, we fixed the data packet generation interval to 0.25 seconds and we increased the number of IoT objects from 4 (one per QoS class) to 12 (three per QoS class). The IoT objects are sending data simultaneously as they start generating data at the same time with the same interval of packet generation.

B. *Performance evaluation*

The evaluation of our proposed QoS based access method is based on different performance parameters concerning the traffic of our QoS classes. The importance of these parameters depends on the characteristics of the corresponding traffic. Indeed, the average delay is very important and critical for the RTMC and RTNMC traffic whereas it is less important for Streaming traffic and not important for NRT traffic. In this context, we considered the following performance parameters.

- Average Delay: It refers to the average time experienced by a generated packet to be received by the destination. It is computed by dividing the total delay experienced for all the packets by the number of packets.
- Packet Delivery Ratio (PDR): It expresses the degree of reliability achieved by the system for successful transmissions. It is obtained by dividing the number of received packets by the number of generated packets. Non received packets are either lost due to a collision or still in the sender buffer waiting for channel access.
- Effective data rate: It evaluates the link bandwidth utilization. It is computed by multiplying the number of received packets by their sizes to obtain the total length of the data frame, which is divided by the simulation time.

Fig. 4 presents the delay evaluation for 4 QoS classes traffic while using our proposed QBAIoT access method and we compare it with the traditional IEEE 802.15.4 slotted CSMA/CA method. The Delay QoS parameter is very sensitive for RTMC and RTNMC traffic. The obtained results in Figure 4 shows that for 4 objects, our proposed method enables better delay for the RTMC traffic (10 ms less than the standard) and the RTNMC traffic (7 ms less than the standard). This difference becomes greater while increasing the number of objects. The better delays that we obtain for Real Time traffic with our proposed method are owing to the fact of giving the Real Time classes a more important number of slots in which they can send their data without any collision with other objects belonging to other non real time QoS classes. Consequently, data packets do not need to wait in buffer for a long time. They are served faster than other traffic types. Although it is not critical for NRT traffic, we notice important delays for this traffic when the total number of objects is equal to 12. This delay comes from the fact that this traffic is served during 2 slots in each superframe and that each traffic class generates the same number of packets in our scenario. So, when the number of objects in the NRT class increases, the delay will increase because the generated traffic is greater than the allocated capacity of 2 slots resulting in a great number of packets in the sending buffer.

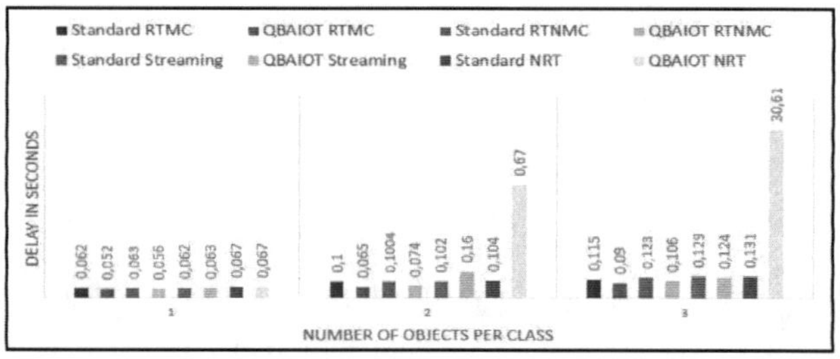

Figure 4. Delay evaluation for different traffic types using QBAIoT and IEEE 802.15.4 Standard

Fig. 5 shows the Packet Delivery Ratio for 4 QoS classes traffic while using our proposed QoS based access method and the IEEE 802.15.4 standard. Our QBAIoT access method is giving, for all QoS classes three times better PDR with one object by class, four times better PDR with two objects by class and 6 times better PDR (except NRT class 1,5 times) with 3 objects by class than IEEE 802.15.4 standard method. We obtain a better PDR with our approach thanks to an optimized channel access per class avoiding collisions between different QoS classes. Indeed, for each QoS CAP, only objects of the corresponding QoS class can compete to access the channel. This way, a lower number of objects are competing for accessing the channel for a given slot. Packets will not run the slotted CSMA/CA algorithm for several times and there is no need to drop packets after several attempts when macMaxCSMABackoffs is reached.

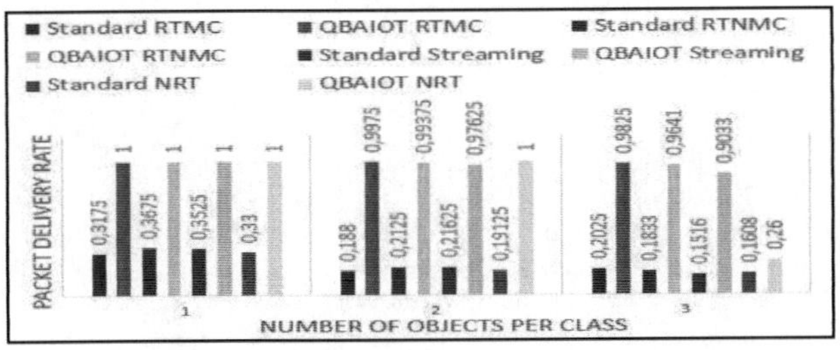

Figure 5. PDR evaluation for different traffic types using QBAIoT and IEEE 802.15.4 Standard

As for the effective data rate, Fig. 6 compares the obtained results using our proposed QBAIoT method and the traditional slotted CSMA/CA of the IEEE 802.15.4.

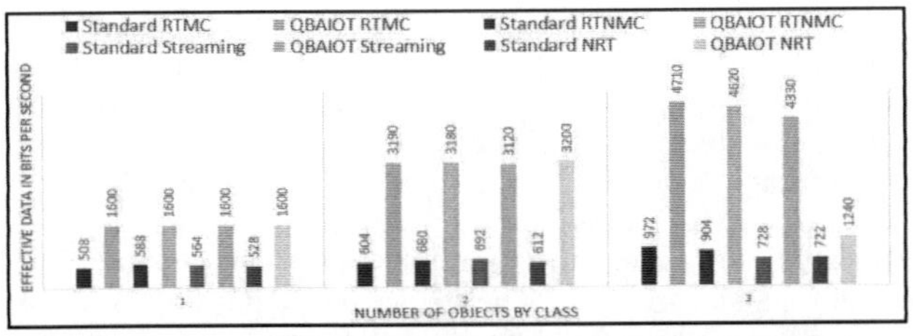

Figure 6. Effective Data Rate evaluation for different traffic types using QBAIoT and IEEE 802.15.4 standard

The obtained results show that QBAIoT allows always better effective data rate than the traditional approach, as the PDR of QBAIoT is always higher.

VI. Conclusion

To ensure better user experience in the Internet of Things environment, researchers try to optimize the delivered services while guaranteeing the QoS. Different access technologies could be used in the sensing layer of the IoT architecture. Several of these technologies are based on the IEEE 802.15.4 standard but the latter does not provide any QoS guarantee for the traffic generated by objects using this standard to access the IoT infrastructure. Therefore, we proposed the QBAIoT access method as an enhancement of the IEEE 802.15.4 slotted CSMA/CA mechanism in order to take into consideration QoS requirements of 4 different kinds of QoS traffic classes generated in the IoT environment. We compared our proposed access method to the IEEE 802.15.4 standard and we showed that we obtain better results while using our QoS based access method to guarantee a reduced delay for Real Time traffic, as well as a greater PDR and effective data rate for all QoS classes.

As ongoing work, we are implementing a closed control loop enabling self-management capabilities within an IoT gateway adopting our QBAIoT access method in order to adapt the superframe configuration according to the environment (slots usage variation within each QoS CAP).

Acknowledgment

The regional council of Bourgogne Franche-Comté, supported and funded this research project.

References

[1] ITU-T Y.2066, "Next Generation Networks – Frameworks and functional architecture models", 32 pages, 2014

[2] P. Thubert, C. Bormann, L. Toutain, and R. Cragie, "Pv6 over Low-Power Wireless Personal Area Network (6LoWPAN) Routing Header", IETF RFC, 37 pages, April 2017

[3] S. Nath, S. Aznabi, N. Islam, A. Faridi, and W. Qarony, "Investigation and Performance Analysis of Some Implemented Features of the ZigBee Protocol and IEEE 802.15.4 Mac Specification", International Journal of Online Engineering (iJOE), vol.13, pp. 14-32, Nov.2017, ISSN: 1861-2121, doi:10.3991/ijoe.v13i01.5984

[4] A. Nordrum, "Popular Internet of Things Forecast of 50 Billion Devices by 2020 Is Outdated", *IEEE Spectrum,* August 2016.

[5] P. Mell and T. Grance, "The NIST Definition of Cloud Computing", NIST, 2 pages. version 15, July 2009

[6] A. Banafa, "Definition of fog computing", IBM, August 2014, https://www.ibm.com/blogs/cloud-computing/2014/08/fog-computing/ (Last access 17 March 2018)

[7] IEEE Standard for Local and metropolitan area networks, Low-Rate Wireless Personal Area Networks, IEEE Computer Society, 311 pages, September 2011

[8] ITU-T E.800, "Definitions of terms related to quality of service", 30 pages, 2008

[9] J.Gubbi, R. Buyya, S. Marusic, and M. Palaniswami, "Internet of Things (IoT): A vision, architectural elements, and future directions", Future Generation Computer Systems, vol. 29, pp. 1645-1660, 2013, doi: 10.1016/j.future.2013.01.010

[10] R. Bhaddurgatte and V. Kumar, "Review: QoS Architecture and Implementations in IoT Environment", Research & Reviews: Journal of Engineering and Technology, ISSN: 2319-9873, pp. 6-12, 2015

[11] Martin Serrano, "OpenIoT D.4.6 Quality of Service (QoS) for IoT services", OpenIoT Consortium, Project Number 287305, 51 pages, 2014

[12] Syarifah Ezdiani, Indrajit S Acharyya, Sivaramakrishnan Sivakumar, and Adnan Al-Anbuky "An IoT Environment for WSN Adaptive QoS", 2015 IEEE International Conference on Data Science and Data Intensive Systems (DSDIS 2015), , 2015, pp. 586-593, ISBN: 978-1-5090-0214-6, doi:10.1109/DSDIS.2015.28

[13] S. Sarode and J. Bakal, "A Slotted CSMA/CA of IEEE 802.15.4 Wireless Sensor Networks: A Priority Approach", International Journal of Computer Trends and Technology (IJCTT), vol. 44, pp. 33-38, Feb. 2017, ISSN: 2231-2803, doi: 10.14445/22312803/IJCTT-V44P106

[14] F. Xia, J. Li, R. Hao, X. Kong, and R. Gao, "Service Differentiated and Adaptive CSMA/CA over IEEE 802.15.4 for Cyber-Physical Systems", The Scientific World Journal, vol. 2013, Article ID 947808, 12 pages, 2013, doi:10.1155/2013/947808

[15] A. Khalil, N. Mbarek, and O. Togni, "Service Level Guarantee Framework for IoT environments", International Conference on Internet of Things and Machine Learning (IML 2017), 2017, ISBN: 978-1-4503-5243-7, doi: 10.1145/3109761.3158393

[16] M. Kirsche, IEEE 802.15.4-Standalone, https://github.com/michaelkirsche/IEEE802154INET-Standalone (Last Access 17 March 2018)

Sectorized Codebook Design for a Polyhedron-Based Antenna Array Structure

Jiyeong Yang and Wonjin Sung
Department of Electronic Engineering
Sogang University
35 Baekbeom-ro, Mapo-gu, Seoul 04107, Korea
E-mail: wsung@sogang.ac.kr

***Abstract*—Utilization of massive Multiple-Input Multiple-Output (MIMO) arrays for reliable data transmission at a very high bandwidth efficiency is one of the key techniques required for the Fifth-Generation (5G) wireless systems. In order to steer data beams to various moving targets including vehicular and aerial objects, new types of array structures are under study. One of promising candidates for such structures is the spherical array based on polyhedrons. In this paper, we investigate how the icosahedron shape can be used to perform full-dimensional beamforming to multiple receivers, and propose codebooks applicable to such a transmission scenario. The correlation performance of the proposal is verified for different codebook sizes, which is shown to exceed the greedy search algorithm performance.**

Keywords-5G; spherical arrays; beamforming; codebook; massive MIMO.

I. INTRODUCTION

For next-generation wireless systems, connectivity to various types of moving objects including self-driving cars and drones is becoming an important issue. In order to provide a sufficient coverage to such objects, full-directional beamforming capable of performing vertical tilting of all zenith angles is required. Utilization of Three-Dimensional (3D) antenna arrays on a spherical structure can be especially advantageous in such transmission scenarios [1]. Spherical arrays are generalization of uniform circular arrays which mainly target azimuthal transmission [2], and can be combined with millimeter-wave carriers to formulate beams based on a sufficiently large number of antenna elements located in a compact-size structure [3]-[5]. Arrays on geodesic domes have been investigated for satellite communication applications [6],[7].

In this study, we investigate an efficient beamforming strategy based on spherical arrays and propose codebooks applicable in a limited-feedback environment. We assume a polyhedron-based array, for which antenna elements are located on vertices of the icosahedron. The boresight of each antenna element form a 3D sector, partitioning the whole isotropic space into 12 sectors. At each antenna location, a set of antenna elements or a subarray can be used for sharper beams with more flexible beam tilting adjustment. This type of sectorization can be regarded as an extension of high-order sectorization used in 3GPP cellular system design in the conventional 2D space [8].

In Section II, the proposed codebook design is explained, followed by the performance evaluation result in Section III. Conclusions are given in Section IV.

II. SECTORIZED CODEBOOK DESIGN

Our strategy is to determine the beamforming vectors for each sector, and apply those vectors to other sectors as well by performing coordinate transformations. Figure 1 shows the sectorization of 3D space using the 12 antennas in the spherical array. As can be seen from the figure, each sector has the form of pentagonal pyramid, and we can indicate the beamforming direction of each vector at its base. Note A_m denotes the m-th coverage sector, (θ_q, ϕ_q) represents the codevector location, and (θ_q', ϕ_q') is the location after transformation. Figure 2 is an illustration of such indication. With a single representative codevector at the antenna boresight, we evenly distribute the remaining vectors at a certain angular distance. The distance is determined by the correlation measure between the geometric channel and the codevector, in such a way that the average correlation is maximized. We progressively use more beamforming vectors to include $Q = 2^B$ entries in the codebook as the number B of feedback bits increases.

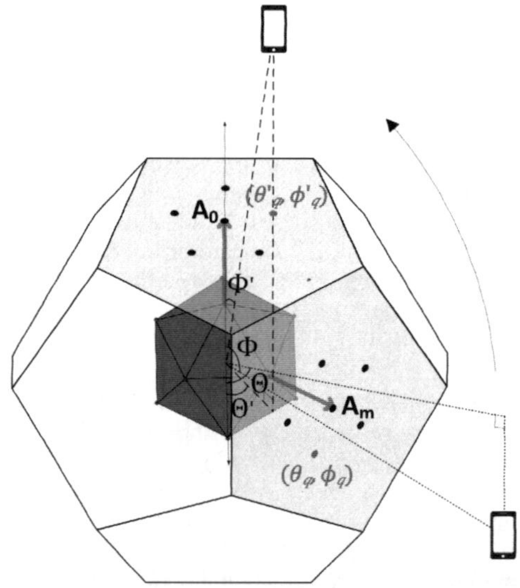

Figure 1. Beamforming vectors for each of 12 sectors in 3D space.

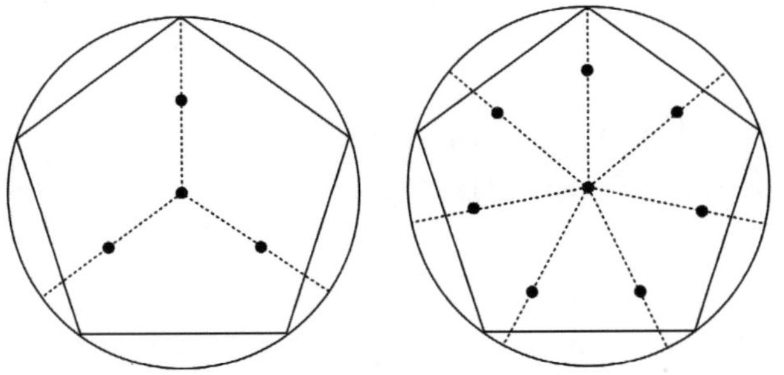

(a) (b)

Figure 2. Beam directions for the chosen codevectors: (a) $B = 2$, (b) $B = 3$.

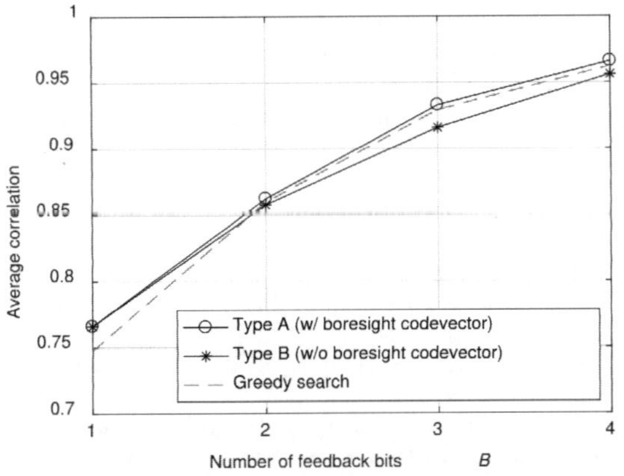

Figure 3. Perfomance of the proposed codebook in comparison to greedy search results.

Constructed codebook $\mathbf{C} = \{\mathbf{w}_1, \mathbf{w}_2, \ldots, \mathbf{w}_Q\}$ includes codevectors $\mathbf{w}_q$ for which the phase vector has the form

$$\text{Phase}(\mathbf{w}_q) = -(2\pi/\lambda)\ [\ d_0, d_1, \ldots, d_{M-1}\ ]^T$$

for $q = 1, 2, \ldots, Q$, where λ is the carrier wavelength, M is the number of antenna elements, and d_m is the distance between the m-th antenna and the target receiver. The distance is determined using the geometry characteristics of the array polyhedron. For the antenna elements located at vertices of icosahedron, the distance has the form of

$$d_m = \sin\theta \sin\alpha \cos(\phi - \beta) + \cos\theta \cos\alpha$$

where ϕ and θ are position angles for the codvector points in Figure 2. Symbols $\alpha \in \{0, 31.7^o, \pi - 31.7^o, \pi\}$ and $\beta \in \{0, \pi/10, 2\pi/10, \ldots, 9\pi/10\}$ are obtained from the geometry information of icosahedron. By computing the distances, the codebook of a given size is obtained and the corresponding performance can be evaluated.

III. Performance

We evaluated the average correlation performance of the proposed sectorized codebook for different codebook sizes. The result is summarized in Figure 3. As the codebook size increases, the correlation rapidly approaches to unity, the performance for beamforming vectors with infinite resolution. We found the case with the codevectors pointing the antenna boresight at the sector center (indicated as Type A in the figure) outperforms the case without them (indicated as Type B). We also have constructed search-based codebooks using the greedy algorithm, by successively selecting the beamforming vector, which is most preferred by the random channel location samples. As can be verified from the figure, the proposed Type A codebook exhibits enhanced performance over the search method.

IV. Conclusion

We proposed the codebook which can be applied to the 3D space covered by spherical arrays. The design can be generalized to different array structures including geodesic-based spheres and those including antenna subarrays. Planned future work is the multi-rank extension exploiting the orthogonality of the spherical beams.

Acknowledgment

This work was supported by the National Research Foundation (NRF) of Korea (NRF-2017R1A2B4002367) and by Commercialization Promotion Agency for R&D Outcomes, MSIP (No. 2017K000348).

References

[1] S. M. Razavizadeh, M. Ahn, and I. Lee, "Three-dimensional beamforming: A new enabling technology for 5G wireless networks," IEEE Signal Process. Mag.,. vol. 31, no. 6, pp. 94-101, Nov. 2014.

[2] Q. U. A. Nadeem, A. Kammoun, M. Debbah, and M. S. Alouini, "Spatial correlation characterization of a uniform circular array in 3D MIMO systems," Proc. IEEE SPAWC '16, pp. 1-6, Edinburgh, UK, July 2016.

[3] H. Seleem, et. al., "Hybrid precoding-beamforming design with Hadamard RF codebook for mmWave large-scale MIMO systems," IEEE Access, vol. 5, pp. 6813-6823, 2017.

[4] 3GPP TR 36.873 V12.2.0, Study on 3D Channel Model for LTE (Release 12), June 2015.

[5] 3GPP TR 38.901 V14.1.1, Study on Channel Model for Frequencies From 0.5 to 100 GHz (Release 14), July 2017.

[6] B. Tomasic, et. al., "The geodesic dome phased array antenna for satellite control and communication - Subarray design, development and demonstration," IEEE Int. Symp. Phased Array Syst. Technol., 2003, pp. 411-416.

[7] S. Liu, B. Tomasic, and J. Turtle, "The geodesic dome phased array antenna for satellite operations support - Antenna resource management," IEEE Int. Symp. Ant. Prop. Soc., Honolulu, HI, 2007, pp. 3161-3164.

[8] R. Joyce, et. al., "Higher order horizontal sectorization gains for 6, 9, 12 and 15 sectored cell sites in a 3GPP/HSPA+ network," IEEE Trans. Veh. Technol., vol. 65, no. 5, pp. 3440-3449, May 2016.

Reducing Link Failure Test Cases for Telecom Networks by Focusing on Topological Similarity

Megumi Shibuya†, Toshihiko Kato†, Teruyuki Hasegawa†† and Hirozumi Yamaguchi‡
†University of Electro-Communications
Tokyo, Japan
e-mail: shibuya@net.is.uec.ac.jp
kato@is.uec.ac.jp
††KDDI, Corp.
Tokyo, Japan
e-mail: teruyuki0077.society@gmail.com
‡Osaka University
Osaka, Japan
e-mail: h-yamagu@ist.osaka-u.ac.jp

***Abstract*—In order to provide high reliable network services for a large number of users, an ideal network test is required to guarantee end-to-end connection for any pair of clients with a failure of any link. However, the time and human resources that can be dedicated to the test are limited, which prevents such an ideal test. In this paper, we propose a method to reduce the number of network failure test cases by focusing on "similarity" among test cases. We leverage topological similarity for the purpose, formulate a problem of minimizing the number of test cases, and conduct simulation experiments to show the effectiveness.**

Keywords- Telecom network; Link failure test; Topological similarity; Optimization.

I. INTRODUCTION

The telecom companies, such as Internet service providers and mobile network operators, are required to provide highly reliable network service for a large number of users. For this purpose, the networks maintained by telecom companies, which we call *telecom networks* in this paper, take the following two approaches. The first is to introduce redundant configuration. At least two paths are guaranteed between any two network node pair. The second is strict testing at changing network configuration, such as introducing new equipment, changing the network configuration, and upgrading software versions.

In general, the testing in telecom networks is conducted as link failure test. In the case that a physical link is disconnected, or network equipment, such as a switch and a router is broken, those failures are detected as failures at the related links. Therefore, it will be common that the testing at the network configuration change is performed in the following way.

- Select a pair of nodes which may communicate together, and determine a communicating path between them.
- Pick up one of the links comprising the path, cause fault artificially on the selected link (*link shutdown*), and verify that a new communication path is set up and the communication between the selected nodes is restarted. This procedure is called a *test case* in this paper.
- Conduct the above test case for all possible node pairs and links in paths.

Recent telecom networks have become large in their size and complex in their structure. This increases the number of test cases in the link failure testing. Furthermore, due to the spread of Internet of Things (IoT) applications, the number of devices connected to network is increased, the number of communication node pairs is increased, and the number of links included in a path between a node pair is increased. As a result, the number of link failure test cases is drastically increased. On the other hand, it is difficult for a telecom company to conduct a vast number of tests exhaustively within a limited time until the start of service. Therefore, it becomes important to reduce the number of failure test cases without deteriorating the reliability.

We focus on the topological similarity in a telecom network to reduce the number of test cases. In general, a telecom network has a tree-like hierarchical structure, consisting of several *link tiers* including core, relay and access. The type of network equipment and the bandwidth of links are selected on a tier basis, and the type of routing protocols also depends on tiers, e.g., border gateway protocol (BGP) at a core tier and open shortest path first (OSPF) at a relay tier.

Therefore, we propose to introduce the topological similarity to selecting the link failure test cases in the following two steps.

Step 1:

We introduce the *similarity of test cases* using an idea of the *abstract path* that considers only the number of links and their tiers in a path.

Specifically, for different communicating node pairs whose paths have the same number of links, each of which has the same link tier (the same abstract path), we suppose that the communications for these node pairs will be processed similarly within the telecom network. Based on this concept, we define that test cases for node pairs and shut down links are *similar*, when the followings are satisfied.

(1) The paths for node pairs before a link shutdown have the same abstract path.
(2) The shut down links are located at the same tier.
(3) The paths for node pairs after a link shutdown have the same abstract path.

For reducing the number of test cases, we suppose that conducting only one of test case will be enough among the similar test cases.

Step 2:

We expand the idea of abstract path so as to include other attributes.

In Step 1, only the number of links and the tier of links are considered. However, other attributes, such as the link bandwidth and the manufacturers or types of network equipment will influence the processing behaviors within the network. So, we add link bandwidth or equipment type in the definition of abstract path.

In this paper, we propose how to reduce the number of link failure test cases by focusing on the topology similarity based on the idea of test case similarity using abstract path. We suppose an IoT oriented telecom network, where end nodes in the network, which we call *clients*, communicate with each other, and the link failure test assuming single link failure. We define as a *test target* a set of communicating client pair and a shut down link over the path between the client pair. We cluster the possible test targets throughout a telecom network into groups of similar test targets based on the idea of abstract path, as described in Steps 1 and 2 above. This will be done by formulating with integer linear programming (ILP) problem. By selecting one test target from a test target cluster, we can reduce the number of test cases drastically.

This paper is organized as follows. Section II summarizes related work and Section III explains the proposed method. Section IV presents the experimental results of applying the proposed method to various types of networks. We conclude this work in Section V.

II. Related Work

As for the network failure test, there are many studies focusing on improving its efficiency by automating network tests [1]-[3]. M. Shibuya et al. [1], our previous paper, proposes an automated network testing system which can automatically construct test environment, check connectivity, test scenario execution, and collect and analyze test results. The work in [2] proposes L1 patch where all OpenFlow switches are virtually monitored in a single L1 patch panel using an OpenFlow technique. By combining this approach with Mininet [4], an OSS-based network testing tool mitigates the operational workload. The dedicated time is just a few minutes per operator, while the conventional work procedure requires a half hour or an hour by two operators. The work in [2] also reports that the number of test types increased to 194, which had been just 90 in the conventional approach because the testing time was shorten. The work in [3] proposes a method to construct an automated test platform for Virtual Network Functions (VNF). Network comprehensive tests, which had required a lot of manual operations so far, can be automatically performed by using the proposed tool [5]. According to [3], 2,736 types of tests can be conducted in 40 hours. These workload mitigation methods are of great help, but we need to design a fundamental methodology to reduce the number of test cases while keeping the test coverage.

As for the topology similarity, there are several studies on the graph similarity based on network metrics, such as hop distance and link degrees [6]-[10]. The graph isomorphism problem [6] is a computational approach to determine whether two finite graphs are isomorphic or not. This approach is able to prove the isomorphism between two graphs, and some algorithms, such as Ullman [7], VF 2 [8], and Naughty [9], are proposed. However, they have an issue that the computational complexity is not known.

G. Kollias et al. [10] proposes a similarity calculation method of topology in a neuro network. This method compares the similarity of partial networks focusing on the number of connections of nodes and links. For network tests, however, we need to take into account of not only the topology but also the end user paring, routing and link failures. Therefore, the challenge is to design an appropriate similarity that actually covers a wide variety of viewpoint.

III. Proposed Method

In this section, we explain how our proposed method reduces the number of link failure test cases by focusing on the topology similarity based on the test case similarity using abstract path.

A. Traditional Failure Test

As described above, a traditional failure test requires that testing be conducted for all combinations of client pairs and shut down links over paths between individual client pairs. Therefore, the number of test cases in a traditional test is given by the following;

$$F = \sum_{c_i, c_j \in C, i<j} H_{ij} \quad (1)$$

where C is the set of clients and H_{ij} is the path length between clients c_i and c_j.

B. Notation

As described in Section I, the purpose of proposed method is to reduce the number of link failure test cases by introducing similarity among test cases in two steps. In order to specify the proposed method, this paper introduces the following notations.

- a path between clients c_i and c_j: *Primary* (c_i, c_j)
- test target focusing on clients c_i and c_j, and link to be shut down (shut down link) e: (c_i, c_j, e)
  Here, $e \in$ *Primary* (c_i, c_j).
- a path between clients c_i and c_j after shut down link e is shut down: *Secondary* (c_i, c_j, e)
- path length of a client pair (c_i, c_j) before link shutdown: q
- path length of a client pair (c_i, c_j) after link shutdown: r
- the link tier of shut down link e: k
- test target attribute vector used in Step 1: (q, r, k)

- name of additional test attribute used in Step 2: α
  In this paper, link bandwidth and equipment type are used as α.
- value of attribute defined dependent of attribute name α: w_α
  In this paper, w is defined as follows;
  - α = bandwidth: w_α = link bandwidth with shut down link e
  - α = equipment_type: w_α = equipment types at both sides of shut down link e
- test target attribute vector used in Step 2: (q, r, k, w_α)
- maximum number of conducting test cases: N

C. Basic Idea

In this subsection, we describe our basic idea using an example shown in Figure 1. Here, we suppose four link tier network with four clients. Figure 1(a) shows the paths between possible client pairs. We suppose the shutdown of links at tier 3 (links *e1* though *e8*). Figure 1(b) shows a test case where link *e1* is shut down. In this case, Paths *Primary* (*c1, c2*) and *Primary* (*c1, c3*) will be rearranged to paths

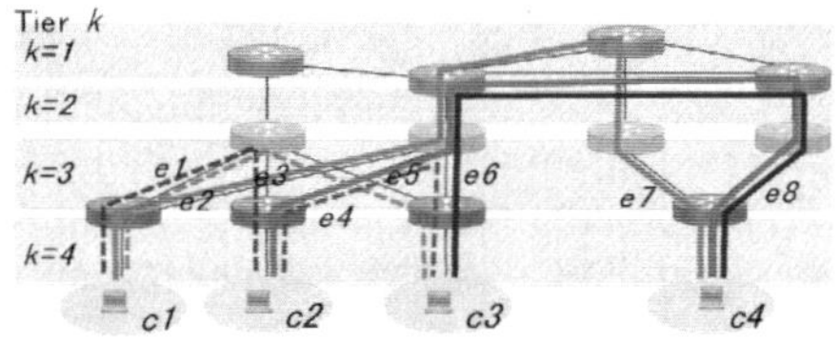

(a) Network configuration and paths between client pairs.

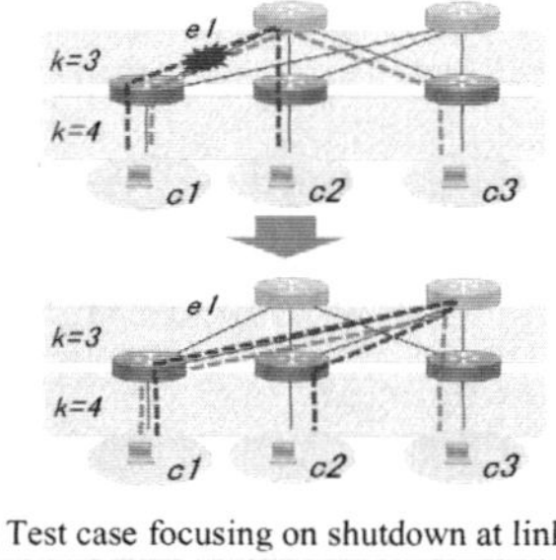

(b) Test case focusing on shutdown at link *e1*.

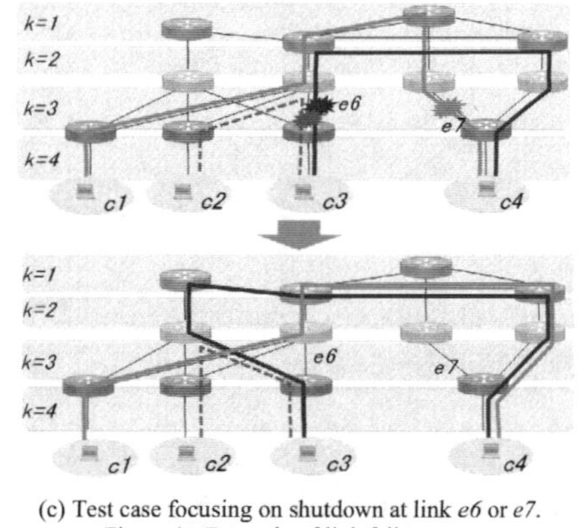

(c) Test case focusing on shutdown at link *e6* or *e7*.

Figure 1. Example of link failure test.

Secondary (*c1, c2, e1*) and *Secondary* (*c1, c3, e1*), respectively, as shown in the figure. Figure 1(c) shows the test cases where link *e6* or *e7* is shut down. When we focus only on the path lengths before and after link shutdown (q and r, respectively), and the tier of shut down link (k), the paths can be modeled as shown in Figure 2. This is abstract paths handled in Step 1. For all the paths among clients *c1, c2,* and *c3*, the paths before and after link shutdown have path length 4, i.e., $q = r = 4$. In this case, we consider that all the test cases whose test targets are specified by (i) in Figure 2 are similar and can be clustered in a group (test target cluster). We propose that one test case can represent this cluster and that checking one test case is enough in the link failure test.

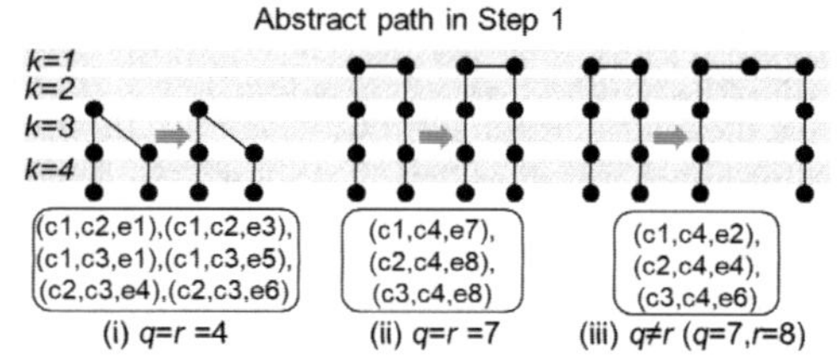

Figure 2. Test target clustering in Step 1.

For the paths between *c1, c2* or *c3*, and *c4*, there are two cases as shown in (ii) and (iii) in Figure 2. The path length before link shutdown, the path length is 7 for all test targets. For test targets (*c1, c4, e7*), (*c2, c4, e8*) and (*c3, c4, e8*), the path length after link shutdown is 7. Figure 1(c) shows the case of test target (*c1, c4, e7*). On the other hand, for test targets (*c1, c4, e2*), (*c2, c4, e4*) and (*c3, c4, e6*), the path length after link shutdown is 8. So, we consider that the behaviors after the link shutdown will be different for these two test case clusters, and we propose that one test target needs to be selected from each of the clusters.

As we explained in Section I, the abstract path in Step 1 is too generalized network features. So, in this paper, we add other attributes, such as link bandwidth and equipment type, in defining abstract paths. Consider that, among links at tier 3, link *e5* has different bandwidth than the others. Say, the bandwidth of link *e5* is 1 and that of others is 2. In this case, the test target cluster given by (iii) in Figure 2 is divided as shown in Figure 3. Specifically, only in the test case for target (*c3, c4, e6*), the path after link shutdown goes through link *e5*, as indicated in Figure 1(c). Therefore, test targets (*c1, c4, e2*) and (*c2, c4, e4*) are classified in a cluster and target (*c3, c4, e6*) is in another.

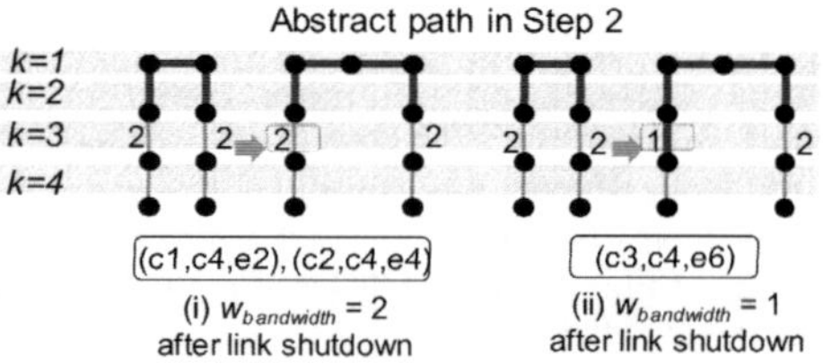

Figure 3. Test target clustering in Step 2.

D. Formulation

In this subsection, we formulate how to group test targets into test target clusters as an optimization problem.

Suppose a network that consists of switches $V = \{v_1, v_2, ..., v_S\}$ and links $E = \{e_1, e_2, ..., e_L\}$, whose sizes are respectively S and L and follows k tiered topology. It is expressed as network graph $G = (V, E)$ with $E \subseteq V \times V$. Each client is a member of the client set $C = \{c_1, c_2, ..., c_M\}$ *where* M denotes the number of clients, and is connected to one of switches as a leaf. Each link has an additional attribute and has an attribute value assigned from $W = \{w_{e1}, w_{e2}, ..., w_{eL}\}$.

Next, we define the similarity function *Sim ()* between two test targets in the following way. That is, if the test target attribute vectors are the same for two test targets, then this function is 1, otherwise 0.

$$Sim\left(\left(c_x, c_y, e\right), \left(c_a, c_b, e_z\right)\right) = \begin{cases} 1 & same \\ 0 & otherwise \end{cases} \quad (2)$$

Using on this function, the set of similar test targets are calculated in the following way, focusing on a specific link e to be shut down, which we denote as $D(e)$.

$$\begin{aligned} D(e) = &\left\{\left(c_x, c_y, e\right) \mid \forall c_x, \forall c_y \in C; x < y\right\} \\ \cup &\left\{\left(c_a, c_b, e_z\right) \mid \forall c_a, \forall c_b \in C;\right. \\ &\forall e_z \in E; \exists c_i, \exists c_j \in C; \\ &i < j;\ a < b; \\ &\left. Sim\left(\left(c_i, c_j, e\right), \left(c_a, c_b, e_z\right)\right) = 1\right\} \end{aligned} \quad (3)$$

Furthermore, we introduce the binary variable *down*(e) that indicates whether the link shutdown at link e is actually conducted (=1) or not (=0). $Z(e)$, a subset of $D(e)$ that only includes test targets associated with actual shutdown links, can be given with *down*(e) as follows.

$$Z(e) = \begin{cases} D(e) & \text{if } down(e) = 1 \\ \varphi & \text{if } down(e) = 0 \end{cases} \quad (4)$$

Here, the number of shut down links must not be greater than N, which is a given limit.

$$\text{s.t.} \qquad \sum_{e \in E} down(e) \le N \quad (5)$$

By selecting $Z(e)$ with the maximum number of test targets, the number of test cases is reduced. Therefore, using (2) through (5), the objective function to be optimized is expressed in (6).

$$\text{maximize} \qquad \sum_{e \in E} \left| \bigcup Z(e) \right| \quad (6)$$

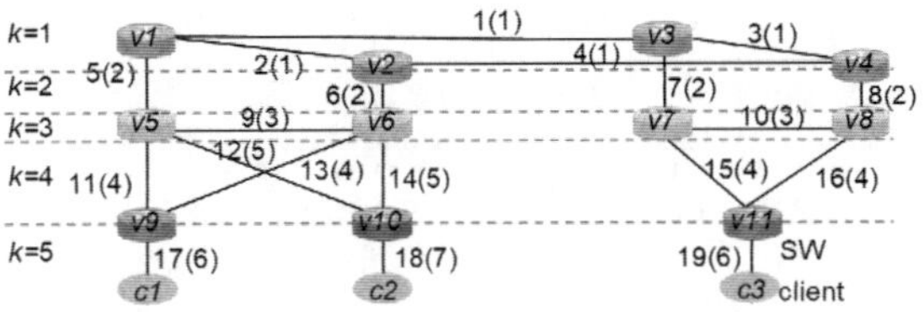

(a) Example network

Z(e)

e	D(e)			
1	(1,3,1)	(2,3,1)		
5	(1,3,5)	(2,3,5)	(1,3,7)	(2,3,7)
7	(1,3,7)	(2,3,7)	(1,3,5)	(2,3,5)
11	(1,2,11)	(1,3,11)	(1,3,15)	(2,3,15)
12	(1,2,12)	(2,3,12)		
15	(1,3,15)	(2,3,15)	(1,3,11)	
17	(1,2,17)	(1,3,17)	(1,3,19)	(2,3,19)
18	(1,2,18)	(2,3,18)		
19	(1,3,19)	(2,3,19)	(1,3,17)	

(b) Similar test targets for example network
Figure 4. Example of test target similarity.

Figure 4 shows an example of calculating similar test targets. Figure 4(a) gives an example network with 5 tiers. Each link is associated with its name and an attribute value in the form of name (attribute). For example, test targets (1,3,11) and (2,3,15) in Figure 4 are similar, i.e., *Sim*((1,3,11), (2,3,15)) = 1, because q, r, k and w of both paths are the same (q=7, r=7, k=4 and w=4).

As the result of applying (2) and (3), the similar test targets are calculated for this network as shown in Figure 4(b). After that, by considering (4) and (6), the optimal test targets are selected. If N = 2, Z(5) and Z(11) are selected as shown in Figure 4(b).

Since this can be treated as an ILP problem, we can calculate the optimal solution by the general programing solver, e.g., IBM ILOG CPLEX.

IV. Experimental Evaluation

We present the experimental results of applying the proposed method to various types of networks in the following subsections.

A. Experimental Setup

In order to evaluate the effectiveness of our proposed method, we have set up the solver IBM ILOG CPLEX Optimization Studio12.6 [11] on Windows PC (OS: Windows 8.1 Pro, CPU: Intel Core (TM) i7-6700@3.40GHz, memory: 16.0GBytes), and calculate the optimal set of shut down links.

As shown in Table I, we have applied 6 topologies, where the numbers of switches, clients, links and link tiers are different each other. Four network topologies (NW1 though NW4) are based on ladder type with path redundancy. The last two topologies (NW5 and NW6) are based on the core network topologies of Japanese telecom company [12] and Japanese internet project [13], by adding relay and access tiers with redundant topologies. The network topology of NW6 is shown in Figure 5.

TABLE I. EXPERIMENTAL NETWORK TOPOLOGIES

NW #	total nodes (#SWs+#Clients)	#links	#link tier k	max. path length q	#band-width	#equipment types
1	14 (11+3)	19	4	7	6	14
2	16 (12+4)	22	4	7	6	12
3	38 (30+8)	54	4	9	6	16
4	72 (56+16)	106	4	13	6	16
5	100 (74+26)	138	6	11	7	29
6	232 (174+58)	346	4	13	11	16

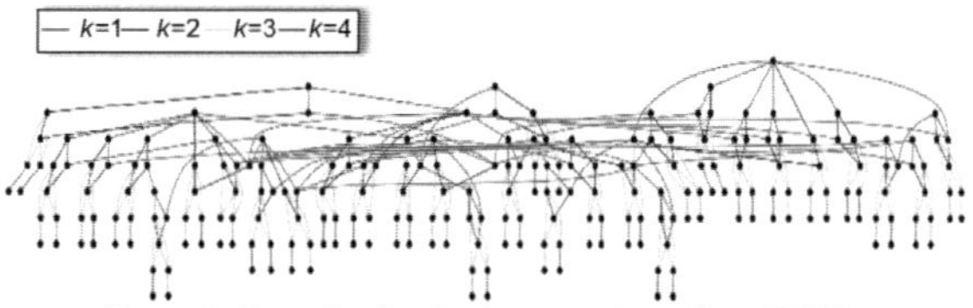

Figure 5. Example of evaluation network topology (NW6).

The paths before and after link shutdown are calculated by the Dijkstra's algorithm. First, the shortest path of each client pair is calculated as Primary (). Next, by removing a shut down link from the primary path, Secondary () is calculated. The similarities between any pair of test targets are calculated according to the elements of the test target attribute vector *q, r, k and w* described in Section III-B.

TABLE II. EVALUATION CASES

Case#	Evaluation Methods	Method
1	Comprehensive test for all test targets (=F)	Traditional
2	Test target attribute vector (q, r, k)	Proposed
3	Test target attribute vector (q, r, k, $w_{bandwidth}$)	
4	Test target attribute vector (q, r, k, $w_{equipment\_type}$)	

To evaluate the effectiveness of proposed method, we compared the four cases as shown in TABLE II. Case1 is a traditional method, and the number of comprehensive test for all test targets is F calculated by (1). Case2, Case3 and Case4 are proposed method, and each their test target attribute vectors are different. Note that the links not comprised in the path between any client pairs are exclude from the calculation.

B. Test Case Count and Reduction Ratio

First, we evaluate the test case count and the reduction ratio compared with comprehensive test for all test targets.

The reduction ratio $E1$ is calculated by (7). The number of test cases and the reduction ratio are shown in TABLE III.

$$E1 = 1 - \frac{N \; in \; CaseX}{F} \quad \left(X = 2,3,4\right) \tag{7}$$

From the table, the number of test cases of the proposed methods of Case2, Case3 and Case4 in each topology were massively reduced compared with the traditional method. In almost all cases, the reduction ratio $E1$ was decreased in order of Case2, Case3 and Case4. Specifically, the reduction ratio $E1$ of Case4 at NW1, and Case2 at NW6 were 0.833 (minimum) and 0.999 (maximum), respectively.

TABLE III. NUMBER OF TEST CASES AND REDUCTION RATIO

NW #	Test case count (reduction ratio) Case# 1	2	3	4
1	36 (0)	4 (0.889)	5 (0.861)	6 (0.833)
2	66 (0)	4 (0.939)	6 (0.909)	7 (0.894)
3	404 (0)	4 (0.990)	7 (0.983)	10 (0.975)
4	2120 (0)	4 (0.998)	19 (0.991)	36 (0.983)
5	5424 (0)	19 (0.996)	19 (0.996)	53 (0.990)
6	29896 (0)	11 (0.999)	91 (0.997)	69 (0.998)

From the above results, it was confirmed that our proposed method is able to reduce the test case count significantly even when the test target attribute is considered.

C. Test Case Count and Test Coverage

Next, in order to complete the link failure tests within a limited time, the number of link failure test cases may be limited. Therefore, we evaluate the test case count N and the test coverage. The test coverage is defined as the ratio of the number of similar test targets at the test case count N against F.

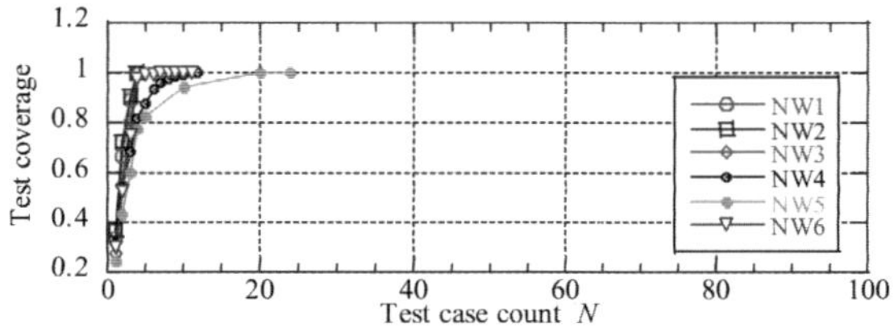

(i) Test target attribute vector (q, r, k) (Case2).

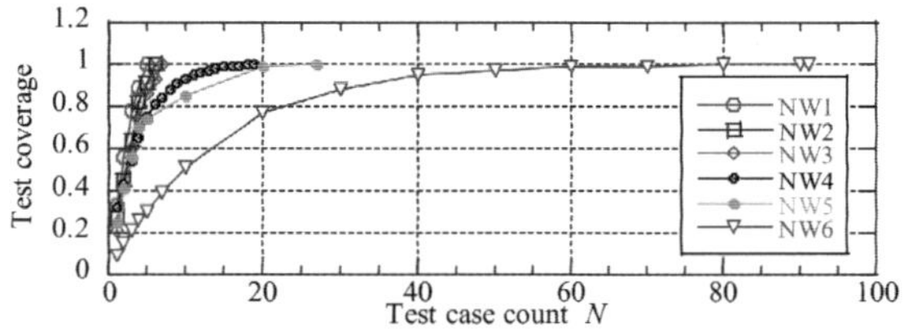

(ii) Test target attribute vector (q, r, k, $w_{bandwidth}$) (Case3).

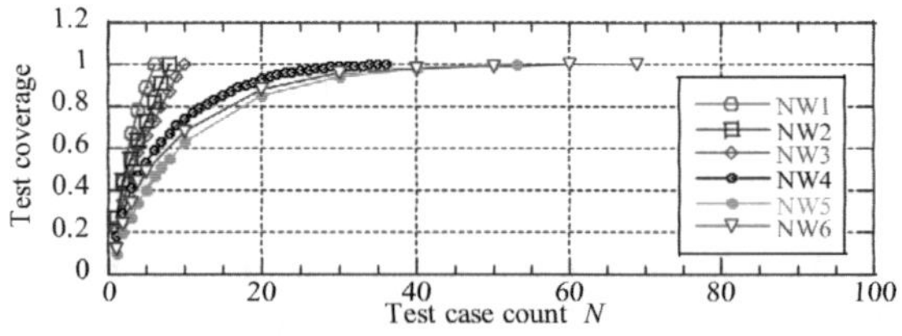

(iii) Test target attribute vector (q, r, k, $w_{equipment\_type}$) (Case4).

Figure 6. Test case count N vs test coverage.

Figure 6 shows the test coverage in response to different test case count (N), in each evaluation case. From this figure, the test coverage increased in response to the number of test case count N in all cases. In addition, the small-scale network, such as NW1, NW2 and NW3, the test coverage was increased rapidly. The test coverage increased in response to N rapidly in order of Case2, Case3, and Case4, except at NW6. In Case4 at NW6 in Figure 6 (iii), the test coverage was almost saturated at N=50, and the test coverage was 1 at N=69, when the whole link failure test was completed. In all the NWs and Cases, the test coverage exceeded 50% when the test case count $N \leq 10$. Furthermore, in Figure 6 (ii), the test coverage in Case3 at NW6 was increased slowly compared with other NWs in Case3 because the number of link bandwidth is larger than that of other NWs.

These experimental results indicate that our proposed method is able to obtain the sufficient coverage even when the number of test count N is small.

D. Link attribute and Test Case Count

In the telecom network consists of the different types of equipment, such as switches, the telecom company decides on own test coverage to satisfy the link failure test. Therefore, we evaluate the number of test target attributes and test case count.

To evaluate it, all $w_{equipment\_type}$ are calculated using the equipment types, which are randomly assigned from 1 to 5 per k to each equipment at both sides of links in NW5. The result showed that the number of equipment types is from 12 to 79.

Figure 7 shows the number of test case count N and the number of equipment types $w_{equipment\_type}$ when the test coverage was varied from 25% to 100% at 25% intervals at NW5. From this graph, the test case count N is (almost) linearly increased as the number of equipment types. The increase ratio of the test case count N when the test coverage was 100%, was larger than that of 50%. When the number of equipment types was 79, the test coverage 100% was 3.1 times larger comparing of the test coverage 50%. For example, when the number of equipment types is 73 and the test coverage sets 75%, the telecom company needs to conduct the link failure test 35 cases.

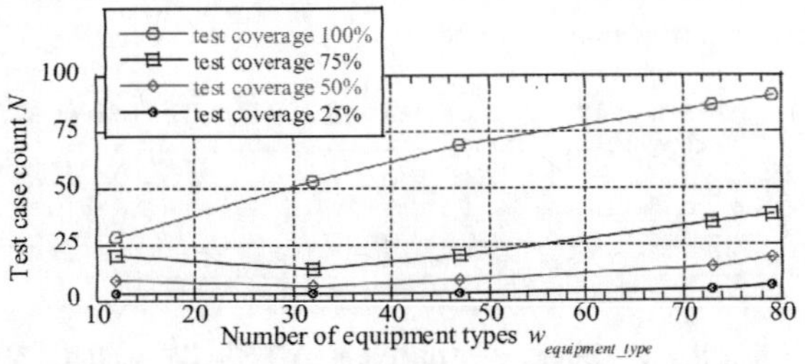

Figure 7. Number of equipment types $w_{equipment\_type}$ vs test case count N (ex. NW5).

From the above results, it indicates that if the target coverage sets higher, the number of test cases increases significantly.

V. CONCLUSION

In this paper, we proposed how to reduce link failure test cases by focusing on the topology similarity based on the idea of test case similarity using abstract path. We supposed a telecom network, where clients in the network, communicate with each other, and the link failure test assume single link failure. In this proposal, we clustered the possible test targets throughout a telecom network into groups of similar test targets based on the abstract path. We utilized topological similarity for the purpose, formulated a problem of minimizing the number of test cases, and conducted simulation experiments for 6 cases including large-scale networks with realistic topology. Through the experiments, we confirmed that our proposed method can drastically reduce the test case count. In future, we plan to verify the similarity based on the degree of the switch, propagation delay, and multiple failures.

REFERENCES

[1] M. Shibuya, H. Kawakami, T. Hasegawa, and H. Yamaguchi, "Design and implementation of support system for network testing with whitebox switches," COLLA 2016, pp.39-44, Nov. 2016.

[2] http://www.sdnjapan.org/2015/1411_torii.pdf (in Japanese), [retrieved: May, 2018].

[3] http://www.okinawaopenlabs.org/wp/wp-content/uploads/20160205_tanabe.pdf (in Japanese), [retrieved: May, 2018].

[4] Mininet, http://mininet.org/, [retrieved: May, 2018].

[5] QualiSystems CloudShell / TestShell, http://www.qualisystems.com/products/cloudshell-add-ons/testshell-overview/, [retrieved: May, 2018].

[6] D. G. Corneil and C. C. Gotlieb, "An Efficient Algorithm for Graph Isomorphism," Journal of the ACM, Vol. 17, Issue 1, pp.51-64, Jan. 1970.

[7] J. R. Ullumn, "An Algorithm for Subgraph Isomorphism," Journal of the ACM, Vol. 23, Issue 1, pp.31-42, Jan. 1976.

[8] B. D. McKay, "Practical Graph Isomorphism," Congressus Numerantium, vol. 30, pp. 45-87, 1981.

[9] L. P. Cordella, P. Foggia, C. Sansone, and M. Vento, "A (Sub) Graph Isomorphism Algorithm for Matching Large Graphs," IEEE Trans. Pattern Analysis and Machine Intelligenc, , vol. 26, no. 10, pp. 1367-1372, Oct. 2004.

[10] G. Kollias, S. Mohammadi, and A. Grama, "Network similarity decomposition (NSD): A fast and scalable approach to network alignment," IEEE Transactions on knowledge and Data Engineering, Vol. 24, No. 12, pp.2232-2243, Dec. 2012.

[11] IBM ILOG CPLEX Optimiazation Studio, https://www.ibm.com/developerworks/downloads/ws/ilogcplex/, [retrieved: May, 2018].

[12] IIJ, https://www.iij.ad.jp/en/company/network/backbone/images/bawckbone_en.gif backbone_en.gif, [retrieved: May, 2018].

[13] WIDE, http://www.wide.ad.jp/About/report/pdf2016/usb/wide-memo-two-report-2016-01.pdf, [retrieved: May, 2018].

The IEEE 802.11p Performance for Different Packet Length and Arrival Rate in VANETs

Osman Toker, A. F. M. Shahen Shah, M.S. Ufuk Tureli
Department of Electronics & Communication Engineering Yildiz Technical University Istanbul, Turkey
e-mail : osmantoker@hotmail.com, shahen.shah@hotmail.com, utureli@yildiz.edu.tr

***Abstract*—The IEEE 802.11p standard uses Enhanced Distributed Channel Access (EDCA) mechanism for the contention-based prioritized Quality of Service (QoS) at the Media Access Control (MAC) layer. The IEEE 802.11p is MAC and physical (PHY) layer standard for Vehicle Ad Hoc Networks (VANETs), which uses the Enhanced Distributed Channel Access Function (EDCAF) to support contention-based prioritized QoS in the MAC layer. VANET aims to provide users with a better, safer and more coordinated approach to their destination. This paper provides an analytical model to compute the performance of the IEEE 802.11p EDCAF for Vehicular Network based on packet size.**

Keywords*—*IEEE 802.11p; EDCA; performance analysis; VANET

I. INTRODUCTION

An Intelligent Transportation System (ITS) is an advanced application, which intelligence as such, aims to provide innovative services relating to different modes of transport, traffic management. ITS allows users to be better informed and use safer, more coordinated and smarter transport networks [1].

ITS is working to increase road safety and to provide on-site information services to improve transport efficiency. For these applications, the vehicles can be equipped with sensors and communication devices to form a network called the Vehicle Ad Hoc Network (VANET).

The IEEE 802.11p standard [2] known as Wireless Access in Vehicular Environments (WAVE) is specially developed to adapt VANETs requirements and supports ITS. The performance of WAVE physical layer is one of the important factors that play a great role in the communication process [3]. The IEEE 802.11p uses an Enhanced Distributed Channel Access (EDCA) mechanism, which is designed for the contention-based prioritized Quality of Service (QoS) support at the MAC layer. The IEEE 802.11p EDCA mechanism defines four access categories (ACs); AC_VO (Voice), AC_VI (Video), AC_BE (Best effort) and AC_BG (Back ground). The priority among ACs is set by different EDCA parameters. An enhanced distributed channel access function (EDCAF) is used for each AC queue at the MAC sublayer to contend for transmission opportunities using its own EDCA parameters. EDCA parameters include the minimum contention window (CW_{min}), maximum contention window (CW_{max}) and Arbitration Interframe Space Number (AIFSN).

Recently performance modeling of the IEEE 802.11p EDCA mechanism has been studied in [1]. In this paper, the performance model was developed considering all important factors that may affect the performance of the IEEE 802.11p EDCA mechanism for different ACs. In these calculations, the effect of the package size on performance and delay has been examined. Strong approximations are avoided to ensure the accuracy of the model. Markov Chain modeling based theoretical analysis is presented where the relationship between EDCA parameters and EDCA performance metrics are shown. Simulation results are provided to demonstrate the accuracy of the analytical model. Simulations were done using MATLAB. The rest of the paper is organized as follows. Section II describes the analytical model and performance analysis. Section III presents the simulation results. Section IV concludes the paper.

II. ANALYTICAL MODEL AND PERFORMANCE ANALYSIS

The 802.11 standard defines EDCA as a mechanism by which one class of frames can be given priority over another in their competition to access the medium. The relationship between EDCA parameters and performance metrics are also established for all AC queues. Based on Markov model, the performance of the IEEE 802.11p EDCA mechanism for all ACs is derived. According to the package size changes, throughput and delay analysis were performed

A. Overview of the Enhanced Distributed Channel Access

The EDCA is a channel access mechanism designed for the contention-based prioritized QoS support at the MAC layer. The EDCA mechanism defines four ACs. The four ACs have four priorities, including CW_{min}, CW_{max} and AIFSN. The contention window parameters are shown in Table I.

TABLE I. DEFAULT EDCA PARAMETER FOR DIFFERENT ACS

AC	CW_{min}	CW_{max}	AIFSN	TXOP Limit
AC_BK	aCW_{min}	aCW_{max}	9	0
AC_BE	aCW_{min}	aCW_{max}	6	0
AC_VI	$(aCW_{min}+1)/2-1$	aCW_{min}	3	0
AC_VO	$(aCW_{min}+1)/4-1$	$(aCW_{min}+1)/2-1$	2	0

Each AC queue uses different AIFS, CW_{min} and CW_{max}. Prioritization of transmission in EDCA is implemented by a new Inter-Frame Space (IFS), namely, Arbitration Inter-Frame Space (AIFS). The duration of AIFS for each AC is derived from the value of AIFSN of that AC. SIFS is the duration of the short inter-frame space and T_{slot} is the duration of a slot time [4]. AIFSN can be expressed as follows

$$AIFS\ [AC] = AIFSN\ [AC] \times T_{slot} + SIFS \quad (1)$$

Prioritization mechanism is shown in Figure 1.

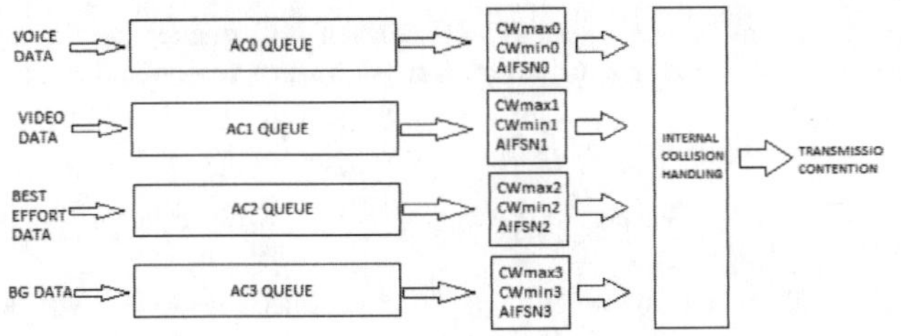

Figure 1. Demonstration of EDCA Mechanism

The EDCA mechanism relies on the Carrier Sense Multiple Access/Collision Avoidance (CSMA/CA) technique to contend and access channel, which a station must probe the channel before transmission to determine whether it is busy or idle. If only one AC queue has backlogged data at a time in a station, and the station will sense the channel idle for the duration of AIFS[AC] before attempting to transmit it. If the channel is sensed as busy, then the station defers its transmission of an additional back-off interval. The back-off interval is calculated as a random number of slot times uniformly selected from [0, CW[AC]]. At the first transmission attempt, the back-off interval for an AC in EDCA is randomly selected from [0, CW_{min}[AC]], and it is doubled at every retransmission with an upper limit equal to CW_{max}[AC]. The smaller is AIFS[AC] or CW_{min}[AC], the higher is the priority in channel access. If the channel is sensed idle in a slot, the back-off counter will be decremented by 1. The packet will be transmitted when the back-off counter becomes 0. For priority reasons, EDCA mechanism employs a separate time for back-off. Therefore, an internal collision occurs inside a station, also called virtual collision. If an internal collision occurs, the station will grant the transmission to the AC queue with the highest priority. In the meantime, the AC queue with lower priorities will start to back-off and then the packet will be transmitted.

B. Markov Model Analysis

A Markov chain is a stochastic model describing a sequence of possible events in which the probability of each event depends only on the state attained in the previous event. The Markov chain describes the withdrawal procedure of any AC. In this Markov chain, k is the value of a back-off counter. The value of k is initially set to from 0 [0, W−1] and is decremented by 1 if the channel is sensed idle in a slot, frozen at the current value when the channel sensed busy. The packet will be transmitted when k becomes zero[7]. T_{slot} is the slot time size. P_c and P_b is the collision probability and channel busy probability in a slot. Figure 2 shows the Markov chain model

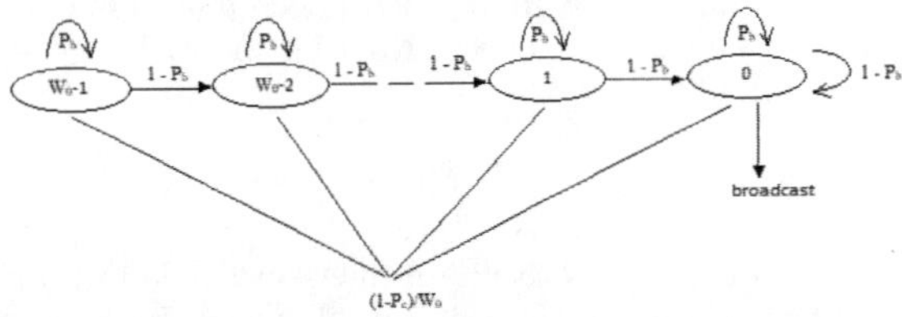

Figure 2. Back-off Process via Markov Chain Model

The back-off time is decremented by 1 when the channel is sensed idle, the calculation is specified in Equation (2). The back-off time is frozen at the current value when the channel is sensed busy, is specified in Equation (3). The packet will be transmitted when the back-off counter becomes 0, is specified in Equation (4).

$$P\{k|k+1\} = 1 - P_b \qquad k \in (0, W_0 - 2) \quad (2)$$

$$P\{k|k\} = \frac{P_b}{W_0} \qquad k \in (0, W_0 - 1) \quad (3)$$

$$P\{k|0\} = \frac{1-P_c}{W_0} \qquad k \in (0, W_0 - 1) \quad (4)$$

The solutions can be obtained from the Markov chain. b(t) be the stochastic process representing the back-off counter for a given vehicle at timeslot t. $b(t) \in (0, W_0 - 1)$. The Markov chain is constructed to describe the back-off procedure of an AC [7]. As the sum of all possible states equal to one, so following relations can be derived

$$1 = \sum_{k=0}^{W_0-1} b_k = \sum_{k=0}^{W_0-1} \frac{W_0 - k}{W_0} b_0$$

from which

$$b_0 = \frac{2}{W_0+1} \quad (5)$$

A vehicle transmits a packet in a randomly chosen slot time probability P_t can be expressed as follows

$$P_t = b_0 = \frac{2}{W_0+1} \quad (6)$$

Considering n number of vehicle, P_c is the probability that, in a slot time, at least one of the n-1 remaining vehicles transmit packet. Each remaining vehicle transmits a packet with probability P_t, the collision probability is given by

$$P_c = 1 - (1 - P_t)^{n-1} \quad (7)$$

If the vehicle competes on the channel and each transmits the probability via P_t, the probability of channel busy can be written as

$$P_b = 1 - (1 - P_t)^{n-1} \quad (8)$$

P_s is the successful transmission probability that a transmission occurring on the channel is successful, which can be calculated as

$$P_s = \frac{2n}{\frac{(W_0+1)^n}{(W_0-1)^{n-1}} - W_0 + 1} \quad (9)$$

P_q is the packet arrival probability that follows a Poisson distribution with a constant arrival rate λ, which can be calculated as

$$P_q(n\ arrivals\ in\ interval\ T_e) = \frac{(\lambda T_e)^n e^{-\lambda T_e}}{n!} \quad (10)$$

where n number of arrivals and T_e is the expected time that a vehicle spends in each Markov state [5]. For n=0

$$P_q = 1 - e^{-\lambda T_e} \quad (11)$$

$$T_e = (1 - P_b)T_{slot} + P_b P_s T_s + P_b(1 - P_s)T_c \quad (12)$$

where T_s and T_c are the time duration when a packet is transmitted collision free and transmitted with collision respectively. Due to vehicular networks broadcast nature T_s and T_c are equal, which can be expressed as

$$T_s = \frac{L_h+L}{R_d} + SIFS + AIFS + T_{delay} \quad (13)$$

where L_h is the MAC layer and physical layer header lengths, L is the packet size, R_d is the system data transmission rate and T_{delay} is the propagation delay.

C. Throughput Analysis

The normalized system throughput S is the average information payload transmitted in a slot time over the average duration of a slot time

$$S = \frac{E[payload\ info]}{E[length\ of\ a\ slot\ time]} \quad (14)$$

The normalized system throughput S can be expressed as follows

$$S = \frac{P_S P_b L}{(1-P_b)T_{slot} + P_b P_S T_S + P_b(1-P_S)T_S} \quad (15)$$

L is the packet size, T_{slot} is the duration of a slot time [6].

For all transmission protocols with CSMA base, the throughput variation equation based on the offered traffic load of the environment can be expressed as follows

$$S = \frac{Ge^{-\propto G}}{(1-e^{-\propto G})+\propto} \quad (16)$$

where G offered traffic load, T packet transmission time, τ propagation delay through the air. The offered traffic load of a cell is typically characterized by average number of mobile stations requesting the service and average length of time the mobile stations requiring the service [8]. The offered traffic load $\propto$ is normalized time unit and can be expressed as $\propto = \frac{\tau}{T}$.

D. Delay Analysis

E[Tw] is the average waiting time of an AC queue at the back-off stage can be calculated by using Equation (12)

$$E[T_w] = \frac{W_0-1}{2}T_e \quad (17)$$

is the average access delay of an AC queue that is the average time for a packet transmission starts to contend for the channel until the packet successfully transmitted or dropped can be derived by using Equation (7) and Equation (17)

$$E[D_{access}] = E[T_w]P_c(1 - P_c) + E[T_w]P_c \quad (18)$$

There are two events may occur, either the packet will be transmitted successfully if a collision occurs and no collision occurs, or the packet is dropped due to collision.

E[Tinterval] is the average packet interval time between two successfully received packets at one receiver can be calculated by using Equation (12)

$$E[T_{interval}] = nT_e \quad (19)$$

E[Tdrop] is the average time to drop a packet can be expressed as

$$E[T_{drop}] = E[X_{drop}]T_e \quad (20)$$

where E[Xdrop] is the average number of slot times for a dropped packet

$$E[X_{drop}] = \frac{W_0+1}{2} \quad (21)$$

E[D] is the average packet delay of an AC queue that is the average delay for a successfully transmitted packet which can be calculated as

$$E[D] = E[T_{interval}] - \frac{P_{fdrop}}{1-P_{fdrop}}E[T_{drop}] \quad (22)$$

where Pfdrop is the probability that a packet will finally be dropped.

III. SIMULATION RESULTS

In previous sections, the performance of the IEEE 802.11p EDCAF and the verification of the theoretical analysis were calculated. The simulations are conducted in MATLAB. The data packets arrive at each AC queue following the mean of the process is 0.5 Mbps. The simulation model includes MAC behavior of IEEE 802.11p in vehicular networks. In this simulation, the number of vehicles is fixed and is calculated as 10. Packet arrival probability is defined as vector. Pfdrop is fixed and calculated as 0.03. Table II provides the parameters value used in the simulation.

TABLE II. VALUE OF PARAMETER USED IN SIMULATION

Parameter	Value	Parameter	Value
CW_{min} [0]	3	CW_{max} [0]	7
CW_{min} [1]	3	CW_{max} [1]	15
CW_{min} [2]	7	CW_{max} [2]	1023
CW_{min} [3]	15	CW_{max} [3]	1023
AIFSN [0]	2	AIFSN [1]	3
AIFSN [2]	6	AIFSN [3]	9
T_{slot}, T_{delay} (μs)	20, 1	SIFS, AIFS (μs)	10, 64
L_h	46	R_d, λ (Mbps)	11, 0.5

Figure 3 shows throughput versus packet arrival probability when the packet size (L) is 512 bytes. The scenario was simulated with the average packet length planned to be used in vehicle-2-vehicle communication. The packet size can contain at least 64 bytes with the header and at most 1518 bytes in the 802.11 standards. Figure 4 and Figure 5 show throughput versus packet arrival probability when the packet size (L) is 64 bytes and 1500 bytes respectively. Figure 3, Figure 4 and Figure 5 shows that the increase of length of the packet size affects the throughput in the right direction. So using largest packet is more efficient. Figure 6 shows the average access delay versus packet arrival probability when the packet size is 64 bytes. Figure 8 shows the average access delay versus packet arrival probability when the packet size is 1518 bytes. According to the Figure 6 and Figure 8, AC [0] provides minimum latency while the packet arrival probability increases. In the calculations, AC [2] and AC [3] values are very close to each other. But we can see that if we use AC [2] and AC [3], we should try to send packages with minimum size. Figure 9 shows the throughput change graph depending on the offered load if 10 vehicles in the environment request are generated during a minute when $\tau = 0.1$.

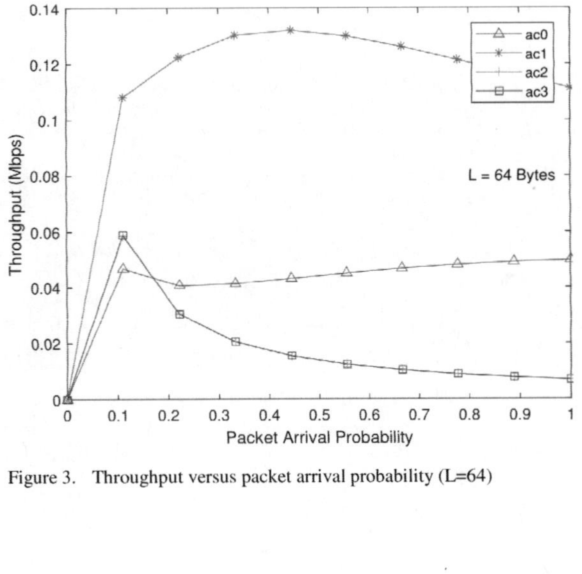

Figure 3. Throughput versus packet arrival probability (L=64)

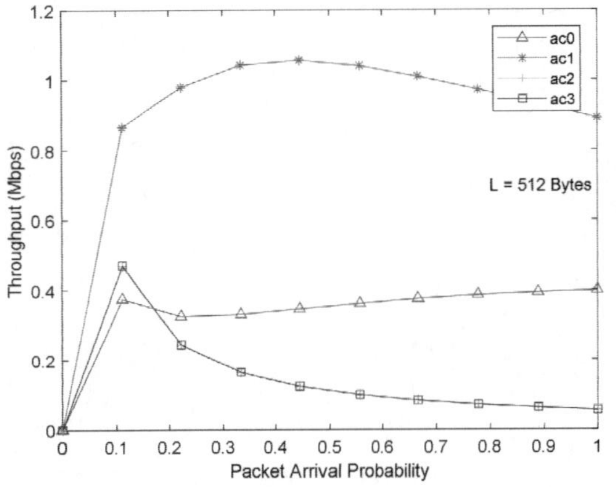

Figure 4. Throughput versus packet arrival probability (L=512)

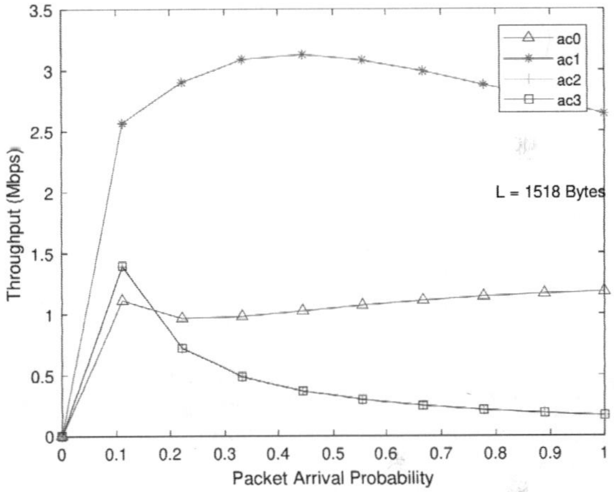

Figure 5. Throughput versus packet arrival probability (L=1518)

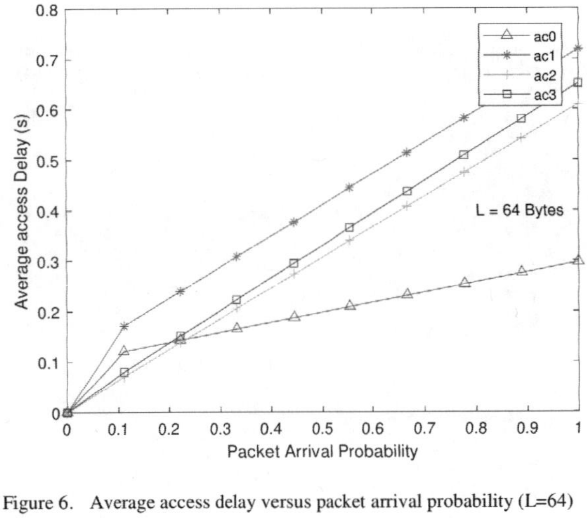

Figure 6. Average access delay versus packet arrival probability (L=64)

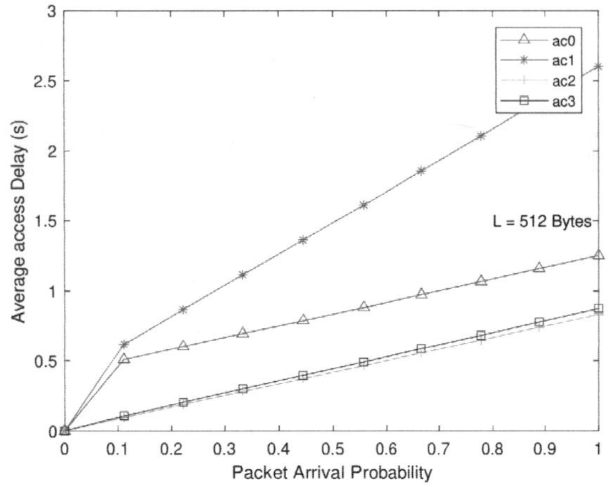

Figure 7. Average access delay versus packet arrival probability (L=512)

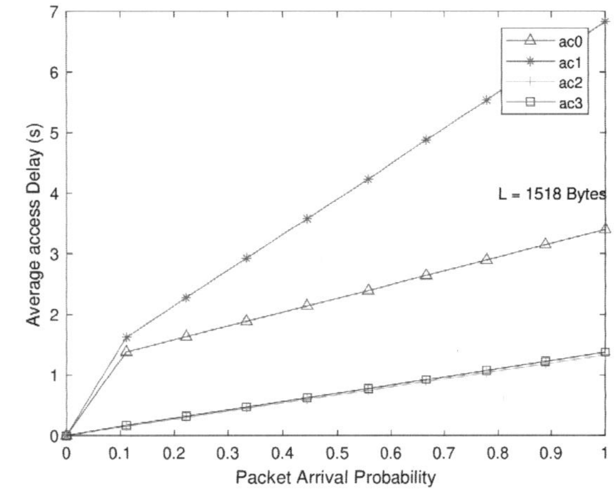

Figure 8. Average access delay versus packet arrival probability (L=1518)

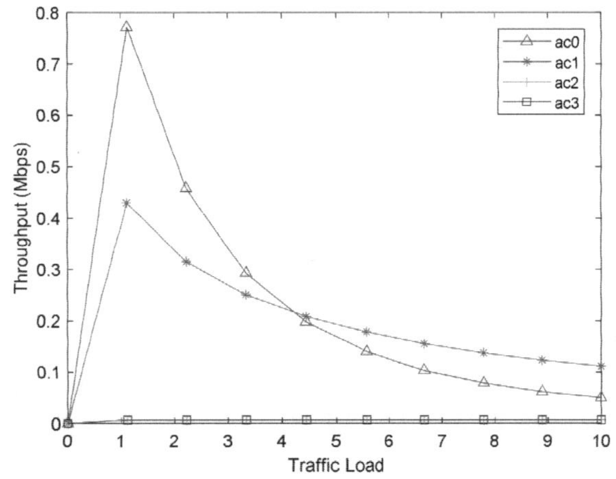

Figure 9. Throughput versus offered traffic load

IV. CONCLUSION

In this paper, a simple analytical model to compute the performance of the IEEE 802.11p EDCAF for vehicular network is presented. The performance model is derived based on Markov chain. The Markov model calculates all important factors that can affect the access performance of the IEEE 802.11p EDCA mechanism for each AC, such as the CW, AIFS and internal collisions. Equation (9), Equation (10), Equation (15) and Equation (18) shows the relationship among the EDCA parameters and performance matric considering transmission probability, collision probability, throughput and delay. Simulation results show that the packet size change affects throughput proportionally. Given the declining throughput because of increased traffic intensity, AC [0] should be preferred up to a certain density for critical messages. With increasing offered load, channel preference can shift to AC [1].

REFERENCES

[1] IEEE Standart for Information technology-- Local and metropolitan area networks—Specific requirements-- Part 11: Wireless LAN Medium Access Control (MAC) and Physical Layer (PHY) Specifications Amendment 6: Wireless Access in Vehicular Environments, IEEE 802.11p-2010, July 15, 2010.

[2] A. F. M. S. Shah and N. Mustari, "Modeling and Performance Analysis of the IEEE 802.11P Enhanced Distributed Channel Access Function for Vehicular Network", FTC 2016 - Future Technologies Conference 2016, pp. 173-178, December 6-7, 2016.

[3] Z. Zhao and X. Cheng, "IEEE 802.11p for Vehicle-to-Vehicle (V2V) Communications", in School of Electronics Engineering and Computer Science, Beijing China, Peking University, March 2016.

[4] C. Song, "Performance Analysis of the IEEE 802.11p Multichannel MAC Protocol in Vehicular Ad Hoc Networks", Sensors(Basel), pii. E2890, doi:10.3390/s17122890, Dec. 2017.

[5] E. Modiano, "Introduction to Queueing Theory", Massachusetts Institute of Technology, 2002

[6] G. Narayanan, "Analysis of Broadcast Non-Saturation Throughput as a Performance Measure in VANETs", International Conference on Advances in Computer Engineering & Applications, IJCA, Ghaziabad, pp. 179-184, 2014.

[7] Y. Y. Nasrallah, I. Al-Anbagi and H. T. Mouftah, "A Realistic Analytical Model of IEEE 802.11p for Wireless Access in Vehicular Networks", International Conference on Connected Vehicles and Expo (ICCVE), Vienna, Austria, doi: 10.1109/ICCVE.2014.7297503, Nov. 2014.

[8] D. P. Agrawal, Q. Zeng, "Introduction to Wireless and Mobile Systems", Cengace Learning, pp. 112, 2011.

Low-Complexity Antenna Selection for Minimizing the Power Consumption of a MIMO Base Station

Rémi Bonnefoi*, Christophe Moy†, Jacques Palicot* and Amor Nafkha*
*CentraleSupélec/IETR, CentraleSupélec Campus de Rennes, 35510 Cesson-Sévigné, France
E-mail: {remi.bonnefoi, jacques.palicot, amor.nafkha}@centralesupelec.fr
†Univ Rennes, CNRS, IETR - UMR 6164, F-35000, Rennes, France. E-mail: christophe.moy@univ-rennes1.fr

Abstract—**In this paper, we study the problem of Transmit Antenna Selection (TAS) for the minimization of a base station power consumption. We propose an algorithm, which solves this problem when the optimal precoding and power allocation are employed, *i.e.*, when an eigenvalue decomposition is employed with a water-filling algorithm. For that purpose, we derive an approximation for the base station power consumption expression that can be used to compute the number of switched-on antennas. Besides, we show that Norm-Based Selection (NBS) policy can be used for selecting the switched-on antennas. Finally, our numerical results show that the proposed low-complexity algorithm provides optimal power consumption performances.**

Keywords–Multiple-Input Multiple-Output; Transmit Antenna Selection (TAS); Energy-Efficient Wireless Networks.

I. Introduction

Multiple-Input Multiple-Output (MIMO) is one of the key technology to meet the ever-growing demand for mobile data. However, increasing the number of transmit and receive antennas increases the number of RF chains and, therefore, the energy consumption of base stations. That is why mitigating the energy consumed by MIMO systems is a big challenge for the development of future wireless networks [1].

The base station energy consumption can be reduced by switching-off some of the transmit antennas. This mechanism is called Transmit Antenna Selection (TAS) [2]. This solution has been widely proposed for maximizing the capacity of MIMO systems [3][4] and can also be used for making green wireless communications networks.

Making wireless communication networks green can be done by either maximizing the Energy Efficiency (EE) or by minimizing the base station power consumption under some constraints on the quality of service (e.g., capacity). An algorithm for maximizing the EE of a point-to-point communication with antenna selection has been proposed in [5]. However, this algorithm has a rather high complexity. In [6], the authors proposed a transmit antenna selection algorithm for maximizing the EE of a MISO system with a large number of transmit antennas. Moreover, in [7], the authors proposed to maximize the EE by selecting antennas on both the transmit and receive sides. Unlike [6][7], which focus on the maximization of the EE, in this paper, we focus on the problem of antenna selection for power consumption minimization. This problem has been studied in [8], in this paper the authors proposed an algorithm to solve it in the case where the transmit power is equally distributed over all the eigenvalues. One of the limitations of the algorithms proposed

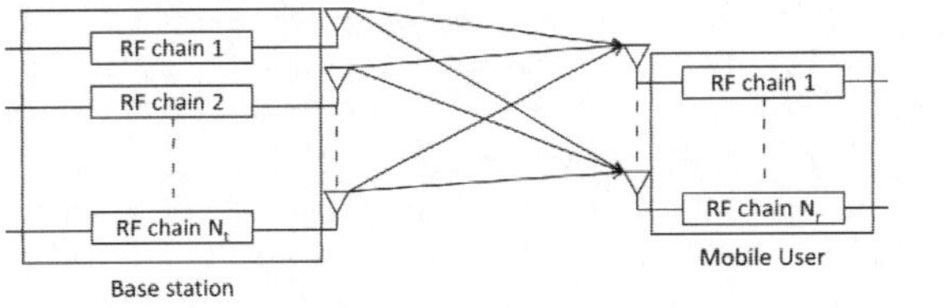

Figure 1. A base station with N_t antennas serves a mobile user with N_r antennas.

in [5]–[8] is the precoding and power allocation. Indeed, in all these papers, the transmit power is equally distributed either over all the antennas or over all the modes. Whereas, in MIMO systems, more efficient performance can be achieved using better precodings. In particular, optimal performance can be achieved using the well-known eigenvalue decomposition and water-filling algorithm [9].

In this paper, we study the problem of transmit antenna selection for the minimization of the power consumption of a base station when the optimal precoding and power allocation is performed. In other words, when the eigenvalue or singular value decomposition is employed with a water-filling algorithm [9]. In addition to improving the performance, the optimal power allocation changes the set of antennas which have to be switched-on to serve the user. We propose a low-complexity two-steps algorithm for the selection of a sub-optimal set of switched-on antennas. For that purpose, we derive an approximation for the base station power consumption and use it for computing N_{on} (the number of switched-on antennas). Moreover, we show that, once this number is known, we can switch-on the N_{on} antennas whose corresponding columns of the channel matrix has the highest norm.

The rest of this paper is organized as follows. The system model is introduced in Section II. In Section III, we recall the expression of the water-filling algorithm and we assess the performance of the antenna selection policy. In Section IV, we propose an approximation for the base station power consumption and we use this approximation for selecting the number of switched-on antennas. Some numerical simulations are conducted in Section V and Section VI concludes this paper.

II. System Model

We consider a point-to-point MIMO system in which a base station with N_t transmit antennas serves a mobile user with N_r receive antennas. As illustrated in Fig. 1, each of the N_t antennas of the base station is linked to an RF chain.

Instead of using all its antennas, the base station switches-off some of them and the corresponding RF chains in order to save energy. We denote $\mathscr{S}_{on}$ the set of switched-on antennas and N_{on} is the cardinal of this set, i.e., the number of switched-on RF chains. Moreover, for the analysis of the base station power consumption, we focus on the power consumed in the RF chains whose power consumption can be modeled as [5] [10]:

$$P = \frac{1}{\eta_a} P_{Tx} + N_{on} P_{ct}, \tag{1}$$

where P is the total base station power consumption, P_{Tx} is the transmit power used to serve the user. This transmit power must be lower than a maximum value denoted $P_{\max} = 20W$. $\eta_a = 0.35$ denotes the efficiency of the power amplifiers, and $P_{ct} = 120$ mW is the static power consumed by each switched-on RF chain. In other words, P_{ct} is the power which can be saved by switching-off an antenna.

In this paper, we suppose that the base station has a perfect Channel State Information (CSI). We denote $\mathbf{H} \in \mathbb{C}^{N_r \times N_{on}}$ the channel matrix when N_{on} antennas are switched-on. Moreover, $\mathbf{h}_k$ denotes the kth column of the matrix $\mathbf{H}$ and $||\mathbf{h}_k||_2$ denotes its Euclidian norm. Furthermore, L denotes the pathloss between the base station and the user and σ^2 denotes the noise power. We denote by $\mathbf{Q}$ the input covariance matrix [9], which verifies $\mathrm{Tr}(\mathbf{Q}) = P_{Tx}$, where Tr(.) denotes the trace operator. With the notations introduced herein, the channel capacity can be written as:

$$C = \log_2 \left(\det \left(\mathbf{I}_{\mathbf{N_{on}}} + \frac{L}{\sigma^2} \mathbf{Q} \mathbf{H}^* \mathbf{H} \right) \right), \tag{2}$$

where $\mathbf{I}_{\mathbf{N_{on}}}$ denotes the identity matrix of size N_{on}, det(.) is the matrix determinant and $\mathbf{H}^*$ denotes the conjugate transpose of $\mathbf{H}$.

In our numerical simulations, we consider Rayleigh fading channel, in such case, the elements of the channel matrix are independent identically distributed (i.i.d.) zero mean complex Gaussian variables with variance one. Moreover, we compute the pathloss with the Winner II 'C1' pathloss model [11] with a 2 GHz central frequency. The thermal noise is equal to $\sigma^2 = k_B T B$, where k_B is the Boltzmann constant, T is the temperature in Kelvin and $B = 1$ MHz is the bandwidth. A $2dB$ noise figure is considered.

Our objective is to minimize the base station power consumption while providing to the user a given quality of service in term of capacity. The optimization problem can be written as:

$$\min_{\mathscr{S}_{on}, P_{Tx}} \frac{1}{\eta_a} P_{Tx} + N_{on} P_{ct}, \tag{3a}$$

$$\text{S.t. } C_c \leq \log_2 \left(\det \left(\mathbf{I}_{\mathbf{N_{on}}} + \frac{L}{\sigma^2} \mathbf{Q} \mathbf{H}^* \mathbf{H} \right) \right). \tag{3b}$$

$$P_{Tx} \leq P_{\max} \tag{3c}$$

In (3b), C_c denotes the capacity constraint of the user. Please note that, this constraint is written as an inequality, however, it is easy to see that the base station power consumption is minimum when this constraint is an equality, i.e., when $C_c = C$. Equation (3c) makes sure that the transmit power is not higher than the maximum transmit power of the base station. In the following, we propose an algorithm to solve the problem of (3).

III. Antenna Selection Policy

In this section, we first recall the optimal MIMO precoding and power allocation. Besides, we assess the performance of the employed antenna selection policy.

A. MIMO precoding

We assume, here, that a set of $\mathscr{S}_{on}$ antennas has been switched-on and we recall the MIMO precoding which minimizes the power consumption. When the set of switched-on antennas has been chosen, minimizing the base station power consumption aims at minimizing the transmit power. Looking at the capacity, finding the optimal MIMO precoding means deriving the matrix $\mathbf{Q}$ which minimizes the transmit power while providing to the user its capacity constraint. It is well-known that the matrix $\mathbf{Q}$ is optimal when the eigenvalue decomposition of $\mathbf{H}^*\mathbf{H}$ is performed [9]. In other words, $\mathbf{Q}$ and $\mathbf{H}^*\mathbf{H}$ must have the same eigenvectors. In that case, the capacity constraint becomes:

$$C_c = \sum_{k=1}^{N} \log_2 \left(1 + \frac{L}{\sigma^2} \mu_k \lambda_k \right), \tag{4}$$

where λ_k denotes the kth eigenvalue of $\mathbf{H}^*\mathbf{H}$, μ_k is the kth eigenvalue of $\mathbf{Q}$ and $N = \min(N_{on}, N_r)$. Then, the eigenvalues μ_k which minimize the transmit power are computed with the well-known water-filling algorithm:

$$\mu_k = \frac{\sigma^2}{L} \left(\frac{2^{\frac{C_c}{N'}}}{\left(\prod_{k=1}^{N'} \lambda_k \right)^{\frac{1}{N'}}} - \frac{1}{\lambda_k} \right)^{\dagger}, \tag{5}$$

where $(.)^\dagger = \max(., 0)$ and N' is the number of non-zero eigenvalues of $\mathbf{Q}$. With this optimal power allocation over the eigenvalues of the system, the total transmit power can be expressed as:

$$P_{Tx} = \frac{\sigma^2}{L} \left(\frac{N' 2^{\frac{C_c}{N'}}}{\left(\prod_{k=1}^{N'} \lambda_k \right)^{\frac{1}{N'}}} - \sum_{k=1}^{N'} \frac{1}{\lambda_k} \right) \tag{6}$$

B. Norm-Based Selection

In this section, we answer the following question: if we want to switch-on N_{on} antennas, which ones must be selected? A good solution for antenna selection lies in switching-on the N_{on} antennas whose corresponding columns of the channel matrix have the highest norm. This solution is called Norm-Based Selection (NBS). This approach has been proposed in [12] for capacity maximization with equal power allocation over the antennas. It has been proven to be optimal at low Signal-to-Noise Ratio (SNR) and in the Multiple-Input Single-Output (MISO) case [13]. Recently, this solution has also been shown to provide near-optimal performance even when the columns of the channel matrix are correlated [14].

In this paper, we propose to use NBS with the optimal power allocation for the purpose of power consumption minimization. In order to assess the performance of NBS, we consider a base station with $N_t = 12$ antennas and we suppose that the capacity constraint is equal to 5 bits/s/Hz. We compare:

- The minimum base station power consumption with NBS. Which is obtained by computing the power consumption with the N_t possible antenna configurations with NBS and by finding the one that minimizes the power consumption.
- The minimum base station power consumption which is computed with an exhaustive search. I.e., by evaluating the base station power consumption for the $2^{N_t} - 1$ possible antenna configurations and by finding the optimal one.

We compute the average base station power consumption, with these two strategies, as a function of the distance between the user and the base station. The results are presented in Fig. 2. They show that, with the selected simulation parameters, NBS and the iterative search provide the same results. As a consequence, this antenna selection strategy provides optimal performance. That is why we can use NBS as a solution for transmit antenna selection.

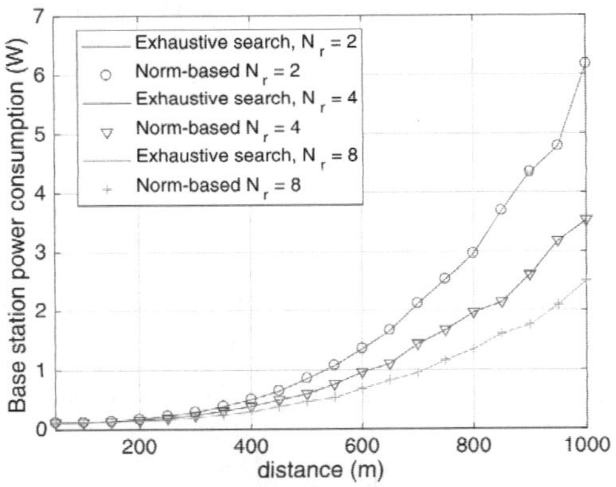

Figure 2. Comparison of NBS with an exhaustive search.

IV. SUB-OPTIMAL NUMBER OF SWITCHED-ON ANTENNAS

In this section, we propose a method to compute N_{on}, the number of switched-on antennas.

A. Number of antennas

In the previous section, we have shown that with an optimal power allocation, NBS is an optimal antenna selection policy. We, now, have to focus on the number of switched-on antennas. Indeed, with NBS, we have N_t possible antenna configurations (one for each number of switched-on antennas). In order to find the one which minimizes the base station power consumption, we can compute the power consumption of the base station for each of them and select the optimal one. However, this iterative computation requires N_t matrix diagonalizations and as many water-filling algorithms. This is too much. That is why, in the following, we derive an approximation for the base station power consumption when N_{on} antennas are switched-on. Once this approximation has been derived, the proposed algorithm can compute the value of N_{on} which minimizes our approximation in order to provide a sub-optimal value for the number of switched-on antennas.

In order to approximate the base station power consumption, we first insert the expression of the transmit power of (6) in (1). We obtain the following expression:

$$P = \frac{\sigma^2}{L\eta_a}\left(\frac{N' 2^{\frac{C_c}{N'}}}{\left(\prod_{k=1}^{N'}\lambda_k\right)^{\frac{1}{N'}}} - \sum_{k=1}^{N'}\frac{1}{\lambda_k}\right) + N_{on}P_{ct}. \quad (7)$$

In the following, in order to make our derivation clearer, we denote α_k the normalized eigenvalue of $\mathbf{H}^*\mathbf{H}$:

$$\alpha_k = \frac{\lambda_k}{\sum_{n\in\mathscr{S}_{on}}||\mathbf{h}_n||_2^2}, \quad \forall k \in [\![1;N]\!]. \quad (8)$$

With this notation $\sum_{k=1}^{N}\alpha_k = 1$. The base station power consumption becomes:

$$P = \frac{N'\sigma^2}{L\eta_a S}\left(\frac{2^{\frac{C_c}{N'}}}{\left(\prod_{k=1}^{N'}\alpha_k\right)^{\frac{1}{N'}}} - \frac{1}{N'}\sum_{k=1}^{N'}\frac{1}{\alpha_k}\right) + N_{on}P_{ct}, \quad (9)$$

where $S = \sum_{n\in\mathscr{S}_{on}}||\mathbf{h}_n||_2^2$. In order to derive an approximation for the base station power consumption, we consider the case where the matrix $\mathbf{H}^*\mathbf{H}$ has exactly N non-zero eigenvalues and where all these eigenvalues are considered in the water-filling algorithm. In other words, we consider the case $N' = N$. In this situation, all the eigenvalues are beneficial to satisfy the user's capacity constraint. This is the best case.

In (9), we have a weighted difference between the geometric and arithmetic means of $\frac{1}{\alpha_k}$, $\forall k \in [\![1;N']\!]$. The geometric mean is always lower than the arithmetic mean and we have an equality in the case where all the α_k are equals to $\frac{1}{N}$. As a consequence, we can approximate the base station power consumption of the base station by its value in the case where all the eigenvalues are equals. We derive:

$$P \approx N_{on}P_{ct} + \frac{N^2\sigma^2}{L\eta_a\sum_{n\in\mathscr{S}_{on}}||\mathbf{h}_n||_2^2}\left(2^{\frac{C_c}{N}} - 1\right). \quad (10)$$

Please, note that, the evaluation of the power consumption with (10) does not require any matrix diagonalization. Moreover, this approximation allows to verify if the constraint on the maximum transmit power of (3c) is satisfied. Indeed, for a given number of switched-on antennas, the transmit power of the base station is approximated by:

$$P_{Tx} \approx P_{Tx}^{\text{app}} = \frac{N^2\sigma^2}{L\eta_a\sum_{n\in\mathscr{S}_{on}}||\mathbf{h}_n||_2^2}\left(2^{\frac{C_c}{N}} - 1\right). \quad (11)$$

For a number N_{on} of antennas, if the approximation of (11) is higher than the maximum transmit $P_{\max}$, the value of P_{Tx} will probably be higher than $P_{\max}$. As a consequence, we can eliminate the antenna configurations for which the transmit power is higher than $P_{\max}$ by eliminating the values of N_{on} for which $P_{Tx}^{\text{app}} \geq P_{\max}(1-\epsilon)$, where ϵ is a security margin which can be equal to 0.05.

Finally, we can find N_{on}^*, the sub-optimal value for the number of switched-on antennas, by finding the value of N_{on} which minimizes (10):

$$N_{on}^* = \underset{N_{on}}{\text{argmin}}\ N_{on}P_{ct} + \frac{N^2\sigma^2}{L\eta_a\sum_{k=1}^{N_{on}}||\mathbf{h}_k||_2^2}\left(2^{\frac{C_c}{N}} - 1\right). \quad (12)$$

1. Sort the columns of the channel matrix by descending order of their norm, $||\mathbf{h}_k||_2$;
2. Eliminate the values of N_{on} for which $P_{Tx}^{\text{app}}(N_{on}) \geq P_{\max}(1-\epsilon)$;
3. $N_{on}^* = \underset{N_{on}}{\text{argmin}}\ N_{on}P_{ct} + \frac{N^2\sigma^2}{L\eta_a \sum_{k=1}^{N_{on}} ||\mathbf{h}_k||_2^2}\left(2^{\frac{C_c}{N}} - 1\right)$;
4. Diagonalize the matrix $\mathbf{H}^*\mathbf{H}$ which contains the N_{on}^* column which have the highest norm;
5. Apply the water-filling algorithm of (5);

Figure 3. Proposed algorithm

B. Algorithm in full

The observations done in the previous sections show that NBS policy provides optimal performance, and that we can provide an approximation for the base station power consumption. So, the antenna selection can be done by first ordering the columns by descending order of their norm. Then, for each value of N_{on}, we can evaluate the base station power consumption with (10) and find the value N_{on}^* for which it is minimum. Finally, the base station can make the eigenvalue decomposition and apply the water-filling algorithm.

The whole algorithm introduced in this paper is summarized in Fig. 3. It is interesting to note that among the five steps of the algorithm, the first three are used for antenna selection and the last two are used for precoding and power allocation. Besides, this algorithm has a low complexity. Indeed, the step with the highest complexity is the matrix diagonalization which is part of the precoding.

V. SIMULATION RESULTS

In this section, we use numerical simulations in order to analyze the effect of the proposed antenna selection policy and of the power allocation on the base station power consumption.

A. Performance of the proposed policy

We first conduct some numerical simulations in order to assess the performance of the proposed algorithm. For that purpose, we compare four different policies:

- The proposed policy.
- The optimal policy with NBS, in which we compute the power consumption for the N_t possible configurations and select the one which consumes the less power.
- A policy in which all the RF chains are switched-on.
- A policy in which the number of antennas is computed using the method proposed in [8].

For each of the antenna selection policies compared here, NBS is applied and after selecting the number of antennas, the base station computes the transmit power with the water-filling algorithm. We consider the simulation parameters introduced in Section II and we suppose that the base station has $N_t = 32$ antennas, that the user has $N_r = 8$ antennas, and that the capacity constraint of the user is equal to 20 bits/s/Hz.

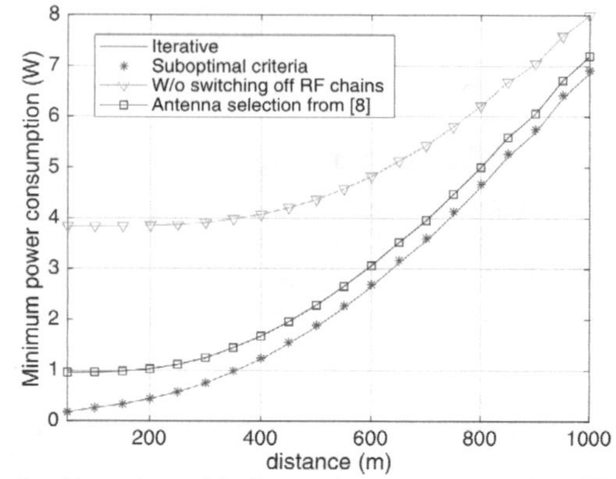

Figure 4. Comparison of the base station power consumption with several antenna selection policies.

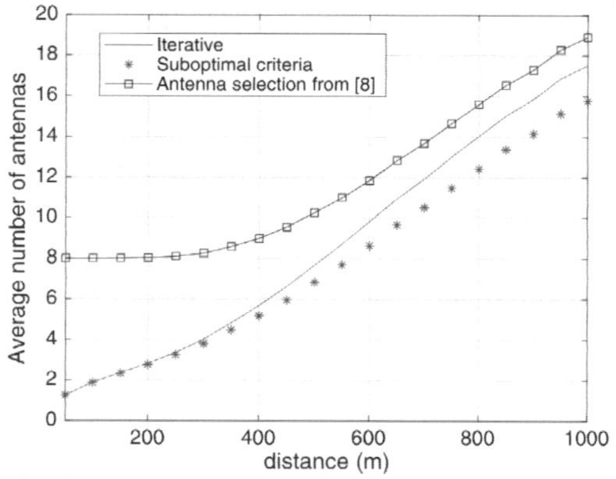

Figure 5. Comparison of the number of switched-on antennas with several antenna selection policies.

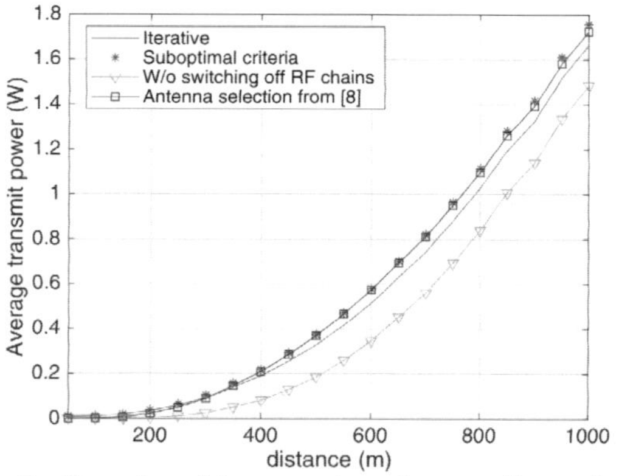

Figure 6. Comparison of the average transmit power with several antenna selection policies.

We display in Fig. 4 the average base station power consumption with the four compared policies. We can see in this figure that the proposed policy provides optimal performance. We first compare the base station power consumption with the proposed policy and with the policy without antenna selection. We can see that the highest gain is obtained when the user is near the base station. In such situation, the base station power consumption is reduced from 4 W to 0.2 W. Moreover, we can see, in Fig. 5, that the number of switched-on antennas is low when the user is near the base station and increases with the distance. Indeed, when the user is near the base station, the transmit power used to serve him is low. In such case, the part of the power consumption which is dependent on the transmit power ($\frac{1}{\eta_a} P_{TX}$) is low. As a consequence, switching-on an antenna increases more the power consumption than increasing the transmit power and, consequently, only one antenna is switched-on. On the contrary, when the user is far from the base station, the part of power consumption which is proportional to the transmit power is high compared to the power needed to switch-on an antenna. In that case, it is beneficial to switch-on more antennas.

By comparing the number of switched-on antennas with the proposed and with the optimal policies, we can see, in Fig. 5, that the number of switched-on antennas is slightly lower with the proposed policy. However, we can see in Fig. 4 that, the error committed on the number of antennas does not have any effect on the power consumption as the water-filling algorithm counterbalances this error by adjusting the transmit power. In other words, when the power is allocated with the water-filling algorithm, it compensates the error committed on the number of antennas. Besides, as the proposed solution uses a little less antennas than the optimal strategy, it requires a little more power to serve the user. This result is shown in Fig. 6.

Furthermore, with the solution proposed in [8], the number of switched-on antennas is computed considering that the transmit power P_{T_X} is equally distributed over all the eigenvalues. With such hypothesis, more antennas are required to serve the users. As more antennas are switched-on, the base station power consumption is higher. This extra-power consumption causes performance loss when the user is near the base station and the transmit power low. That is why, our solution outperforms the one proposed in [8]. When the distance increases, the transmit power increases and the impact of the error in the number of antennas has less impact on the base station power consumption.

B. Impact of the power allocation

We now analyze the impact of the power allocation. For that purpose, we still consider that the base station has 32 antennas and that the user has 8 antennas. We consider three different power allocations: the water-filling one, an equal power transmission over the transmit antennas and an equal power transmission over the eigenvalues. For this evaluation, we suppose that the capacity constraint is equal to 10 bits/s/Hz and we do not consider the constraint on the maximum transmit power. The results are displayed in Fig. 7. It is important to note that, with equal power transmissions (over the transmit antennas or over the eigenvalues of $\mathbf{H}^*\mathbf{H}$) the value of the transmit power which satisfies the capacity constraint of the user has to be computed using an iterative algorithm such as the bisection method.

This figure shows that the water-filling algorithm outperforms the two others power allocations. More precisely, the water-filling algorithm provides a large gain compared to the allocation where the RF power is equally distributed over all the antennas. Besides, even if the water-filling algorithm provides a small gain compared to the power allocation with equal transmit power over the eigenvalues, both solutions require perfect CSI and the water-filling algorithm is more convenient for antenna selection as we can more easily express the base station power consumption.

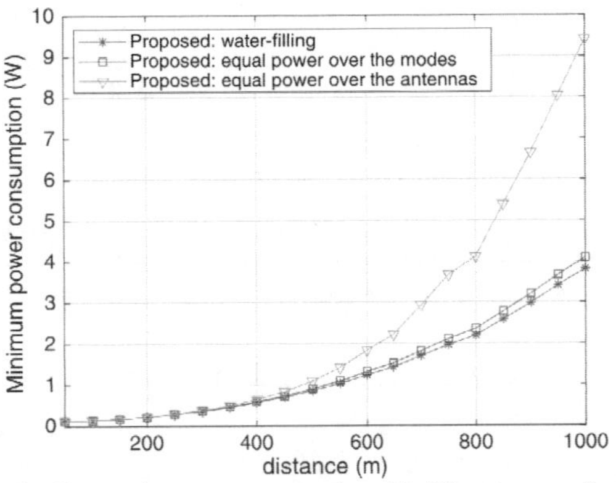

Figure 7. Base station power consumption with different power allocations.

VI. Conclusion

In this paper, we studied the problem of transmit antenna selection with an optimal precoding, *i.e.*, with the eigenvalue decomposition and a water-filling algorithm. We proposed a low-complexity algorithm for minimizing the base station power consumption. Our results show that, when the water-filling algorithm is employed, a small error in the number of switched-on antennas has no effect on the base station power consumption. This result highlights the possibility to reach optimal performance with simple algorithms. For our future work, we plan to study the combination of antenna selection and Cell Discontinuous Transmission.

Acknowledgement

Part of this work is supported by the project SOGREEN, which is funded by the French National Research Agency, under the grant agreement coded: N ANR-14-CE28-0025-02 and by Région Bretagne, France.

References

[1] K. N. R. S. V. Prasad, E. Hossain, and V. K. Bhargava, "Energy Efficiency in Massive MIMO-Based 5G Networks: Opportunities and Challenges," *IEEE Wireless Communications*, vol. 24, pp. 86–94, June 2017.

[2] X. Zhou, B. Bai, and W. Chen, "Invited Paper: Antenna selection in energy efficient MIMO systems: A survey," *China Communications*, vol. 12, no. 9, pp. 162–173, 2015.

[3] D. A. Gore, R. U. Nabar, and A. Paulraj, "Selecting an optimal set of transmit antennas for a low rank matrix channel," in *2000 IEEE ICASSP*, vol. 5, pp. 2785–2788 vol.5, 2000.

[4] Y. Pei, T.-H. Pham, and Y. C. Liang, "How many RF chains are optimal for large-scale MIMO systems when circuit power is considered?," in *2012 IEEE GLOBECOM*, pp. 3868–3873, Dec 2012.

[5] X. Zhou, B. Bai, and W. Chen, "Iterative Antenna Selection for Multi-Stream MIMO under a Holistic Power Model," *IEEE Wireless Communications Letters*, vol. 3, pp. 82–85, February 2014.

[6] H. Li, L. Song, D. Zhu, and M. Lei, "Energy efficiency of large scale MIMO systems with transmit antenna selection," in *2013 IEEE ICC*, pp. 4641–4645, June 2013.

[7] C. Jiang and L. J. Cimini, "Antenna Selection for Energy-Efficient MIMO Transmission," *IEEE Wireless Communications Letters*, vol. 1, pp. 577–580, December 2012.

[8] Z. Xu, C. Yang, G. Y. Li, S. Zhang, Y. Chen, and S. Xu, "Energy-Efficient MIMO-OFDMA Systems Based on Switching off RF Chains," in *2011 IEEE Vehicular Technology Conference (VTC Fall)*, pp. 1–5, Sept 2011.

[9] I. E. Telatar, "Capacity of multi-antenna Gaussian channels," *European Transactions on Telecommunications*, vol. 10, pp. 585–595, 1999.

[10] S. Cui, A. J. Goldsmith, and A. Bahai, "Energy-constrained modulation optimization," *IEEE Transactions on Wireless Communications*, vol. 4, pp. 2349–2360, Sept 2005.

[11] P. Kyosti *et al.*, "Winner II Deliverable 1.1.2.: Winner II Channel Models," tech. rep., September 2007.

[12] S. Sanayei and A. Nosratinia, "Antenna selection in MIMO systems," *IEEE Communications Magazine*, vol. 42, pp. 68–73, Oct 2004.

[13] M. Gharavi-Alkhansari and A. B. Gershman, "Fast antenna subset selection in MIMO systems," *IEEE Transactions on Signal Processing*, vol. 52, pp. 339–347, Feb 2004.

[14] T. H. Tai, W. H. Chung, and T. S. Lee, "A low complexity antenna selection algorithm for energy efficiency in massive mimo systems," in *2015 IEEE DSDIS*, pp. 284–289, Dec 2015.

A New Clipping Function for PAPR Mitigation: The Gaussian Clipping Function

Jacques Palicot*, Yves Louet* and Désiré Guel†
*CentraleSupélec/IETR, CentraleSupélec Campus de Rennes, 35510 Cesson-Sévigné, France
{email: jacques.palicot, yves.louet}@centralesupelec.fr
† Nokia Networks 7 Route de Villejust, 91620 Nozay, France
email: desire.guel@nokia.com

Abstract—**A Gaussian function to clip multicarrier modulation is presented in this paper in order to decrease their Peak to Average Power Ratio (PAPR). The Gaussian clipping (GC) function is a soft non-linear function which keeps constant the average power of the signal, what is a characteristic of great importance in real transmission. The characteristics and performance of this GC is analysed both theoretically and by simulation. Furthermore, in the application context of Wifi IEEE802.11, this GC is compared to several other clipping functions well known in the literature such as hard clipping, smooth clipping and deep clipping. The results prove that the average power is kept constant which was our objective.**

Index Terms— PAPR; Clipping; Gaussian Clipping.

I. Introduction

Orthogonal Frequency Division Multiplexing (OFDM), although used in standards such as IEEE 802.11a/g, IEEE 802.16, Digital Video Broadcasting (DVB) [1] and 4G cellular system/LTE suffers from the high Peak-to-Average Power Ratio (PAPR). Large PAPR requires a linear High Power Amplifier (HPA), which is inefficient. Moreover, the combination of a non linear HPA and large PAPR leads to in-band distortion and out-of-band radiation [2]. Several PAPR reduction techniques have been proposed [3]- [6]. The simplest way to reduce PAPR is to deliberately clip and filter the OFDM signal before amplification. However, clipping is a nonlinear process and may cause significant distortions that degrade the Bit Error Rate (BER) and increase adjacent out-of-band carriers [7]. The contribution of this paper is the following:

- first, we propose a new clipping function, the Gaussian Clipping (GC) function, which has the main advantage, compared to other clipping functions from the literature, to keep constant the average power.
- second, we analyse both theoretically and by simulation the performance of this GC, in terms of PAPR reduction gain and average power variation.
- third, we compare the GC performance with those of other clipping functions in terms of average power and BER in a Wireless Local Area Network (WLAN) context.

In Section II, we recall the basic idea of OFDM and we describe the PAPR problem. In Section III, we first describe clipping functions already known in the literature. In Section IV, we present our Gaussian clipping function. Section V deals with theoretical performance. Then Section VI presents some results and performance comparison, in a WLAN environment, of different clipping functions and finally we conclude the paper.

II. OFDM Systems and PAPR Issue

The basic idea underlying OFDM systems is the division of the available frequency spectrum into several subcarriers. To obtain a high spectral efficiency, the frequency responses of the subcarriers overlapp in an orthogonal way, hence the name OFDM. This orthogonality can be completely maintained with a small price in SNR degradation, even though the signal passes through a time dispersive fading channel, by introducing a Cyclic Prefix (CP).

The continuous-time baseband representation of an OFDM symbol is given by

$$x(t) = \frac{1}{\sqrt{N}} \sum_{k=0}^{N-1} X_k e^{j2\pi f_k t}, \quad 0 \leq t \leq T_s \ , \qquad (1)$$

where N data symbols X_k form an OFDM symbol $\mathbf{X} = [X_0, \cdots, X_{N-1}]$, $f_k = \frac{k}{T_s}$ and T_s is the time duration of the OFDM symbol.

In practice, OFDM signals are typically generated by using an Inverse Discrete Fourier Transform (IDFT).

The OFDM symbol represented by the vector $\mathbf{X} = [X_0 \cdots X_{N-1}]^T$ is transformed via IDFT into T_s/N-spaced discrete-time vector $\mathbf{x} = x[n] = [x_0 \cdots x_{N-1}]^T$, i.e.

$$x_n = \frac{1}{\sqrt{N}} \sum_{k=0}^{N-1} X_k e^{j2\pi \frac{n}{N} k}, \quad 0 \leq n \leq N-1 \ . \qquad (2)$$

In this paper, the discrete-time indexing $[n]$ denotes Nyquist Rate samples. Since oversampling may be needed in practical designs, we will introduce the notation $x[n/L]$ to denote oversampling by L. Different oversampling strategies of $x[n/L]$ can be defined. From now on, the oversampled IDFT output will refer to oversample of equation (2), which is expressed as follows:

$$x[n/L] = \frac{1}{\sqrt{N}} \sum_{k=0}^{NL-1} X_k e^{j2\pi \frac{n}{NL} k}, \ 0 \leq n \leq NL-1 \ . \qquad (3)$$

The above expression (3) can be implemented by using a length-(NL) IDFT operation with the input vector

$$\mathbf{X}^{(\mathrm{L})} = \left[\begin{array}{ccc} X_0, \cdots, X_{\frac{N}{2}-1}, & \underbrace{0, \cdots, 0}_{(L-1)N \text{ zeros}} & X_{\frac{N}{2}}, \cdots, X_{N-1} \end{array} \right].$$

Thus, $\mathbf{X}^{(\mathrm{L})}$ is extended from $\mathbf{X}$ by using the so-called zero-padding scheme, i.e., by inserting $(L-1)N$ zeros in the middle of $\mathbf{X}$, i.e.,

$$X_k^{(\mathrm{L})} = \begin{cases} X_k, & k \in \mathcal{S}_1 \\ 0, & k \in \mathcal{S}_2 \end{cases},$$

where $\mathcal{S}_1$ and $\mathcal{S}_2$ are the set of In-Band (IB) indices and Out-Of-Band (OOB) indices respectively.

In the literature, the envelope variations of $x[n/L]$ are often described in terms of the crest-factor (CF), peak-to-mean envelope power ratio (PMEPR) or simply peak-to-average power ratio (PAPR). In this paper, we adopt the term PAPR to quantify the envelope excursions of the signal. The PAPR of the signal $x(t)$ may be defined as

$$\mathrm{PAPR}_{[x]} \triangleq \frac{\max\limits_{t\in[0,T_s]} |x(t)|^2}{\mathcal{P}_x}, \quad (4)$$

where $\mathcal{P}_x = E\left\{|x(t)|^2\right\}$ is the average signal power and $E\{.\}$ is the statistical expectation operator. Note that, in order to avoid aliasing distortion into the data bearing subcarriers and in order to accurately describe the PAPR, an oversampling factor $L \geq 4$ is required.

In the literature, it is customary to use the Complementary Cumulative Distribution Function (CCDF) of the PAPR as a performance criterion. It is denoted as

$$\mathrm{CCDF}_{[x]}(\psi) \triangleq \Pr\left\{\mathrm{PAPR}_{[x]} \geq \psi\right\}.$$

If N is large enough, based on the central limit theorem, the real and imaginary parts of OFDM $x(t)$ follow a Gaussian distribution and its envelope will follow a Rayleigh distribution. This implies a large PAPR.

III. Some Clipping Functions

In this Section, we present the clipping techniques family [8]. Whatever the clipping technique to reduce OFDM PAPR is, the output signal y_n, in terms of the input signal x_n is given as follows:

$$y_n = f(|x_n|)\, e^{j\varphi_n}, \quad (5)$$

where φ_n is the x_n phase and $f(.)$ is the clipping function.

A. Classical Clipping (CC) technique

The Classical Clipping (CC) proposed in [7] is one of the most popular clipping technique for PAPR reduction known in the literature [9] [7]. It is sometimes called hard clipping or soft clipping. To avoid any confusion, it is called Classical Clipping (CC) in this paper. In [7], its effects on the performance of OFDM, including the power spectral density, the PAPR and BER are evaluated. The function-based clipping used for CC technique is defined below and depicted in Figure 1 (a).

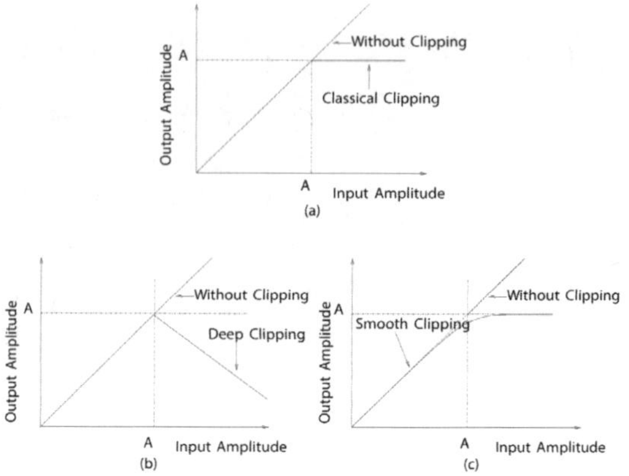

Fig. 1: Functions-based clipping for PAPR reduction

$$f(r) = \begin{cases} r, & r \leq \mathrm{A} \\ A, & r > \mathrm{A} \end{cases}, \quad (6)$$

where A is the clipping threshold.

B. Deep Clipping (DC) technique

Deep Clipping has been proposed in [10] to solve the peaks regrowth problem due to the out-of-band filtering of the classical clipping and filtering method. So, in DC technique, the clipping function is modified in order to "deeply" clip the high amplitude peaks. A parameter called clipping depth factor has been introduced in order to control the depth of the clipping. The function-based clipping used for DC technique is defined below and depicted in Figure 1 (b).

$$f(r) = \begin{cases} r & , \quad r \leq \mathrm{A} \\ \mathrm{A} - \beta(r - \mathrm{A}) & , \quad \mathrm{A} < r \leq \frac{1+\beta}{\beta}\mathrm{A} \\ 0 & , \quad r > \frac{1+\beta}{\beta}\mathrm{A} \end{cases},$$

where β is called the clipping depth factor.

C. Smooth Clipping (SC) technique

In [11], a Smooth Clipping technique is used to reduce the OFDM PAPR. In this paper, the function based-clipping for SC technique is defined below and depicted in Figure 1 (c).

$$f(r) = \begin{cases} r - \frac{1}{b}r^3, & r \leq \frac{3}{2}\mathrm{A} \\ \mathrm{A}, & r > \frac{3}{2}\mathrm{A} \end{cases},$$

where $b = \frac{27}{4}\mathrm{A}^2$.

These three clipping functions are drawn on Figure 1 and have been completely studied and compared in [8]. We may notice that the 'invertible clipping' of [12] is a variant of SC.

To the best of authors's knowledge, since 2008 with the DC [10], no new clipping functions has been proposed in the literature. Of course, a lot of papers deal with OFDM clipping but from many others point of view as the threshold computation of the CC [16] [17] [18] or the mitigation of the clipping noise [10] [13] [15] ..., but no new clipping function have been proposed so far as the GC introduced in this paper.

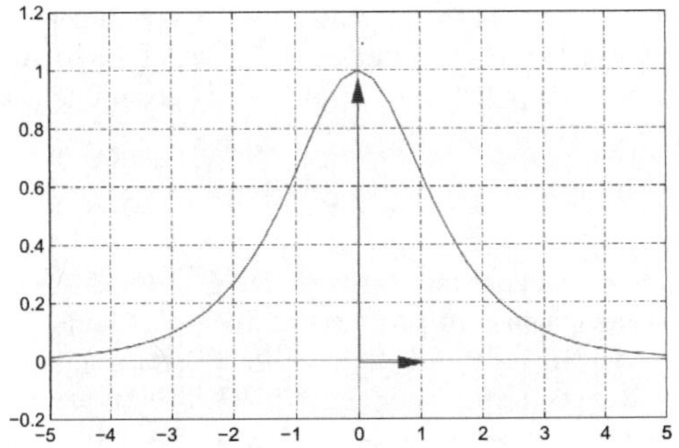

Fig. 2: Gaussian function curve.

IV. Gaussian Clipping

In this Section, we present the Gaussain clipping for PAPR reduction. We start from the Gaussian function, which is drawn in Figure 2. It will act on the multicarrier signal amplitude in order to decrease its PAPR. In this context, only positive values are taken into account, because the signal modulus is always a positive value.

The Gaussian Clipping function $f(.)$, associated to this Gaussian function, is expressed as:

$$f(r) = Ae^{-(\eta r)^2}, \quad r \geq 0. \tag{7}$$

The parameters A and η control the performance of the method (the transmitted mean power variation and the PAPR reduction capability).

The GC technique equation (7) can reduce the OFDM PAPR by increasing low amplitudes samples and by decreasing high amplitudes samples, as illustrated in Figure 3.

Figure 3 shows that for samples r_n such that $r_n = |x_n| \leq r^{(\text{threshold})}$, the signal is amplified whereas for samples r_n such that $r_n \geq r^{(\text{threshold})}$ the signal is attenuated.

The threshold value, $r^{(\text{threshold})}$, which corresponds to the threshold between amplification and reduction of the signal is obtained by solving equation (8) and is given by equation (9).

$$f[r] = Ae^{-(\eta r)^2} = Ar. \tag{8}$$

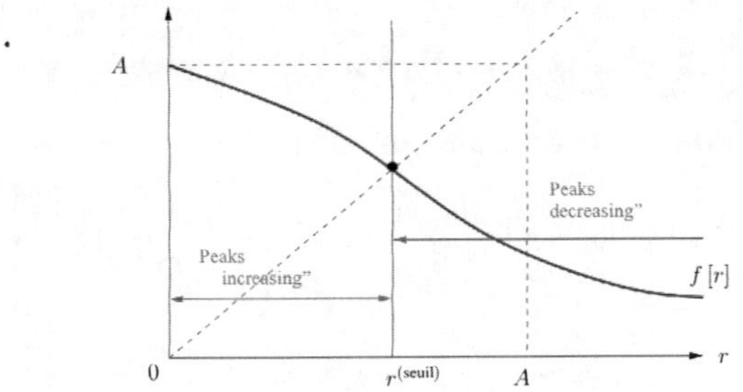

Fig. 3: Behavior of Attenuation/Amplification of the signal versus A and r parameters.

What gives:

$$r^{(\text{threshold})} = \sqrt{\frac{W(2\eta)}{2\eta}}, \tag{9}$$

where W is the Lambert function. The equation (9) shows that $r^{(\text{threshold})}$ depends only on the η parameter of the GC (see equation (7)). It is therefore clear that $r^{(\text{threshold})}$ and consequently η, drives the PAPR reduction gain of the GC.

We will now explain the influence of A in the PAPR reduction gain. We remind that one of our main objective is to keep constant the average power between the input and the output of clipping. Therefore, we would like to have $\mathcal{P}_y = \mathcal{P}_x$, where $\mathcal{P}_x$ is the average power of the signal before and $\mathcal{P}_y$ is the average power of the signal after the PAPR mitigation technique. Considering equation (7) $\mathcal{P}_y$ is given by equation (10):

$$\mathcal{P}_y = \int_0^\infty f(r)^2 p(r)dr = A^2 \int_0^\infty \mathrm{e}^{-2(\eta r)^2} p(r)dr. \tag{10}$$

Therefore, the ratio γ between the two powers $\mathcal{P}_x$ and $\mathcal{P}_y$ is expressed as follows:

$$\gamma = \frac{\mathcal{P}_y}{\mathcal{P}_x} = \frac{A^2}{\mathcal{P}_x} \int_0^\infty \mathrm{e}^{-2(\eta r)^2} p(r)dr. \tag{11}$$

As shown by equation (11), A and η influence the ratio γ. This means that it is possible to drive the ratio γ between the two powers thanks to parameter A without modifying the PAPR reduction gain, for a given η . In fact we schowed that the PAPR reduction gain only depends on η parameter.

The A parameter value which give $\mathcal{P}_y = \mathcal{P}_x$ is given by the equation (12)

$$A^{(\text{opt})} = \frac{\sqrt{\mathcal{P}_x}}{\left[\int_0^\infty \mathrm{e}^{-2(\eta r)^2} p(r)dr\right]^{\frac{1}{2}}}. \tag{12}$$

To summarize, we have shown, theoretically, that η parameter drives the PAPR reduction gain whereas A parameter drives the average power variation for a given η.

V. Theoretical Study of Gaussian Clipping

In this Section, we analyse theoretically the behavior of the GC function. We focus (subsectionV-A) on the average power variation given by the following equations:

$$\gamma = \frac{\mathcal{P}_y}{\mathcal{P}_x}, \tag{13}$$

$$\Delta \mathrm{E} = 10 \log_{10}(\gamma). \text{ [dB]} \tag{14}$$

In subsectionV-B, we focus on the PAPR CCDF at the ouput of the GC function. We are interested in the PAPR reduction gain ΔPAPR for a CCDF value of 10^{-2} before and after clipping.

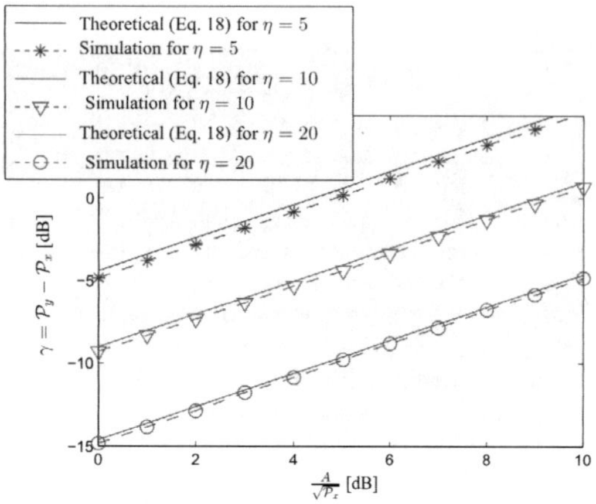

Fig. 4: Theoretical and simulation average power variation comparison for several values of $\frac{A}{\sqrt{\mathcal{P}_x}}$.

A. Average power variation analysis

The expression of the transmitted mean power $\mathcal{P}_y$ as a function of the OFDM mean power $\mathcal{P}_x$ can be expressed as:

$$\mathcal{P}_y = \int_0^{+\infty} [f(r)]^2 p_x(r)\, dr, \tag{15}$$

where $p_x(r)$ is the probability density function (PDF) of the OFDM envelope and can be assimilated to a Rayleigh distribution for a large number of OFDM subcarriers:

$$p_x(r) = \tfrac{2r}{\mathcal{P}_x} e^{-\frac{r^2}{\mathcal{P}_x}}, \quad r \geq 0. \tag{16}$$

By sustituting the expression of $p_x(r)$ in equation (15), the expression of the transmitted mean power $\mathcal{P}_y$ is given by:

$$\mathcal{P}_y = \int_0^{+\infty} \left[Ae^{-(\eta r)^2}\right]^2 \frac{2r}{\mathcal{P}_x} e^{-\frac{r^2}{\mathcal{P}_x}} = \frac{A^2}{1+2\eta^2\mathcal{P}_x}. \tag{17}$$

Let us consider γ the output-to-input mean power ratio; using equation (17), γ is expressed below

$$\gamma \triangleq \frac{\mathcal{P}_y}{\mathcal{P}_x} = \frac{A^2}{(1+2\eta^2\mathcal{P}_x)\,\mathcal{P}_x}. \tag{18}$$

From equation (18), it is easy to compute the value of $A^{(\text{opt})}$ (that means the A value which gives $\mathcal{P}_y = \mathcal{P}_x$) and is expressed as:

$$A^{(\text{opt})} = \left[(1+2\eta^2\mathcal{P}_x)\,\mathcal{P}_x\right]^{\frac{1}{2}}. \tag{19}$$

Equation (19) shows that $A^{(\text{opt})}$ depends on η (which controls the PAPR reduction gain) and the average power of input signal.

The average power variation related to the Gaussian clipping given by equation (14) is compared with simulation results in Figure 4. Results show a good match between theory (equation 18) and simulation. For a given η value, the average power is a linear function of A. Therefore, for a given η parameter value, it is possible to find the value of $A^{(\text{opt})}$ which keeps constant the average power (our objective). This is given by the value $\gamma = 0$.

B. PAPR distribution analysis

In this subsection, the PAPR CCDF is derived anatyically for the ouput signal. To perform this analysis, like in [19] for the classical OFDM PAPR analysis, we assume that the signals $x(t)$ and $y(t)$ (input and ouput of the Gaussian clipping respectively) are sampled at the Nyquist rate (that means, oversampling factor $L = 1$). Therefore, input and output samples x_n and y_n are respectively given by:

$$\begin{aligned} x_n &= x\left(\frac{n}{N}T_s\right), \\ y_n &= y\left(\frac{n}{N}T_s\right), \end{aligned} \tag{20}$$

where $0 \leq n < N$, N is the subcarriers number and T_s the OFDM symbol period. The signals x_n and y_n may also be written:

$$\begin{aligned} x_n &= r_n e^{j\phi_n}, \\ y_n &= f[r_n]\, e^{j\phi_n} = v_n e^{j\phi_n}, \end{aligned} \tag{21}$$

where r_n is the amplitude of x_n et ϕ_n its phase; $v_n = f(r_n)$ is the amplitude of y_n.

The PAPR of y_n is defined as:

$$\text{PAPR}_{[y]} = \frac{\max\limits_{0\leq n<N} |y_n|^2}{\mathcal{P}_y} = \frac{\max\limits_{0\leq n<N} {v_n}^2}{\mathcal{P}_y}. \tag{22}$$

By applying the same development as in [19], and by assuming v_n independance values we derive:

$$\begin{aligned} \text{CCDF}_{[y]}\left(\tilde{\psi}\right) &= \Pr\left[\text{PAPR}_{[y]} \geq \tilde{\psi}\right] = \Pr\left[\frac{\max\limits_n v_n^2}{\mathcal{P}_y} \geq \tilde{\psi}\right] \\ &\simeq 1 - \prod_{n=0}^{N-1}\left\{\Pr\left[\frac{f(r_n)^2}{\mathcal{P}_y} \leq \tilde{\psi}\right]\right\}, \\ &\simeq 1 - \prod_{n=0}^{N-1}\left\{\Pr\left[f(r_n) \leq \sqrt{\tilde{\psi}\mathcal{P}_y}\right]\right\} \end{aligned} \tag{23}$$

where $f[r]$ is the Gaussian clipping function given by equation (7).

By using equation (7), we get:

$$\text{CCDF}_{[y]}\left(\tilde{\psi}\right) \simeq 1 - \prod_{n=0}^{N-1}\left\{\Pr\left[r_n \geq \frac{1}{\eta}\left[\ln\left(\frac{A}{\sqrt{\tilde{\psi}\mathcal{P}_y}}\right)\right]^{\frac{1}{2}}\right]\right\}. \tag{24}$$

As r_n is a Rayleigh i.i.d random variable whose probability density function is given by equation (16), equation (24) becomes:

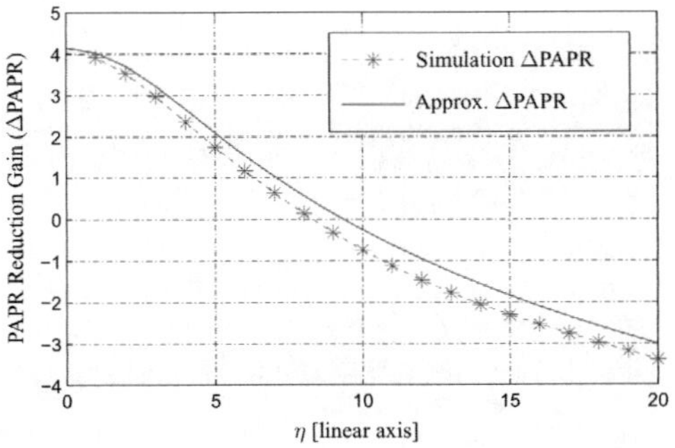

Fig. 5: PAPR reduction gain comparison between theoretical and simulation results versus η parameter for $\frac{A}{\sqrt{\mathcal{P}_x}} = 3$ dB.

$$\mathrm{CCDF}_{[y]}\left(\tilde{\psi}\right) \simeq 1 - \prod_{n=0}^{N-1}\left[e^{-\frac{\ln\left(\frac{A}{\sqrt{\tilde{\psi}\gamma\mathcal{P}_x}}\right)}{\eta^2\mathcal{P}_x}}\right], \qquad (25)$$
$$\simeq 1 - e^{-N\frac{\ln\left(\frac{A}{\sqrt{\tilde{\psi}\gamma\mathcal{P}_x}}\right)}{\eta^2\mathcal{P}_x}},$$

where $\mathcal{P}_x$ is the OFDM average power and γ the ratio between output average power and input average power given by equation (18).

The PAPR reduction gain is compared to simulations results and is presented in Figure 5 for several values of η parameter. It shows that the theoretical approximation of equation (25) is very close to simulation results.

The PAPR reduction gain decreases when η parameter increases. This result provides us an upper bound of η. In fact it should be smaller then 8 to have a positive PAPR reduction gain, which, of course, is our objective.

VI. COMPARATIVE RESULTS STUDY WITH OTHER CLIPPING FUNCTIONS

In this subsection, GC performance are compared with classical clipping [7] (Section III-A), Deep clipping [10] (Section III-B) and Smooth clipping [11] (Section III-C) performance. This comparative study is performed in the context of the WLAN standard IEEE 802.11 a/g, whose parameters are given in Table I.

TABLE I: SIMULATION PARAMETERS.

Paramètres du Système	Valeurs
Modulation type	16-QAM
Carriers number	N = 64
Data sub carriers number	48
Pilots number	4
Oversampling factor	$L = 4$
Channel type	AWGN

In Figure 6 the PAPR reduction gain, ΔPAPR, is analysed for the four clipping techniques in function of the average

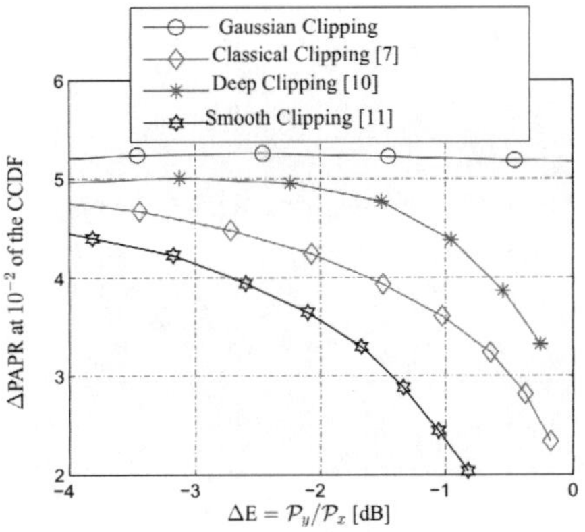

Fig. 6: PAPR reduction gain versus ΔE for the four clipping techniques.

power variation ΔE. For the Classical, Deep and Smooth clipping functions, the PAPR gain decreases with ΔE and becomes very small for ΔE $\simeq 0$ dB. At the opposite, this PAPR gain with the GC is quasi constant in function of ΔE. In fact, whatever the value of ΔE is, the PAPR gain ΔPAPR of GC is equal to around 5.2 dB. This result is the great advantage of the GC, because it offers a PAPR reduction of 5.2 dB without modifying the average power. To reach this result it is necessary to set $\frac{A}{\sqrt{\mathcal{P}_x}}$ at 0.45 dB as it is shown in Figure 7. In this figure, the influence of the A parameter is presented. The results show that parameter A could control the average power variation without modifying the PAPR reduction gain. This result is very important. In fact, it is possible to choose A in such a way that $\mathcal{P}_y = \mathcal{P}_x$ without modifying the PAPR reduction gain. In other words, with the GC function it is possible to reach a PAPR reduction gain of 5 dB with an average power variation ΔE $= 0$.

Figure 8 presents the BER for the four clipping techniques. As expected, these techniques degrade the BER. In fact the signal resulting from clipping functions is useful for PAPR reduction but is also the interferer signal which deteriorates the signal both in band and out of band. Generally out of band

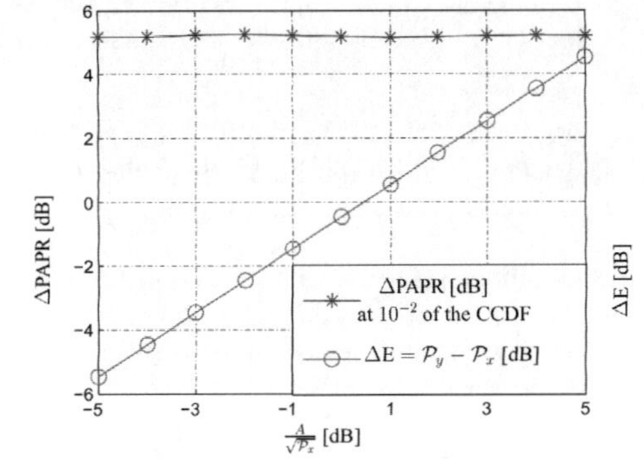

Fig. 7: PAPR reduction gain and average power variation of the GC function versus parameter A .

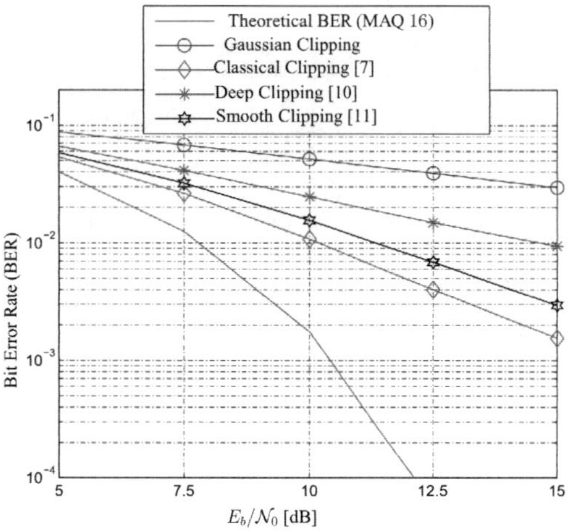

Fig. 8: BER Comparison for the four clipping techniques.

degradation is suppressed by filtering (it is why clipping techniques are generally named clipping and filtering techniques). As it could be seen GC is the one which degrades the most the BER. This was expected because the PAPR reduction was the greatest. That means that GC (as every clipping function) could not be used without BER improvement. To improve BER degradation due to clipping noise (whatever the clipping function is), several techniques could be performed:

- by inverting the clipping function or by iterative subtraction of the noise regenerated with the clipping function at the receiver [13]. Iterative methods to substract the estimated noise have been proposed in [14] and in [15]. The main drawbacks, in our point of view, is that these techniques become no more backward compatible and add complexity at the receiver side. Furthermore, the OOB noise, will degrade the signal in the ajacent band (the so called shoulders), which is, of course, not acceptable.
- Another alternative consists in turning the clipping method into a Tone Reservation (TR) method. By principle TR does not deteriorated the BER. This technique has several advantages: i) to be performed at the transmitter side, ii) to be backward compatible, iii) to be very simple to realize. It is this technique we have studied in [20] .

VII. Conclusion

Gaussian Clipping has been proposed in this paper. We studied its theoretical performance in terms of PAPR reduction and average power variation. These performances were also evaluated trough simulations and compared to other clipping techniques. The main conclusion is that the proposed GC is a very interesting clipping method when keeping the average power constant is a strong requirement.

Of course, as all the other clipping functions, due to their non linear characters, GC degrades the BER, which means that this clipping technique should be used in addition with filtering and/or with TR method.

References

[1] *DVB: Frame structure channel coding and modulation for a second generation digital terrestrial television broadcasting system (DVB-T2)*, DVB, June 2008.

[2] R. van Nee and R. Prasad, *OFDM for Wireless Multimedia Communications*, Boston: Artech House Publishers, March 2000.

[3] H. Ochiai and H. Imai, *Peak power reduction schemes on OFDM systems: a review*, in Proc. 11th Wireless Personal Multimedia Communications Symposium, pp. 247–252, 8–11 Sept. 1998.

[4] S. H. Han and J. H. Lee, *An overview of peak-to-average power ratio reduction techniques for multicarrier transmission*, IEEE Transactions on Wireless Communications, vol. 12, pp. 56–65, April 2005.

[5] T. Jiang and Y. Wu, *An Overview: Peak-to-Average Power Ratio Reduction Techniques for OFDM Signals*, IEEE Transactions on Broadcasting, vol. 54, pp. 257–268, June 2008.

[6] Y. Louet and J. Palicot, *A classification of methods for efficient power amplification of signals*, Annals of Telecommunications, vol. Volume 63, pp. 351–368, 2008.

[7] X. Li and J. L. J. Cimini, *Effects of clipping and filtering on the performance of OFDM*, IEEE Communication Letters, vol. 2, pp. 131–133, May 1998.

[8] D. Guel and J. Palicot, *Analysis and Comparison of Clipping techniques for OFDM Peak-to-Average Power Ratio Reduction*, in International Conference on DSP, July 2009.

[9] J. Armstrong, *Peak-to-average power reduction for OFDM by repeated clipping and frequency domain filtering*, Electronics Letters, vol. 38, pp. 246–247, 28 Feb. 2002.

[10] S. Kimura, T. Nakamura, M. Saito, and M. Okada, *PAR reduction for OFDM signals based on deep Clipping*, 3rd International Symposium on Communications, Control and Signal Processing, vol. 2, pp. 911–916, March 2008.

[11] P. Boonsrimuang, E. Puttawong, H. Kobayashi, and T. Paungma, *PAPR Reduction Using Smooth Clipping in OFDM System*, The 3rd Information and Computer Engineering Postgraduate Workshop 2003 (ICEP'2003), vol. 2, pp. 158–161, Jabuary 2003.

[12] S. Ragusa, J. Palicot, Y. Louet, and C. Lereau, *Invertible Clipping for Increasing the Power Efficiency of OFDM Amplification*, in IEEE International Conference on Telecommunications,, May 2006.

[13] R Déjardin, M. Colas, and G. Gelle, *Comparison of iterative receivers mitigating the clipping noise of OFDM based systems*, in European Wireless Proceedings, 2007.

[14] H.Chen and A. M. Haimovich, *Iterative estimation and cancellation of clipping noise for OFDM signals*, IEEE Communications Letters, vol. 7, pp. 305–307, July 2003.

[15] R Déjardin, M. Colas, and G. Gelle, *On the iterative mitigation of clipping noise for COFDM transmissions*, European Transactions on Telecommunications pp. 247–252, 1998.

[16] H. J. Kim, S. C. Cho, H. S. Oh, and J. M. Ahn, *Adaptive clipping technique for reducing PAPR on OFDM systems*, In Vehicular Technology Conference,2003, VTC 2003-Fall, volume 3,pages 1478-1481.

[17] B. M. Lee and Y. Kim *An adaptive clipping and filtering technique for PAPR reduction of OFDM signals*, Circuit, Systems and Signal Processing Journal,(2013),Vol 32, pages 1335-1349.

[18] L. M. Diallo, J. Palicot, and F. Bader *Achieving a Desired Deterministic Upper Bounded PAPR Value Using a Fast Adaptive Clipping Algorithm*, The Eleventh Advanced International Conference on Telecommunications,June 2015,Brussels, Belgium

[19] H.Ochiai and H.Imai, *On the distribution of the peak-to-average power ratio in OFDM signals*, IEEE Trans. Commun., vol. 49, pp. 282–289, Feb 2001.

[20] J. Palicot, Y. Louet, and D. Guel, *Tone Reservation Based Gaussian Clipping and Filtering for OFDM PAPR Mitigation*, International Conference on Telecommunications,Saint Malo, France, June 2018.

Dynamic Resource Allocation and Balanced Cell Loading - a Stochastic Meanfield Control Approach

Abheek Saha
Hughes Systique Corporation,
India
Email: abheek.saha@hsc.com

***Abstract*—Mean-field theory is a significant recent step for the field of stochastic optimal control. By allowing the optimal control functions to take into account not only the state of the controlled node, but also the mean-field state of an entire ensemble of nodes, mean-field theory allows us to model inter-dependent networks of agents in an analytically tractable manner. In this paper, we show its application to a very standard problem of cellular network optimization, the cell loading problem. By modelling the cell-loading problem as a combination of the loading of the individual cell, as well as the loading of the entire network, we show that a distributed optimal control function exists that can be individually implemented at nodes, and that is capable of reaching network wide equilibrium.**

Keywords*—*mean field games; stochastic control; cell loading; admission control

I. Introduction and Problem Statement

Stochastic optimal control is a powerful technique to control time-varying systems with randomly varying inputs. Developed over the last fifty years from the base of variational inequality and deterministic optimal control theory, it has been applied in multiple disciplines, ranging from finance to oil exploration and medical trials. The fundamental strength of optimal control is the ability to develop an optimal control function which can optimize performance over a time interval, as opposed to a single instant of time, in the face of unknown, time varying inputs.

Application of stochastic optimal control to wireless networks, however, has been limited [1][2][3]. A fundamental problem in the application of optimal control techniques in this domain is that of inter-node inter-dependency. Wireless networks of the 4th and 5th generation are increasingly built around the principles of shared resources, overlapping coverage areas and inter-cell and even inter-radio technology coordination. This change, from the days of isolated cells of fixed boundaries in 2nd generation networks, has come about because of two reasons. The first is the ability of individual user terminals to use larger and larger bands of spectrum. The second is the need for networks to dynamically adapt to large variations in demand, both spatially and temporally. Cellular networks are being moved towards newer and newer business cases such as wide-area connectivity for cellular networks supporting *Internet Of Things*, connected vehicles, etc. Most of these use cases are dependent on network nodes being able to flexibly adapt to new patterns in user behaviour. Hence, the paradigm of dynamically shared resources and network node cooperation is here to stay. For a few examples, we see Coordinated Multipoint networks in 4G, Hetnets and Inter-Cell Interference Coordination (ICIC/eICIC). Indeed, the 3rd Generation Partnership Project (3gPP) has introduced the X-interface between network nodes as an explicit means of inter-node coordination in real-time, in order to make coordinated cooperative network operation possible.

A. Optimal Control for Wireless Networks

Applying any kind of optimal control to wireless network nodes hence needs to model the network nodes impact on each other. Network nodes are independent, yet coexisting agents, tied together by the constraints of shared resources and shared environments. In this situation, it is not really possible to model each network as independent of the other nodes. To apply optimal control, one would to simultaneously solve the optimal control equation for all network nodes simultaneously, i.e., the network state becomes a vector of states, one for each agent. This however leads to the dimensionality problem as the number of degrees of freedom increase as $\mathcal{O}(n^2)$. It also requires a degree of simultaneous coordinated control that is not feasible in most wireless networks. A strictly adversarial approach (such as used in game theoretic techniques) is also not appropriate, since network nodes are not necessarily operating in competition of each other. It may make sense for a given node to hand over load to another node or to take over loading from another node cooperatively. To a large extent, we are optimizing overall network capacity, not individual node capacity.

B. The Mean-Field Extension to Stochastic Optimal Control

In the 2000s, Lasry and Lions [4] and independently, yet nearly simultaneously Minyi Huang and his team [5] kicked off a concerted research effort on optimal control of multiple interacting stochastic processes with mean field constraints. Optimal control problems of this nature are called Mean Field Games (henceforth MFG). The MFG technique is an extension to stochastic optimal control that allows the empirical distribution of individual network node states to be included in the transition and cost functions. This provides us a mechanism for incorporating the network state variables into individual node decision control algorithms. For example, Huang et al. in [6] use mean-field stochastic control as a way of optimal power control in wireless networks. Wireless nodes have to set transmission power so as to maximize the Signal to Interference Ratio (SIR), yet minimize cross-neighbour interference. In this case, the latter is modelled in terms of the empirical power distribution across the network.

In this paper, we apply stochastic control with mean field constraints to an associated problem, that of cell loading. We will show how this powerful new technique can be applied to this crucial and very basic problem of cellular resource management. The rest of the paper is organized as follows. In Section II, we introduce the cell loading problem. In Section III, we give an introduction to Stochastic Optimal Control and its extension to Mean-field constraints. Finally, in Section IV, we show how we model the cell loading problem in terms of mean-field constraints and stochastic demand and provide a framework for its solution.

II. THE CELL LOADING PROBLEM

The cell-loading problem has been studied as part of the load balancing problem since a long time and is seen as a fundamental component of the Self Optimizing Network (SON) [7][8].

A relatively recent analysis of the current status and open areas is given by Andrews et al. in [9]. In this work, the authors also discuss the myths surrounding cell loading and QoS. One of the myths identified by the authors is that the capacity of a cell is rarely a property of the link SIR, but also has to take into account the loading of the cell itself. In our opinion, this underlies the need to do active load balancing as discussed in the rest of the paper.

1) Problem Description: The problem is briefly described as follows: we have a network of overlapping cells covering a given coverage area. Each cell is controlled by a network node (base-station). The state variable $X(t)$ for a given cell is the demand for bandwidth from the associated network node. The network nodes negotiate with a central controller for allocation of resources; the resources available to a given network are a measure of its capacity $c(t)$. The resources allocated to a cell (network node) may be a combination of various different physical and computational resources, such as spectrum, power and backhaul capacity. All of these combine in some way to determine the overall load handling ability $c()$ of a given network node. Since these are shared resources, nodes in a SON can flexibly deploy them, while keeping with overall network constraints, from one cell to the other as demand changes.

We make the problem more interesting by making some additional assumptions on the part of the users; that they are bandwidth hunting and self-optimizing. A bandwidth hunting entity constantly increases demand as its current demand is met; this attribute is typically used for TCP congestion management algorithms, which hunt for spare bandwidth in the network and then fill it up. Since modern wireless networks are dominated by data traffic, this is not a far-fetched assumption. The second attribute refers to the user equipments agency in terms of selecting the cell to attach to; an individual user terminal will tend to detach from over-crowded cells with less available bandwidth and attach to less crowded cells using a mixture of measurements and network feedback. 5th generation user terminals will have the capability to interrogate the network for this kind of information and the algorithms to use the information for optimal network selection.

It is clear that the likelihood of input demand rising further is tied to the expressed demand not only in the current cell, but also in the neighbouring cells; for example, if the demand for a given cell is low and that of the neighbouring cells higher, it is possible for users to handoff to one of the neighbouring cells, hence decreasing expressed demand in the given cell. Here we can use the difference of the local demand and the average of the empirical network-wide demand to express this preference. Similarly, we can place constraints on the final distribution, by making $g()$ a function both of the final value of X, as well as the final distribution; for example, by providing an incentive for users to stay within a certain range of the mean.

Given this scenario, the challenge is to design an algorithm for the optimal allocation of resources. The input to the algorithm is the demand as measured at each network node, and information of the network wide distribution of this variable; since we are only interested in a single moment of the distribution, the amount of information to be circulated network wide is relatively limited. Based on this input, individual network nodes will compute the optimal capacity they wish to deploy and then execute that strategy. The objective is to minimize the demand allocation gap while maximizing the total served demand. For reasons we shall describe below, we shall formulate and solve the algorithm as a stochastic optimal control problem with a meanfield constraint.

2) Previous Work: The existing literature in load balancing in cellular networks is vast, even if we limit it to distributed cooperative algorithms. Broadly, the approaches in the literature can be divided into two categories. One set of research tends to focus on user redistribution, using intra-cellular and inter-cellular handoffs [10][11]. In other words, rather than moving resources, the users are moved between cells. In these approaches, the decisions are typically taken at the endpoints with the network nodes providing information about current loading. Alternately, one can move the decision logic to the network nodes themselves. In the second set of approaches, the network nodes autonomously learn the *optimal* loading limit individually and then act to achieve this. In [12], the authors propose reinforcement learning techniques for network nodes to tune specific configuration parameters to achieve the optimal load. In contrast, in [13] Bigham et al. describe a method of structured direct negotiation between the network nodes, using the gap between demand and capacity as a distance factor between nodes in a graph. In [14], the authors model the negotiation process as a game between an individual loaded cell and underloaded neighbour cells.

In this paper we have proposed load balancing using mean-field stochastic optimal control. We replace the inter-network node negotiation by a distributed stochastic optimization process, where the network node has visibility of its own load as well as the network wide load. The network wide load is a *mean field* statistic, sampled at a central location from feedback from individual nodes, computed, filtered and broadcast back to the network nodes as an input variable. User load is modelled as an exogenous variable, where individual users seek to maximize their own utilities.

III. Stochastic Optimal Control and Mean Field Games

In this section, we shall present the basics of mean-field stochastic optimal control.

A. Fundamentals

We start with the basic stochastic optimal control problem. We consider a system whose state variable X is controlled by the transition function (1) given below

$$dX_t^k = b(X_t^k, u_t)dt + \sigma(X_t^k, u_t)dW_t^k \tag{1}$$

The variable $u_t = U(X_t^k, t)$ is the output of a control function at time t, where said function is adapted to the filtration generated by the stochastic process W_t^k , which is a brownian motion. $b()$ and $\sigma()$ are Lipschitz continuous bounded functions as required for the standard definition of a Wiener process. The system governed by this equation has a long term cost function as in (2).

$$\begin{aligned}\Phi\left(x^0, u, T\right) = \mathbb{E}\left[g(X_T) + \int_0^T f\left(X_t^k, u_t\right) dt\right] \\ X(0) = x^0\end{aligned} \tag{2}$$

Our aim is to find the optimal control function $u^*(t)$ from a set of possible control functions $u \in \mathscr{U}$ so as to minimize the expected minimum total cost $\Phi(x0, a, T)$, over the time period $[0, T]$. Computing the optimal value of $u(t)$ is, in a nutshell, the stochastic optimal control problem.

The general solution technique is derived from the corresponding deterministic optimal control problem, with an important caveat. Whereas, in a deterministic control problem, the cost corresponding to each choice of $u()$ can be forecast, here we are faced with uncertainty in the future. At each point t, the value of $u(t)$ has to be based on the information regarding X as known upto then. This is what we mean by being adapted to the filtration of X.

1) Solution Technique : HJB equation : The classic way to solve a stochastic optimal control problem is to construct the Hamilton Jacobi Bellman (HJB) equation, which, for the above problem is given in (3).

$$\begin{aligned}&\frac{\partial \phi}{\partial s}(y, u) + b(y, u)\nabla_x \phi + \frac{\sigma^2(y, u)}{2}\nabla_x^2 \phi + f(y, u) = 0 \\ &\Rightarrow \frac{\partial \phi}{\partial s}(y, u) + \mathcal{H}(b, \nabla_x \phi, f, u) + \frac{\sigma^2}{2}(y, u)\nabla_x^2 \phi = 0 \\ &\phi(Y) = g(Y)\end{aligned} \tag{3}$$

The value of $u = u^*$ which solves this equation for all y gives the optimal value of u. Note the second derivative term, which makes the solution rather complex. The function $\mathcal{H}(y, b, f, x, u) = \langle y(x, u), b(x, u)\rangle + f(x, u)$ is called the Hamiltonian; the solution to the above equation depends, to a very large extent, on the structure of the Hamiltonian.

2) The Adjoint Equation Approach: A second method is to construct the adjoint equation based on the Stochastic Maximum Principle (SMP), in a manner analogous to the Lagrangian for a deterministic optimization problem. The stochastic maximum principle [15] is conceptually similar to the Pontryagin maximum principle for the deterministic case. However, it is more complex to solve because the solution is not time reversible [16].

The SMP requires us to find two stochastic variables p_t, q_t, such that the equation pair (4) holds.

$$\begin{aligned}-dp_t &= \nabla_x \mathcal{H}\left(p_t, q_t, b, f, X_t^k, u\right) dt + q_t dW_t^k \\ p_T &= \nabla_x g\left(X_T\right)\end{aligned} \tag{4}$$

In this equation, the Hamiltonian takes the extended form defined as in (5).

$$\begin{aligned}&\mathcal{H}(p, q, b, f, x, u) \\ &\quad = \langle p, b(x, u)\rangle + \text{tr}\left\{q^T.\sigma(x, u)\right\} + f(x, u) \\ &\partial_u \mathcal{H}(p, q, b, f, x, u^*) = 0\end{aligned} \tag{5}$$

The solution of p_t, q_t if they exist, provide an optimal control function u. Note that this is a backward stochastic differential equation again because the termination value of p is provided. We note that this is a simplified version of the SMP, where the function $\sigma()$ is independent of X_t^k. If $\sigma()$ is a function of X, then we need to add a second pair of variables to take care of the additional risk of modifying the diffusion term in dX_t^k. The interested reader should consult Yong [16, Section 3.1] for more information. For the rest of this article, we will only consider problems where $\sigma()$ is independent of u.

B. Adding the Meanfield Constraint

We now consider the problem of adding the meanfield constraint. In this version of the problem, the equations (1), (2) change to the form given in (6). The term z_t is the meanfield term. In the simplest case, it is the scaled average of the empirical states of the other agents in the game, i.e., $z_t = \eta/(N-1)\sum X_t^{j \neq k}$. In real life, it can be expressed as more complex moments of the empirical distribution μ_t^X or functions thereof.

$$\begin{aligned}dX_t^k &= b(X_t^k, u_t, z_t^k)dt + \sigma(X_t^k, u_t, z_t)dW_t^k \\ \phi\left(x^0, u\right) &= E\{g\left(X_T, z_t\right) + \int_0^T f\left(X_t^k, u_t, z_t\right) dt\} \\ \mu_t^X(Y) &= \frac{1}{N}\sum_{j=1}^N \mathcal{I}_{X_j = Y} \\ z_t &= \text{Average}\left(\mu_t^X\right)\end{aligned} \tag{6}$$

The existence of the term z_t represents the coupling between the states of the different agents. It requires us to take into account the global ensemble of states, when computing the optimal strategy $u^*()$ for the kth agent. The meanfield term thus allows us to model the interdependence of the agents. Most explicit solutions that we have encountered use the empirical average. However, more complex functions may also be used at the cost of complexity.

1) Convergence to Equilibrium: The incorporation of the meanfield term μ_t^X raises an interesting problem of evolution of the meanfield distribution μ_t^X in response to a given strategy $u()$. This is important because we would like a solution where the optimal strategy $u^*()$ drives μ_t^X to stable equilibrium (or at least a stable value of the feedback term z_t). Huang et al. in [5] address this problem by considering the case where the number of agents is very large. By taking the limit to infinity, Huang et al. demonstrate that there is a Nash equivalent solution (NCE) wherebe μ_t^X tends to a long term stable distribution μ_t^X which leads to a Nash equilibrium for all agents. This is very important, because it lets us relate the term μ_t^X to the evolution of X; we shall see the solution technique in The HJB-KFP approach section below.

A second interesting problem is that of differentiating the Hamiltonian function with respect to a distribution function; Lasry [4] has shown that this can be done using the Wasserstein space of probablity measures on a Borel space and using a suitably defined lifting function.

Unfortunately, solutions for stochastic optimal control problems with mean-field games are not easy. There are three main techniques, two of which depend on solving Forward Backward Stochastic Differential Equations (FBSDE). To date, most of the research in solutions of MFGs pertain to a special class of MFGs, the so-called Linear Quadratic MFG [17][18][19]. There are two main approaches that we shall discuss below; these approaches have been studied mostly in the context of LQMFGs. Recently, a paper has been published by Pham and Wei [20], which discusses a dynamic programming solution to these games. However, we have not covered it here.

The linear quadratic MFG (LQMFG) consists of an optimization problem where the transition function of X_t^k is linear (7) and the value function is quadratic (8).

$$dX_t = bX_t + au_t + \hat{b}z_t \tag{7}$$

$$\phi = qX^2 + r.u^2 + \hat{q}\,(X - z)^2 \tag{8}$$

While simple in nature, the LQMFG can be applied to a large number of situations with interesting results. As we shall see below, we have modelled the cell loading problem as an LQMFG.

2) The HJB-KFP approach: The fundamental idea behind this approach is that as the number of agents becomes large, the distribution for the states of the individual agents approaches the probability distribution for the state of each individual agents. In [5] Huang et al. have shown that this assumption leads to a Nash equilibrium. The solution comes from utilizing the Kolmogorov Backward equation (sometimes called the Kolmogorov Fokker Planck equation) to model the probability distribution of X for a given agents, together with the HJB equation, as shown below (9), given the probability distribution of the starting state. In theory, in a stable equilibrium, the long term probability distribution of X_t^k under the Fokker Plank equilibrium should match the empirical distribution of X_T^k as $T \to \infty$, leading to a stable solution for the HJB equation and thereby making the equilibrium self-sustaining. In this situation, we can postulate that $X_T^k \to z_t$ as the distribution evolves, for large values of T.

$$\begin{aligned}
&\partial_t \phi + \frac{\sigma^2}{2}\nabla^2\phi + \mathcal{H}(\nabla_x\phi, b, f, X_t^k, u_t, z_t)\\
&\phi_T = g\,(X_T)\\
&z_t = \mathbb{E}\left[X_t^k\right],\ X_0^k = x_0\\
&\partial_t z_t = -b()\nabla_x z_t + \frac{1}{2}\sigma^2(x)\nabla^2 z_t,\ z_0 = X_0^k
\end{aligned} \tag{9}$$

Note that the HJB equation is a backward stochastic differential equation, whereas the KFP is a forward equation. Once again, the value of u which solves both equations simultaneously is the optimal control function. The KFP-HJB technique has been used successfully for LQMFGs in many papers; a good example is that of Bardi [17].

C. Constructing the Adjoint Equation

An alternate approach to solve the mean field problem is to extend the adjoint equation described in (4) to take into account the presence of the mean field term z_t [21]. To do this, we have to extend the Hamiltonian as shown in (10) .

$$\tilde{\mathcal{H}}\left(X, y, z, \tilde{X}, u\right) = \mathcal{H}\left(X, y, z, \mu_t^X, u\right) \tag{10}$$

Here $\tilde{X}$ is a random variable with a probability distribution function matching μ_t^X. The extended Hamiltonian $\tilde{\mathcal{H}}$ thus becomes a *lifted* version of the standard Hamiltonian, allowing us to take the derivative with respect to the distribution μ_t^X. The Stochastic Maximum Principle is as in (11)

$$\begin{aligned}
-dp_t &= \nabla_x \mathcal{H}\left(X_t^k, u_t, p_t, q_t, \mu_t^X\right) dt\\
&\quad + \mathbb{E}\left[\partial_\mu \mathcal{H}(X_t^k, u_t, p_t, q_t, \mu_t^X)\right] + q_t dW_t^k\\
p_T &= \nabla_x g\,(X_T) + \mathbb{E}\left[\partial_\mu g\,(X_T)\right]
\end{aligned} \tag{11}$$

The challenge with solving (11) is that we have no idea of μ_t^X or even of the form of μ_t^X. One possible way out of this is to treat it as a variational inequality problem as suggested by Bensoussan in [18]. In this approach, we assume that all the agents, other than the kth agents is using the optimal strategy, which leads to the term μ_t^X being replaced by a deterministic z_t as the moment of the distribution that we are interested in. The optimal strategy, if it is deviation proof, will lead to a fixed point solution, where by $x_t = \mathbb{E}\left[X_t | g(z_t)\right] = z_t$, where $g(z_t)$ represents the moment of the distribution that we are interested in. Bensoussan et al. apply this to the solution of a Linear Quadratic MFG and demonstrate the solution is ϵ Nash compliant.

IV. Application to the Cell-Loading Problem

We now see if this technique can be applied to the cell-loading problem. We recall that the purpose of the cell loading problem is to ensure that cell-loads are as uniform as possible, given the variations in demand. We measure the expressed demand ,i.e., actual request for service at any given kth cell as the state variable X_k. The variation in demand is based on two parts. One is the natural variation, captured through a random diffusion term. The second is the variation of demand in response to the offered service. For our control variable u, we have selected the gap between the request for service $X_k(t)$ and the actual capacity assigned to that cell, $C_k(t)$. $u_t^k = X_t^k - C_t^k$.

A. Feedback Loop Between Demand and Offered Capacity

The majority of modern data-based applications use the Internet Transport Control Protocol (TCP) as the backbone transport protocol. This is true for Internet browsing, as well as video streaming using Dynamic Adaptive Streaming over HTTP (DASH). TCP by its very design uses a bandwidth hunting algorithm to determine the appropriate transmission rate. As a result, TCP endpoints react to the available bandwidth in the network. When the network is congested, the TCP back off and reduce the data injection rate and hence, the network load. On the other hand, if they sense the availability of bandwidth in the network, they increase the network load gradually. The success of the TCP bandwidth hunting algorithm is such that even non TCP connections are nowadays required to maintain *TCP like* transmission rate management protocols. For example, the Tcp Friendly Rate Control [22] is now an Internet standard for bandwidth control of media flows such as those proposed in Web real-time communication (WebRTC). The assumption of bandwidth hunting endpoints is important, because it allows us to model demand as a continuous process. If, on the other hand, the bandwidth demand changed in discrete bands, we would have to use a jump-diffusion process, which makes the analysis more complex.

For wireless networks, the bandwidth hunting behaviour of individual endpoints is augmented by the bandwidth sensing capability of the access network user; for example, User Equipment (UE) triggered handoffs between cells as a response to congestion. We can postulate that expressed demand will decrease in the face of a demand capacity gap ($u > 0$) and increase in the face of surplus capacity being deployed ($u < 0$). We further postulate that this has to take into account the overall distribution of demand. In other words, if a given kth cell is heavily loaded and facing a demand supply gap, its users will have an incentive to migrate to neighbouring cells. Hence, we define the state transition function as in (12), using the term z_t as introduced above.

$$dX^k(t) = -Au_t^k + B\left(X_t^k - z_t\right)) + \sigma dW_t^k \qquad (12)$$

We note that the diffusion term is independent of the empirical distribution, for the reasons described above. A and B are constants.

B. Network Cost

We now come to the cost function. As expected, we penalize the admission control function for high values of u; if positive, because of the large demand supply gap and if negative, because of the oversupply and consequent wastage of capacity. The final reward function is purely a function of the empirical distribution of X.

$$f() = M.u_t^2 - NX_t^2 \qquad (13)$$
$$g() = \eta\left(X_T - z_T\right)^2 \qquad (14)$$

C. Existence of a Solution

We will now show that a unique solution exists, for suitable values of M, N, A and B. We can use the technique given in Bensoussan [18, Section 3], by taking the derivative of the cost function at the optimal u and then setting it to zero. The cost function can be written in terms of the perturbed optimal cost $u_t(\theta) = u_t^* + \theta v_t)$ as in (15).

$$\phi(u_t) = \eta\mathbb{E}\left[X_T - z_T\right]^2 + \mathbb{E}\left[\int_0^T \left(Mu_t^2 - NX_t^2\right) dt\right]$$
$$dX_t^k = Au_t + B\left(X_t^k - z_t\right)$$
$$X_t^k\left(u_t^* + \theta v_t\right) = y_t + \theta\tilde{x}_t,\ dx_t = Av_t + Bx_t \qquad (15)$$

Taking the derivative of $\phi(u_t + \theta v_t)$ with respect to θ and setting it to 0,

$$\mathbb{E}\left[\int_0^T 2Mu_tv_t - 2N\tilde{x}_t.y_t dt\right] + \mathbb{E}\left[\eta\tilde{x}_T y_T\right] = 0 \qquad (16)$$

We choose an adjoint variable ω_t with the properties shown in (17).

$$\frac{d\omega_t}{dt} = -B\omega_t + 2Ny_t,\ \omega_T = \eta y_T \qquad (17)$$

Expanding $d(\omega_t\tilde{x}_t)$ and substituting suitable in (16), we get the following pair of adjoint equations.

$$\frac{d\omega_t}{dt} = -B\omega_t + 2Ny_t,\ \omega_T = \eta y_T$$
$$dy_t = -\frac{A^2}{2M}\omega_t dt + B\left(y_t - z_t\right)dt + \sigma dW_t \qquad (18)$$

The optimal u is given by (19). The form of $p(t)$ has to be chosen so that $u^*()$ is anticipatory (because ω_t is not guaranteed to be $\mathscr{F}(Y)$ adapted.

$$u_t^* = -A/2Mp(t), p(t) = \mathbb{E}\left[\omega_t|\mathscr{F}(Y)\right] \qquad (19)$$

By the fixed point theorem, a solution exists if $z_t = [E]\left[y_t\right]$. Setting $\mathbb{E}\left[\omega_t\right] = \epsilon_t$ and $\mathbb{E}\left[y_t\right] = Y_t$, we can write the above equation as (20). It is clear that a fixed point solution exists, because the matrix is invertible.

$$\frac{d}{dt}\begin{bmatrix}\epsilon_t \\ Y_t\end{bmatrix} = -\begin{bmatrix} B & -2N \\ \frac{A^2}{2M} & 0\end{bmatrix}\begin{bmatrix}\epsilon_t \\ Y_t\end{bmatrix} \qquad (20)$$

The equation pair in (18) has to be solved using numerical techniques [23]. In some rare cases an analytical solution is available. The output of the solution is an approximate control function $u(x,z)$, which is a function of the current state value x and the network state z. The control function may be stored as a two-dimensional table or as a polynomial function and computed at appropriate intervals. In a future paper, we shall present the challenges of solving the MFG and the associated performance for a large network of nodes.

V. Conclusion and Future Work

In this paper, we have demonstrated the application of mean-field stochastic optimal control to a very standard and well-studied problem of wireless network control. As we have seen here, even a simplified network model can capture a rich network interaction structure and yield a sophisticated, yet realizable solution to this problem. We have demonstrated that a solution exists for a simple linear format of the game, which can be solved numerically.

It is arguable that our particular model for the cell loading problem can be significantly enhanced. For example, we can put further constraints on the solution space. This may include domain specific constraints, i.e., a maximum limit on the capacity per cell or the total capacity in the network, etc. Since our primary purpose is to demonstrate the applicability of the Mean-field technique, we have used a simplified model in this paper for the sake of analytical tractability. Most existing solution techniques for MFGs are limited to very specific models. We hope to extend our work to more complete models as our ability to solve more complex MFGs evolves.

References

[1] L. Georgiadis, M. J. Neely, L. Tassiulas *et al.*, "Resource allocation and cross-layer control in wireless networks," Foundations and Trends in Networking, vol. 1, no. 1, 2006, pp. 1–144.

[2] M. J. Neely, E. Modiano, and C.-P. Li, "Fairness and Optimal Stochastic control for Heterogeneous Networks," IEEE/ACM Transactions On Networking, vol. 16, no. 2, 2008, pp. 396–409.

[3] T. Holliday, A. Goldsmith, N. Bambos, and P. Glynn, "Distributed power and admission control for time-varying wireless networks," in Information Theory, 2004. ISIT 2004. Proceedings. International Symposium on. IEEE, 2004, pp. 352–352.

[4] J.-M. Lasry and P.-L. Lions, "Mean field games," Japanese journal of mathematics, vol. 2, no. 1, 2007, pp. 229–260.

[5] M. Huang, R. P. Malhamé, P. E. Caines *et al.*, "Large population stochastic dynamic games: closed-loop McKean-Vlasov systems and the Nash certainty equivalence principle," Communications in Information & Systems, vol. 6, no. 3, 2006, pp. 221–252.

[6] M. Huang, P. E. Caines, and R. P. Malhamé, "Individual and mass behaviour in large population stochastic wireless power control problems: centralized and Nash equilibrium solutions," in Decision and Control, 2003. Proceedings. 42nd IEEE Conference on. IEEE, 2003, pp. 98–103.

[7] O. G. Aliu, A. Imran, M. A. Imran, and B. Evans, "A survey of self organisation in future cellular networks," IEEE Communications Surveys & Tutorials, vol. 15, no. 1, 2013, pp. 336–361.

[8] D. Liu, L. Wang, Y. Chen, M. Elkashlan, K.-K. Wong, R. Schober, and L. Hanzo, "User association in 5G networks: A survey and an outlook," IEEE Communications Surveys & Tutorials, vol. 18, no. 2, 2016, pp. 1018–1044.

[9] J. G. Andrews, S. Singh, Q. Ye, X. Lin, and H. S. Dhillon, "An overview of load balancing in hetnets: old myths and open problems," IEEE Wireless Communications, vol. 21, no. 2, April 2014, pp. 18–25.

[10] H. Kim, G. De Veciana, X. Yang, and M. Venkatachalam, "Distributed alpha-optimal user association and cell load balancing in wireless networks," IEEE/ACM Trans. Netw., vol. 20, no. 1, Feb. 2012, pp. 177–190. [Online]. Available: https://doi.org/10.1109/TNET.2011.2157937

[11] K. Son, S. Chong, and G. D. Veciana, "Dynamic association for load balancing and interference avoidance in multi-cell networks," IEEE Transactions on Wireless Communications, vol. 8, no. 7, July 2009, pp. 3566–3576.

[12] P. Muñoz, R. Barco, J. M. Ruiz-Avilés, I. de la Bandera, and A. Aguilar, "Fuzzy rule-based reinforcement learning for load balancing techniques in enterprise lte femtocells," IEEE Transactions on Vehicular Technology, vol. 62, no. 5, 2013, pp. 1962–1973.

[13] L. Du, J. Bigham, L. Cuthbert, P. Nahi, and C. Parini, "Intelligent cellular network load balancing using a cooperative negotiation approach," in 2003 IEEE Wireless Communications and Networking, 2003. WCNC 2003., March 2003, pp. 1675–1679 vol.3.

[14] A. Awada, B. Wegmann, I. Viering, and A. Klein, "A game-theoretic approach to load balancing in cellular radio networks," in Personal Indoor and Mobile Radio Communications (PIMRC), 2010 IEEE 21st International Symposium on. IEEE, 2010, pp. 1184–1189.

[15] S. Peng, "A general stochastic maximum principle for optimal control problems," SIAM Journal on control and optimization, vol. 28, no. 4, 1990, pp. 966–979.

[16] J. Yong and X. Y. Zhou, *Stochastic controls: Hamiltonian systems and HJB equations*. Springer Science & Business Media, 1999, vol. 43.

[17] M. Bardi, "Explicit solutions of some linear-quadratic Mean field games," Networks and heterogeneous media, vol. 7, no. 2, 2012, pp. 243–261.

[18] A. Bensoussan, K. Sung, S. C. P. Yam, and S.-P. Yung, "Linear-quadratic Mean field games," Journal of Optimization Theory and Applications, vol. 169, no. 2, 2016, pp. 496–529.

[19] O. Guéant, "Mean field games - equations with quadratic Hamiltonian: a specific approach," Mathematical Models and Methods in Applied Sciences, vol. 22, no. 09, 2012, p. 1250022.

[20] H. Pham and X. Wei, "Dynamic Programming for McKean-Vlasov dynamics," Control and Optimization, SIAM Journal on, vol. 55, no. 2, 2017, pp. 1069–1011.

[21] R. Carmona, F. Delarue *et al.*, "Forward–backward stochastic differential equations and controlled McKean–Vlasov dynamics," The Annals of Probability, vol. 43, no. 5, 2015, pp. 2647–2700.

[22] M. Handley, S. Floyd, J. Padhye, and J. Widmer, "TCP Friendly Rate Control (TFRC): Protocol Specification," Internet Requests for Comments, RFC Editor, RFC 3448, January 2003. [Online]. Available: http://www.rfc-editor.org/rfc/rfc3448.txt

[23] J. Douglas, J. Ma, P. Protter *et al.*, "Numerical methods for forward-backward stochastic differential equations," The Annals of Applied Probability, vol. 6, no. 3, 1996, pp. 940–968.

PAPR and Spectral Control Procedure for OFDM Wireless Systems Using CAZAC Equalization

Yoshitsugu Sugai, Yushi Shirato, Tomotaka Kimura and Masahiro Muraguchi

Department of Electrical Engineering, Tokyo University of Science
6-3-1 Niijuku, Katsushika-ku, Tokyo, Japan
E-mail: 4317614@ed.tus.ac.jp, yshirato@sea.plala.or.jp, kimura, murag@ee.kagu.tus.ac.jp

Abstract— **A major drawback of Orthogonal Frequency Division Multiplexing (OFDM) signals is extremely high Peak-to-Average Power Ratio (PAPR). The CAZAC equalization scheme makes the PAPR of M-array Quadrature Amplitude Modulation (M-QAM) OFDM signals into the PAPR of M-QAM single-carrier signals. Therefore, it dramatically improves the PAPR of OFDM signals. However, severe bandpass filtering of CAZAC-OFDM signal lead to unacceptable degradation of the PAPR. The paper provides available control procedure for PAPR and spectrum managements. It is confirmed that the CAZAC-OFDM signal controlled by our procedure maintains enough low PAPR and can clear the spectrum mask specifications in IEEE802.11 standard.**

Keywords-OFDM; CAZAC; spectrum mask; PAPR.

I. INTRODUCTION

Orthogonal Frequency Division Multiplex (OFDM) systems that attain high speeds and high capacity have recently been attracting attention in wireless applications, e.g., Wireless Local Area Networks (WLANs), third Generation Partnership Project Long-Term Evolution (3GPP LTE), and the Digital Video Broadcasting-Terrestrial (DVB-T) standard [1][2]. However, the main drawback of OFDM is its high Peak-to-Average Power Ratio (PAPR), which decreases the efficiency of Power Amplifiers (PAs) and increases transmitter power consumption [3][4]. Therefore, a number of techniques have been proposed to reduce the PAPR [3]. Well-known techniques are clipping-and-filtering, Partial Transmit Sequences (PTSs), and Selected Mapping (SLM). Clipping-and-filtering limits the peak amplitude of the transmission signal. However, non-linear distortion causes BER to degrade. PTS partitions input data into disjoint sub-blocks. Moreover, each sub-block are weighted by a phase factor. This technique chooses the phase factor to minimize the PAPR of combined signals. SLM generates multiple candidate data blocks. All data blocks represent the same information. Although PTS and SLM can be expected to create a certain reduction in PAPR, both techniques need side information in the receiver, which decreases spectral efficiency. The most practical solution to improving PAPR is to introduce Single Carrier Frequency Division Multiplexing Access (SC-FDMA). The 3GPP LTE system adopts SC-FDMA for uplink multiple access systems [2][5]. However, SC-FDMA has not been considered to be suitable for next-generation high-speed communications.

A new PAPR reduction technique with Constant Amplitude Zero Auto-Correlation (CAZAC) equalization was recently proposed [6][7]. The CAZAC equalization scheme makes the PAPR of M-array Quadrature Amplitude Modulation (M-QAM) OFDM signals into the PAPR of M-QAM single-carrier signals [8]. Therefore, it dramatically improves the PAPR of OFDM signals. However, severe bandpass filtering of CAZAC-OFDM signal lead to unacceptable degradation of the PAPR.

The paper provides available control procedure for PAPR and spectrum managements for the CAZAC-OFDM system. One simplest approach of improving the PAPR is to clip the amplitude of the signal to a fixed level. An accurate clipping boundary is easily defined, because we can manage the amplitude of the time-domain signal of CAZAC-OFDM like a single-carrier signal. As the correct demodulation of CAZAC-OFDM signals requires only values of the original signal points, we can improve the PAPR without any degradation of BER and spectrum performances by clipping. We have confirmed that the CAZAC-OFDM signal controlled by our procedure maintains enough low PAPR and can clear the spectrum mask specifications in IEEE802.11 standard.

The rest of this paper is organized as follows. In Section 2, we describe the CAZAC-OFDM system. In Section 3, we describe the proposed spectral control. In Section 4, we describe the PAPR reduction method. Finally, we conclude this paper in Section 5.

II. CAZAC-OFDM SYSTEM

In this section, we describe the CAZAC-OFDM System. We first describe the OFDM system, and then we explain the CAZAC equalizing technique.

A. OFDM system

In OFDM system, the frequency domain symbol $\boldsymbol{X} = [X_0, X_1, \ldots, X_{N-1}]^T$ is modulated by N size inverse Fast Fourier Transform (IFFT). The discrete-time OFDM signal with N subcarriers is represented as

$$x_n = \sum_{k=0}^{N-1} X_k e^{j2\pi kn/N}, \tag{1}$$

where $j = \sqrt{-1}$ and n is discrete time index. On the other hand, receiver acquires frequency domain symbol $\boldsymbol{Y}$ by applying FFT to received signal $\boldsymbol{y}$.

$$Y_k = \sum_{n=0}^{N-1} y_n e^{-j2\pi kn/N} = \sum_{n=0}^{N-1} (x_n + Noise) e^{-j2\pi kn/N}. \quad (2)$$

The PAPR of the OFDM signal (1) can be expressed as

$$PAPR = \frac{\max_{0 \le n \le N-1} |x_n|^2}{\mathrm{E}[|x_n|^2]}, \quad (3)$$

where E[·] is expectation operator. PAPR represents amplitude fluctuation of each symbol. In order to improve the accuracy of PAPR, the OFDM signal x_k is converted to L-times oversampled time domain signal [1].

As shown from (2), the OFDM signal is composed of a plurality of subcarrier signals, which causes an increase in amplitude fluctuation. A high PAPR signal increases the Input Back Off (IBO) at the power amplifier in order to amplify the transmit signal without distortion. In general, increasing in IBO causes decreasing the efficiency of PA.

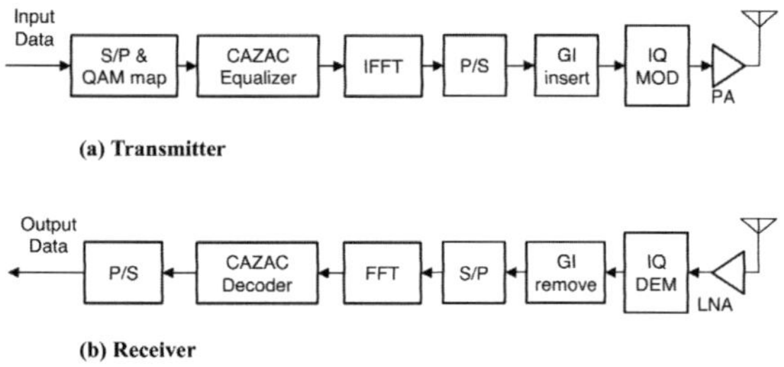

Figure 1. CAZAC-OFDM system.

B. *CAZAC equalizing technique*

Figure 1 shows a transmitter and receiver block diagrams for a CAZAC-OFDM system. The CAZAC sequence is an orthogonal sequence and the autocorrelation function is a delta function. In addition, the CAZAC sequence has a characteristic that the amplitude exhibits a constant value in both time and frequency domain. Zadoff-Chu (ZC) sequences is one of the CAZAC sequence. The ZC sequence C_k of length L is defined as

$$C_k = \begin{cases} exp\left(\dfrac{j\pi k(k-1)r}{L}\right) & (L \text{ is odd}) \\ exp\left(\dfrac{j\pi (k-1)^2 r}{L}\right) & (L \text{ is even}) \end{cases}, \quad (4)$$

where L is the length of the CAZAC sequence and r is the sequence number, $k = 1, 2, \cdots L$. L is a natural number, and r is a prime integer with respect to L. CAZAC sequences are generated by cyclic shift of the original CAZAC sequence. The periodic cross-correlation function ρ is defined as

$$\rho(m) = \sum_{n=1}^{L-1} c_n c^*_{(c-m) \bmod L} = \begin{cases} L \ (m = 0) \\ 0 \ (m \neq 0) \end{cases}, \quad (5)$$

where m is integer variables.

CAZAC equalization uses a square matrix M generated from the equation in the case where L in equation (4) is an even number. The matrix equation is defined as

$$M = \frac{1}{\sqrt{N}} \begin{bmatrix} c_1 & c_2 \cdots & c_N \\ c_{N+1} & c_{N+2} \cdots & c_{2N} \\ \vdots & \vdots \ \ddots & \vdots \\ c_{(N-1)N+1} & \cdots \ \cdots & c_{N^2} \end{bmatrix}, \quad (6)$$

where matrix M is the rearrangement of in equation (4) in the row direction, and N is the number of subcarriers and $L = N^2$, $r = 1$. N is an even number, so L is also an even number.

Multiply the signal before IFFT by the matrix as shown in Figure 1 calculate the product of the transposed the frequency domain symbol $X = [X_1, X_2, \cdots, X_N]$ and the matrix M, and create a CAZAC equalized signal X'. X' is represented as

$$X' = M \cdot X^T = \frac{1}{\sqrt{N}} \begin{bmatrix} c_1 & \cdots & c_N \\ c_{N+1} & \cdots & c_{2N} \\ \vdots & \ddots & \vdots \\ c_{(N-1)N+1} & \cdots & c_{N^2} \end{bmatrix} \cdot \begin{bmatrix} X_1 \\ X_2 \\ \vdots \\ X_N \end{bmatrix}. \quad (7)$$

An IFFT operation is performed on this signal. The OFDM time domain signal x_n of the sample is represented as

$$x_n = \frac{1}{N} \sum_{k=0}^{N-1} X'_k e^{j2\pi kn/N}$$
$$= \sum_{k=0}^{N-1} \left\{ \sum_{m=0}^{N-1} e^{j\pi(m+kN)^2/L} X_m \right\} e^{j2\pi kn/N}$$
$$= \sum_{m=0}^{N-1} e^{j\pi m^2/N^2} X_m \left\{ \sum_{k=0}^{N-1} e^{j2\pi k(m+n)/N} e^{j\pi k^2} \right\}, \quad (8)$$

where k is an integer not less than 0, so the following equation is developed.

$$\exp(j\pi k^2) = \begin{cases} 1 & (k : \text{even}) \\ -1 & (k : \text{odd}) \end{cases}. \tag{9}$$

To lead (10) from (9).

$$\exp(j\pi k^2) = (-1)^k. \tag{10}$$

Substituting (10) into (8) leads to (11).

$$x_n = \sum_{m=0}^{N-1} e^{j\pi m^2/N^2} X_m \left\{ \sum_{k=0}^{N-1} \{-e^{j2\pi(m+n)/N}\}^k \right\}. \tag{11}$$

The inside of {} in equation (11) is the sum of the geometric progression. Therefore, equation (12) is derived.

$$\sum_{k=0}^{N-1} \{-e^{j2\pi(m+n)/N}\}^k = \begin{cases} N & (-e^{j2\pi(m+n)/N} = 1) \\ 0 & (-e^{j2\pi(m+n)/N} \neq 1) \end{cases}. \tag{12}$$

When $2\pi(m+n)/N = 1$, $2(m+n)/N$ is an integer and odd number. Also, n and m are $0 \leq n \leq N-1, 0 \leq m \leq N-1$. These relationships satisfy the relationship of equation (13).

$$m = \frac{N}{2} - n \ (mod\ N). \tag{13}$$

Equation (14) is derived from equations (11), (12) and (13).

$$\begin{aligned} x_n &= e^{j\pi\{N/2 - n\ (mod\ N)\}^2/N^2} X_{\frac{N}{2}-n(mod\ N)} \\ &= c_{\frac{N}{2}-n(mod\ N)} X_{\frac{N}{2}-n(mod\ N)}, \end{aligned} \tag{14}$$

Equation (14) shows that CAZAC equalization converts the PAPR of the OFDM time domain signal into the PAPR of a single-carrier signal. Figure 2 shows the image diagram of the CAZAC-OFDM time domain signal. Among the components of the coefficient X, only one was reinforced, all others cancel each other.

Figures 3 (a) and (b) show the constellation of CAZAC-OFDM, which shows time-domain signal points at the IQ-MOD input in Figure 1. The discrete-time signal points of QPSK CAZAC-OFDM line up on the unit circle orbit as shown in Figure 3 (a), and the discrete-time signal points of 16QAM CAZAC-OFDM signal are on the three concentric circle orbits as shown in Figure 3 (b).

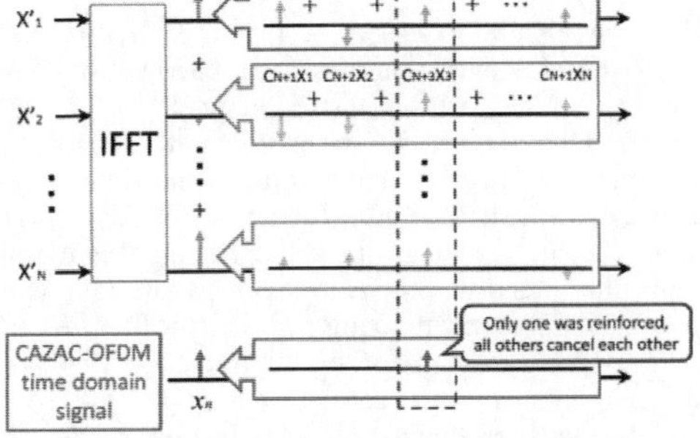

Figure 2. The time domain signal of CAZAC-OFDM

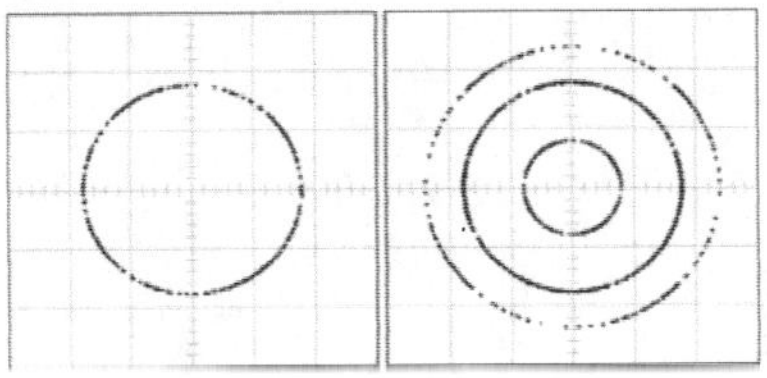

(a) QPSK (b) 16QAM

Figure 3. Constellation examples of the CAZAC-OFDM Signals.

III. SPECTRAL CONTROL

In this section, we explain the proposed spectral control method. We first describe the procedure of the proposed method, and then we evaluate the performance of the spectral control method through simulation experiments.

A. *Procedure of Spectral Control*

The CAZAC-OFDM signal at the IQ-MOD output in Figure 1 is an analog signal wave, which deals with the passband signal with a carrier frequency of f_c in the continuous time domain. Since f_c in general is much higher than $1/T_s$, a continuous-time baseband OFDM signal with the symbol period T_s and the corresponding passband signal with the carrier frequency f_c have almost the same waveform. However, in general, the waveform for the discrete-time baseband signal may not be the same as that for the continuous-time baseband signal. In practice, the PAPR for the continuous-time baseband signal can be measured only after implementing the actual hardware, including Digital-to-Analog Convertor (DAC). In other words, measurement of the PAPR for the continuous-time baseband signal is not straightforward. Therefore, there must be some means of estimating the PAPR from the discrete-time signal. Fortunately, it is known that the discrete-time baseband signal can show almost the same PAPR as the continuous-time baseband signal if it is four times interpolated (oversampled).

To make the discrete-time OFDM signal with the proper passband characteristics which satisfy the IEEE 802.11 specifications, we set the subcarrier allocation as shown in Figure 4. Here, we set the FFT size of CAZAC-OFDM to 64. Therefore, four times interpolated (oversampled) FFT size becomes 256.

The first task to consider is that the CAZAC-OFDM spectrum of 64 subcarriers with the bandwidth (BW) of 16MHz is centered on the carrier frequency of f_c, 24MHz bandwidth to the left, i.e., the space of 96 null subcarriers, and in the same way 24 MHz bandwidth to the right. Figure 5 shows a block diagram of the generation of CAZAC-OFDM symbols. The second step to produce the signal is to apply a transmit filtering with proper roll-off by an FFT-window processing, and to avoid aliasing by low-pass filtering. Figure 6 shows a block diagram of the reproduction of CAZAC-OFDM symbols. In receiver side, multiply the received symbol in frequency domain and the inverse matrix $\{M^T\}^H$ after FFT shown by figure 6.

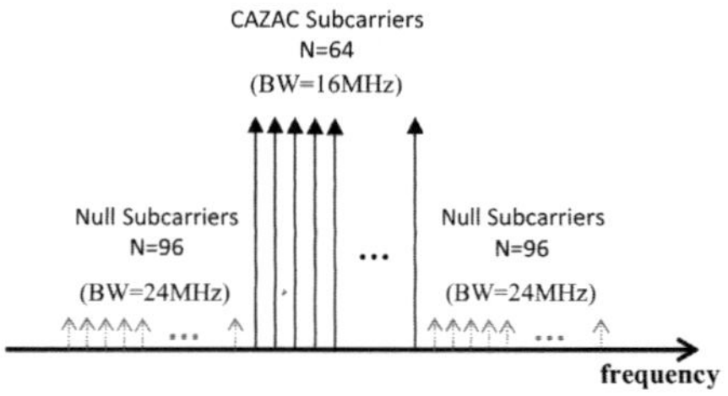

Figure 4. Subcarrier allocation based on four times interpolated (oversampled) FFT processing.

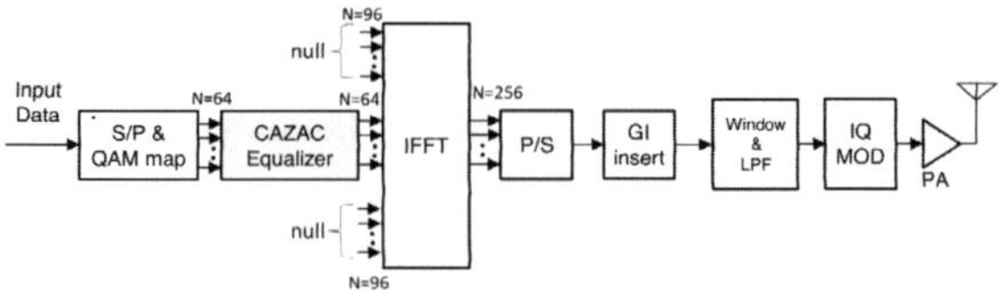

Figure 5. The CAZAC-OFDM transmitter based on four times interpolated (oversampled) FFT processing.

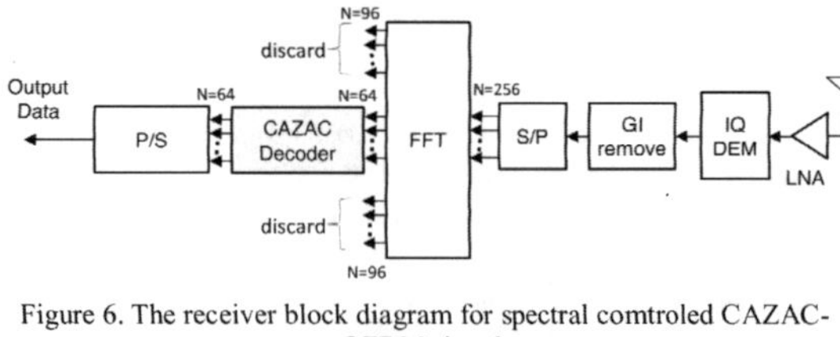

Figure 6. The receiver block diagram for spectral comtroled CAZAC-OFDM signal.

B. Simulation results

We carried out our simulation with the MATLAB/ Simulink to evaluate the performance of the system. Table I summarizes the simulation parameters.

Figure 7 shows the spectrum for the 16QAM CAZAC-OFDM system. It is confirmed that the spectrum satisfied the spectrum mask standardized by the IEEE 802.11 specifications [1].

TABLE I. MAJOR SIMULATION RAMETERS

Number of CAZAC Subcarriers	64 [Data: 60, Pilot: 4]
IFFT & FFT size	256
Sampling Rate	16MHz
Symbol Period T_s	5 μ sec
Guard Interval	1 μ sec
Modulation of Subcarriers	QPSK, 16QAM
Channel Model	AWGN
	Flat Rayleigh Fading - Doppler Frequency($f_D T_s$): 7.5×10^{-5} 18-Ray Rayleigh Fading with Exponential Decay Profile - Doppler Frequency($f_D T_s$): 7.5×10^{-5} - Delay Spread(τ / T_s): 2×10^{-2}

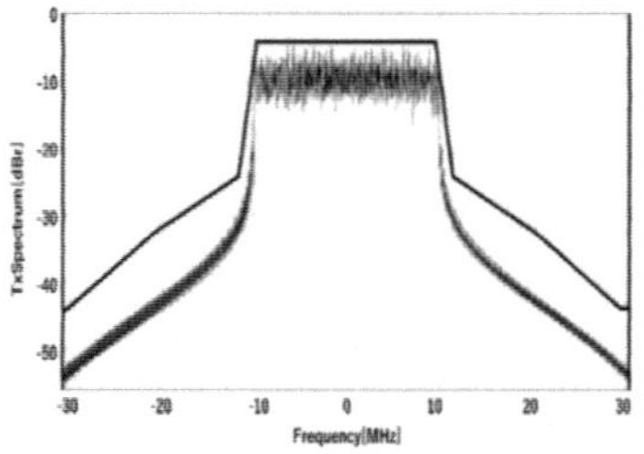

Figure 7. The spectrum comtroled 16QAM CAZAC-OFDM signal.

IV. PAPR CONTROL

This section describes the proposed PAPR control method. We first explain the procedure of the PAPR control method, and then we present simulation results to discuss the performance of the proposed PAPR control method.

A. Procedure of PAPR control

The CAZAC equalization scheme makes the PAPR of M-array Quadrature Amplitude Modulation (M-QAM) OFDM signals into the PAPR of M-QAM single-carrier signals. Therefore, it dramatically improves the PAPR of OFDM signals. However, severe bandpass filtering of the CAZAC-OFDM signal lead to unacceptable degradation of the PAPR.

Figure 8 shows the amplitude of bandpass and four times oversampled QPSK CAZAC-OFDM signal with subcarrier allocation shown in Figure 4. The original sample points of QPSK are on the line of unity amplitude. However, many of the interpolating points go above the line of unity amplitude. This means obvious degradation of the PAPR.

One simplest approach of reducing the PAPR is to clip the amplitude of the signal to a fixed level. Fortunately, correct demodulation of CAZAC-OFDM signals requires only values of the original sample points, and it is possible to skip out the values of the interpolating points. Therefore, we can clip amplitude of the interpolating points at the unity amplitude level as the clipping boundary in case of the QPSK CAZAC-OFDM signal.

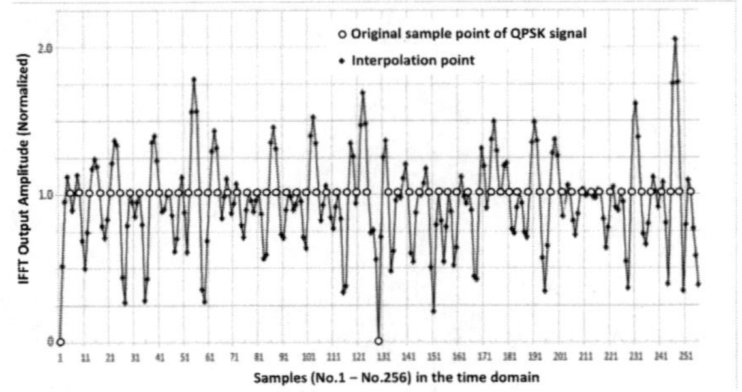

Figure 8. Amplitude of bandpass and oversampled QPSK CAZAC-OFDM signal in the time domain.

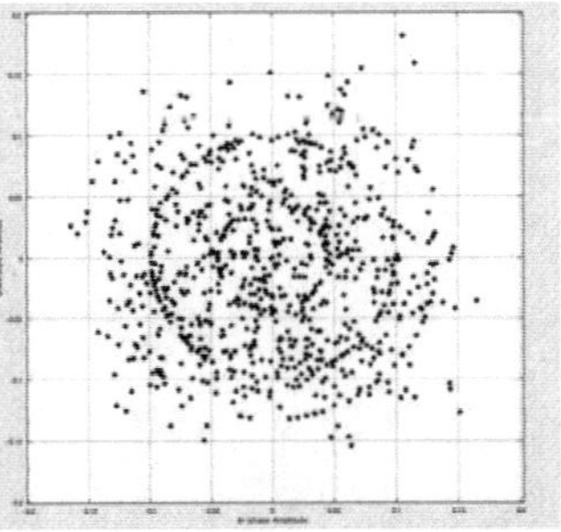

Figure 9. The constellation of bandpass and oversampled 16-QAM CAZAC-OFDM signal.

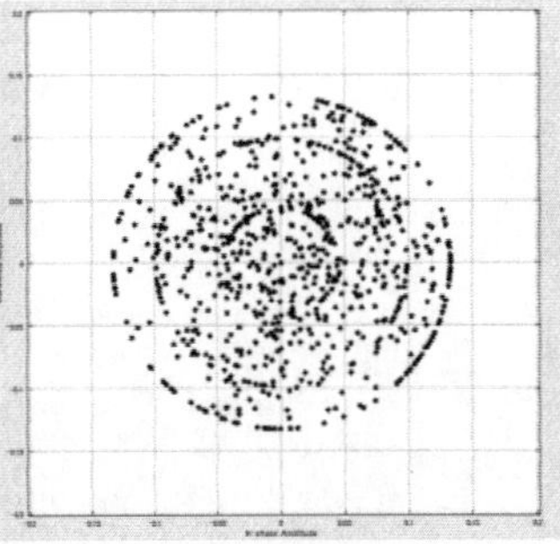

Figure 10. The constellation of bandpass and oversampled 16-QAM CAZAC-OFDM signal with clipped amplitude processing.

B. Simulation results

Figure 9 shows the constellation of bandpass and four times oversampled 16QAM CAZAC-OFDM signal with subcarrier allocation shown in Figure 4. The original sample points of 16QAM CAZAC-OFDM signal are on the three concentric circle orbits as shown in Figure 3 (b). However, many of the interpolating points overfly to outer side of the largest circle orbit. This means obvious degradation of the PAPR.

As noted previously, correct demodulation of CAZAC-OFDM signals requires only values of the original sample points, which are all in the inner-side of the largest circle orbit of 16QAM CAZAC-OFDM signal, and it is possible to clip amplitude of the interpolating sample points. Figure 10 shows the constellation of bandpass and oversampled 16-QAM CAZAC-OFDM signal with clipped amplitude processing.

We first considered the Complementary Cumulative Distribution Function (CCDF) of PAPR to evaluate the performance of PAPR, which is the probability that PAPR will be higher than a certain PAPR value PAPR0, i.e., Pr(PAPR > PAPR0). Figure 11 plots the CCDF of PAPR of 16QAM CAZAC-OFDM system with and without clipping, as well as the conventional 16QAM OFDM and single-carrier 16QAM systems. We found that the PAPR of the 16QAM CAZAC-OFDM system with clipping was almost equal to that of the single-carrier 16QAM system. Moreover, the PAPR of the 16QAM CAZAC-OFDM system with clipping was improved by 5 dB at the CCDF of 10^{-3} compared with the conventional 16QAM OFDM system.

Figure 12 shows spectrum for the 16QAM CAZAC-OFDM system with clipping. It is confirmed that the spectrum also satisfied the spectrum mask standardized by the IEEE 802.11 specifications. The result indicates the clipping does not bring serious effect to the spectrum.

We next examined the Bit Error Rate (BER) of the proposed system. We considered three channels: Additive White Gaussian Noise (AWGN) and tow type of Rayleigh fading with AWGN.

Figure 13 shows the BER performances of the QPSK and the 16QAM CAZAC-OFDM systems with clipping which are applied for AWGN channels. The results indicate that the CAZAC-OFDM system with clipping does not degrade BER performances.

Figure 14 shows the BER performances of the 16QAM CAZAC-OFDM system with clipping which are applied for fading channels. We found that the BER of the system was comparable to that of the conventional OFDM system under the Flat Rayleigh Fading channel. In contrast, under the 18-Ray Rayleigh Fading channel, which is a type of frequency selective fading channel, the BER of the 16QAM CAZAC-OFDM system with clipping is improved because the influence of fading is spread to all sub-carriers. This indicates that the CAZAC-OFDM system has excellent capabilities to resist frequency selective fading.

V. CONCLUSIONS

The paper provides available control procedure for PAPR and spectrum managements for the CAZAC-OFDM system. One simplest approach of improving the PAPR is to clip the amplitude of the signal to a fixed level. An accurate clipping boundary is easily defined, because we can manage the amplitude of the time-domain signal of CAZAC-OFDM like a single-carrier signal. As the correct demodulation of

CAZAC-OFDM signals requires only values of the original signal points, we can improve the PAPR without any degradation of BER and spectrum performances by clipping. We have confirmed that the 16QAM CAZAC-OFDM signal controlled by our procedure maintains enough low PAPR of 6dB and can clear the spectrum mask specifications in IEEE802.11 standard. Moreover, under the 18-Ray Rayleigh Fading channel, which is a type of frequency selective fading channel, the BER of the 16QAM CAZAC-OFDM system with clipping is improved, compared with the conventional OFDM system, because the influence of fading is spread to all sub-carriers. This indicates that the CAZAC-OFDM system has excellent capabilities to resist frequency selective fading.

REFERENCES

[1] IEEE, "Part 11: Wireless LAN Medium Access Control (MAC) and Physical Layer (PHY) Specifications," IEEE Std 802.11-2012 (Revision of IEEE Std 802.11-2007), Mar. 2012, pp. 1-2695.

[2] A. Ghosh, R. Ratasuk, B. Mondal, N. Mangalvedhe, and T. Thomas, "LTE-advanced: Next-generationWireless Broadband Technology," IEEE Wireless Communications, vol. 17, no. 3, June 2010, pp. 10–22.

[3] H. Seung, Hee and L. Jae, Hong, "An Overview of Peak-to-average Power Ratio Reduction Techniques for Multicarrier Transmission," IEEE Wireless Communications, vol. 12, no. 2, Apr. 2005, pp. 56–65.

[4] J. Joung, C. K. Ho, K. Adachi, and S. Sun, "A Survey on Power-Amplifier-Centric Techniques for Spectrum- and Energy-Efficient Wireless Communications," IEEE Communications Surveys & Tutorials, vol. 17, no. 1, Jan. 2015, pp. 315–333.

[5] H. Myung, J. Lim, and D. Goodman, "Single Carrier FDMA for Uplink Wireless Transmission," IEEE Vehicular Technology Magazine, vol. 1, no. 3, Sep. 2006, pp. 30-38.

[6] I. Baig and V. Jeoti, "PAPR Reduction in OFDM Systems: Zadoff-Chu Matrix Transform Based Pre/Post-Coding Techniques," in Proc. of the 2nd International Conference on Computational Intelligence, Communication Systems and Networks, July 2010, pp. 373-377.

[7] Z. Feng, et al., "Performance-Enhanced Direct Detection Optical OFDM Transmission With CAZAC Equalization," IEEE Photonics Technology Letters, vol. 27, no. 14, July 2015, pp. 1507-1510.

[8] R. Ishioka, T. Kimura, and M. Muraguchi, "A Proposal for a New OFDM Wireless System using a CAZAC Equalization Scheme," Proc. AICT 2017, June 2017, pp. 47-51.

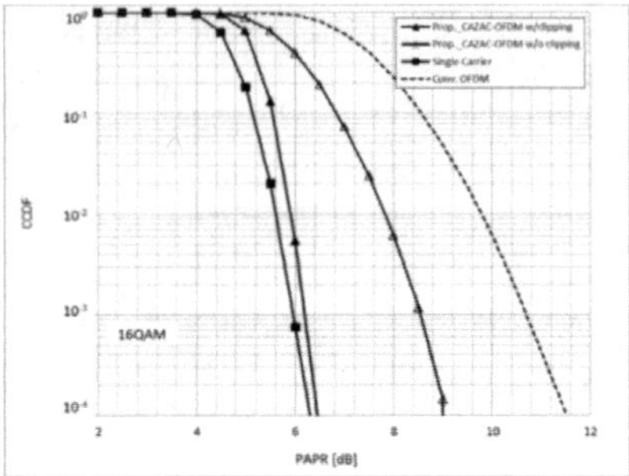

Figure 11. PAPR of the proposed CAZAC-OFDM.

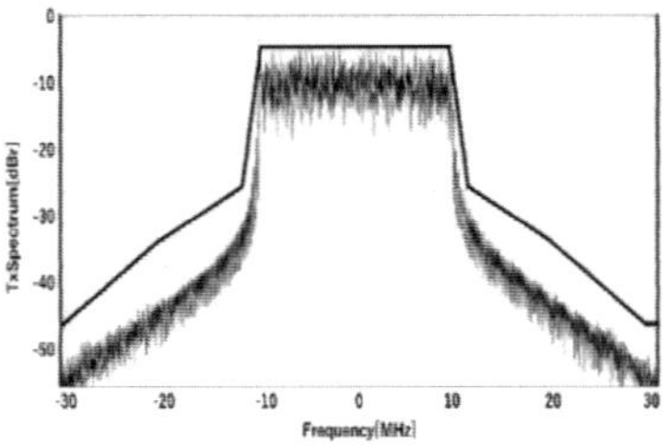

Figure 12. Spectrum of the 16QAM CAZAC-OFDM Signal with clipping.

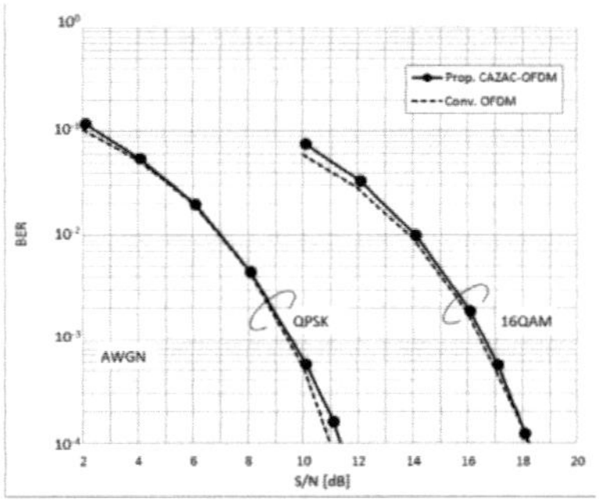

Figure 13. BER performances of the systems under AWGN channels.

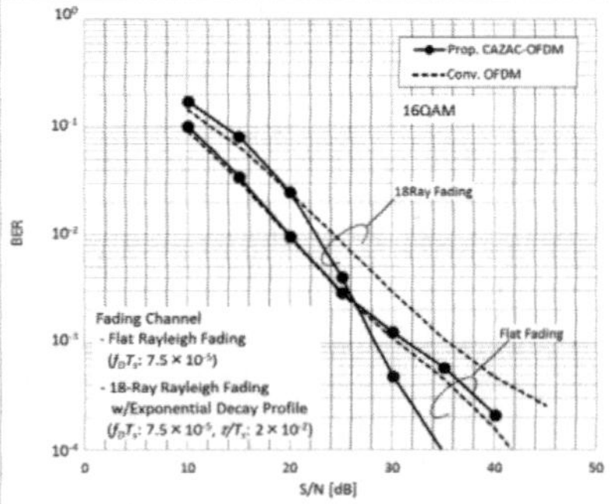

Figure 14. BER performances of the systems under fading channels.

Receiver Sensitivity Improvement for IoT

MohammaMahdi Asgharzadeh, Emil Novakov, Ghislaine Maury
Institut de Microélectronique, Electromagnétisme et Photonique (IMEP-LAHC)
University of Grenoble Alpes
Grenoble, France
Email: {asgharzm, novakov, maury}@minatec.grenoble-inp.fr

***Abstract*—In this paper, we present two basic communication techniques for Internet of Things (IoT), as well as a new software-based solution to increase the receiver sensitivity and to improve the communication link budget. The methodology and the experimental results are also presented at the end. The complexity of the experimental setup is reduced, but it demonstrates how a simple method may be efficient for very low SNR. We apply the Time Synchronous Averaging (TSA) as a powerful signal processing technique to improve receiver sensibility. This technique is very useful for the constraints which occur during narrow band RF communications. The most important disadvantage of TSA is due to synchronization. To overcome this problem, an innovative signal processing method for synchronization in phase and in frequency is applied. The result of Averaging applied with innovative synchronization method, is the remarkable enhancement in signal detection in the presence of a very strong noise (Signal to Noise ratio near zero). The proposed solution can also be applied on large band transmissions.**

Keywords-synchronization; sensitivity; signal processing; IoT; LPWAN.

I. INTRODUCTION

The communication between the objects, Machine-to-Machine (M2M) and Internet of Things (IoT), is the revolutionary movement toward controlling almost all the aspects of costs and resources. IoT could also help us overcome the global challenges like environmental pollution, resource depletion and energy crisis [1]. IoT applications vary between several sectors and consist mainly: smart cities, tele-operation, smart metering, industrial assets and critical infrastructure monitoring, logistics, home automation and also agriculture and wild life tracking. Several studies have proven the huge growth in volume and revenue of the IoT and M2M. The number of connected objects is predicted to surpass the number of human subscribers using smart phones, tablets, laptop and PCs by 2020 [2]. The overall IoT market is also expected to reach a revenue of 4.3 trillion dollars by 2043 [3]. Cellular networks and wireless short range communication technologies were traditionally used for IoT application. These two techniques are limited by their short range of communications or the vast power consumption. Low Power Wide Area Networks (LPWAN) as a novel communication paradigm has been examined as a solution for increasing the communication range while increasing the power efficiency. In the IoT applications, the size of the data packet is very small and therefore the data rate is considered to be lower than data rate in Cellular networks. Lowering the data rate could help us achieving the higher communication range. A brief demonstration of the relationship between the different communication standards, their data rates and the communication ranges is shown in Figure 1. Unlike the data packet size, which is not an issue for IoT applications, the power efficiency, data range and the ability to communicate with large number of devices are the most important concerns in this domain. There are various techniques employed by LPWAN technologies to satisfy the desire conditions of IoT.

The desired link budget for LPWAN technologies is about 150±10 dB which is sufficient to cover a range of few kilometers for urban areas and tens of kilometers for rural areas. There is always the compromise between the data rate and the energy consumption. The receiver should be capable of decoding the noisy and weak signals. The sensitivity of such a receiver reaches as low as -130 dBm. Different LPWAN technologies are based on two main modulation techniques, narrowband and spread spectrum techniques.

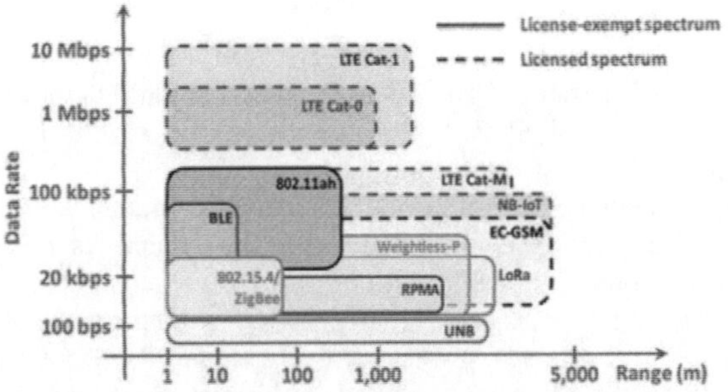

Figure 1. Data rate vs communication range

Assigning a narrow band to each carrier provides a higher link budget. The experienced noise is reduced as well. This will give us a far greater range of communication. However the data rate is also reduced. The main difficulty of narrowband communication is the frequency generation systems. This is mostly related to the oscillator's stability and phase noise. It is hard to achieve the frequency synchronization in the case of very weak signals at the receiver.

On the other hand, the spread spectrum technique spread the information signal over a wider frequency band but keeps the same power. This communication is more robust to interference and jamming. However, this technique is less efficient in terms of spectrum usage. SIGFOX and LoRa are two well-known examples of technologies, which use Narrowband and Spread spectrum techniques, respectively. Here, we introduce a novel technique to increase the receiver sensitivity. In consequence the increase in receiver sensitivity will cause more power efficiency as well as longer ranger of communication. The proposed method is applicable for both LPWAN technologies (Narrowband and spread spectrum). In state-of-the-art TSA approaches, the same information is transmitted K times. The signal must have sufficient energy to be correctly synchronized in receiver before averaging. There is a high risk of data distortion in averaging process in case of losing the synchronization. The most important advantage of our method is its robustness to the noise for achieving the synchronization. In simulations we had a non-zero two-way communication for SNR = -37 dB while in practical measurement, due to some physical limits we achieve a level of SNR = 0.3 dB. These limits and the solution to remove them are explained at the end of the article.

II. Time Synchronous Averaging

The sensitivity of a digital receiver is the minimum input signal power P_{MIN} in dBm required for a particular quality of the received information in terms of Bit Error Rate (BER) [4].

$$P_{min} = -174 + 10 \log (B) + NF + SNR \qquad (1)$$

NF is the noise figure, B is the receiver equivalent noise bandwidth, and SNR is the detector input signal-to-noise ratio (SNR) needed to achieve a fixed BER.

The smaller contribution of the receiver, which means the lower power to encode the receiving signal is mostly translated to the better sensitivity.

By using advanced signal processing methods, we are capable of increasing the receiver sensitivity. Since the processing method is a software technique there is no need to change any in-use hardware. Coherent averaging is a software processing method to apply on the coherent component (a periodic signal). The received signal is damaged by a non-coherent component (stationary additive noise) [5]. An uncorrelated stationary white Gaussian noise is supposed to affect the data during the transmission. Averaging the repeated data at the receiver node will reduce the noise power K times. [6][7]. Let s(t) is a periodic signal with period T and power P_S, and n(t), an additive white Gaussian noise (AWGN) with variance σ_n^2 . The signal to-noise ratio SNR is:

$$SNR = \frac{P_S}{\sigma_n^2} \qquad (2)$$

By averaging the K signals synchronously, the SNR of the averaged signal becomes [5]:

$$SNR_{TSA} = \frac{P_S}{(\frac{\sigma_n^2}{K})} = K.SNR \qquad (3)$$

TSA is widely used in communications [8], medicine [9], mechanics [10], electronics and all scientific fields which treat periodic weak signals corrupted by noise [11].

III. Methodology

The most critical problem of averaging method is related to the synchronization. This is also the main issue for using the narrowband receivers.

Synchronization for averaging concerns synchronization in phase and in frequency. These correspond to the data repetition period and data stream starting point. It is very difficult to recognize and distinguish the data period and data start point when the noise power becomes very strong in comparison to the signal power (low SNR). In reality we cannot apply averaging anymore since there is no information about start and end of each period. Here we use an innovative software signal processing method to achieve the synchronization. This method is based on the periodic behavior of the signal. The main stages for applying this technique are shown in Figure 2.

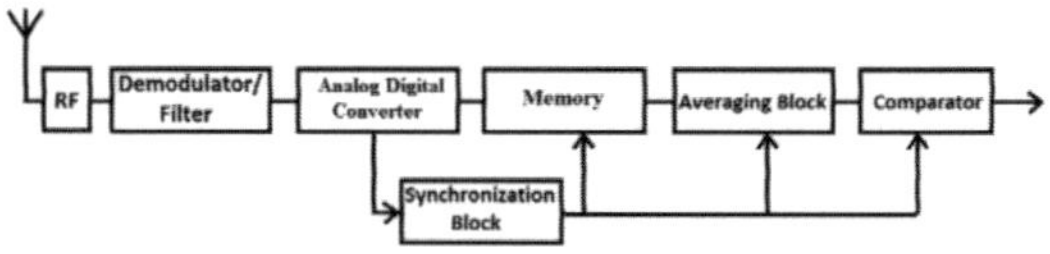

Figure 2. Principle of the Time Synchronous Averaging

The novel signal processing technique has been realized by MATLAB. For the experimental measurement, a signal generator is used to generate a series of data which are periodic.

The incoming data will be registered in a memory block. The synchronization block and the memory block work in parallel. The synchronization block drives also the averaging and comparator blocks. The output is a multi-level signal. The comparator converts it to the binary data signal. The modulation type and the SNR at the comparator (threshold circuit) input define the BER at the receiver output.

The BER for the minimum shift key (MSK) modulation, which is very common for low data rate communication systems, in the presence of AWGN is [6]:

$$BER = Q\left(\sqrt{2\frac{E_B}{N_0}}\right) \qquad (4)$$

E_B is the energy per bit and N_0 is the noise power spectral density. The last equation is valid only if we consider a perfect synchronization for the coherent demodulator / matched filter. The noise power P_n is:

$$P_n = N_0 B_n \qquad (5)$$

B_n is the equivalent noise bandwidth of the Demodulator / Filter circuit in Figure 2. Using (2), (3) and (5) (D is the data rate in bit/s.):

$$\frac{E_B}{N_0} = \frac{P_S}{P_n}\frac{B_n}{D} = SNR_{TSA}\frac{B_n}{D} = K.SNR\frac{B_n}{D} \qquad (6)$$

As we can see the TSA method improves the SNR at the comparator input K times and the corresponding BER is:

$$BER_{SA} = Q\left(\sqrt{2K\frac{E_B}{N_0}}\right) \qquad (7)$$

K is the number of retransmission of the data frame. This repetition will increase K times the energy per bit since each bit is repeated K times. It is good to notice that the transmitted power remains the same. This is one of the important advantages of this method since the communication standards limit the transmitted RF power. In other words, with no need to increase the signal power, the signal energy can be improved significantly. This technique spread the signal in the time but keeps the same bandwidth for the system as well as the same RF power. The time diversity, which is due to the providing the receiver with several replicas of the transmitted signal is useful to overcome the fading problem and will improve the overall performance of the radio link.

IV. THE MEASUREMENT SETUP

Signals are generated and processed via MATLAB and Simulink. For the transmission, we use MSK modulation technique. The received signal is demodulated first and then TSA method is applied.

To transmit and receive data, an ADF70XX evaluation board with ADF7021 transceiver was used. At the transmitter, the data generated by MATLAB is transferred to Keysight 33622A digital signal generator. The output of signal generator is connected to ADF70XX board. The transceivers are adjusted in a way to establish a MSK modulation. At the receiver, we use another ADF70XX and ADF7021 board. A manual attenuator is also applied at the first stage of receiver to attenuate the signal strength and to control the SNR. The output signal is driven from the analog port at the ADF7021 and can be seen with an oscilloscope. Registered data from oscilloscope at the receiver node is analyzed with MATLAB. The schematic of the measurement setup for transmitter and receiver are shown in Figures 3 and 4.

Figure 3. Schematic of the transmitter

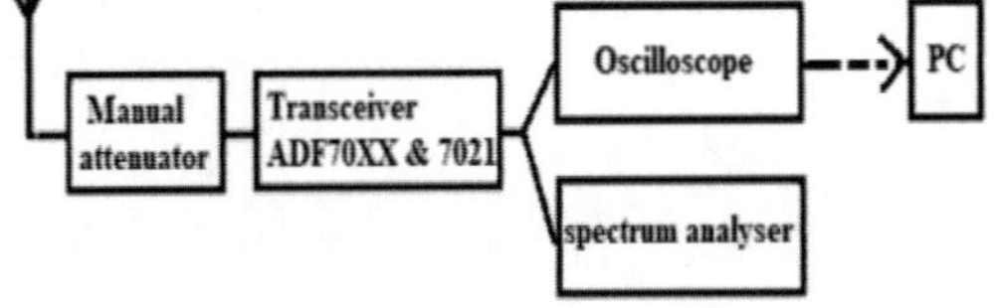

Figure 4. Schematic of the Receiver

The decision over the value of each bit has to be made after signal processing in MATLAB. To ignore any other effects during the measurements, any potential RF coupling has to be removed.

Here, we present an experiment in which we use a series of 15 bits [010100001111101], which is the length of the data frame or one period of data. It will be repeated 80 times at the rate of 2 k.Samples/s. The over sampling rate at the receiver node on oscilloscope is 5, which makes 75 samples in each period of data repetition. The information binary data rate $\mathbf{D_b}$ at the receiver node, after processing is calculated by dividing the samples data rate $\mathbf{D_s}$ by Total number of repetitions and equal to:

$$D_b = \frac{D_s}{Number\ of\ repetitions} = \frac{2000}{5*80} = 5_{bit/s} \qquad (8)$$

The received signal power was about -119.7 dBm while noise power at the receiver was -120 dBm, so, the SNR = 0.3 dB. The registered signal from oscilloscope at the receiver is shown in Figure 5 as a function of sample index (Time interval between two samples is equal to 0.5 ms). Please note that, this is the noisy signal before applying the signal processing methods.

To synchronize the data and apply TSA we need the data start point as well as each repetition period. The calculating method is based on the periodic behavior of the information signal.

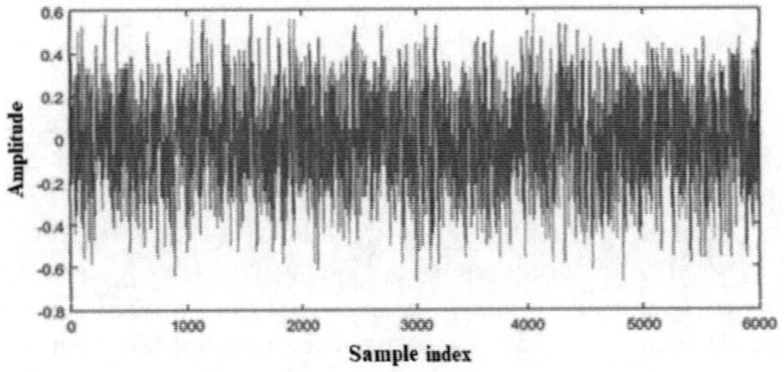

Figure 5. Received signal

The calculated values from received signal are presented bellow (corresponding peak index in Figures 6 and 7).

In this experiment, there were 1400 non data zero samples before data stream. In Figure 6, the peak point value is 1401 which is exactly the position of the first chip of data in the memory. The length of the data frame for one period multiply by the over sampling rate at the oscilloscope is 75, which is the period of data repetition. This is exactly the peak value calculated and demonstrated in Figure 7. These two values are essential for synchronization in phase and in frequency.

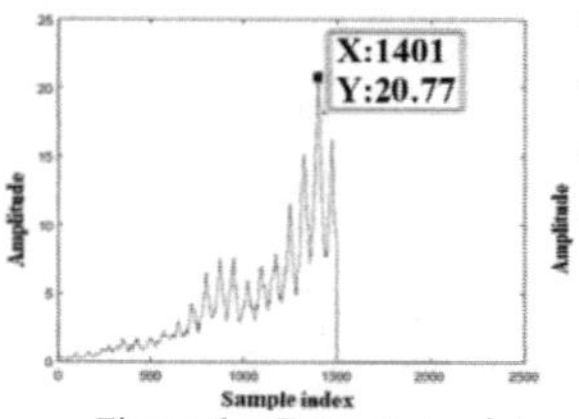

Figure 6. Data start point

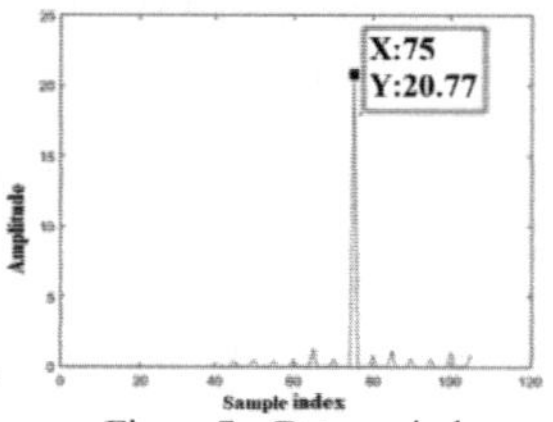

Figure 7. Data period

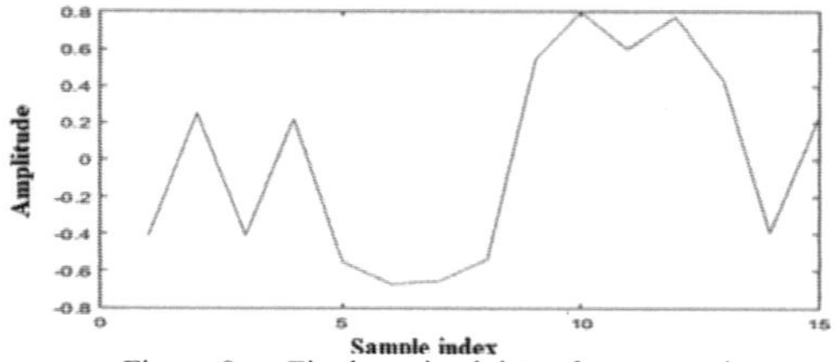

Figure 8. Final received data after processing

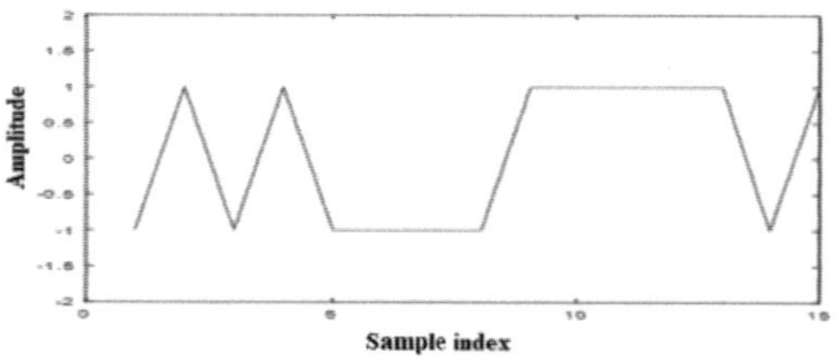

Figure 9. Data at the comparator block

Finally, the result of averaging after applying TSA and before making decision is shown in Figure 8. The overall gain due to synchronized averaging techniques is significant. Using the comparator gives the digital signal (presented in Figure 9). The result after comparator block is [010100001111101] which is the transmitted data with no error.

V. Conclusion

Averaging helps to establish a link in the presence of a very strong noise. The cost of averaging is the size of repeated data (more bits than information bits are needed). The limitations of averaging are due to synchronization in phase and in the frequency. In other words, the exact instant at which the data starts as well as the period of each repetition are needed. One solution is to manipulate the data before sending. These manipulation parameters are used later at the receiver to reveal this information. The gain of whole process (averaging plus synchronization in phase and in the frequency) becomes infinity, as long as, there are no limitations in terms of data repetitions and memory size. But, in real measurements for SNR close to zero, it becomes more difficult to measure the received signals. It is mostly due to heavy coupling effect while the transmitter and receiver are near to each other (in the presented experiment). One solution to overcome this problem is to put a sufficient distances between receiver and transmitter to avoid the electromagnetic coupling. We also have to avoid using the same power line for both receiver and transmitter. In very low SNR the signals propagated over the powerlines are comparative to free space propagation. Therefor repeating the measurement in an anechoic chamber will reduce this effect as well. The other difficulty is the lack of memory in experimental devices in case of large information block. WE have to break the information into small block or add more memory at receiver node.

Acknowledgment

This work was financed by the EC-ENIAC project Things2DO.

References

[1] Usman Raza, Parag Kulkarni, and Mahesh Sooriyabandara, "Low Power Wide Area Networks: An Overview", IEEE Communications surveys & tutorials, VOL. 19, No. 2, Second quarter 2017.

[2] "Cellular networks for massive IoT: Enabling low power wide area applications", Ericsson, Stockholm, Sweden, Tech. Rep. UEN 284 23-3278, [retrieved: May 2018]. [Online]. Available: https://www.ericsson.com/res/docs/whitepapers/wp_iot.pdf

[3] E.Berthelsen and J.Morrish, "Forecastingthe Internet of things revenue opportunity", Machina Res., London, U.K., Tech. Rep., [retrieved: May 2018]. [Online]. Available: https://machinaresearch.com/report/forecasting-the-internet-of-things-revenue-opportunity/

[4] Emil Novakov, Mohammadmahdi Asgharzadeh, and Ghislaine Maury, "Enhancement of the Sensitivity of a Digital Receiver by Time Synchronous Averaging", URSI GASS, Montreal, 2017.

[5] R. Lyons, "Understanding Digital Signal Processing", Third Edition, Pearson Education Inc., 2011, pp. 562-589.

[6] L. W. Couch, "Digital and Analog Communication Systems" Seventh Edition, Pearson Prentice Hall, 2007, pp. 476-508.

[7] M. Sahmoudi, M. Amin, and R. Landry, "Acquisition of Weak GNSS Signals Using a New Block Averaging Tre-Processing", IEEE 2008.

[8] J. Jarret and N. Flowers, "Signal-Averaged Electrocardiography: History, Techniques, and Clinical Applications", Ciln. Cardiol. 14, 984-994, 1991.

[9] L. Zhu, H. Ding, and X.-Y. Zhu, "Extraction of Periodic Signal Without External Reference by Time-Domain Average Scanning", TEEE Trans. on Industrial Electronics, vol. 55, NO2, February 2008, pp.918-927.

[10] D. Hochmann and M. Sadok, "Theory of Synchronous Averaging", 2004 IEEE Aerospace Conference Proceedings, pp.3636-3653.

Pulsar Signal Detection Using Hough Transform

Ivan Garvanov
University of Library Studies and Information Technologies
Sofia, Bulgaria
e-mail: i.garvanov@unibit.bg

Abstract—**Pulsars are rotating neutron stars that emit electromagnetic radiation at regular intervals and can be used for navigation and for detection of meteoroids and asteroids. The detection of a pulsar signal for a short time (in real time) is difficult because the signals are very weak. In this paper, we develop a detection algorithm, which includes three basic stages: moving average filter with a jumping window, Hough transform and detector. The algorithm proposed in the paper was verified with pulsar signals from Jodrell Bank Centre for Astrophysics.**

Keywords-Pulsar signal detection, Hough transform, signal processing, moving average filter with a jumping window

I. INTRODUCTION

Pulsars are fast rotating neutron stars (see Figure 1) that periodically emit broadband electromagnetic pulses [1]. The emission period is thought to be the same as the rotation period. Although individual pulsar pulses vary in strength and shape, the average pulse shape is stable and characterizes each pulsar.

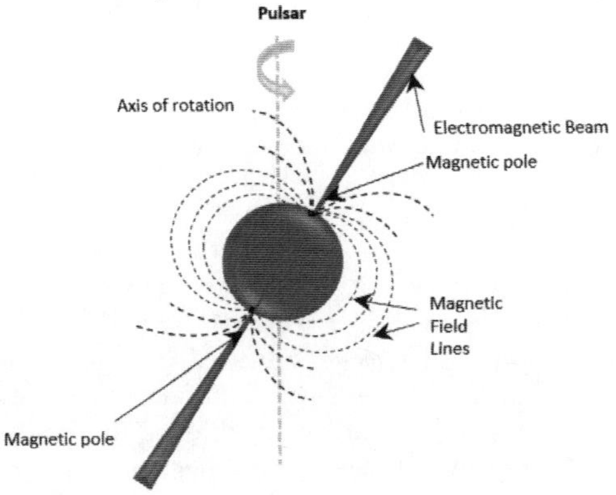

Figure 1. Pulsar

The idea of using pulsars, rapidly rotating neutron stars, for orientation in space is not new [2]-[4]. It is similar to the oldest idea - navigation of ships centuries ago through observation of the visible stars with sextants and using the star and sea charts. This approach is similar, but the difference is in the reception of radio signals instead the light emission of stars.

A similar approach for navigation by satellites is in Global Navigation Satellite System (GNSS). This requires to search very specific, fast and effective methods and algorithms for detection and estimation of their parameters.

Earlier, the practical realization of the idea of space navigation was difficult, first, the insufficient number of known pulsars, and secondly - sophisticated technology to detect them. But in recent years, the situation has changed significantly. Since the discovery of the first pulsar in 1967, approximately 2100 pulsars have been found.

The pulsar signal can be used also for observation and detection of falling cosmic objects as asteroids and meteoroids [14]. This information would be useful in creating early warning systems.

The main difficulty in detecting a signal from the pulsar by radio telescopes is the low Signal-to-Noise Ratio (SNR) at the receiver input (from -40 dB to -90 dB). Another difficulty in the study of the pulsars is a great consumption of time needed for detecting the signal from them, about 1-2 hours [5]-[11], [15].

Since each pulsar has a unique period, in [4] is applied epoch folding algorithm to shape the pulsar pulse, remove noise, and find the pulsar. Folding is similar to integration except that in folding, the data is broken into a sequence of discrete intervals corresponding to the period of the expected pulsar and then added (or folded) ensuring that the pulsar signal is reinforced with each fold, while the noise approaches a mean zero. The epoch folding method is convenient, but the integration time is too much. It is equal to the number of period of repetition of the signal from the pulsar multiplied by the length of the period.

In [5] it is discussed the possibility to improve the signal to noise ratio by using Moving Average Filter with a Jumping Window (MAFJW) in time domain signal. As a result of this processing, the number of samples in the record will be reduced in proportion to the number of cells in jumping window. The small number of samples will increase the further signal processing.

In this paper, we propose the use of Hough transform as method for detecting of pulsar pulse sequence. This algorithm is tested over real pulsar signals. In the previous works, the Hough Transform is used to detect straight lines in image. This transformation is also used in algorithms for detecting of target and trajectories of moving targets [13], [16]. In this paper, we offer an unconventional approach to detecting pulsar signal using Hough transform. In the further work will be evaluated the efficiency of the proposed algorithm.

Section 2 describes the algorithm for signal processing. Section 3 discusses the experimental results. Finally, section 4 draws conclusions based on the obtained results.

II. Signal Processing

The considered algorithm of signal processing of the pulsar signals experimental data is shown in Figure 2. It includes the following stages: filtration by the MAFJW; Hough transform and, finally detector.

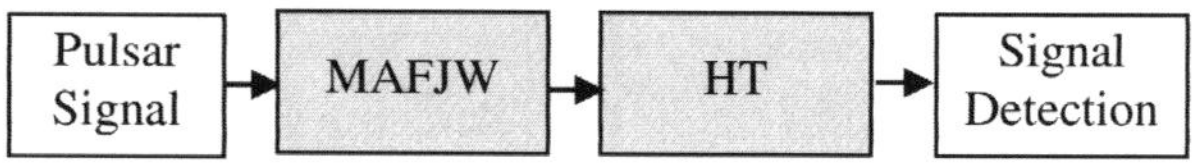

Figure 2. Block-scheme of signal processing

A. *Filtering by the MAFJW*

The aim of this study is to examine the possibility to increase the signal to noise ratio of the received pulsar signal by means of one modification of a Moving Average Filter, which uses the Jumping Window (MAFJW). It takes N samples of input at a time and take the average of those N-samples and produces a single output point. It is a very simple structure that comes handy for scientists and engineers to filter an unwanted noisy component from the input data.

$$y[n] = \sum_{k=-N}^{N} \frac{1}{2N+1} x[n-k], \quad n=N+1, 2N+1, \ldots, MN+1 \qquad (1)$$

Where n contrary to the traditional Moving Average Filter (MAF) where the number of output samples is equal to the number of input samples, the MAFJW reduces the number of output samples N times, where N is the length of the Jumping Window. The number of input samples is MN, and the number of output samples is M. Therefore in contrary to the traditional Moving Average window, the MAFJW acts not only as a low-pass filter but a decimator as well. When the signal processing is carried out in the time domain, the use of the MAFJW can be very useful in the sense of reducing the processing time.

B. *Hough Transform*

The standard Hough transform and the related Radon transform have received much attention in recent years [13]. Using them makes possible the transformation of two-dimensional images with lines into a domain of possible line parameters, where each image line corresponds to a peak, positioned at the respective line parameters. For these reasons, many line detection applications appeared within the image processing, computer vision, and seismic research areas. The use of the standard Hough transform (SHT) for target detection and track determination in white Gaussian noise is introduced by Carlson, Evans and Wilson in [12]. The standard Hough transform maps points from trajectory of the observation space termed as range-time $(r-t)$ data space into curves in Hough parameter space. The trajectory from the observation space can be defined by the angle θ of its perpendicular from the origin and the distance ρ from the origin to the line along the perpendicular.

$$\rho = r\cos(\theta) + t\sin(\theta) \qquad (2)$$

where r and t are coordinates measured from the origin of ρ and θ axis in the lower left. The result of transformation is a sinusoid with magnitude and phase depending on the value of the point in range-time $(r-t)$ space.

Each point in the Hough parameter space corresponds to one straight line in the $(r-t)$ space with two parameters (ρ, θ). Each of the sinusoids corresponds to a set of possible straight lines through the point. If a straight line exists in the $(r-t)$ space, by means of the Hough transform it can be viewed as a point of intersection of sinusoids defined by the Hough transform. The parameters ρ and θ define the linear trajectory in the Hough parameter space, which could be transformed back to the $(r-t)$ space showing the current distance to the target.

C. *Detection algorithm*

The detection algorithm is based on threshold processing of the cells in the Hough parametric space [13]. According to this algorithm, we tested a simple hypothesis H1 (pulsar signal is present) against a simple alternative H0 (pulsar signal is absent). Each cell from the Hough parameter space is intersected by a limited set of sinusoids obtained by Hough transform. If the number of intersections in any of the cells in the parameter space exceeds a fixed threshold (T_M), pulsar signal detection is indicated.

III. Results

In this study, the experimental records of the signal received from the pulsar B0329+54 provided by Jodrell Bank Centre for Astrophysics are used. This is the brightest radio pulsar in the northern sky. Otherwise this pulsar is a typical, normal pulsar, rotating with a period of 0.714520 seconds, hence the star makes about one and a half turn in a second, giving it a locomotive kind of sound. We can see in Figure 3 that each pulse has a different structure, hence the beam of this cosmic lighthouse is constantly changing in shape. This recording has been made with the Lovell telescope in Jodrell Bank.

The signal in Figure 3 is obtained after signal processing procedure which is about 2 hours. When the SNR is about -20 dB, the pulsar signal will be as in Figure 4. The representation of the pulse signal in a matrix so that each pulse period is in a separate order is shown in Figure 5. When we use moving average filter with jumping window

(MAFJW), the output SNR increases. The filter output for length of the jumping window N=100 is shown in Figure 6. The contour of the MAFJW output is shown in Figure 7. In the Figure 8 is shown Binary integration of data in Hough parameter space. If the number of binary integrations (BI) of data in the Hough parameter space (of intersections in any of the cells in the parameter space) exceeds the detection threshold, then pulsar signal is detect.

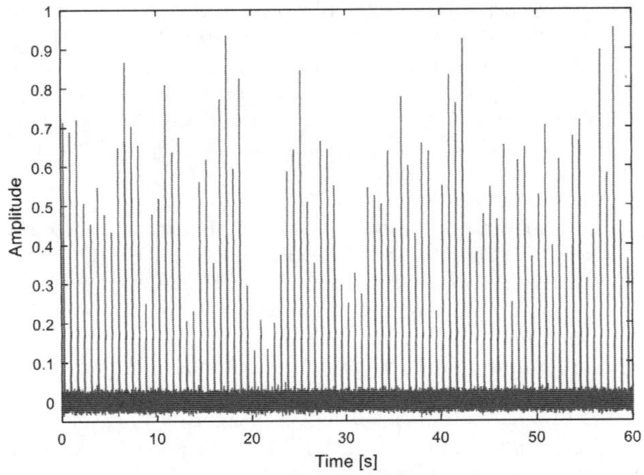

Figure 3. Pulsar signal (B0329+54)

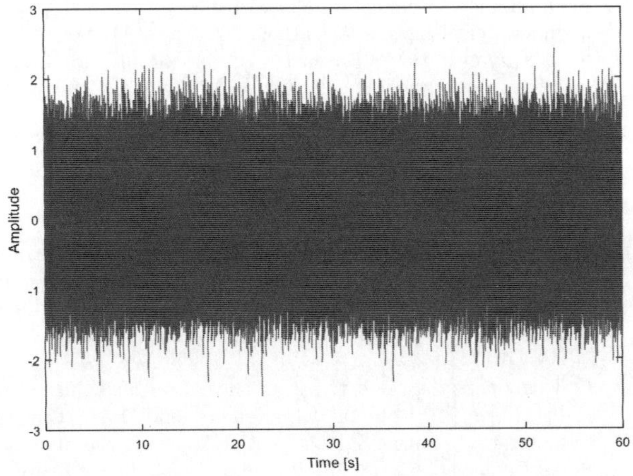

Figure 4. Pulsar signal B0329+54 and noise (SNR= - 20dB)

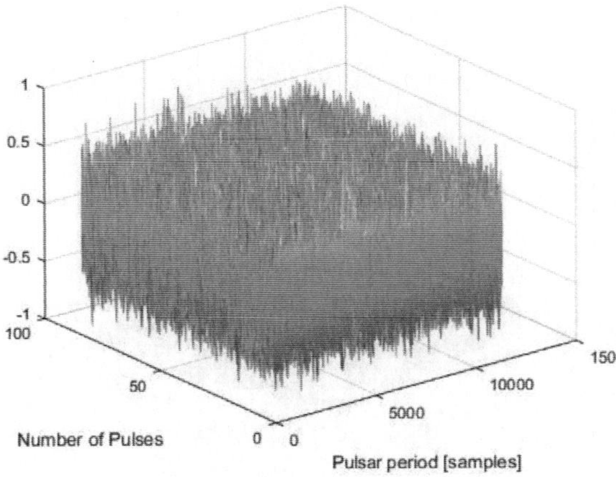

Figure 5. Pulsar signal

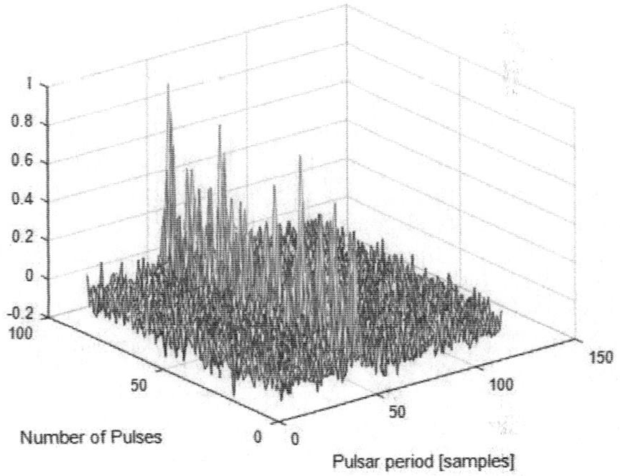

Figure 6. Pulsar signal after MAFJW (N=100)

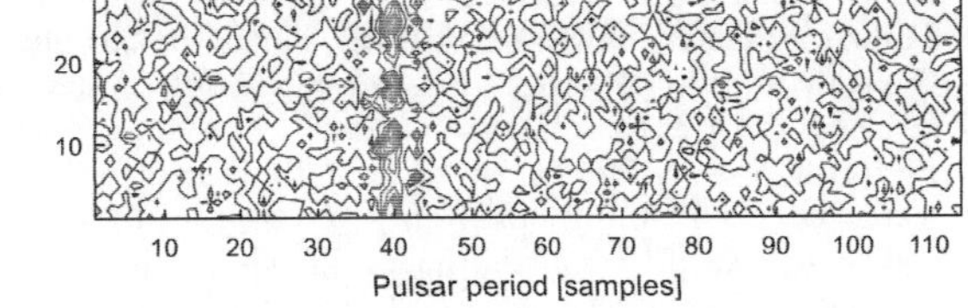

Figure 7. Contour of the pulsar signal after MAFJW (N=100)

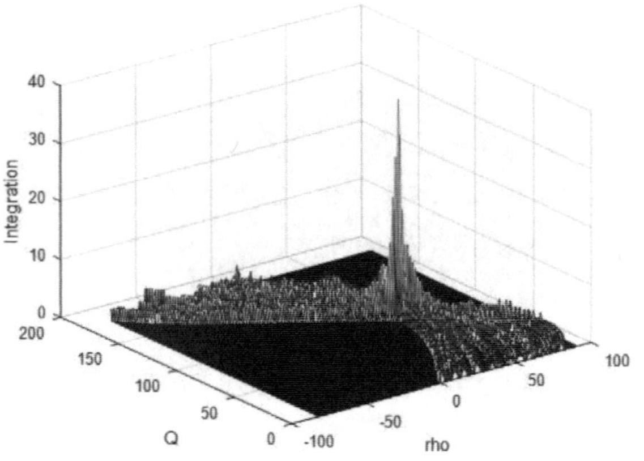

Figure 8. Hough transform the pulsar signal after MAFJW (N=100)

IV. CONCLUSIONS

The obtained results show that the presented algorithm can be successfully used for processing and detection of pulsar signals. The signals from pulsars are very weak and difficult to detect. The SNR can be improved using the Moving Averaging Filter with a Jumping window. The pulsar signals are periodic with a highly stable pulse-repetition frequency allowing the pulse signal to form a straight line in the computer space. The Hough transform is a popular tool for line detection due to its robustness to noise and missing data. The presence of the Hough transform further enhances the detection of the pulsar signal. In the next work, the efficiency of the proposed algorithm will be evaluated.

ACKNOWLEDGMENT

This work is supported by the project "Investigation of parameters, properties and phenomena of radio signals from pulsars and their interaction with objects", DN 07/1 from 14.12.2016.

REFERENCES

[1] J. Sala, A. Urruela, X. Villares, R. Estalella and J. Paredes, "Feasibility study for a spacecraft navigation system relying on pulsar timing information", Final Report, 03/4202, ARIADNA Study, June 2004, p. 92.

[2] P. Buist, S. Engelen, A. Noroozi, P. Sundaramoorthy, S. Verhagen and C. Verhoeven, "Principles and Potential of Pulsar Navigation", Proceedings of the 24th International Technical Meeting of The Satellite Division of the Institute of Navigation (ION GNSS 2011), Portland, OR, September 2011, pp. 3503-3515.

[3] P. Buist, S. Engelen A. Noroozi, P. Sundaramoorthy, S. Verhagen and C. Verhoeven, „Overview of Pulsar Navigation: Past, Present and Future Trends", Journal of the Institute of Navigation, vol.58, № 2, 2011, pp.153-164.

[4] N. White, F. Nagase and A. Parmar "X-Ray Binaries", Cambridge Astrophysics Series, 1995, p. 662.

[5] I. Garvanov, C. Kabakchiev, V. Behar, and M. Garvanova, " The Experimental Study of Possibility for Pulsar Signal Detection", The Second International Conference "Engineering & Telecommunications – En&T 2016", Noevember 28-30, Moscow-Dolgoprudny, Russia, 2016, pp. 68-72, doi: 10.1109/EnT.2016.023.

[6] C. Kabakchiev, V. Behar, P. Buist, I. Garvanov, D. Kabakchieva, N. Gaubich and M. Bentum, "Study of CFAR Algorithms for Signal Acquisition in Radio Pulsar-Based Navigation", 21st Saint Petersburg International Conference on Integrated Navigation Systems 2014, Saint Petersburg, Russian Federation, 2014, pp. 186-194.

[7] C. Kabakchiev, V. Behar, P. Buist, I. Garvanov, D. Kabakchieva and M. Bentum, "Time of Arrival Estimation in Pulsar Based Navigation Systems", Signal Processing Symposium, Debe, Poland, 2015, pp. 1-5, doi: 10.1109/SPS.2015.7168287.

[8] C. Kabakchiev, V. Behar, P. Buist, R. Heusdens, I. Garvanov and D. Kabakchieva, "Detection and Estimation of Pulsar Signals for Navigation", International Radar Symposium, Dresden, Germany, 2015 pp. 688-693, doi: 10.1109/IRS.2015.7226320.

[9] I. Garvanov, C. Kabakchiev, V. Behar and M. Garvanova, "Target detection using a GPS Forward-Scattering Radar". IEEE Second International Conference "Engineering & Telecommunications – En&T 2015", Moscow-Dolgoprudny, Russia, 2015 -pp. 29-33, doi: 10.1109/EnT.2015.20.

[10] D. Izvorska, "On the something application of axial and central symmetry to work on construct problems", II International seminar Symmetry: theoretical and methodological aspects, Astrakhan, 2007, pp. 194-199.

[11] S. Slavova and D. Izvorska, "Using Maple in Linear Algebra", International Scientific and Methodical Conference, Penza, 2008, pp. 218-230.

[12] B. Carlson, E. Evans and S. Wilson, "Search Radar Detection and Track with the Hough Transform", IEEE Trans., vol. AES - 30.1.1994, Part I, pp. 102-108; Part II, pp. 109-115; Part III, pp. 116-124.

[13] I. Garvanov I., "Multisensor Data Association by Using the Polar Hough Transform", Book Title "Practical Issues of Intelligent Innovations", Chapter No.: 11, Springer International Publishing, 2018, pp. 255-276, doi:10.1007/978-3-319-78437-3.

[14] C. Kabakchiev, V. Behar, I. Garvanov, D. Kabakchieva, A. Kabakchiev, H. Rohling, M. Bentum and J. Fernandes, "Separation of Pulsar Signals in FSR System", International Radar Symposium 2018, 28-30 June, 2018, Bonn, Germany.

[15] H. Liang and Y. Zhan, "A Fast Detection Algorithm for the X-Ray Pulsar Signal", Mathematical Problems in Engineering, Volume 2017, pp. 1-5, doi:10.1155/2017/9607821

[16] E. Davies, "The generalized Hough transform", Book Title: Computer Vision: Principles, Algorithms, Applications, Learning, Chapter No.: 11, Elsevier, 2018, pp. 299-340, doi:10.1016/B978-0-12-809284-2.00011-3

Fixed Complexity Soft-Output Detection Algorithm Through Exploration and Exploitation Processes

Bastien Trotobas, Amor Nafkha
SCEE/IETR UMR CNRS 6164, CentraleSupélec
Avenue de la Boulaie, 35576 Cesson Sévigné, France
Email: {bastien.trotobas,amor.nafkha}@centralesupelec.fr

***Abstract*—In this paper, we propose a soft-output Multiple-Input and Multiple-Output (MIMO) detector algorithm, which is based on two complementary techniques: *exploration* and *exploitation*. The proposed detector, called List Exploration and Exploitation (L2E), achieves near-optimal performance with low and fixed computational complexity. It has a high parallelism degree, which makes it suitable for efficient practical implementation. The soft-output values are calculated by means of squared Euclidean distances in a max-Log Likelihood Ratio (LLR) approximation. The average Bit Error Rate (BER) performances of the L2E are compared to the well-known List Sphere Decoding (LSD) algorithm and it is shown that our method considerably reduces the computation complexity while maintaining near-optimal performance in comparison to LSD algorithm.**

Keywords-MIMO detection; sphere-decoding; soft demodulation.

I. INTRODUCTION

MIMO systems can be used to increase data rates by adopting spatial multiplexing method or to improve the reception reliability by exploiting spatial diversity. In spatial multiplexing systems, the maximum likelihood (ML) detection leads to the optimal method for minimizing transmission errors. However, it involves high computation complexity and requires a brute-force search over all of the transmitted vectors. A promising and efficient alternative, with reduced computational complexity, is the original sphere decoding (SD) algorithm by Fincke and Phost and its variants [1]–[4].
Nevertheless, the computational complexity of the sphere decoding algorithm is still exponential in problem size [5]. Fast but suboptimal ML detection algorithms such zero forcing, minimum mean-squared error, semi-definite programming, and interference cancellation detectors have already been proposed in the literature [6]. This wide variety of detectors is mainly due to a lack of optimum performances and/or higher computational complexity.

It has already been shown that the soft-output detector improves the error performance compared with a hard-output detector [8]. A soft-output detector generates the LLR value of each bit, defined as the ratio of the probabilities that a zero or a one has been transmitted conditioned on the received vector. However, the computation complexity of exact a-posteriori probabilities (APP) is exponential in the MIMO system dimensions [9]–[11]. Recently, a number of soft-output MIMO detectors have been reported, which approximate the APP and provide soft outputs [7]. Several demodulation schemes use a list of candidate data vectors to obtain approximate LLRs. To the best of our knowledge there are three families of candidate list generation algorithms for the suboptimal soft-output maximum a-posteriori (MAP) detector. The first type of algorithms is a modified version of well-known hard tree search detector where the goal of is to find one tree leaf with the best metric. The goal of soft-output is to find and keep a list in which one seeks to efficiently identify all bit vectors that dominate the LLRs. The mostly well-known list type of soft-output MIMO decoding algorithms are LSD algorithm [8], sequential sphere decoding (LISS) algorithm [12], and the M-Algorithm [13]. The second type of algorithms is based on simple bit flips around the hard solution [14]. Therefore, a hard decoder is employed to find a maximum a posteriori symbol estimate, and a candidate list is generated by bit-flipping of the MAP estimate. This technique may produce a LLRs approximation with high probability. The third type of techniques is based on lattice-reduction (LR) aided detector following by bit-flipping technique, which generates a list from which it computes the APP of all bits comprising the symbol vector. The channel matrix properties can be improved using an efficient lattice reduction and by this way we can reduce the complexity of the hard demodulator.

Our contribution in this paper is multi-fold: Based on previous MIMO detection studies of the hard detector [15][16], we propose a new near-optimal soft-output demodulator based on list generation algorithm. The algorithm list's size is controlled using the number of considered candidates, N_c, during the exploitation phase, and the number of considered direction, N_d. The proposed soft-output MIMO detection algorithm L2E was closely approximate the max-log LLR functions based on the generated initial solutions list with a reduced and fixed computational complexity. In contrary, the List Sphere-Decoding algorithm has a variable computational complexity depending on the MIMO channel conditioning. Moreover, the growth of the LSD complexity is exponential in the low Signal-to-noise ratio (SNR) region.

The computation complexity of the proposed L2E algorithm is independent from the SNR and thus has a constant value over all SNR regions. In our algorithm, the complexity depends only on the number of transmitter/receiver antennas, the number of considered candidates N_c, and the number of considered directions N_d. Monte Carlo simulations show that the proposed soft-output list detector has better complexity and performance trade-offs than the well-known LSD detector. Moreover, the L2E detector has an inherent parallel structure, thus it is very suitable for massive parallel architectures.

The remainder of this paper is organized as follows. Section II introduces the mathematical model of the studied MIMO bit-interleaved coded modulation (BICM-MIMO) system and the associated maximum likelihood detection (MLD) problem. The hard-output version of the exploration and exploitation detector algorithm (H2E) will be introduced and it is extended to compute soft-outputs. The proposed algorithm will be called as list exploration and exploitation detector (L2E). Computational complexity issues are given in Section IV. Section V provides Monte Carlo simulation results of the proposed algorithm and gives same discussions. Finally, Section VI is devoted to concluding remarks;

II. Mathematical Model

In this section, we introduce the BICM-MIMO model and the LLR generation with perfect channel state information (CSI) at the receiver is described.

A. MIMO-BICM system Model

Herein, we consider a MIMO system with N transmit antennas and M receive antennas associated to a BICM schema where a block of information bits is mapped to transmit symbols through a channel encoder and a symbol mapper separated by a code-bit interleaver [17] [18]. Let us consider a MIMO-BICM system with $M \times N$ channel matrix $\mathbf{H}_c$. At the receiver, a detector calculates the log-likelihood ratios for the coded bits, which are deinterleaved and passed to the subsequent channel decoder. The coded bit stream is mapped to N-dimensional transmit vector symbols $\mathbf{x}_c \in \phi^N$, where ϕ is a 2^Q-QAM modulation. The individual coded bits are denoted by b_{ij}, where the indexes i and j refer to the ith bit in the binary label of the jth entry of the transmitted symbol vector $\mathbf{x}_c = [x_1^c, x_2^c, ..., x_N^c]^T$. In considered MIMO-BICM system, the transmitted signal and the received signal are related through a complex baseband input-output relation as:

$$\mathbf{y}_c = \mathbf{H}_c\mathbf{x}_c + \mathbf{w}_c \tag{1}$$

where $\mathbf{w}_c$ is an independent and identically distributed complex zero-mean Gaussian noise with variance $\sigma^2/\sqrt{2}$ per complex entry, $\mathbf{y}_c$ is the received symbol vector, and $\mathbf{x}_c$ is the transmitted symbol vector with the average transmit power of each antenna normalized to one, *i.e.* $E[\mathbf{x}_c\mathbf{x}_c^H] = \mathbf{I}_N$. The $M \times N$ channel matrix $\mathbf{H}_c$ contains uncorrelated complex Gaussian fading gains where the element h_{ij}^c represents the complex transfer function from the jth transmit antenna to the ith receive antenna. Thus, the channel matrix $\mathbf{H}_c$, which is assumed to be known by the receiver, is modelled as an independent and identically distributed complex Gaussian variable with zero mean and variance $1/2$ per complex entry. Treating real and imaginary part of (1) separately, and with the real-valued channel matrix and the real-valued vectors, the system model can be rewritten as

$$\begin{bmatrix} \Re(\mathbf{y}_c) \\ \Im(\mathbf{y}_c) \end{bmatrix} = \begin{bmatrix} \Re(\mathbf{H}_c) & -\Im(\mathbf{H}_c) \\ \Im(\mathbf{H}_c) & \Re(\mathbf{H}_c) \end{bmatrix} \begin{bmatrix} \Re(\mathbf{x}_c) \\ \Im(\mathbf{x}_c) \end{bmatrix} + \begin{bmatrix} \Re(\mathbf{w}_c) \\ \Im(\mathbf{w}_c) \end{bmatrix}$$

where $\Re(z)$ and $\Im(z)$ denote the respective real and complex parts of a complex number z. Let $m = 2M$ and $n = 2N$, then the dimension of the real channel matrix is given by $m \times n$. Likewise, the dimension of the vectors are given by $\mathbf{y} \in \mathbb{R}^m$, $\mathbf{w} \in \mathbb{R}^m$, and $\mathbf{x} \in \xi^n$ where $\xi \equiv \Re(\mathcal{O})$. In this paper, we restrict our study to the case where $\xi^n \equiv \{\pm 1\}^n$.

B. Optimum Soft-output Demodulation

Given the channel matrix $\mathbf{H}$, the received vector $\mathbf{y}$, and assuming an ideal interleaver, the optimum soft-output maximum a posteriori decoder minimizes the BER by evaluating the LLRs of the a posteriori probability of each bit b_{ij}.

$$\mathcal{L}(b_{ij}) = \log \frac{P(b_{ij} = 1|\mathbf{y})}{P(b_{ij} = 0|\mathbf{y})} \tag{2}$$

where $P(b_{ij}|\mathbf{y})$ is the probability mass function of the code bits conditioned on $\mathbf{y}$. The exhaustive evaluation of (2) has a high computational complexity. Thus, using Bayes' theorem and the max-log approximation as shown in [7][9], the equation (2) can be further rewritten as:

$$\mathcal{L}(b_{ij}) \approx \min_{\mathbf{x}\in\mathcal{X}_{ij}^0} \|\mathbf{y} - \mathbf{H}\mathbf{x}\|^2 - \min_{\mathbf{x}\in\mathcal{X}_{ij}^1} \|\mathbf{y} - \mathbf{H}\mathbf{x}\|^2 \tag{3}$$

where $\mathcal{X}_{ij}^1$ and $\mathcal{X}_{ij}^0$ are the sets of symbols vectors having b_{ij} equal to 1 and 0, respectively. The set ξ^n can be seen as the union of the previous two subsets $\xi^n = \mathcal{X}_{ij}^1 \cup \mathcal{X}_{ij}^0$. The computation complexity of (3) is exponential in the number of transmit antennas. Thus, we propose a novel soft-output detector, called L2E, which keeps a limited number of candidates in order to evaluate the equation (3). Hence, the LLR of the ith bit b_{ij} in the jth symbol x_j can be approximated as

$$\mathcal{L}(b_{ij}) \approx \min_{\mathbf{x}\in\Gamma\cap\mathcal{X}_{ij}^0} \|\mathbf{y} - \mathbf{H}\mathbf{x}\|^2 - \min_{\mathbf{x}\in\Gamma\cap\mathcal{X}_{ij}^1} \|\mathbf{y} - \mathbf{H}\mathbf{x}\|^2 \tag{4}$$

where Γ denotes the candidates list, which is the subset of the feasible set ξ^n. The computational complexity the soft-output detector is affected by the list size and it increases approximately linearly (see Section IV).

III. Proposed soft-output detector

In this section, we propose an soft-output MIMO detector based on the exploration and exploitation strategies. The proposed L2E detector allows a sub-optimal solution for the optimum soft-output demodulation problem that limits the complexity of the receiver design.

A. Exploitation technique

The exploitation step can be defined as a simple and naive local search technique. This section gives a mathematical basis to understand how the exploitation (*intensification*) is applied on the subset $\xi_{st}^n \subset \xi^n$. The subset ξ_{st}^n is generated by the first phase, which is the exploration (*diversification*) step. In the remainder of this section, we show that a simple greedy policy of position switching between neighbouring feasible solutions to locally minimize the objective function $f(\mathbf{x}) = \|\mathbf{y} - \mathbf{H}\mathbf{x}\|^2$ over the subset ξ_{st}^n.

1) Definition 1: A neighbourhood operator is a function $\mathcal{Z} : \xi^n \longmapsto \mathcal{Z}(\xi^n)$ that assigns to every solution $\mathbf{u} \in \xi^n$ a set of neighbours $\mathcal{Z}(\mathbf{u}) \subseteq \xi^n$. The subset $\mathcal{Z}(\mathbf{u})$ is called neighbourhood of $\mathbf{u}$ and it is equivalent to a neighbourhood graph, which has ξ^n as vertex set, and which contains directed edge $\mathbf{v} \longmapsto \mathbf{u} \Leftrightarrow \mathbf{v} \in \mathcal{Z}(\mathbf{u})$.

2) Definition 2: A local minimum solution with respect to a neighbourhood operator $\mathcal{Z}$ is a solution $\mathbf{u}^*$, such that for all $\mathbf{u} \in \mathcal{Z}(\mathbf{u}^*) \Rightarrow f(\mathbf{u}^*) \leq f(\mathbf{u})$. The exploitation technique starts at a given solution $\mathbf{u} \in \xi^n$ and makes it as the current solution $\mathbf{x}_0 = \mathbf{u}$. At each iteration, it examines all the neighbours of the current solution and seeks to best one having a better objective function value than $\mathbf{x}_0$, *i.e.*, $\mathbf{v} \in \mathcal{Z}(\mathbf{x}_0)$ such that $f(\mathbf{v}) \leq f(\mathbf{x}_0)$. If such a solution is found, it becomes the current solution, *i.e.*, $\mathbf{x}_0 = \mathbf{v}$. These iterations are repeated until there is no better solution in the neighbourhood $\mathcal{Z}(\mathbf{x}_0)$ of the current solution. For the exploitation step, we perform a simple 1-flip local search algorithm where only one variable is flipped, per step, to reach the nearest neighbour. The local neighbourhood is the Hamming ball with distance one. More expensive, p-flip methods can be adopted where at most p variables are simultaneously flipped. In general, for a total number of n variables, the cardinality of the neighbourhood set is equal to $\binom{n}{p}$.

B. Exploration technique

Given a channel matrix $\mathbf{H}$, the singular value decomposition of this matrix is defined as $\mathbf{H} = \mathbf{UDV}^T$, where the diagonal matrix $\mathbf{D}$ contains the singular values $[\lambda_k]_{k=1}^n$, supposed to be indexed in increasing order, i.e., $\{\lambda_i \leq \lambda_j, 1 \leq i < j \leq n\}$. The unitary matrices $\mathbf{U}$ and $\mathbf{V}$ contain, respectively, the left $[\mathbf{u}_k]_{k=1}^m$ and right $[\mathbf{v}_k]_{k=1}^n$ singular vectors of the matrix $\mathbf{H}$.

Let's now $\mathbf{x}_{zf} = \mathbf{H}^+\mathbf{y}$, where $\mathbf{H}^+$ is the pseudo-inverse of channel matrix $\mathbf{H}$, be a linear solution given by the zero-forcing (ZF) detector. For all $\mathbf{x} \in \xi^n$, the vector $\mathbf{z} = \mathbf{x} - \mathbf{x}_{zf}$ can be expressed as a linear combination of the basis vectors formed by the columns of the matrix $\mathbf{V}$. Moreover, the value of the objective function $f(\mathbf{x})$ can be expressed as

$$\begin{aligned} f(\mathbf{x}) &= \|\mathbf{H}(\mathbf{x} - \mathbf{x}_{zf})\|^2 \\ &= \Sigma_{k=1}^n a_k^2 \lambda_k^2 \end{aligned} \quad (5)$$

where the coefficients $[a_k]_{k=1}^n$ are real numbers. Since the singular values of the channel matrix are ordered increasingly, we can note that the increase in the objective function is much slower along the first N_d singular values than the last $(n - N_d)$ values. Let us consider an n-dimensional line Δ_k passing through the point $\mathbf{x}_{zf}$ with the directed vector $\mathbf{v}_k$, i.e $\Delta_k = \{\mathbf{z} \in \mathbb{R}^n; \mathbf{z} = \mathbf{x}_{zf} + \gamma\mathbf{v}_k, \gamma \in \mathbb{R}\}$. It is obvious that if we choose $\mathbf{x} \in \xi^n$ that are close to the first N_d lines $\{\Delta_k\}_{k=1}^{N_d}$ associated to the N_d smallest singular values, we can create a subset ξ_{st}^n that contains N_c possible solutions in the vicinity of each line. The purpose of the exploration step is to create a subset $\xi_{st}^n \subset \xi^n$, which contains $N_c N_d$ feasible solutions.

C. L2E algorithm

By construction, the exploration step generates a subset ξ_{st}^n of feasible solutions where each solution will be processed independently by the exploitation step. The latter step will iterate once over each element of the subset ξ_{st}^n. In this exploration and exploitation optimization process, the objective function will be evaluated nN_dN_c times. The L2E will create the list Γ of $2nN_dN_c$ elements, which yielded the lowest objective function values, and then the Γ list will be used to evaluate the output soft metrics. A summary of the proposed soft-output MIMO detector is shown in Figure 1.

```
Data: Channel matrix H, received vector y, N_d and
      N_c.
Result: LLR-values of the sub-optimal solution's
        entries.
begin
  Extract the N_d right singular vectors of the channel
    matrix {v_k}_{k=1}^{N_d};
  Compute H^+;
  Compute x_zf = H^+ y;
  for k = 1..N_d do
    Generate the line Δ_k defined by x_zf and
      directed vector v_k;
    Find all intersection points between the line Δ_k
      and all hyperplanes x(i) = 0 and project them
      on ξ^n;
    Evaluate the objective function for all feasible
      solution and keep the best N_c solution in order
      to update ξ^n_st;
  Create Γ using ξ^n_st;
  Perform the exploitation step over Γ;
  Compute LLR-values;
```

Figure 1. L2E Algorithm

IV. L2E Complexity

The complexity is measured in terms of the number of real multiplications required to decode one block of transmitted information bits. The assumption of a block-constant channel is almost universal in the analysis of MIMO systems. Thus, computing the pseudo-inverse matrix $\mathbf{H}^+$ is not needed for each received vector. We assume that each block contains L transmitted vector. To find the linear solution $\mathbf{x}_{zf}$, the received signal vector will be multiplied by the pseudo-inverse of channel matrix. The resulting complexity for L transmitted vectors is hence equal to Ln^2 multiplications. For the N_d studied directions, the exploration step produces an initial list of feasible solutions using the intersection points between lines $\{\Delta_k\}_{k=1}^{N_d}$ and hyperplanes $\{\mathbf{x}(i) = 0\}_{i=1}^n$. Thus, the computation complexity of the exploration step would be LN_dn^2 multiplications. The exploitation step will be performed on subset ξ_{st}^n of feasible solutions (the ξ_{st}^n subset's cardinality is N_dN_c). The exploitation step needs $2nN_dN_c$ multiplications. Finally, the LLR-values computation needs $4nN_dN_c$.

For a given N_d and N_c, the computational complexity of the proposed soft-output L2E detector is constant, over the entire SNR range, compared to that of the list sphere-decoding.

V. Simulation Results

In this section, we carry out some simulation results to evaluate the bit error rate performances of the soft-output L2E MIMO detector. We consider a MIMO-BICM system as proposed in [8], with N transmit antennas and M receive antennas. This system use a parallel concatenated turbo error control coding with rate $R = 1/2$. Each constituent convolutional code has memory 2, feedback polynomial $G_r(D) = 1 + D + D^2$, and feedforward polynomial $G(D) = 1 + D^2$. The interleaver size of the turbo code is 512 information bits. We choose the number of inner iterations for the turbo decoding module to be 10. As in [8], we generate independent Rayleigh flat fading channels between transmit/receive antennas and we assume a perfect channel estimation at the MIMO receiver side.

In the $N \times M$ MIMO system (i.e., $n = m = 8$) case, the Figure 2 compares the performance of proposed soft output L2E algorithm versus the list sphere decoding (LSD) with candidate list of maximal length $N_{cand} = 1024$ as show in [8] and the shifted spherical list APP detector [19]. It can be seen that for this MIMO systems scenario, the shifted spherical list APP detector, with $N_{cand} = 1024$, has a slightly better performance than the L2E decoder with parameters ($N_d = 3$ and $N_c = 4$). However, the soft-output L2E use not more than nN_dN_c feasible solutions to generate the log-likelihood ratios of different outputs.

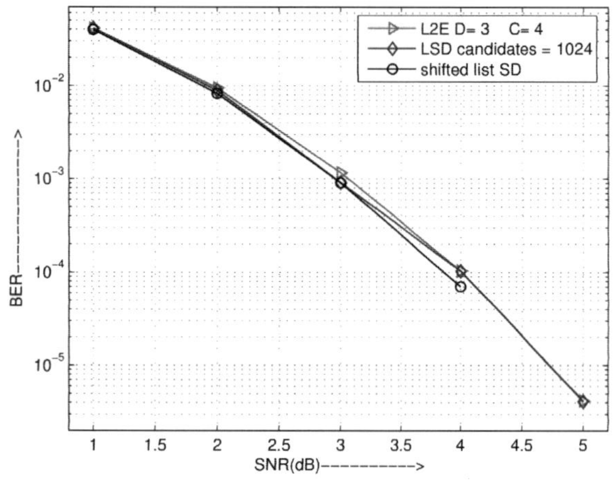

Figure 2. BER performances versus the SNR of L2E, LSD and shifted list sphere decoder, $N = M = 4$.

In Figure 3, the bit error rate performances between following soft-output MIMO detectors has been compared: list sphere-decoding, list exploration and exploitation detector, and soft-output semi-definite programming (SDP). Numerical results are presented for a MIMO system with $N = 8$ and $M = 8$ in a Rayleigh fading channel. The bit error rate difference is not even noticeable between the L2E with parameters $N_d = 3$ and $N_c = 4$ and the soft output SDP. At the bit error rate of 10^{-4}, L2E performance is only less than 0.2 dB from the LSD with candidates list length $N_{cand} = 1024$.

VI. Conclusion

In this paper, we proposed a soft-output MIMO detector algorithm called the list exploration and exploitation. We have shown that the proposed algorithm achieves near-optimal performance with low and fixed computational complexity. Furthermore, it is suitable for efficient practical implementation because of its parallelism. We have compared the bit error rate performances of the proposed detector are compared to the well-known list sphere decoding algorithm and it is shown that our method maintains near-optimal performances in comparison with LSD while considerably reducing the computation complexity.

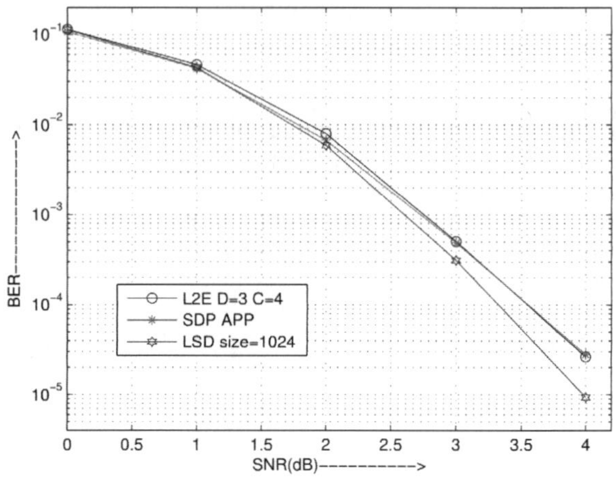

Figure 3. BER performances versus SNR of L2E, LSD and soft-output SDP detector, $N = M = 8$.

References

[1] U. Fincke and M. Pohst, "*Improved methods for calculating vectors of short length in a lattice, including a complexity analysis,*" Math. Comput., vol. 44, pp. 463-471, Apr. 1985.

[2] B. Hassibi and H. Vikalo, "*On the sphere-decoding algorithm I. Expected complexity,*" in IEEE Transactions on Signal Processing, vol. 53, no. 8, pp. 2806-2818, Aug. 2005.

[3] J. Jalden and B. Ottersten, "*On the complexity of sphere decoding in digital communications,*" in IEEE Transactions on Signal Processing, vol. 53, no. 4, pp. 1474-1484, April 2005.

[4] T. Kailath, H. Vikalo, and B. Hassibi, MIMO Receive Algorithms, Cambridge, U.K.:Cambridge Univ. Press, 2005.

[5] H. Vikalo and B. Hassibi, "*On the sphere-decoding algorithm II. Generalizations, second-order statistics, and applications to communications,*" in IEEE Transactions on Signal Processing, vol. 53, no. 8, pp. 2819-2834, Aug. 2005.

[6] L. Bai, J. Choi, and Q. Yu, Low Complexity MIMO Receivers. Springer Publishing Company, Incorporated, 2014.

[7] R. Asvadi, A. H. Banihashemi, M. Ahmadian-Attari, and H. Saeedi,"*LLR Approximation for Wireless Channels Based on Taylor Series and its Application to BICM With LDPC Codes,*" IEEE Transactions on Communications, vol. 60, no. 5, pp. 1226-1236, May 2012.

[8] B. M. Hochwald and S. T. Brink, "*Achieving near-capacity on a multiple antenna channel,*" IEEE Transactions on Communications, vol. 51, no. 3, pp. 389399, March 2003.

[9] C. Xu, D. Liang, S. Sugiura, S. X. Ng, and L. Hanzo, "*Reduced-Complexity Approx-Log-MAP and Max-Log-MAP Soft PSK/QAM Detection Algorithms,*" in IEEE Transactions on Communications, vol. 61, no. 4, pp. 1415-1425, April 2013.

[10] F. Jiang, C. Li, and Z. Gong, "*A low complexity soft-output data detection scheme based on Jacobi method for massive MIMO uplink transmission,*" IEEE International Conference on Communications (ICC), Paris, 2017, pp. 1-5, 2017.

[11] X. Qin, Z. Yan, and G. He,"*A Near-Optimal Detection Scheme Based on Joint Steepest Descent and Jacobi Method for Uplink Massive MIMO Systems,*" IEEE Commun. Lett., vol. 20, no. 2, pp. 276-279, Feb. 2016.

[12] S. Baro, J. Hagenauer, and M. Witzke,"*Iterative detection of MIMO transmission using a list-sequential (LISS) detector,*" IEEE International Conference on Communications, pp. 2653-2657, vol.4, 2003.

[13] K. Wong and P. McLane, "*A low-complexity iterative MIMO detection, scheme using the soft-output M-algorithm,*" In Proceedings of the IST Mobile Summit, June 2005.

[14] W. Shin, H. Kim, M. h. Son, and H. Park, "*An Improved LLR*

Computation for QRM-MLD in Coded MIMO Systems," IEEE 66th Vehicular Technology Conference, Baltimore, MD, pp. 447-451, 2007.

[15] A. Nafkha,"*Near maximum likelihood detection algorithm based on 1-flip local search over uniformly distributed codes,*" IEEE International Conference on Communications (ICC), Budapest, pp. 4900-4904, 2013.

[16] A. Nafkha, E. Boutillon, and C. Roland, "*Quasi-maximum-likelihood detector based on geometrical diversification greedy intensification,*" IEEE Transactions on Communications, vol. 57, no. 4, pp. 926-929, April 2009.

[17] A. Stefanov and T. M. Duman, "*Turbo-coded modulation for systems with transmit and receive antenna diversity over block fading channels: system model, decoding approaches, and practical considerations,*" IEEE Journal on Selected Areas in Communications, vol. 19, no. 5, pp. 958-968, May 2001.

[18] S. H. Muller-Weinfurtner, "*Coding approaches for multiple antenna transmission in fast fading and OFDM,*" IEEE Transactions on Signal Processing, vol. 50, no. 10, pp. 2442-2450, Oct 2002.

[19] J. Boutros, N. Gresset, L. Brunel, and M. Fossorier, "*Soft-input soft-output lattice sphere decoder for linear channels,*" IEEE Global Telecommunications Conference, GLOBECOM '03, pp. 1583-1587 vol.3, 2003.

Pedagogical Design Principles Guided Integration of Social Media Concepts in a Hybrid Learning Environment

Analysing and Reporting Focus Group Results

Manal Assaad
Faculty of Information and Technology
Hochschule Emden/Leer
Emden, Germany
e-mail: manal.assaad@hs-emden-leer.de

Tiina Mäkelä
Finnish Institute for Educational Research
University of Jyväskylä
Jyväskylä, Finland
e-mail: tiina.m.makela@jyu.fi

Dimitris Pnevmatikos
Department of Primary Education
University of Western Macedonia
Florina, Greece
e-mail: dpnevmat@uowm.gr

Panagiota Christodoulou
Department of Primary Education
University of Western Macedonia
Florina, Greece
e-mail: pchristodoulou@uowm.gr

***Abstract*—The current study aims to identify trends in users' wishes and requirements regarding the integration of social media in teaching and learning. Social media has been widely adopted in everyday life, facilitating communication and collaboration, as well as community development and knowledge exchange between users. Although the added value of social media for learning and instruction has been highlighted widely, still students' and teachers' perceptions on their use and implementation are incongruent with the current state of the art in their pedagogical exploitation. Science, Technology, Innovation, Mathematics, Education for the Young (STIMEY), a European funded project, aims at developing a pedagogical framework exploiting the full potential of social media, particularly for Science, Technology, Engineering and Mathematics (STEM) education. A participatory co-design methodology, with focus group techniques, was employed for the identification of the project stakeholders' wishes, forming the basis of more concrete requirements regarding the use of social media in teaching and learning. Moreover, a qualitative approach was followed for their analysis. Findings are presented and discussed in terms of their relationship with pedagogical design principles and social media concepts previously identified within the project research.**

Keywords-E-Learning; E-Teaching; Europe; Pedagogy; Social Media; STEM; Technologies.

I. INTRODUCTION

With the universal adoption of social media in everyday life, efforts in educational research have focused on its use in learning, mostly in out-of-school context, where it's often used. However, studies are mostly concerned with the use of popular social networking sites by students and teachers. Only very few studies investigate students' and teachers' perceptions and practices of social media use in formal learning environments, especially in middle and secondary school settings [1].

Social media encompass technologies that facilitate communication and collaboration between users, enabling them to construct communities and exchange knowledge. Educational researches have also recognized them as valuable tools that can be used for learning and teaching purposes [2]. Still, using such technologies as learning tools can be challenging to students and teachers given the lack of pedagogical support [3] and the lack of understanding how different functions of social media tools can be used efficiently in learning tasks [4]. Thus, students and teachers need to collaborate on reconstructing their views of pedagogy to come to a shared vision for enabling the learning experience, in order to leverage the potential of social media technologies for broadening the learning context, blending information and learning resources, and sharing expertise [5].

The Science, Technology, Innovation, Mathematics, Education for the Young (STIMEY) project, funded by European Union's Horizon 2020 H2020-SEAC-2015-1 program, with partners in Belarus, Finland, Germany, Greece, and Spain, aims to develop a hybrid learning environment that connects students and teachers, as well as parents and organizations. One of its main objectives is to create a pedagogical framework that exploits the full potentials of social media, especially for Science, Technology, Engineering, and Mathematics (STEM) subjects, in formal and informal learning contexts, as well as to develop recommendations and guidelines that can be used widely beyond the project [6]. To successfully integrate social media technologies within the STIMEY hybrid learning environment, their use then must be linked to the achievement of learning goals, following a pedagogic strategy. Identifying which features users already use, find interesting and consider important, and recognizing how their use can be endogenous to learning goals is one way to achieve that objective [7].

This study builds upon previous research, where key social media concepts and features, such as user profiles, status updates, and discussion, were identified for their potential roles as support tools that can enable and facilitate learning tasks and goals [8]. As part of the research, co-design focus groups with students, teachers, parents, and professionals were conducted in 5 different countries. The participants discussed and shared their views on using social media in learning and teaching context, thus fulfilling the approach of participatory co-design of pedagogical principles. In this paper, the participants' wishes related to the use of social media in learning and teaching context, and the resulting pedagogical design principles, are presented and discussed, for their integration in the social media concepts within the STIMEY platform.

In the following background subsection, the key social media concepts and pedagogical design principles identified in the previous research are briefly reiterated. In Section 2, the research questions, and methodology are described in detail. In Section 3, the results of the focus group are presented, with a discussion of how the previously identified social media concepts fulfill the pedagogical design principles based on participants' wishes and requirements in Section 4, and the study limitations in Section 5. In Section 6, a conclusion is drawn with guidance for future research.

A. Background

So far, researchers and educators have had to deal with a lack in the understanding and identification of the social media features that the youth find most appealing and important, and in defining and assessing learning and communication using social media. In the review of 24 studies from the educational research literature that examine the use and perception of social network sites by learners and teachers in primary and secondary education, it was concluded that most studies focus on common uses in students' informal learning outside of school. Only some studies investigated students' formal learning in schools and classrooms. However, none of the studies researched social media technologies' effectiveness at improving student learning and their impact on teaching pedagogy [1].

Therefore, efforts in this research first focused on the theoretical understanding of key social media concepts, identified based on the common features in popular networking sites, and their potential role as learning tools in the progressive inquiry model, to demonstrate their support of pedagogical learning approaches [8]. The concepts identified in that analysis are:

- *User profile:* the foundation of the user's activity on the e-learning platform, and the digital representation of their personal data, which can help identify their personal interests to find like-minded learners based on their expertise areas.
- *Status Update:* the most basic form of communication on the platform, which allows users to share their thoughts, opinions, and important information with others, to enable brainstorming, presenting and unstructured discussions.
- *Social Feedback:* an effective tool in learning context, by supporting the co-creation of working theories and critical evaluation through likes, comments, replies, etc.
- *Social Connecting:* a feature that enables communication, collaboration, knowledge sharing and network building on a social platform, with functions like "add friend" or "follow account", thus driving multiple pedagogical frames that depend on interactions among the various roles in a pedagogical model (i.e., learners, tutors, facilitators/mentors, and group members/leaders).
- *Activity Stream:* the most common method of displaying the list of recent activities on a platform from a user's network, which supports generating context and receiving or providing feedback on those activities.
- *Social Messaging:* rich text chatting that enables deeper private or group discussions, collaboration, brainstorming and sharing expertise, between the various roles.
- *Community:* a feature that allows users to find and connect with like-minded people, in interest and niche-specific private or public forums, enabling learning tasks, such as communicating, assimilating and producing information and knowledge, etc.
- *Discussion Forum:* a common feature in most e-learning platforms, which enables learners to cooperate and collaborate on constructing knowledge, by supporting the learning tasks' types and techniques.

Previous research efforts in the STIMEY project also focused on identifying pedagogical principles to guide the design of a hybrid (physical, virtual, formal, and informal) STEM Learning Environment (STEM LE), such as the STIMEY LE. In the preliminary research, design principles were created based on focus group discussions collecting the wishes of Finnish (n = 27) and Greek (n = 24) primary, lower, and upper secondary school students, teachers, school directors, parents, and STEM professionals on teaching, learning, assessment, and motivation both in general and in relation to STEM studies [9]. In that analysis, 22 pedagogical design principles were formulated, based on the research literature and supported by participants' wishes, in 3 areas:

- General Principles, such as:
  - *Versatility* in teaching, learning, and assessment;
  - *Novelty* in use of methods and tools for learning; and
- Ways of Teaching and Learning, such as:
  - *Reflective learning*, e.g., reflection, deep thinking, critical thinking;

  - *Learning outside the school*, e.g., field trips, visits to workplaces;
- Socio-emotional aspects, such as:
  - *Joy of learning* referring, e.g., to the importance of enjoyment, learner satisfaction, and having fun;
  - *Justice and equity*, equal treatment of all students, no discrimination, fair assessment, etc.

In this paper, the pedagogical design principles that the participants related in their social media wishes are presented and considered in employing the previously identified key social media concepts [8].

II. RESEARCH QUESTIONS

This paper extends on the previous research [9] to include the data of focus group discussions conducted in Belarus, Finland, Germany, Greece, and Spain, considering participating stakeholders' wishes related to the use of social media in STEM learning environments. The main research question is: What are the wishes of the participating stakeholders concerning the social media use in learning and teaching context?

The answer thus lies in recognizing which previously identified pedagogical design principles can be pinpointed in the focus group data on social media use in learning and teaching.

B. Methodology

Participatory design approach [10] and focus group techniques [11] [12] were combined in the focus group co-design sessions [9].

1) Participants

TABLE I. PARTICIPANTS

Stakeholder groups	**Countries**					***Total*** *n =*
	Belarus *n =*	***Finland*** *n =*	***Germany*** *n =*	***Greece*** *n =*	***Spain*** *n =*	
Primary school students	2	4	11	2	4	23
Lower sec. school students	6	6	2	2	5	21
Upper sec. school students	2	2	7	2	4	17
Teachers	3	3	2	6	2	16
Directors	3	3	3	3	2	14
Parents	4	5	3	6	4	22
STEM professionals	2	2	-	3	1	8
University students	5	2	2	-	2	11
Total n =	27	27	30	24	24	132

Table I displays information on participants per each stakeholder group and each country. The largest groups of participants were primary, lower secondary and upper secondary school students. Focus group discussions included no STEM professionals (business or research) in Germany, and no university students in Greece. The number of participants per each country was relatively homogenous ranging from 24 to 30 participants. There were slightly more female ($n = 73$) than male ($n = 59$) participants.

2) Materials

Materials for the focus group sessions involving various stakeholders in the learning environment co-design were developed in collaboration with the partners participating in the STIMEY project, first in English, and then translated into local languages.

Focus group discussions collected participants' wishes related to the main topics covered in the STIMEY project: Teaching and learning, STEM subjects, cross-curricular skills, social media, games and gamification, digital platform, radio, social robots, gender, and safety issues. These topics were presented to the participants in slides, accompanied by images of each topic for inspiration and to evoke discussions. Participants' wishes related to various topics were collected by using an online form with open-ended questions. Focus groups discussions were also recorded.

This paper concentrates on the analysis of the stakeholders' wishes related to social media, more concretely with the following statements:

- I wish the means of social communication…
- I wish user profiles…
- I wish social networking…

Materials were designed based on the grounded theory approach [13]. Instead of referring to specific theories and pre-defining these concepts for participants, we were interested in their ideas and understandings related to these topics.

3) Procedures

The main focus groups' co-design sessions were organized in all project countries at a primary school, lower secondary school, and upper secondary school during the school year 2016-17. Some participants, who could not be present during the main sessions provided their contributions in separate, additional sessions. Participants' written consents, and in the case of minors, also their parents' consents, were asked in advance. After a short description of the STIMEY project, researchers presented the topics to be discussed one by one, using the presentation slides.

Sessions lasted from 90 to 120 minutes with approximately 5 to 10 minutes time to discuss and write down the wishes related to each topic. While open conversation enabled collaborative idea elicitation between stakeholder groups, writing wishes down enabled expressing oneself without feeling constrained to voice their views in front of the others [11]. It also gave less extrovert participants chances to participate. Researchers were careful so as not to influence participants' ideas. In the case there was a need to clarify some concepts or give some examples, participants were reminded that there were no right or wrong responses. Participants were, however, encouraged to think and express their wishes as representatives of their stakeholder group instead of thinking only personal preferences [9].

4) Data Analysis

When analyzing what pedagogical design principles could be identified in stakeholders' wishes related to social media, the previously formulated design principles were used as categories or themes to be coded in the data. For instance, under the principle named as *connectedness*, responses wishing that students would learn how to use social media tools in real-life situations, such as job search were coded. Under *collaborative methods*, responses referring to the use of social media in communication and interaction both within and outside the school community, were coded.

The frequencies of wishes related to each category or theme were calculated. As the purpose of this paper is to identify the connection between the pedagogical design principles and the social media design, the focus is on the most frequent learning and social media related wishes as a whole (n = 132), not as an exact numeric data, but as overall trends and tendencies. Possible country-, gender-, group- or age-based differences are out of the scope of this analysis. Although commonly mentioned in the data, stakeholders' wishes concerning social media aspects which were not related to teaching and learning, such as safety and privacy issues, are not included or discussed herein.

III. RESULTS

The results in this paper focus on the identification of stakeholders' wishes and requirements with respect to social media concepts use in learning, and teaching. In the analysis of these results, seven pedagogical principles were identified to be relevant in the integration of social media concepts, as presented and discussed herein:

- *Teaching and learning aid* was the most commonly cited category of wishes expressed among stakeholders in all countries; it was related to the use of social media as a *Learning/Instructional aid*. Wishes related to the use of social media concepts as supporting aids during learning and instruction processes were grouped under "*Teaching and learning aid*". This refers to the teacher's role in facilitating effective teaching, learning, and assessment, and motivating students [9] through social media tools. For instance, a female upper secondary student in Spain wished that "social communication becomes a tool, and not a waste. That is, it could, for example, bring people to answer questions in real time". A teacher from upper secondary education in Germany highlighted in his statement that "social networks would provide not only superficial information, but deep conversations, good information exchange, and constructive reasoning". Also, a female parent representing upper secondary education in Belarus suggested that social media "could offer information only with informative character".
- *Collaborative methods* were among the most commonly cited categories; this category included ideas and wishes that referred to the use of social media concepts in different forms of group activities in teamwork and/or group work and communication, and collaboration. For example, a female primary education student from Germany mentioned the importance of "having a smartphone and a group, the teacher writes down homework in that group". Furthermore, a male student from upper secondary education in Germany suggested that "[when using social media], you could text with friends, for example, and solve tasks with them or discuss with them".
- *Connectedness with future life and careers* was outlined by many participants who stated that using social media should be connected to the user's future life and choice of career as it offers an opportunity to relate with companies and industries. Such a wish was expressed by a male primary education teacher in Greece, who indicated that "user profile in social media should be restricted only to professional contexts", as well as by a female director in lower secondary in Finland, who suggested that social media "would support professional development". Also, a female upper secondary student in Germany suggested that user profiles "could be of interest to companies for subsequent application submissions. So special activities or accomplishments on STIMEY should be stored in a user profile".
- *Personalization (including also aspects related to customization)* was a category often endorsed by stakeholders in all countries. Personalization in pedagogy mainly refers to considering personal competence level and differences in knowledge, skills, rhythm, and ways of learning [9]. Under this category, wishes related with the ability of users to adopt and adjust the social media according to their preferences were included. For instance, a male STEM professional in Spain wished that a user profile is "designed [by] myself", while a female parent in upper secondary education in Greece wished for "users to register with a name in their profiles, which in turn they would be able to control". In some cases, personalization and customization were related with visibility, namely that users could gain more visibility by showcasing their interests when using social media. This attitude is expressed particularly in the statement of a male student from a primary school in Germany who stated that "[a

user profile should] show my interests like cars, but I do not want to show my grades to other students".

- *Multiple representations* were often highlighted by participants expressing their need to employ multiple types of media and tools in learning and instruction processes. Specifically, wishes which referred to combining any kind of digital or non-digital forms of presenting information including visual, multimedia, audio, text, simulations and animations [9] were included here. As a female student in lower secondary education in Finland suggested: "[An instant messaging tool] could be used in biology classes to upload images and discuss nature and animals". Moreover, a male student from primary education in Germany stated the desire to "share posts about my interests, [using] microphone and audio because I can't type". This desire is also illustrated by a female student in upper secondary education in Spain who hoped to use social media features in learning to ask questions, send photos or make a video call when needing help with homework.
- *Active knowledge construction* was less commonly referred by the participants. Active knowledge construction is conceptualized considering learners' active agency during learning and instruction processes [9]. Particularly, participants related to it in social media concepts with user-generated content. This is reflected in the statement of a female student in upper secondary education in Germany: "[In social networks], one could see videos that other students had created, aiming to instruct and facilitate knowledge learning of a subject, instead of having a teacher teaching the same subject". Finally, a quite informative argument was offered by a female parent in primary education in Greece suggesting that "[social media] could [be used to] provide news, digital tools for ICT, materials in text form and could be used by students, parents, and teachers."
- *Participation and Involvement* appeared more sporadically in data, as the final category. In this category, items referring to participatory, interactive and conversational teaching-learning interaction [9] were included. To illustrate, a male university student in Belarus wished that social networking would "bring together all trainees and trainers into a unified whole, and there would be no barriers in communication between them."

IV. DISCUSSION

With a myriad of social media features, which are continuously changing and growing, it can be a difficult task to list and identify the ones that stakeholders find most interesting and crucial. This might explain the lack of research in this area, as pointed out earlier. To tackle this task, bottom-up and top-down approaches are employed in this study. In the bottom-up approach, the participating stakeholders' wishes on the use of social media in learning and teaching are collected and analyzed for emerging themes and pedagogical design principles. These themes and principles then guide the selection, design and development of various features in the pre-identified social media concepts [8] within the STIMEY platform in a top-down approach. Using various pedagogic scenarios, the approach examines how these social media concepts and features fulfill the pedagogical design principles:

- **User profiles and Social Connections** are designed with functionalities that allow users to register and partake in the platform's learning activities, under the various roles of student, tutor or facilitator/mentor, and connect with each other based on their roles, interests or expertise. Thus, user profiles are fundamental in facilitating students' self-regulated learning and personalized learning while still being connected to teachers who can be present as guides (pedagogical design principle named as *teaching and learning aid).* Functioning as a resume, a user profile also encloses other functionalities, such as an **e-portfolio** that collects a student's learning achievements on the platform and can then be shared with potential employers or educational institutions and personnel (*Connectedness to Future Life and Careers*). User profiles also give users the ability to personalize and customize their presence on the platform with text and images (*Personalization*). Users can express their individual identity and interests in an "**About**" section, as well as on other functionalities in the profile like the **timeline** (or the "wall" [14]) where they can post status updates with *multiple representations* of various rich media (text, images, videos, documents, links, etc.). Finally, in order to participate in (*participation and involvement)* and collaborate on (*collaborative methods)* the *active knowledge construction* on the platform, users need first to register and create profiles that give them access and enable them to utilize the other social media features, such as **connecting** with each other to build networks, by **adding friends** to have permission and access to each other's private profiles, and timeline, or **following users** for their public profiles and timelines. In one pedagogic scenario, we have elaborated based on these considerations, an upper secondary chemistry teacher can search the platform for a Pharmacologist (based on her experience and skills, found on her user profile), connect with her, and message her to invite her to join a discussion with his students on the platform.
- **Status updates and Social Feedback** are designed with functionalities that enable teachers to set up contexts in various pedagogic scenarios (*teaching and learning aid)*, and allow students to share knowledge among each other, as well as with facilitators/mentors as experts, and provide or receive critical feedback (*participation and involvement, collaborative methods and active knowledge construction)*. Status updates also enable self-expression of interests, preferences,

opinions, expertise, etc., (*personalization*)) through functionalities that enable posting media-rich user-generated content containing text, images, videos, etc. (*multiple representations*). The accompanying social feedback functionalities, such as comments and replies, enable the furthering of discussions and knowledge sharing by providing critical feedback on users' status updates. In one possible pedagogic scenario, a primary biology teacher can post a **status update**, asking students to list different types of summer flowers that they will be tasked to plant for a class project. Students can then **comment** on the teacher's status update with photos, videos or links to different types of flowers that they'd like to grow. The teacher can then provide feedback by **replying** to students' comments, to confirm or correct their selections. She can also further the discussion by asking the students to post instructional videos and links to growing their selected flower in their replies. She can also ask the students to read their peers' comments and find a few who have made the same flower selection, in order to form a group that can be tasked with growing their selected flower.

- **Social messaging** is designed with functionalities that enable knowledge sharing and discussions in private bilateral conversations, such as between two peers discussing classwork, or among a predefined group of users, such as a teacher and his/her students continuing an in-class discussion outside of the classroom (*teaching and learning aid*). The rich media (text, images, videos, links, files, etc.) that can be shared in one-on-one or group chat messages, also enable *personalization* with *multiple representation*. The instant nature of social messaging enables quick discussions and easy participation (*participation and involvement*) that are useful during the collaboration between two users or a group of users (*collaborative methods*). In one pedagogic scenario, two lower secondary students working together on a group project can privately message each other when out of class to discuss the nature and structure of the work, share text, images and videos that can be used in the project, and refer to these messages whenever necessary. The students can also share the project file with each other as a message attachment.
- **Communities and Discussions** are designed with functionalities that enable teaching and learning in groups (*collaborative methods*), mirroring a classroom environment online. Teachers can take on a leading role by creating communities or discussion forum topics (*teaching and learning aid*), or a facilitating role by letting students create their own public or private communities and discussion forum topics under his/her supervision and guidance (*active knowledge construction*). At their fundament, communities and discussions are a collection of status updates with accompanying social feedback (*multiple representations*), confined to a preset list of users, who are members of these communities or discussions (*participation and involvement*), that is specific to an interest or topic, usually identified in the community name and description, or the discussion's title and its location under a topic or a course (*personalization*)). In one pedagogic scenario, a lower secondary physics teacher can create a discussion topic, title it "Collision Examples", under her course on crashes and collisions, and ask her students to create their discussions under that topic, listing examples of collisions from everyday life. The students can further their knowledge by researching questions and constructing hypotheses on how the velocity and mass of an object, and the variable of time can affect momentum in these different examples, by reading their peers' discussion posts and the teacher's feedback and providing peer evaluation. The teacher can also encourage the students work in groups. They can create their own private communities, personalize them with a name and photo representing their group, and use them throughout the duration of the project or the course to discuss their work and collaborate on an assignment.

V. Limitations

This study has statistical limitations, stemming from the study design. Particularly, the focus group data collected and analyzed may not be representative of the general population of European students, teachers, parents and professionals targeted by the STIMEY project, due to the small number of participants represented from the 5 European countries. However, focus groups were used to provide qualitative data, that shed light on trends of pedagogical design principles that are in common among stakeholders, and to enrich the understanding of the main findings from the literature review and the researchers' expertise with relevant examples. Moreover, the analysis of the results was limited to the social media concepts that have been previously identified, while there may be several other social media features that can be apt in fulfilling the stakeholders' wishes and requirements, based on the identified pedagogical principle designs.

VI. Conclusion and Future Research

Although social media has gotten increased attention in educational research in the recent decade, most studies focus on the use of popular social networks and technologies outside of the classroom, and how they are perceived by students and teachers, mostly in higher education. There is, however, a lack in studies that examine the perceptions and practices of learners and teachers in primary and secondary education. More research is especially required on the use of social media features in the classroom based on preference and importance, and their impact on students' learning and teacher's pedagogy. One of the objectives of the STIMEY project is to research and adapt a pedagogical framework that exploits the full potential of social media in learning, especially in STEM education. Initial research was geared towards identifying eight key social media concepts, or features, based on popular social networking sites and their potential role as learning tools in a pedagogical learning model. Concurrently, research was carried out on identifying 22 pedagogical design principles in hybrid STEM learning environments, based on focus group data from two European countries, and literature review. In this study, focus group data, from all five European countries represented in the STIMEY project, relevant to the participating stakeholders' wishes on the use of social media in learning and teaching were analyzed. Results from participants' wishes and statements indicated trends of seven pedagogical design principles, such as collaborative methods, teaching and learning aid, and multiple representations. The previously identified social media concepts were then further examined for which features and functionalities they include to fulfill the stakeholders' needs, based on the seven resulting pedagogical design principles. The study has its limitations concerning the size of the focus groups, and the number of social media concepts taken into consideration. However, these limitations have been taken into account for future research, where the focus is on identifying additional social media features and functionalities based on previously collected and emerging stakeholders' requirements, and diverse pedagogical scenarios involving students, teachers, organizations and parents. Finally, user testing and feedback on the STIMEY platform is planned to conduct a mixed qualitative and quantitative study with a larger number of participants which aims to analyze and assess the social media concepts and pedagogical design principles in this study.

ACKNOWLEDGMENT

This project has received funding from the European Union's Horizon 2020 research and innovation programme, Science Technology Innovation Mathematics Engineering for the Young 2016-2019, under grant agreement No 709515.

Any opinions, findings, and conclusions or recommendations expressed in this material reflect only the authors' views and the Union is not liable for any use that may be made of the information contained therein.

REFERENCES

[1] C. Greenhow and E. Askari, "Learning and teaching with social network sites: A decade of research in K-12 related education," *Education and Information Technologies*, vol. 22, no. 2, pp. 623–645, 2015.

[2] J. Kimmerle, J. Moskaliuk, A. Oeberst, and U. Cress, "Learning and Collective Knowledge Construction With Social Media: A Process-Oriented Perspective," *Educ. Psychol.*, vol. 50, no. 2, pp. 120–137, Apr. 2015.

[3] T. Iiyoshi, M. J. Hannafin, and F. Wang, "Cognitive tools and student-centred learning: rethinking tools, functions and applications," *EMI Educ. Media Int.*, vol. 42, no. 4, pp. 281–296, 2005.

[4] B. Kim and T. C. Reeves, "Reframing research on learning with technology: in search of the meaning of cognitive tools," *Instructional Science*, vol. 35, no. 3, pp. 207–256, 2007.

[5] S. Manca and M. Ranieri, "Is it a tool suitable for learning? A critical review of the literature on Facebook as a technology-enhanced learning environment," *Journal of Computer Assisted Learning*, vol. 29, no. 6, pp. 487–504, 2013.

[6] M. Assaad *et al.*, "Attracting European Youths to STEM Education and Careers: A Pedagogical Approach to a Hybrid Learning Environment," *World Academy of Science, Engineering and Technology International Journal of Educational and Pedagogical Sciences*, vol. 11, no. 10, pp. 1216–1222, 2017.

[7] E. Rosenfeld Halverson, "Do social networking technologies have a place in formal learning environments?," *On the Horizon*, vol. 19, no. 1, pp. 62–67, 2011.

[8] M. Assaad and T. Mäkelä, "Integrating Social Media Concepts as Tools in a Pedagogical Approach for a Technology-enhanced Learning Environment," in *AICT 2017 : The Thirteenth Advanced International Conference on Telecommunications*, Venice, Italy, pp. 67–73, 2017.

[9] T. Mäkelä, D. Pnevmatikos, H. Immonen, N. Fachantidis, M. Kankaanranta, and P. Christodoulou, "Considering Various Stakeholders' Views in the Design of a Hybrid STEM Learning Environment - Perceptions From Finland and Greece," in *EDULEARN17 Proceedings*, pp. 5517-5526, 2017, doi:10.21125/edulearn.2017.2257

[10] T. Mäkelä and S. Helfenstein, "Developing a conceptual framework for participatory design of psychosocial and physical learning environments," *Learning Environments Research*, vol. 19, no. 3, pp. 411–440, 2016.

[11] A. Duarte, L. Veloso, J. Marques, and J. Sebastião, "Site-specific focus groups: analysing learning spaces in situ," *International Journal of Social. Research Methodology*, vol. 18, no. 4, pp. 381–398, 2014.

[12] T. Georgiadou, O. Fotakopoulou, and D. Pnevmatikos, *Exploring Bioethical Reasoning in Children and Adolescents Using Focus Groups Methodology*. SAGE Research Methods Cases, 2018, doi:10.4135/9781526445025.

[13] J. Corbin and A. Strauss, *Basics of qualitative research (3rd ed.): Techniques and procedures for developing grounded theory,* Thousand Oaks, CA: SAGE Publications Ltd, 2008, doi: 10.4135/9781452230153.

[14] "What is a Facebook Wall? - Definition from Techopedia," *Techopedia.com*. [Online]. Available: https://www.techopedia.com/definition/5170/facebook-wall. [Accessed: 09-Jul-2018].

Improvement of an Existing Microservices Architecture for an E-learning Platform in STEM Education

David Alessandro Bauer, Benjamin Penz, Juho Mäkiö, Manal Assaad
Department of Informatics and Electronics
University of Applied Sciences Emden/Leer
Emden, Germany
Email: david.bauer@hs-emden-leer.de, benjamin.penz@hs-emden-leer.de, juho.maekioe@hs-emden-leer.de, manal.assaad@hs-emden-leer.de

***Abstract*— This paper demonstrates and evaluates the technical improvement of an existing prototype of the STIMEY e-learning platform based on a microservices architectural pattern. The first approach is using our page fragments technology that allows to integrate contents of other microservices in a superordinate context but lead to difficulties regarding maintenance. The second approach holds all page fragments in one microservice, and the specific data is provided separately by domain-specific microservices which makes it easier to work with them, in case of the STIMEY platform, because domain-specific designers can now be assigned to just one respective microservice. Additionally, a conception to migrate the platform to Amazon Web Services (AWS) in the future is shown. A novel three-dimensional architecture model is introduced to visualize the used microservices' architectural pattern. Three patterns are shown for the data access of the individual microservices and for their interconnectedness. At the end, it is discussed how the database design can be implemented.**

Keywords-STEM Education; E-learning; Web platform; Microservices; Architecture; Page fragments; Data Access; Database Design.

I. INTRODUCTION

As modern IT-technologies, like cloud computing and mobile computing, get more and more complex, difficulties with development and maintenance increase as well, thus driving innovation and research pressure to cope with these problems. This led to the construction of concepts like Domain-Driven Design, Continuous Integration, scalable systems and Software as a Service, which form the base of the idea of microservices. Microservices are applications that consist of a set of small, independent services in contrast to the large, monolithic kind of software systems [1]. Each microservice follows its own task but works together with other microservices to fulfill a more general purpose. This approach has several advantages such as [1]:

- the use of different technologies. Because every microservice is isolated, they can run on different platforms, and can even be implemented in different programming languages.
- that it is highly scalable. In contrast to monolithic architectures, the different parts of an architecture based on microservices can be scaled independently.
- a better exchangeability. Microservices can be exchanged independently, instead of the need to exchange the whole system, as it is the case with monolithic architectures
- a more convenient deployment. Each microservice can be deployed separately. With the monolithic approach, the whole system needs to be deployed in one, even if only small amounts of code have been changed.

Although the importance of microservices continually increases, research about this topic is mainly limited on the theoretical concept of microservices itself. [1] Therefore, this paper focuses on the applied architecture of a practical use-case. The explained architecture in this article has been developed for a project to research and create a Science, Technology, Engineering and Mathematics (STEM) related e-learning platform called Science, Technology, Engineering and Mathematics for the Young (STIMEY). The STIMEY [2] project is funded by the European Union and started in September 2016. The purpose of the platform is to interest young people to STEM and to bring teachers, students and their parents together to support STEM related learning and to increase the continent's international competitiveness in that regard.

This paper aims at:

- a concrete use-case of an microservice architecture, the STIMEY platform,
- a conception for migrating to Amazon Web Services (PaaS) is shown,
- a novel visualization of the microservice architecture is illustrated,
- a novel page fragments technology will be introduced, and
- an overview of database implementation in context of microservices is given.

The paper is divided in five sections, starting with a brief description of the STIMEY platform in Section 2. The following section proffers a literature review on microservices is provided in related works. The fourth section presents and discusses the architecture of the STIMEY platform that uses microservices as a basic building block. The section covers mainly the above listed contributions. The paper then concludes with a conclusion in the last section.

II. THE STIMEY PLATFORM

This section first motivates and then gives a brief overview of the STIMEY platform.

The international competitiveness of Europe strongly depends on the availability of good educated engineers [3]. To get good educated engineers, the STEM education must be more relatable to European youths to raise their interests and involvement in STEM careers. This interest needs to be awoken already at the school. This is the aim of the STIMEY project. To reach this overall goal, STIMEY project proposes a multichannel hybrid e-learning platform for STEM-Education. The platform provides e-learning components that are designed and developed on the base of a well-researched pedagogical framework [4] that is to be developed in the STIMEY project. By doing so, STIMEY aims to lower the barrier of young people to consider a STEM career as an attractive career alternative.

The participation of multiple parties is needed, unified in the STIMEY platform to reach the overall goal of the STIMEY project. Consequently, within the STIMEY platform not only students come together with their teachers. Additionally, other stakeholders, like universities, schools, parents, business and media partners need to join together to reach the common goal and to make STEM a natural part of the daily life of youths. By doing so we hope to give students the feeling that what they do is important and valuable, and we open all stakeholders an ability to demonstrate their engagement for the STEM education [5].

One of the central ideas of the STIMEY project is to get close to the interests and social identity of the students. For this, the STIMEY is constructed to be a socially motivational platform that supports and motivates students towards STEM subjects.

To do so, the STIMEY contains components that the students are familiar with, like social media and games to stimulate the emotional and educational engagement. There also exists a gamification-oriented [6] reward system that enables students to earn badges. These components are there to help with the intrinsic motivation of the students towards STEM subjects.

For example, the integrated social media tools enable the students to communicate about the STEM topics or to help each other in making exercises. The integrated games in turn are constructed such that the students can learn during gaming. The STIMEY-robot is a socially-assistive learning buddy that supports students and gives them feedback. The idea is to effectively use robot fellow artefacts for pupils' emotional engagement, community bonding, efficient learning and motivation. Additionally, within the platform it will be possible to program the STIMEY-robot using a simple command set that is integrated in the STIMEY platform. The STIMEY-radio allows students to get on demand broadcasting programs about STEM subjects [7]. The integrated STIMEY e-portfolio provides the possibility for the students individually to collect information about courses and activities the student has participated in. Additionally, the STIMEY platform will contain entrepreneurial tools for engaging schoolchildren in innovations and stimulating their creative thinking. In order to integrate a wide array of existing educational tools, we have created in cooperation with SCIENTIX a mechanism to integrate existing tools such as solutions provided from SCIENTIX (Community for science education in Europe) in the STIMEY-platform.

The platform is constructed gender-neutral, so that boys and girls alike can identify with the components contained therein. The challenge of STIMEY is to reach even those students who are not enthusiastic about STEM. Especially girls are underrepresented in the STEM-sector. To be gender-inclusive means for STIMEY means that it supports a wide range of user behavior to provide low-threshold access to the platform.

The second central idea of the STIMEY project is to provide teachers the necessary modern tools to teach STEM in an attractive and engaging manner in-class or remotely, while also following up on students' progress. For this, the platform allows teachers to create their own courses and curse materials, to reuse the materials when creating new courses. Whether the content is more theoretical, or more practical and interactive, is determined by the teacher. The teachers are also able to reuse their created materials when creating new courses. Additionally, teachers may share their courses and course materials with other teachers. This supports the community building among teachers for example to share experiences in using the STIMEY in classes.

Other stakeholders, like parents and companies, are supported in suitable way. For example, parents are able to get information about the current state of the studies of their children or to communicate with their teachers and companies are able to add educational material into the platform.

For security reasons, it is considered to store personal data on different servers, to prevent developers and administrators who work on the platform, and possible attackers, to link data which is stored on the platform to personal information. Every user can determine who has access to his/her shared data.

The STIMEY components are based on a thorough research. The fundamental research focuses among others the following questions:

- Why STEM education is an issue today?
- Why STEM careers are not popular among young people?
- How to motivate and encourage young people to go for STEM careers? and
- What makes STEM unattractive or uninteresting and how positive aspects can be emphasized more?

To answer these questions, we are currently creating and implementing a novel pedagogical framework that exploits the full potentials of Social Media for STEM subjects in formal and informal contexts. Therefore, the major target groups and stakeholders are integrated into the development process. Additionally, to track the students' performance progress, suitable measurements methods, algorithms and tool are under development

All components integrated in the STIMEY-platform serve the goal to raise the attractiveness of STEM subjects among European youth. From the European perspective, it is important that the STIMEY-platform harmonizes with the STEM education in European schools. This is important to reach a critical mass of end users who will be motivated for a STEM career.

III. Related Work

Microservices is a young architectural pattern, which follows the idea of service-oriented computing (SOA). SOA started as an attempt to overcome the drawbacks of monolithic software architectures. It provides loosely coupled services, each usually focused on one specific business process. The services are reusable and could be put together dynamically to address issues in continually changing business environments [8]. Although software that follows SOA architecture can consist of several internal services, the whole product has to be deployed as one unit, leaving it still monolithic, as [9] point out. To maintain scalability, copies of the whole application have to be used, which is not efficient regarding memory consumption. While such architecture makes it easy to develop and deploy large software, it also makes it costly to modify and maintain these applications, because they are difficult to understand. [9]

These problems lead to the development of alternative architectures that aim to conform to modern needs by breaking down the application into smaller independent services [9]. In 2012, a group of software architects chose the term microservices as the most fitting one for the common architectures they had been examining in recent time [1]. Before that, the concept of microservices has been known under different names, e.g. Adrian Cockcroft at Netflix called it "Fine grained SOA" [11]. Dragoni et al. say that there is no common definition of microservices, and therefore the concept is still in its infancy [12]. However, principal features of microservices have been defined by M. Fowler and J. Lewis [11]. For instance, microservices based architectures consist of small independently upgradable, replaceable and reusable components that can be deployed separately. If the code of one microservice is altered, only the microservice itself is affected and must be redeployed, instead of needing the whole application to be deployed again. Another feature of microservices is decentralized governance. The used technology for implementing a specific microservice can be chosen independently. Therefore, different Microservices can use different kinds of databases. The code of microservices can also be written in different programming languages, as long as a common interface is used to handle the communication between the microservices [1]. Other authors like S. Newman, E. Wolff and A. Gupta built on the work of M. Fowler and J. Lewis to make concrete suggestions for conceptions and designs of architectures based on microservices [14][15][16][17]. Villamizar et al. [10] show a slight cost reduction by using microservices instead of a monolithic architecture. The average response time does not differ so much for the microservice architecture (although there is an overhead, through additional server instances). [10] Microservices were introduced in a lot of large companies, to overcome their growing needs of more scalability. For example, Google, Amazon, Microsoft, Netflix and Zalando have successfully introduced microservices for their business [10][13].

A systematic literature research has been conducted by Pahl and Jamshidi to collect and review the existing research on microservices. They discovered that a great amount of research about microservices is only theoretical and just a minor part of studies deals with actual technological solutions [18], leaving a research gap in that department.

One possible use case of microservices is web-based e-learning platforms like the STIMEY platform. D. Chandran and S. Kempegowda [17] state that irrespective of free or commercial products, the implementation of the hardware and software infrastructure are highly cost intensive. Although free e-learning software like Moodle is free to use, the high cost of installation, maintenance, as well as the high learning curve, could make them even more expensive then commercial products. In addition, existing e-learning solutions are often unable to collaborate with other educational facilities or dynamically scale the application. Also, the integration with other systems is expensive due to the proprietary nature of the existing e-learning solutions. Another issue is that in many cases the available hardware is not suitable for web 2.0 applications. D. Chandran and S. Kempegowda therefore propose a cloud-based solution for three defined scenarios to overcome these disadvantages [19]. With cloud-computing free resources can be allocated efficiently, thus providing reduced energy consumption and less costs.

Fazakas et al. [20] propose a technical solution for a collaborative e-learning platform based on microservices. The platform aims at making teaching and learning objectives easier by implementing loosely-coupled software modules. These modules provide synchronous learning functionalities like video communication or text-based chats, and asynchronous functionalities like multimedia authoring.

Martin et al. [21] describe and compare the two different approaches virtual machines and containers for the realization of cloud-based computing. Virtual machines are therefore fully functional operating systems that are running on top of a virtual hardware layer. The advantages of virtual machines are that they can be installed very quickly and booted within a few seconds. They also can be cloned and stacked with centralized tools. Disadvantages are that the additional layers for emulated hardware and operating system come with a significant overhead in performance. In contrast, containers come with performance near that of single-tenant physical servers. In addition, with containers, multiple instances of applications can be run on one single machine. Containers are also very lightweight, because of the absence of system libraries, which makes the boot-process very fast, and makes it possible to create and move containers almost instantly. This enables high scalability [21][22]. Docker is the most used container technology. Based on that it exists also a Kubernetes [23] (orchestrator of containers) solution, former provided by Google (see also

Borg [24], predecessor to Kubernetes). An alternative to Kubernetes is Docker Swarm.

Another paradigm that supports large-scale cloud computing applications is serverless computing or function as a service (FaaS) that is an event-driven approach, utilizing lightweight processes that react to an event. The first service that follows serverless computing is AWS Lambda by Amazon Web Services [25]. For example, Google and Microsoft provide serverless computing services. [26][27]

An evaluation of different cloud computing services has been made by McGrath et al., showing the potential of the underlying technology on two use cases. For instance, systems using serverless computing are more scalable and flexible than previous technologies. [28] Using of AWS Lambda can reduce costs significantly, by 50-60% instead of using microservices [29].

IV. Architecture of the STIMEY Platform

It was decided to use microservices for the entire platform, which allows for development to take place in small separate teams. Microservices are autonomous, isolated services that are loosely coupled with other services. In general, every microservice has its own data storage (i.e., database, so redundancies are accepted). However, sharing the database may be appropriate for simplification. The data models must be kept separate from each other. Microservices can, for example, communicate via REST or WebSockets but they can also have a web interface. Furthermore, microservices are easily scalable, if they are stateless (no use of sessions). All required data must be loaded from the cache or the database directly.

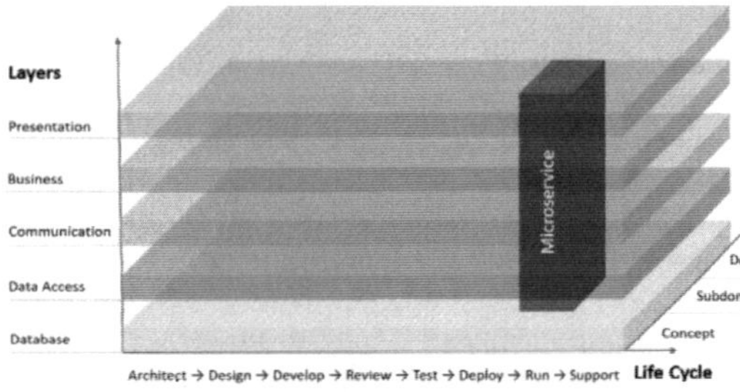

Figure 1. Microservice Architecture Model.

In Figure 1 a novel visualization of the microservice architecture model is presented. In this model microservices may implement multiple layers. Normally, a microservice includes the business logic layer (inclusively offering of services to the outside) and the data access logic to the database (persistence). The communication layer as described above can be implemented using web protocols. In addition, a presentation layer may be included (HTML, JSON and XML). DDD stands for Domain Driven Design by Eric Evans ([30][31]). A concept is the smallest unit within a subdomain (categorization of related concepts). A bounded context is a subset that can be spanned in multiple subdomains. A domain can contain several functional subdomains. The life cycle consists of steps that a microservice goes through: the beginning design, development, testing and production. Maintenance and support are the last stage, or the microservice will be replaced by a better solution and the life cycle starts again. The Reference Architecture Model Industry 4.0 (RAMI4.0) [32] had significant influence in creating Figure 1, which depicts the Microservice architecture model.

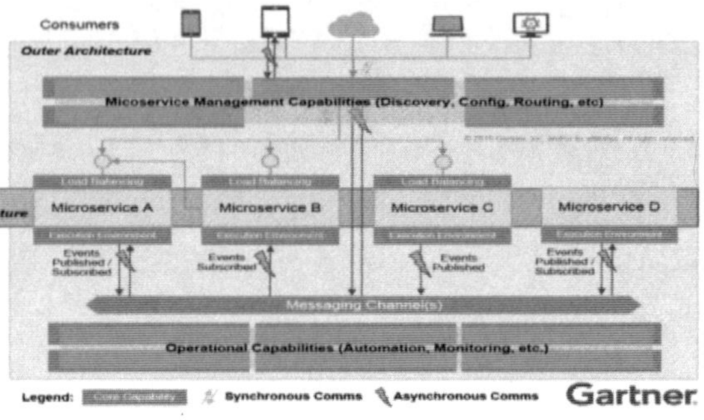

Figure 2. Inner and outer architecture of microservices. [33]

According to Olliffe [33], the platform's internal and external architecture is described in connection with microservices (see Figure 2). The external architecture includes, among other things, tools for configuration, routing, discovery of other microservices, monitoring, and automation (deployment). The microservices themselves are described in the internal architecture and are developed independently from each other. The communication among them is best done asynchronously, while there may be multiple instances of one microservice. A load balancer can be connected to all individual microservices to improve the distribution of workloads, for which the round-robin strategy is commonly used. State changes or notifications can be exchanged by microservices via the so-called messaging channels.

Every microservice on STIMEY platform belongs to one domain, whereas a domain consists of related topics. Each microservice is assigned to one responsible team. All microservices make use of the same technology, for better maintenance. For one, it is easier for the small core team to cope with only one technology. For another, there is a high fluctuance of additional team members (internships, project work, bachelor and master thesis), who can be trained faster that way. One advantage of microservices is that they are fine granular, so they can be easily scaled. There is also no single point of failure, because there are redundant instances for each microservice, and all microservices are not deployed together, like it is the case with a monolithic architecture. That way, older versions of microservices can be replaced during runtime.

A. *Use of Microservices in the STIMEY Platform*

The STIMEY platform in the actual version is divided into several independently developed domains (here: middle-tier, see Figure 3) that are researched, identified and detailed in previous research [4], such as:

- User profile: a visual display of the personal data associated with a specific user in the platform [34].

- Activity stream: typically, a dashboard, where tracked activities or events relevant to a user, community, topic or anything in the platform it's built in [35].
- Community: an online space where individuals can feel part of a group and interact on a common topic or interest by creating posts, commenting, reading in such interest- and niche-specific forums [36].
- Social messaging: refers to the exchange of text messages through a chat tool in real-time [37].
- Online-Course: a supervised learning option for web browsers or mobile applications, that consists of a series of lessons [38].

The communication between microservices works by either calling each other's REST-API, or by messaging (Publish-subscribe), whereas subscribers will be notified by the occurrence of new messages belonging to the subscribed topic. For instance, the gamification microservice (topic: "gamificationstream") must be informed by rewardable activities from other microservices to improve the motivation and experience of the users. Also, for the activity stream, it is necessary to interact with other microservices to access their data which is necessary to calculate the ranking, so that activities or events relevant to the user can be shown in descending order corresponding to the given rank, starting by the highest rank for an activity or event.

The backend includes the microservices for the data access layer (stored files, cache, messaging system, and database for persisting data). The main microservice is part of the frontend, especially for login and sign-up and as a relaying layer (implemented as a proxy) to the underlying middle-tier microservices. It also contains the superordinate web pages of the STIMEY platform (using the technology of page fragments) where the individual microservices are embedded. These should be scalable for further development. Within the microservices, no classic server-based session data is held (data access is via the backend). It should also be noted that a REST-API exists for the platform/robot communication. Furthermore, the platform-to-robot (P2R) communication can be established by an Message Queue Telemetry Transport (MQTT) - Adapter (robot has subscribed on specific topic), which is an integrated part of the messaging service.

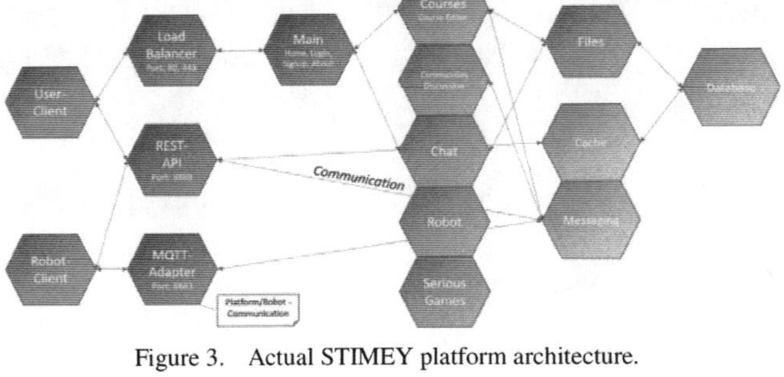

Figure 3. Actual STIMEY platform architecture.

During the login process in the main microservice, an access token is stored as a cookie on the user's browser, which is used for subsequent authentication. Furthermore, a language cookie is also stored for the purpose of multi-language support.

The microservices are deployed in Docker containers, running on CoreOS (Container Linux). This ensures an increased failure safety, as the containers can be restarted accordingly in the event of a failure. The entropy of the system, and hence the error rate, is reduced since the same conditions are always present for the system (in the form of containers, operating system virtualization). There exists also a Kubernetes solution, called Tectonic, which comes from the CoreOS team as well.

This microservice architecture was chosen at first, to follow a different approach for research, instead of the classical approach (mainly over REST-API's). The main microservice uses the page fragments technology, which is explained more in detail in the Section B. Different from the classical approach the microservices provide also their own web pages in the presentation layer. This avoids the maintenance of all web pages in a centralistic way. The main microservice aggregates them in a superordinate context and sends the final web page to the client. In general, the page fragments technology works as intended, but it has to be extended, or further research is necessary, to find a way how it works more smoothly. In the current situation, the whole site will be newly rendered when the page is aggregated, including header, footer and side-menu. A possible solution could be to update only the changing fragment. This has to be further considered.

At the moment, we are planning to migrate to our new architecture model (Figure 4), that is similar to the classical approach of a microservice architecture. The development team recognized that it is more efficient to have the web pages on the same place, because there is an imbalance of developers to designers (much more developers). It is considered as ideal to have interdisciplinary teams working on microservices [15]. One is responsible for the frontend, one for the backend and one for the overall design. We currently do only server-side rendering (using Spring MVC, Model-View-Controller pattern) and plan to switch to client-side rendering (using Vue.js and React.js). This could at least reduce server load. Of course, this also has the disadvantage for the client that it has the costs of processing. One important aspect of the future of the STIMEY platform is also, to make it long-term production ready, as it is only a prototype as of now. This enables the possibility to migrate the STIMEY platform to a PaaS in the future. This reduces the risks involved with self-realizing a microservice architecture. PaaS from established vendors are much more optimized in scalability, resilience, managing, efficiency and uptime. The long-term costs can be reduced, because not so much manpower is needed, and vendors can organize the distribution of their service more efficiently over the world.

The main difference between the old and new architecture (Figure 4) is that with the new architecture only REST-API microservices are used for the communication of the corresponding domains, without providing additional web pages for each microservice. The REST-Service can be called by the REST-API-Gateway that can orchestrate other services or proxies them to the right target. Instead of a main microservice that assembles page fragments coming from different microservices, there is now a storage microservice that holds all the web pages. All teams are working on this microservice and the corresponding REST-API microservice, for which they are responsible. Additionally, there can be used a FaaS service [39] optionally, which is using Vert.x (a Java alternative to Node.js) in combination with actor4j [40] (an actor-oriented framework). The advantage, in comparison to REST-Services, is that they are finer granulated and light weighted. That way, thousands of stateless functions (or actors) can be deployed easily, in contrast to REST-API microservices, which are heavy weighted. Normally, functions are isolated in containers [41], for security and resilience reasons. In an own maintaining FaaS service this is not mandatory, because the underlying functions can be trusted. It would be otherwise, if different contributors were involved. This results in further performance advances. The serious games microservice is using the Apache web server and PHP and is developed from our partner from Belarus. The REST-API-Gateway can be monitored for generating statistics and further analysis of collected data.

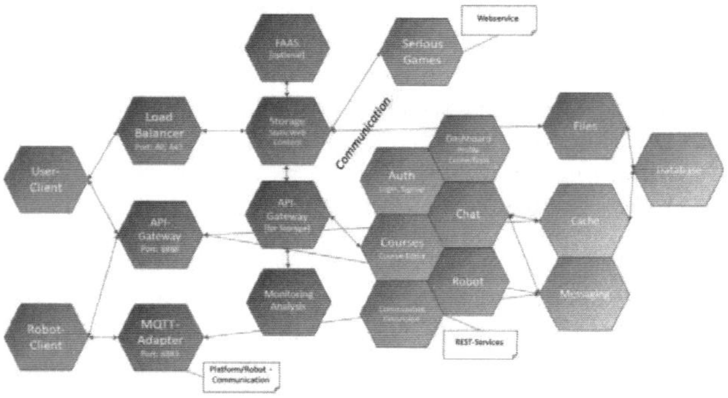

Figure 4. Planned STIMEY platform architecture.

The above described architecture, without page fragments technology, is very suitable to a possible migration to Amazon Web Services (Figure 5). The storage in Figure 4 corresponds to Amazon S3 in Figure 5. In both architectures, there is an API-Gateway for handling according requests sent from the client. Amazon Web Services has an authentification service called Amazon Cognito. This was implemented in the architecture shown in Figure 4 as an independet REST-Service called Auth. The API-Gateway can be monitored in both concepts (in Amazon called CloudWatch). Underlying services can use caching systems, also combined with data storage. It is also possible to use a publish-subscribe system, e.g. for the intercommunication of the services. In Amazon, there are also the Lambda Functions that are more cost-effective than API-calls shown by Villamizar [29]. Our REST services, as seen in Figure 4, are deployed in Docker Containers, so they can be easily migrated to Amazon ECS (Elastic Container Service) later. FaaS has its advantages, but it still has to be proven in practice, whether it is worthwhile to use it with accompanying greater complexity (thousands of light weighted functions) [42].

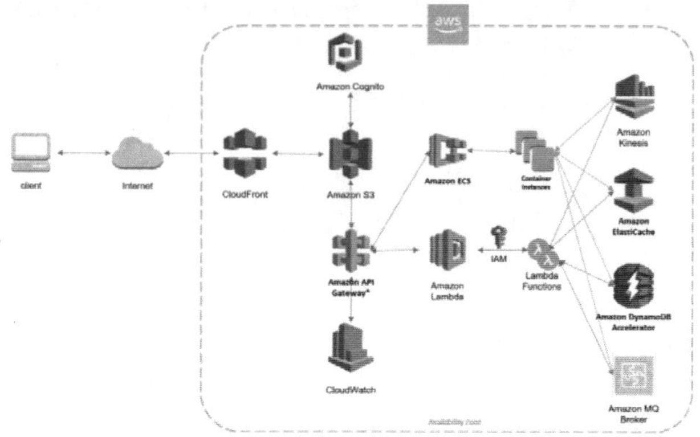

Figure 5. Conception of STIMEY platform architecture with Amazon AWS.

From the beginning, it was not planned to use Amazon Web Services or other PaaS, such as Microsoft Azure and Google Cloud Platform. For some companies, for privacy reasons and protection of intellectual property, an on-premise solution is more preferable. One of the requirements is to use only open-source software to keep the costs low. We decided to use Java as a core-language, because it is widely used and taught on universities. As mentioned before, it is difficult to realize and to maintain an own solution of a microservice architecture, especially in the long-term perspective. In contrast to that, there are open-source solutions like Serverless Framework [43], which makes it easy to switch between different cloud-computing providers (Azure Functions, AWS Lambda, Google Cloud Functions). There are also different providers for container solutions, like Google Kubernetes Engine or, like mentioned above, Amazon ECS and Azure Container Service (also over Kubernetes). "Kubernetes is an open-source system for automating deployment, scaling, and management of containerized applications." [23] At the current stage of prototyping, an on-premise approach is for us the best solution to fulfill the above mentioned requirements and initial goals.

B. *Use of Page Fragments Technology in the STIMEY Platform*

A microservice that uses the page fragments technology can integrate outputs of microservices in a superordinate defined web page.

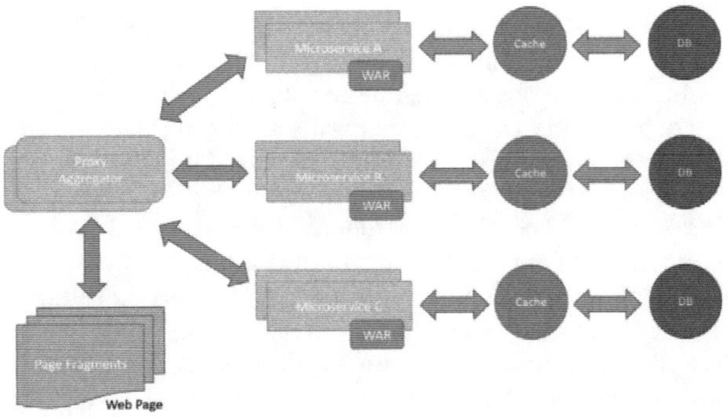

Figure 6. Proxy-Aggregator Design Pattern for page fragments technology, adapted from Gupta. (adapted to [44]and [16])

Here, a proxy server is used that aggregates the individual page fragments (Proxy-Aggregator Design Pattern, see Figure 6), that are references to a microservice that is embedded in the superordinate web page. According to Gupta [16][44], this pattern can be seen as a mixture of the Proxy Microservice Design Pattern and the Aggregator Microservice Design Pattern. It differs only in that way that the microservices are not only REST endpoints. Instead, they are microservices which have also their own web pages (the so-called page fragments) in the presentation layer.

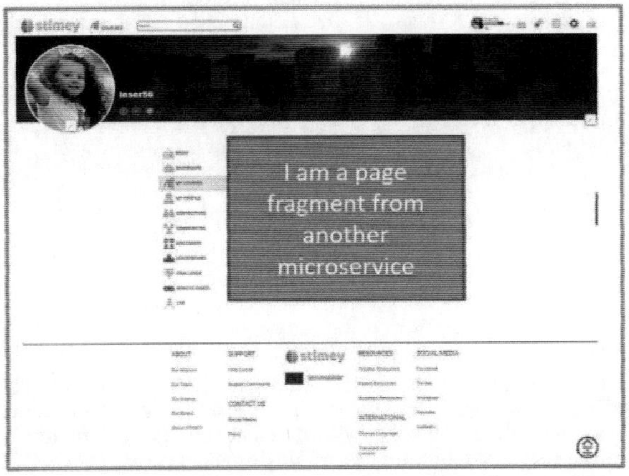

Figure 7. Illustrated example to our platform, showing an embedded microservice.

Figure 7 displays an example based on our future platform, whereas the content of a microservice is embedded in the superordinate web page.

The implementation [45] of the page fragments technolgy is a developed derivative of Smiley's HTTP-Proxy-Servlet (maintained by the MITRE Corporation). Zalando has a similar concept [46] and [47], where fragments (parts of a microservice) where developed by diverse teams (see Figure 8). The "layout service assembles the fragments and streams them to the client" [46]; see also BigPipe [48] by Facebook mentioned in [47].

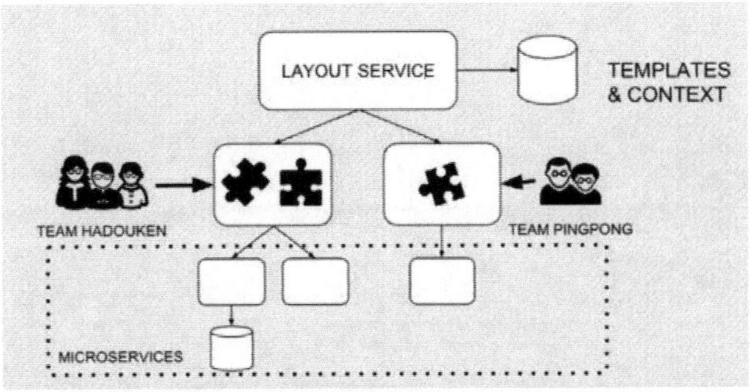

Figure 8. Layout service for front-end microservices [46][47]

C. *Use of Caching/Volatile caching and messaging in the STIMEY platform*

In the previous architecture, for caching/volatile caching and messaging the library was divided into two parts. Either an actor-oriented approach (Actor4j [40] comparable to Akka), or a classic implementation could be used (Redis as cache, NoSQL for persistence, RabbitMQ for messaging). The patterns: "non-volatile caching", "volatile caching", and "messaging", offer the possibility to use messaging channels (state changes and notifications) via appropriate interfaces. The messaging pattern is a special pattern for chatting and message-based content. Only the caching and messaging patterns allow persistence of content.

D. *Design of Database Structure*

As shown in Figure 9, the model is split into different domains. The new database model is a separate model tailored to the needs of individual microservices (largely independent database models). A document-oriented NoSQL database is used as a database. This ensures efficient data processing even with large amounts of data. Known document-oriented NoSQL databases are, for example, MongoDB and CouchDB. A major advantage is the simple serialization / deserialization of the data binding objects into a database document and vice versa (document is stored in the form of a readable JSON string). For the documentation, it is helpful to not only display persistent data structures, but also data structures in the cache, because the data structure of the database is not necessarily the same as the data structure of the cache. Furthermore, the data flow between client and server should be shown in the superordinate context, because the data depends on external triggers. Because of the complexity of the microservice architecture, an extended view is necessary that includes all data structures and the corresponding processes. The whole system is developed in an agile environment so the data structures (and their underlying processes) are subject to evolutionary development processes.

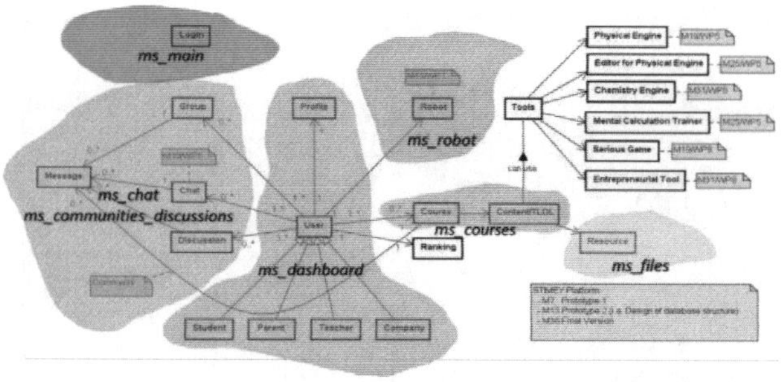

Figure 9. General database structure illustrating microservices affiliation.

V. CONCLUSION

This paper aims at contributing an example of how microservice architecture can be used to build a web platform in practice. This goal has been achieved by introducing the STIMEY platform as a use-case for microservice architecture, and how the architecture has been structured to fulfill the requirements. In addition, the first conception of a future architecture is shown, that builds on the lessons the development team has learned from the work on the current architecture.

The STIMEY platform is divided in several domains, each focused on one specific task, such as user profile, activity streams, and communities. With the microservices approach, each domain is realized by its own microservice. The current architecture of the STIMEY platform has a main microservice as the central hub for server-client communication.

In the current architecture, the main microservice uses the page fragments technology to assemble the outputs of other microservices to a resulting web page and streams them to the client. However, it turned out to be more efficient to have the web pages on one place. For one, the designers can work on only one microservice. For another, the concept of separation of concerns is followed more strictly that way, which makes it easier for the software developers to divide their work. Now they can work in pairs on a domain. One developer is responsible for the REST-API, and the other developer is responsible for the implementation of the front-end with client-side-rendering.

No session data is stored on the server-side, but an access token is stored as a cookie in the client-side browser. To increase failure-safety, docker containers are used for deployment of the microservices. The current system does server-side rendering, using Spring MVC. To reduce server-side cost, it is planned to use client-side rendering with the utilization of Vue.js and React.js in the future. The current architecture uses REST-API for the communication between microservices.

For future-proof scalability, resilience, and efficiency, it is also planned to use FaaS. This is going to make the microservices more lightweight, and to increase the performance significantly. The shift to the new architecture is also suitable for the usage of cloud services like Amazon Web Services that could be used in the future as an option.

The STIMEY platform supports volatile caching, non-volatile caching, and messaging, whereas non-volatile caching and messaging enable persistent data storage.

To fulfill the needs of particular microservices, largely independent database models are used, each modeled specifically to meet the requirements of their corresponding microservice. To allow efficient processing of data, a document-oriented NoSQL database is used.

It is planned to develop testing scenarios in the future to cater with multiple test-cases. Also, a case study that is focused on the research questions introduced in section II is going to be conducted.

ACKNOWLEDGMENT

This project has received funding from the European Union's Horizon 2020 Research and Innovation Program under Grant Agreement Nº 709515 — STIMEY.

REFERENCES

[1] D. Namiot and M. Sneps-Sneppe, "On Micro-services Architecture," International Journal of Open Information Technologies ISSN: 2307-8162 vol. 2, no. 9, 2014.

[2] STIMEY, "Grant Agreement," no. 709515, 2015.

[3] European Union, "EU STEM Coalition: STEM Skills for a Future-Proof Europe," April 2016.

[4] M. Assaad and T. Mäkelä, "Integrating Social Media Concepts as Tools in a Pedagogical Approach for a Technology-enhanced Learning Environment," in K. Daimi and S. Semenov (Eds.), *AICT 2017: The Thirteenth Advanced International Conference on Telecommunications* (pp. 67-73), IARIA, 2017, [Online]. Available from: http://www.thinkmind.org/download.php?articleid=aict_2017_4_30_10061 [retrieved: June, 2018]

[5] M. Assaad, J. Mäkiö, T. Mäkelä, M. Kankaanranta, N. Fachantidis, V. Dagdilelis, A. Reid, C. Rioja del Rio, E. V. Pavlysh, and S. V. Piashkun, "Attracting European Youths to STEM Education and Careers: A Pedagogical Approach to a Hybrid Learning Environment," World Academy of Science, Engineering and Technology International Journal of Educational and Pedagogical Sciences, vol. 11, no. 10, 2017

[6] M. Assaad and S. Shi, "Using the Thematic Approach in Integration with Social Media and Gamification for Concept Design in a Hybrid STEM Learning Environment," 1st International Conference on Educational Technology, 2017.

[7] A. Reid, J. Mäkiö, R. Serrano, and C. Rioja Del Rio, "Conventional radio, the latest motivation to learn science among European youth," International Conference on Education and New Learning Technologies, March 2017

[8] L. Ismail, D. Hagimont, and J. Mossi'ere, "Evaluation of the mobile agents technology: Comparison with the client/server paradigm," Information Science and Technology (IST), vol. 19, 2000.

[9] D. Namiot and M. Sneps-Sneppe, "On micro-services architecture," International Journal of Open Information Technologies, vol. 2, no. 9, 2014.

[10] M. Villamizar et al., "Evaluating the monolithic and the microservice architecture pattern to deploy web applications in the cloud," 2015 10th Computing Colombian Conference (10CCC), Bogota, pp. 583-590, 2015.

[11] M. Fowler and J. Lewis, "Microservices," 2014, [Online]. Available from: http://martinfowler.com/articles/microservices.html [retrieved: June, 2018]

[12] N. et al. Dragoni, “Microservices: Yesterday, Today, and Tomorrow,” in M. Mazzara, B. Meyer (eds) Present and Ulterior Software Engineering, Springer, Cham, 2017.

[13] T. Mauro, “Adopting microservices at netflix: Lessons for team and process design,” 2015, [Online]. Available from: http://nginx.com/blog/adopting-microservices-at-netflix-lessons-for-team-and-process-design/ [retrieved: June, 2018]

[14] S. Newman, “Building Microservices,” O'Reilly Media, Inc, 2015.

[15] E. Wolff, “Microservices,” dpunkt.verlag GmbH, 2016.

[16] A. Gupta. "Getting Started with Microservices," DZone refcardz, Refcard #215, Former version.

[17] V. Reynolds and A. Gupta. "Getting Started with Microservices. Design Patterns for Decomposing the Monolith," DZone refcardz, Refcard #215, [Online]. Available from: https://dzone.com/refcardz/getting-started-with-microservices [retrieved: June, 2018]

[18] C. Pahl and P. Jamshidi, “Microservices: A Systematic Mapping Study,” 2016, [Online]. Available from: https://www.researchgate.net/publication/302973857_Microservices_A_Systematic_Mapping_Study [retrieved: June, 2018]

[19] D. Chandran and S. Kempegowda, "Hybrid E-learning platform based on cloud architecture model: A proposal," 2010 International Conference on Signal and Image Processing, Chennai, pp. 534-537, 2010.

[20] B. P. Fazakas, O. C. Iuonas, C. Porumb, and B. Iancu, "Collaborative learning tools for formal and informal engineering education," 2017 16th RoEduNet Conference: Networking in Education and Research (RoEduNet), Targu Mures, pp. 1-6, 2017.

[21] A. Martin, S. Raponi, T. Combe, and R. Di Pietro, “Docker ecosystem – Vulnerability Analysis,” Computer Communications, vol. 122, pp. 30-43, 2018.

[22] V. Singh and S. K. Peddoju, "Container-based microservice architecture for cloud applications," 2017 International Conference on Computing, Communication and Automation (ICCCA), Greater Noida, pp. 847-852, 2017

[23] Kubernetes, [Online]. Available from: https://kubernetes.io/ [retrieved: June, 2018].

[24] Kubernetes, Kubernetes Blog, “Borg: The Predecessor to Kubernetes,” 2015, [Online]. Available from: https://kubernetes.io/blog/2015/04/borg-predecessor-to-kubernetes [retrieved: June, 2018]

[25] Amazon, “Amazon Lambda (AWS Lambda),” [Online]. Available from: https://aws.amazon.com/lambda/ [retrieved: June, 2018]

[26] Google, “Google Cloud Functions,” [Online]. Available from: https://cloud.google.com/functions/ [retrieved: June, 2018].

[27] Microsoft, “Microsoft Azure Functions,” [Online]. Available from: https://azure.microsoft.com/en-in/services/functions/ [retrieved, June, 2018].

[28] G. Mcgrath, J. Short, S. Ennis, and B. Judson, P. Brenner, “Cloud event programming paradigms: Applications and analysis,” in: 2016 IEEE 9th International Conference on Cloud Computing, CLOUD, pp. 400–406, 2016.

[29] M. Villamizar et al., "Infrastructure Cost Comparison of Running Web Applications in the Cloud Using AWS Lambda and Monolithic and Microservice Architectures," 2016 16th IEEE/ACM International Symposium on Cluster, Cloud and Grid Computing (CCGrid), Cartagena, pp. 179-182, 2016.

[30] Eric J. Evans, “Domain-Driven Design. Tackling Complexity in the Heart of Software,” Addison Wesley, 2003.

[31] InfoQ 2006, “Domain Driven Design Quickly. C4Media,“ [Online]. Available from: https://www.infoq.com/minibooks/domain-driven-design-quickly [retrieved: June, 2018]

[32] DIN, "DIN SPEC 91345. Reference Architecture Model Industrie 4.0 (RAMI4.0), " 2016.

[33] G. Olliffe, “Microservices: Building Services with the Guts on the Outside,” 2015, [Online]. Available from: http://blogs.gartner.com/gary-olliffe/2015/01/30/microservices-guts-on-the-outside [retrieved: June, 2018]

[34] Wikimedia Foundation Inc, “User profile,” [Online]. Available from: https://en.wikipedia.org/wiki/User_profile [retrieved: June, 2018]

[35] Gartner IT Glossary, “Gartner IT Glossary: Activity Stream,” 2012, [Online]. Available from: http://www.gartner.com/it-glossary/activity-stream/ [retrieved: June, 2018]

[36] H. Baxter, “An Introduction to Online Communities,” [Online]. Available from: http://www.providersedge.com/docs/km_articles/An_Introduction_to_Online_Communities.pdf [retrieved: June, 2018]

[37] M. Rouse, “instant messaging (IM or IM-ing or AIM)” SearchUnifiedCommunications, [Online]. Available from: http://searchunifiedcommunications.techtarget.com/definition/instant-messaging [retrieved: June, 2018]

[38] M. Kerres, "Mediendidaktik. Konzeption und Entwicklung mediengestützter Lernangebote," Oldenburg Verlag, 2016.

[39] D. A. Bauer, "Template for using Vert.x and Actor4j (inclusiveley as FaaS)," 2017, [Online]. Available from: https://github.com/relvaner/relvaner-vertx-template [retrived, June, 2018]

[40] D. A. Bauer, “Actor4j an actor implementation,” 2017, [Online]. Available from: https://github.com/relvaner/actor4j-core [retrieved: June, 2018]

[41] G. McGrath and P. R. Brenner, "Serverless Computing: Design, Implementation, and Performance," 2017 IEEE 37th International Conference on Distributed Computing Systems Workshops (ICDCSW), Atlanta, GA, pp. 405-410, 2017.

[42] M. Asay. "Why AWS Lambda and serverless computing won't kill Docker in the enterprise. AWS Lambda and Docker containers may be at odds, but both have a place in a modern enterprise," in TechRepublic, 2017. [Online]. Available from: https://www.techrepublic.com/article/why-aws-lambda-and-serverless-computing-wont-kill-docker-in-the-enterprise/ [retrieved: June, 2018]

[43] Serverless Framework, [Online]. Available from: https://github.com/serverless/serverless [retrieved: June, 2018]

[44] A. Gupta, “Microservice Design Patterns,” 2015, [Online]. Available from: http://blog.arungupta.me/microservice-design-patterns/ [retrieved: June, 2018]

[45] D. A. Bauer, "Derivative of Smiley's HTTP-Proxy-Servlet," 2017, [Online]. Available from: https://github.com/relvaner/HTTP-Proxy-Servlet [retrived: June, 2018]

[46] R. Schaefer, "From Monolith to Microservices at Zalando", in GOTO Conferences, 2016. [Online]. Available from: https://www.youtube.com/watch?v=gEeHZwjwehs [retrieved: June, 2018]

[47] Zalando, "A streaming layout service for front-end microservices," [Online]. Available from: https://github.com/zalando/tailor [retrieved: June, 2018]

[48] C. Jiang, "BigPipe: Pipelining web pages for high performance," in Facebook, Facebook Engineering, 2010, [Online]. Available from: https://www.facebook.com/notes/facebook-engineering/bigpipe-pipelining-web-pages-for-high-performance/389414033919/ [retrieved: June, 2018]

Multicast Activation Scheme based on LoRaWAN for Multicast MAC Transmission

Sun Hwa Lim, Kang Bok Lee
IoT Research Division
Electronics and Telecommunications Research Institute
218, Gajeong-Ro, Yuseong-gu, Daejeon, Korea
e-mail: {limsh, kblee}@etri.re.kr

Abstract—**Internet of Things (IoT) is a rapidly emerging technology which involved both a variety of research and a very wide range of industrial fields. It is increasingly interested in the use of a long range wide area network (LoRaWAN) to remotely monitor and manage the number of devices in real-time. In order to better manage and control a lot of devices, multicast is sometimes more suitable than unicast. However, in the LoRaWAN specification, unicast MAC transmission is only described but multicast MAC transmission is not specified. In this paper, we propose the multicast activation scheme to support multicast MAC transmission based on LoRaWAN. The presented scheme can reduce the energy consumption required for downlink and be used as a guideline for developing LoRaWAN-based IoT applications.**

Keywords- IoT; LPWA; LoRaWAN; multicast; activation.

I. INTRODUCTION

Internet of Things (IoT) have been studied [1]-[3] and applied to a very wide range of fields such as intelligent buildings, manufacturing, agriculture, and goods transportation to remotely monitor and better manage things in real-time [4]-[7]. The devices in these applications typically send tiny amounts of data with limited low power in a long coverage area. In order to guarantee the characteristics of the devices, low power wide area (LPWA) technologies have become more popular than Wi-Fi or LTE [8][9]. Many LPWA technologies have arisen in the licensed spectrum (LTE Cat-0, LTE-M, NB-IoT, etc.) as well as unlicensed (LoRaWAN, SigFox, Ingenu, etc.). Among LPWA technologies, a long range wide area network (LoRaWAN) is widely employed in various applications (for example, shipping and transportation for industrial applications, temperature and moisture monitoring for agriculture, waste management for smart city) [10]-[13].

A large number of devices need to be grouped so as to better manage and control devices (e.g., configuring parameters, initializing devices). Multicast is more suitable than unicast to send small amounts of control information to a lot of devices. However, in the LoRaWAN specification [14], unicast MAC transmission is only described but multicast MAC transmission is not specified. Therefore, in this paper, we propose the detailed and possible multicast activation scheme to provide multicast MAC transmission based on LoRaWAN. The presented scheme can be used as a guideline for developing LoRaWAN-based IoT applications.

This paper is organized as follows. In Section II, we briefly introduce the LoRaWAN network architecture and protocol stack for a multicast activation. In Section III, we propose the multicast activation scheme based on LoRaWAN. In Section IV, we compare unicast and multicast in terms of energy consumption of transmitter over the air. Finally, Section V presents the conclusions.

II. LORAWAN NETWORK

In this section, we introduce the LoRaWAN network architecture and protocol stack for a multicast activation.

A. Architecture

Fig. 1 shows the network architecture of LoRaWAN for a multicast activation. There are an end device, a gateway, a network server, an authentication, authorization, and accounting (AAA) server, and an application server. The end device can transfer and receive data packet to and from the gateway with PHY of LoRa. The gateway shall forward data packet between end devices and the network server. The network server can route data packet from the gateway to the AAA server or the application server, and back. The AAA server shall perform an authentication procedure for the end device and generate session keys such as a network session key and an application session key. The application server can collect and analyze data receiving from the network server. It is also able to process an authentication function without the AAA server.

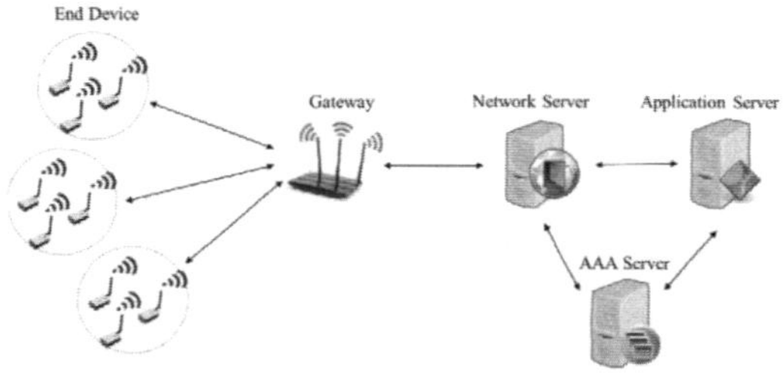

Figure 1. LoRaWAN-based network architecture for a multicast.

B. Protocol Stack

Fig. 2 shows the protocol stack of LoRaWAN for a multicast activation. An end device is composed of the LoRa

PHY layer, the LoRaWAN MAC layer, and the application layer. For the radio interface, a gateway is communicated with the end device based on the LoRa technology. The gateway is connected to a network server over IP networks. The network server is connected to an AAA server based on RADIUS [15] over UDP/IP networks.

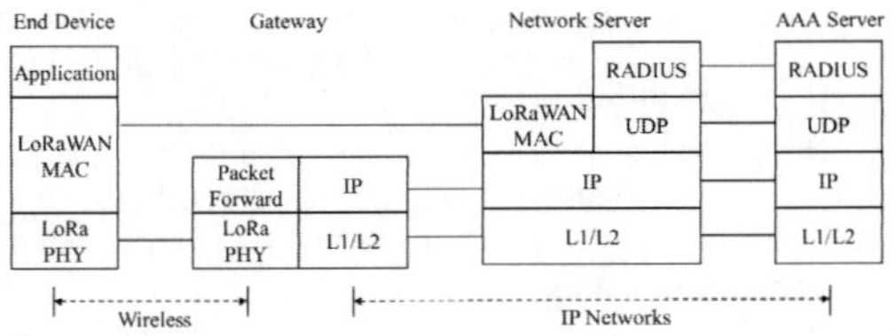

Figure 2. LoRaWAN-based protocol stack for a multicast activation.

III. PROPOSED MULTICAST ACTIVATION SCHEME

In this section, we present the multicast activation scheme to provide multicast MAC transmission based on LoRaWAN.

A. New defined multicast MAC messages

For an end device to join a multicast group over LoRaWAN, it is necessary for us to define new multicast MAC message types. Table 1 shows the newly defined MAC message types. The LoRaWAN specification allows the use of 3-bits message type (MType) and already defines six different MAC message types. The MAC types of a *multicast join request* message and a *multicast join accept* message are defined by 110 and 111, respectively.

TABLE I. MAC MESSAGE TYPES

Message Type	Description
000	Join Request
001	Join Accept
010	Unconfirmed Data Up
011	Unconfirmed Data Down
100	Confirmed Data Up
101	Confirmed Data Down
110	Multicast Join Request
111	Multicast Join Accept

Fig. 3(a) and Fig. 3(b) illustrate the detailed format of a *multicast join request* message and a *multicast join accept* message. In order to generate session keys, the messages can contain the following parameters.

Size(bytes)	8	4	4
Multicast Join Request	MultiAppEUI	DevAddr	DevNonce

(a)

Size(bytes)	8	4
Multicast Join Request	MultiAppEUI	DevAddr

(b)

Figure 3. New defined multicast MAC messages. (a) Multicast Join Request. (b) Multicast Join Accept.

A *multicast join request* message contains MultiAppEUI, DevAddr, and DevNonce. MultiAppEUI is a multicast application identifier, i.e., the MultiAppEUI is a global application ID that uniquely identifies the entity able to process a *multicast join request* message. DevAddr is used to identify an end device within the current network. DevNonce is a random value generated by an end device. A *multicast join accept* message contains MultiNonce and MultiAddr. MultiNonce is a random value generated by an AAA server. MultiAddr is an identifier to identify a multicast group.

B. Integrity of Multicast MAC Messages

In order to ensure the integrity of multicast MAC messages, a message integrity code (MIC) should be appended to the end of the messages. For a *multicast join request* message integrity, MultiAppKey, MHDR, MultiAppEUI, DevAddr, and DevNonce are used as input parameters of the CMAC algorithm. An end device has been pre-configured with MultiAppEUI and MultiAppKey. MultiAppKey is an AES-128 root key specific to a multicast group. MHDR is the MAC header field. | is represented the concatenation of character strings. The MIC can be calculated by

cmac = aes128_cmac (MultiAppKey, MHDR | MultiAppEUI | DevAddr | DevNonce),

MIC = cmac[0..3].

For a *multicast join accept* message integrity, MultiAppKey, MHDR, MultiNonce, and MultiAddr are used as input parameters of the CMAC algorithm. An AAA server has been pre-configured with MultiAppKey. The MIC can be calculated by

cmac = aes128_cmac (MultiAppKey, MHDR | MultiNonce | MultiAddr),

MIC = cmac[0..3].

For a network server to send a secure *multicast join accept* message to an end device, the message is encrypted with MultiAppKey as follows:

aes128_decrypt (MultiAppKey, MultiNonce | MultiAddr | MIC).

MultiAppKey is pre-configured in a network server and the MIC is the value calculated above.

C. Derivation of Multicast Session Keys

After verifying the MIC of multicast MAC messages, an end device and an AAA server can derive the two multicast session keys which are a multicast network session key (MultiNwkSKey) and a multicast application session key (MultiAppSKey). The session keys are calculated as follows:

MultiNwkSKey = aes128_encrypt (MultiAppKey, 0x03 | MultiNonce | MultiAddr | DevNonce | pad16),

MultiAppSKey = aes128_encrypt (MultiAppKey, 0x04 | MultiNonce | MultiAddr | DevNonce | pad16).

MultiNwkSKey is used to encrypt and decrypt the payload field of multicast MAC data messages between end devices of a multicast group and a network server. MultiAppSKey is used to encrypt and decrypt the payload field of application-specific data messages between end devices of a multicast group and an application server.

D. Multicast Activation Procedure

Fig. 4(a) shows a unicast join procedure and Fig. 4(b) shows a multicast join procedure. The detailed description of each step is as follows:

- Once initialization for the LoRaWAN wireless link access is finished, a unicast join procedure is performed between an end device and an AAA server via a gateway and a network server.
- If this procedure is successful, the end device and the AAA server should generate a network session key (NwkSKey), and an application session key (AppSKey).
- The end device may already have the pre-configured multicast group information that it wants to join.
- For joining a multicast group, the end device sends a *multicast join request* message to the network server including MultiAppEUI, DevAddr, and DeviceNonce through a gateway over LoRaWAN.
- The network server sends an *access request* message which includes the parameters of the *multicast join request* message to the AAA server based on the RADIUS protocol.
- If the end device is successfully authenticated, the AAA server shall respond to the network server with an *access accept* message which includes MultitNonce and MultiAddr.
- After the AAA server can generate the two session keys which are MultiNwkSKey and MultiAppSKey, it sends MultiNwkSKey to the network server. The AAA server also sends MultiAppSKey to the application server.
- Upon receiving an *access accept* message, the network server shall send a *multicast join accept* message with the above parameters (MultiNonce and

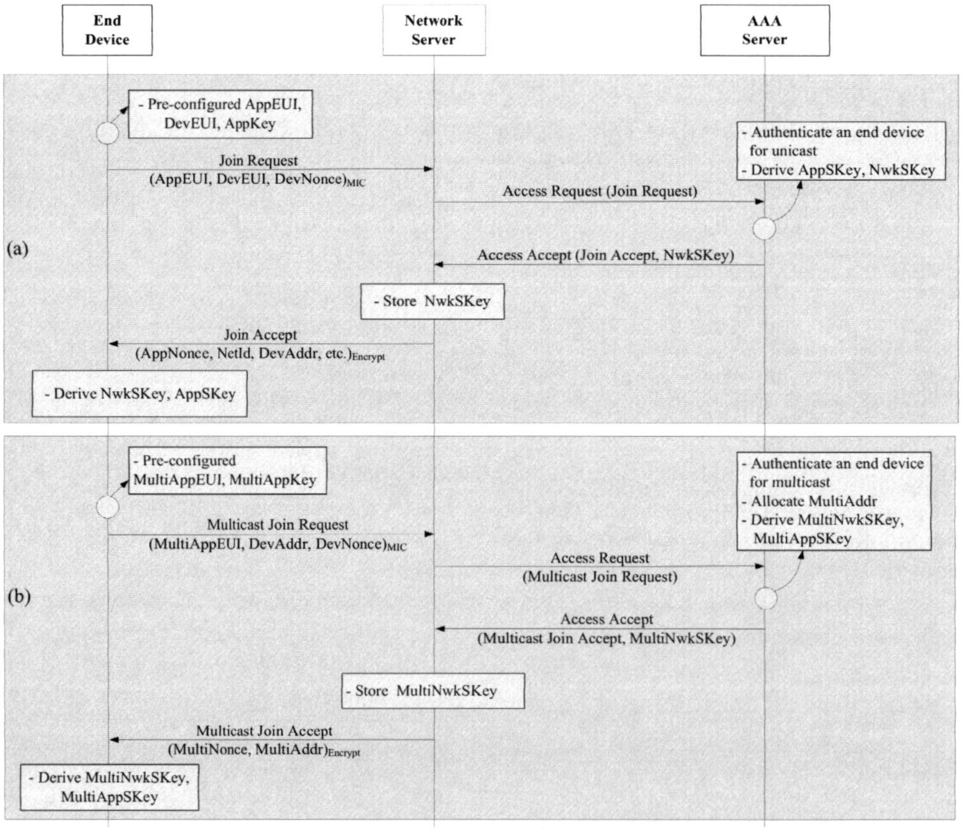

Figure 4. Over-the-air activation procedure based on LoRaWAN. (a) Unicast join activation procedure. (b) Multicast join activation procedure.

MultiAddr) to the end device through the gateway over LoRaWAN.

- The network server shall store MultiNwkSKey receiving from the AAA server.
- When the end device receives a *multicast join accept* message from the network server, it should derive MultiNwkSKey and MultiAppSKey.

We have designed a similar multicast join procedure based on a unicast join procedure described in the LoRaWAN specification. We believe that the proposed scheme is helpful to developers in implementing MAC multicast protocols based on LoRaWAN.

IV. PERFORMANCE ANALYSYS

We compare unicast and multicast in terms of energy consumption of transmitter over the air. A transmitter is a gateway and a receiver is an end device or a multicast group. Energy consumption of transmitter which is located in the distance of d with n bit can be expressed as follows [16]:

$$E_{Tx}(n,d) = E_{Tx-elec}(n) + E_{Tx-amp}(n,d) = E_{elec} \times n + E_{amp} \times n \times d^2. \quad (1)$$

Energy consumption of receiver can be expressed as

$$E_{Rx}(n) = E_{Rx-elec}(n) = E_{elec} \times n. \quad (2)$$

In unicast and multicast, to analyze the total energy consumption of transmitter with the number of end devices and multicast groups, the following terms are defined:

- *unitCost* : the energy consumption of transmitter, i.e., $E_{Tx}(n, d)$,
- *deviceNum* : the number of end devices,
- *groupNum* : the number of multicast groups.

In unicast, the total energy consumption of transmitter can be calculated by

$$E_{Tx\_unicast}(n,d) = unitCost \times deviceNum. \quad (3)$$

In multicast, the total energy consumption of transmitter can be calculated by

$$E_{Tx\_multicast}(n,d) = unitCost \times groupNum. \quad (4)$$

In unicast and multicast, we assume that energy consumption of receiver is equal and examine the total energy consumption of transmitter with the varied weight value of *unitCost* as Sets 1, 2, 3 followed by Table 1.

TABLE II. SETS OF UNITCOST

	unitCost
Set 1	0.1
Set 2	0.2
Set 3	0.4

For our experiments, we consider that *deviceNum* is increased by 10 from 1 to 100 and *groupNum* is given by 1, 2, 4, 5, and 10 with a 100-end devices. We can use the Gnuplot as a performance analysis tool. The simulation results are shown in Fig. 5 and Fig. 6. As illustrated in Fig. 5 and Fig. 6, as *deviceNum* and *groupNum* become increased, the total energy consumption of each transmission increases linearly. Especially, we note that *groupNum* is smaller, the difference of the total energy consumption of unicast and multicast is larger. Therefore, multicast can help to manage and configure a lot of end devices with less energy consumption of transmitter than unicast.

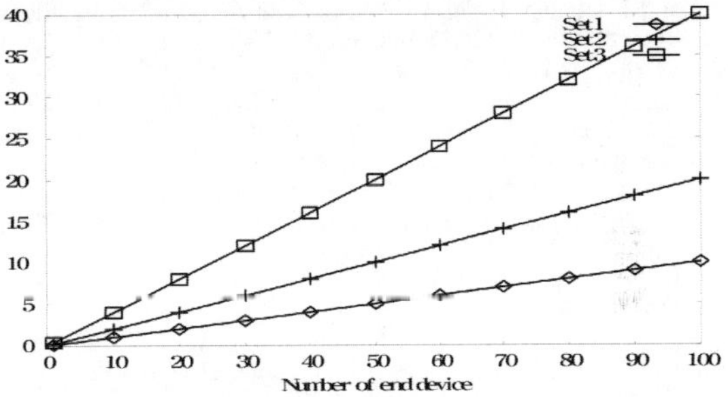

Figure 5. Energy consumption of transmitter in unicast.

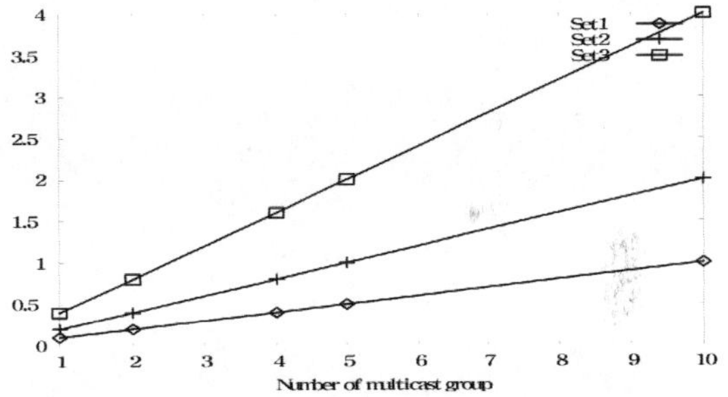

Figure 6. Energy consumption of transmitter in multicast.

V. CONCLUSIONS

We presented the multicast activation scheme to efficiently control the number of end devices based on LoRaWAN in this paper. We defined new multicast MAC messages, create the MIC, and generated multicast session keys. Additionally, we proposed a multicast join procedure for an end device. Finally, we compared unicast and multicast in terms of the total energy consumption of transmitter over the air. The presented scheme can reduce the energy consumption required for downlink. The proposed scheme can be used as a guideline for developing LoRaWAN-based IoT applications.

ACKNOWLEDGMENT

This work was supported by Electronics and Telecommunications Research Institute (ETRI) grant funded by the Korean government. [18ZH1120, Distributed Intelligence Core Technology of Hyper-Connected Space]

REFERENCES

[1] I. Lee and K. Lee, "The Internet of Things (IoT): Applications, investments, and challenges for enterprises," *Business Horizons*, vol. 58, pp. 431-440, Aug. 2015.

[2] A. AI-Fuqaha, M. Guizani, M. Mohammadi, M. Aledhari, and M. Ayyash, "Internet of Things: A Survey on Enabling Technologies, Protocols, and Applications," *IEEE Communications Surveys & Tutorials*, vol. 17, pp. 2347-2376, June, 2015.

[3] M. Tahmassebpour and A. Otaghvari, "Increase efficiency big data in intelligent transportation system with using IoT intergation cloud," *Journal of Fundamental and Applied Sciences*, vol. 8, pp. 2443-2461, 2016.

[4] K. Zheng, S. Zhao, Z. Yang, X. Xiong, and W. Xiang, "Design and Implementation of LPWA-Based Air Quality Monitoring System," *IEEE Access*, vol. 4, pp. 3238-3245, 2016.

[5] M. Centenaro, L. Vangelista, A. Zanella, and M. Zorzi, "Long-range communications in unlicensed bands: the rising stars in the IoT and smart city scenarios," *IEEE Wireless Communications*, vol. 23, pp. 60-67, Nov. 2016.

[6] K. Akkaya, I. Guvenc, R. Aygun, N. Pala, and A. Kadri, "IoT-based occupancy monitoring techniques for energy-efficient smart buildings," *Wireless Communications and Networking Conference Workshops* (WCNCW), Mar. 2015, pp. 58-63, ISBN: 978-1-4799-8760-3.

[7] M. Hassanalieragh, et al. "Health Monitoring and Management Using Internet-of-Things (IoT) Sensing with Cloud-Based Processing: Opportunities and Challenges," *Services Computing* (SCC), Jun. 2015, pp. 285-292, ISBN: 978-1-4673-7281-7.

[8] U. Raza, P. Kulkarni, and M. Sooriyabandara, "Low Power Wide Area Networks: An Overview," *IEEE Communications Surveys & Tutorials*, vol. 19. pp. 855-873, Jun. 2017.

[9] K. Mekki, E. Bajic, F. Chaxel, and F. Meyer, "A comparative study of LPWAN technologies for large-scale IoT deployment," *ICT Express*, Available online, Jan. 2018.

[10] R. Sinha, Y. Wei, and S. Hwang, "A survey on LPWA technology: LoRa and NB-IoT," *ICT Express*, vol. 3, pp. 14-21, Mar. 2017.

[11] Y. Beyene, et.al, "NB-IoT Technology Overview and Experience from Cloud-RAN Implementation," *IEEE Wireless Communications*, vol. 21, pp. 26-32, Jun. 2017.

[12] A. Wixted, et.al, "Evaluation of LoRa and LoRaWAN for wireless sensor networks," *IEEE SENSORS*, Nov. 2016. pp. 1-3, ISBN: 978-1-4799-8287-5.

[13] M. Shirvanimoghaddam, M. Dohler, and S. J. Johnson, "Massive Non-Orthogonal Multiple Access for Cellular IoT: Potentials and Limitations," *IEEE Communications Magazine*, vol. 55, pp. 55-61, Sep. 2017.

[14] LoRaWAN Specification, V1.0.2, 2016.

[15] RFC 2865, Remote Authentication Dial In User Service (RADIUS), IETF, Jun. 2000.

[16] A. Wang, W. Heinzelman, and A. Chandrakasan, "Energy-scalable protocols for battery-operated microsensor networks," *Proc. 1999 IEEE Workshop Signal Processing Systems* (SiPS), pp. 483–492, Oct. 1999.

Proposal of Power Saving Techniques for Wireless Terminals Using CAZAC-OFDM Scheme

Takanobu Onoda, Ryota Ishioka and Masahiro Muraguchi
Department of Electrical Engineering, Tokyo University of Science
6-3-1 Niijuku, Katsushika-ku, Tokyo, 125-0051, Japan
E-mail: 4317614@ed.tus.ac.jp, 4316609@ed.tus.ac.jp, murag@ee.kagu.tus.ac.jp

Abstract— **A major drawback of Orthogonal Frequency Division Multiplexing (OFDM) signals is extremely high Peak-to-Average Power Ratio (PAPR). Signals with high PAPR lead to a lowering of the energy efficiency of the Power Amplifiers (PAs) and the shortened operation time causes a serious problem in battery-powered wireless terminals. In this paper, we propose a new power saving technique for wireless terminals. It is the combination of a polar modulation technique and Constant Amplitude Zero Auto-Correlation (CAZAC) equalizing technique. Proposed the polar modulation technique for the PA employs a current control by changing the common-gate stage bias in a cascade amplifier circuit. The CAZAC equalization scheme makes the PAPR of M-array Quadrature Amplitude Modulation (M-QAM) OFDM signals into the PAPR of M-QAM single-carrier signals. By using CAZAC-OFDM signal, proposed polar modulation PA exhibits overall efficiency of 40% at Error Vector Magnitude (EVM) of -32dB. Furthermore, a breakthrough technique which transcends barrier of 50% efficiency has been proposed. A prototype of Single Ended Push-Pull amplifier (SEPP AMP) exhibits power gain of 15dB over 100MHz to 1GHz, the maximum efficiency of 65% without polar modulation scheme.**

Keywords-OFDM; CAZAC; polar modulation; SEPP;

I. Introduction

Orthogonal Frequency Division Multiplex (OFDM) system for high speed and high capacity communications is recently attracting attention in wireless applications, e.g., 3GPP LTE, Wi-Fi and WiMAX. It is well known that one of the most serious drawbacks of the OFDM system is its high peak-to-average power ratio (PAPR), which decreases the energy efficiency of power amplifier (PA) and increases transmitter power consumption. In mobile communications, high PAPR signal negatively affects device battery life.

To overcome the above problem, many techniques are proposed: Partial Transmit Sequence (PTS), Selected Mapping (SLM), etc. [1]. PTS and SLM techniques choose respectively the phase factor and candidate data block to minimize the PAPR of transmission signal, which improves PAPR performance. However, those techniques need side-information in the receiver side, i.e., phase factor and candidate number information, in order to demodulate the received signal correctly, which result in degradation of spectral efficiency, and additional power consumption of DSPs.

On the other approach to overcome the problem, some circuit topology for high-efficiency OFDM power amplifier design have been proposed [2]. Here, a polar modulation PA, or an envelope tracking PA, is the most promising one. In the polar modulation, OFDM signal is separated into phase modulation (PM) component and amplitude modulation (AM) one. The PM component is input to the PA as the quadrature signal with constant amplitude. On the other, the AM component is used as envelope tracking data, which supplies to the PA as drain DC biasing from adaptive output power supply using a DC-DC converter. In general, the efficiency of PAs operating in saturation region is higher than one in linear region. Therefore, the polar modulation PA improves energy efficiency under full-time operation in the saturation region.

In this paper, we propose a new power saving technique for wireless terminals. It is the coupling technique between envelope tracking operation of PAs and CAZAC (Constant Amplitude Zero Auto-Correlation) equalizing. Here, we had reported an original polar modulation PA using a cascade circuit topology [3]. One can control output power by changing common-gate stage biasing in accordance with signal envelope, which improves energy efficiency of PA by full-time operation in saturation region. Since the polar modulation is a simple method of separating into amplitude information and phase information, it can cope with all modulation schemes. We also reported that one CAZAC sequence in cooperation with IFFT signal-process converted the PAPR of the M-QAM OFDM signal into the PAPR of an M-QAM single-carrier signal. Here, this fact was our original discovery [4].

In this paper, this coupling technology has novelty and effectiveness in combining the features of CAZAC-OFDM which is constant amplitude and the characteristics of this PA which is power saving, where a more power-saving system can be created. The coupling technique reduces the PAPR of 5 dB at the 16QAM-OFDM signal while the system imposed no penalties on the BER performances. By using CAZAC-OFDM signal, proposed polar modulation PA exhibits overall efficiency of 40% or more at error vector magnitude (EVM) of -32dB which satisfies the requirement of IEEE 802.11 ac specification [5].

Moreover, a breakthrough technique, which transcends barrier of 50% efficiency has been proposed. As well-known, a Class-B amplifier allows operating at a power efficiency of

78.5%, while a Class-A amplifier operates at a power efficiency of 50%. The Class-B amplifiers, however, are strongly difficult to achieve high frequency and high linearity operations at the same time.

Our proposal of new circuit topology is certain kind of single ended push-pull amplifier, or SEPP AMP, using a complementary MOSFET technology. The circuit topology is suitable for monolithic circuit configuration and easily applied commercially available process of CMOS foundries. A prototype of the SEPP AMP exhibits power gain of 15dB over 100MHz to 1GHz and the maximum efficiency of 65% with no use of polar modulation scheme.

Up to now we have shown that the polar modulation system is effective with various modulation schemes [3][4]. On the other hand, the contribution of this paper is to demonstrate the achievement of unprecedented power efficiency by combining CAZAC-OFDM which achieved the same PAPR as the single carrier in the world and power-saving polar modulation system.

This paper is organized as follows. Section II presents the proposed the operating principle of the coupling technique between envelope tracking operation of PAs and CAZAC. In Section III, a performance of proposed system is presented. In Section IV, the operating principle of further improvement of OFDM-PAs with SEPP and simulation results are given. Finally, Section V concludes this paper.

II. PROPOSED SYSTEM

In the proposed system, CAZAC-OFDM and polar modulation are used together to improve energy efficiency. Below, we explain CAZAC-OFDM and polar modulation and propose a system with improved efficiency. A description of OFDM system in section A, CAZAC equalizing technique in section B, and polar modulation technique in section C are shown.

A. OFDM system

In OFDM system, the frequency domain symbol $\boldsymbol{X} = [X_0, X_1, \dots, X_{N-1}]^T$ is modulated by N size inverse Fast Fourier Transform (IFFT). The discrete-time OFDM signal with N subcarriers is represented as

$$x_n = \sum_{k=0}^{N-1} X_k e^{j2\pi kn/N}, \tag{1}$$

where $j = \sqrt{-1}$ and n is discrete time index. On the other hand, receiver acquires frequency domain symbol $\boldsymbol{Y}$ by applying FFT to received signal $\boldsymbol{y}$.

$$\begin{aligned} Y_k &= \sum_{n=0}^{N-1} y_n e^{-j2\pi kn/N} \\ &= \sum_{n=0}^{N-1} (x_n + Noise) e^{-j2\pi kn/N}. \end{aligned} \tag{2}$$

The PAPR of the OFDM signal (1) can be expressed as

$$PAPR = \frac{\max_{0 \le n \le N-1} |x_n|^2}{\mathrm{E}[|x_n|^2]}, \tag{3}$$

where $\mathrm{E}[\cdot]$ is expectation operator. PAPR represents amplitude fluctuation of each symbol. In order to improve the accuracy of PAPR, the OFDM signal x_k is converted to L-times oversampled time domain signal [1].

As shown from (2), the OFDM signal is composed of a plurality of subcarrier signals, which causes an increase in amplitude fluctuation. A high PAPR signal increases the Input Back Off (IBO) at the power amplifier in order to amplify the transmit signal without distortion. In general, increasing in IBO causes decreasing the efficiency of PA.

B. CAZAC equalizing technique

CAZAC sequence is constant amplitude and provides a good cross-correlation property. Therefore, CAZAC sequence is used in wireless communication systems such as channel estimation and time synchronization. The Zadoff-Chu sequence c_k which is one of the CAZAC sequences is represented as

$$c_k = e^{j\pi k^2/N^2}, \tag{4}$$

where $k = 0, 1, \dots, N^2 - 1$ denotes the sequence index. In this paper, CAZAC $N \times N$ matrix $\boldsymbol{M}$ is represented as

$$\boldsymbol{M} = \begin{bmatrix} c_0 & c_1 & \cdots & c_{N-1} \\ c_N & c_{N+1} & \cdots & c_{2N-1} \\ \vdots & \vdots & \ddots & \vdots \\ c_{(N-1)N} & c_{(N-1)N+1} & \cdots & c_{N^2-1} \end{bmatrix}. \tag{5}$$

In CAZAC-OFDM system, multiply the signal with M before the IFFT of the transmitter. frequency domain symbol $\boldsymbol{X}' = [X'_0, X'_1, \dots, X'_{N-1}]^T$ is represented as

$$\boldsymbol{X}' = \boldsymbol{M}\boldsymbol{X}. \tag{6}$$

Therefore, the CAZAC-OFDM time signal x' is represented as

$$\begin{aligned} x'_n &= \sum_{k=0}^{N-1} X'_k e^{\frac{j2\pi kn}{N}} \\ &= N \cdot c_{(N/2-n) \bmod N} \cdot X_{(N/2-n) \bmod N}. \end{aligned} \tag{7}$$

Receiver side can demodulate the original frequency domain symbol with using conjugate $\boldsymbol{M}^H$ [4].

Figure 1 shows PAPR performance of OFDM, CAZAC-OFDM and single carriers with using complementary cumulative distribution function (CCDF). Each signal has 64 subcarriers and oversampling factor $L = 4$. As shown from Figure 1, CAZAC equalization improves PAPR performance about 2.5 dB of PAPR when CCDF value is 10^{-3}. In addition, the PAPR of CAZAC-OFDM and M-QAM signal is same performance, which results from (7).

C. Polar modulation technique

In polar modulation system, AM and PM components are input separately into PA as power voltage and quadrature modulation signal respectively. General polar modulation system supplies AM component into PA by using dc-dc

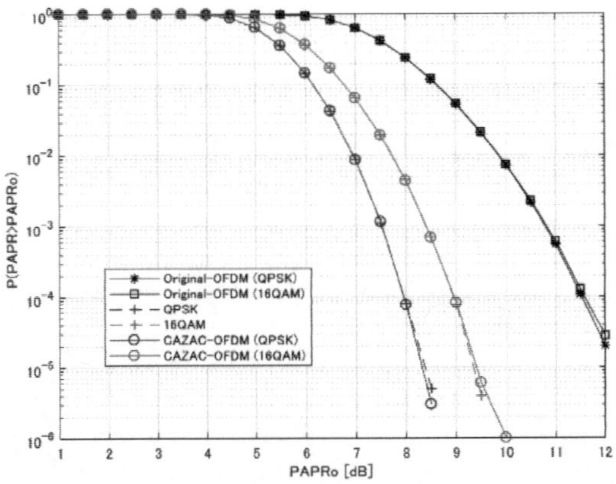

Figure 1. CCDF performance as compared with CAZAC-OFDM, OFDM and single carrier signal.

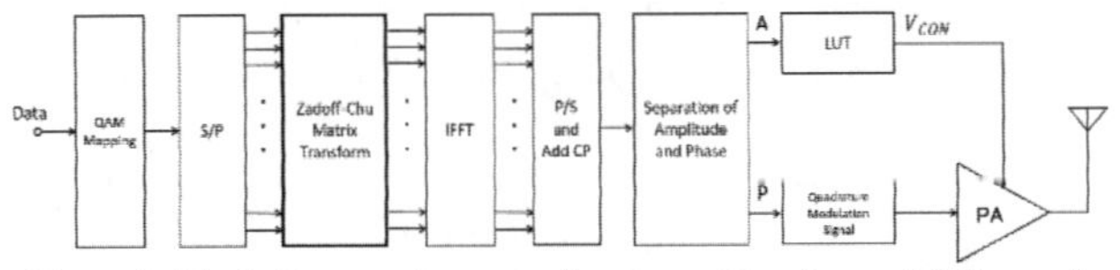

Figure 2. Block diagram of proposed system with polar modulation and CAZAC-OFDM.

converter. However, efficiency of dc-dc converter is around 90%, which affects overall efficiency of transmission system [6]. We have proposed new polar modulation technique without dc-dc converter [3]. In this system, quadrature modulation signal and AM component are input to the common-source and common-gate stage in cascade PA.

Figure 2 shows a block diagram of the proposed system. Mapping data after serial-parallel conversion is applied CAZAC precoding matrix $\boldsymbol{M}$. Secondly, CAZAC-OFDM signal after IFFT is separated into PM and AM component.

Quadrature modulation signal which is composed of PM component of CAZAC-OFDM is input to cascade PA. Lookup table converts AM component to V_{CON} to control envelope of output signal. V_{CON} applies to the common-gate stage in cascade PA.

We suppose OFDM signal in IEEE 802.11 specifications. Therefore, CAZAC-OFDM system must limit bandwidth [4]. In proposed system, we increase the number of data subcarriers and decrease the symbol rate to meet spectrum mask defined IEEE 802.11 specification, which doesn't affect data rate of proposed system.

Prototype cascade PA is shown in Figure 3. In proposed system, the quadrature modulation signal is input to prototype PA as RF_{IN}. On the other hand, proposed system changes the common-gate stage voltage V_{CON} to control envelope of output signal RF_{out}. Figure 4 shows the amplitude and phase shift of output at prototype cascade PA with 10dBm of quadrature modulation signal as input. As shown from Figure 4, changing the common-gate voltage V_{CON} affects the power of output signal RF_{out}. Proposed system controls V_{CON} to linearly amplify the input signal.

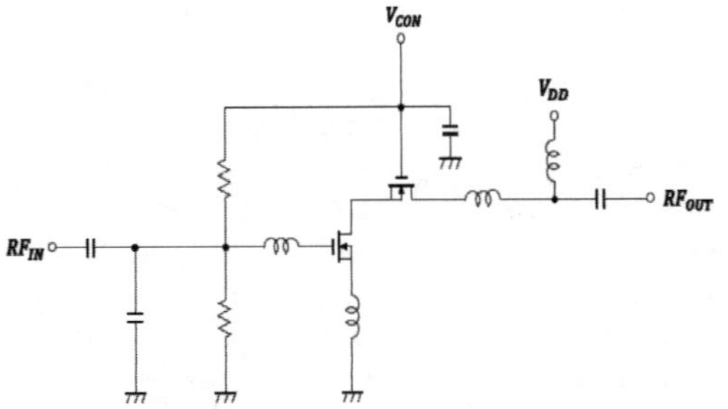

Figure 3. Prototype cascade PA ($\boldsymbol{V_{DD}} = \mathbf{1.8V}$)

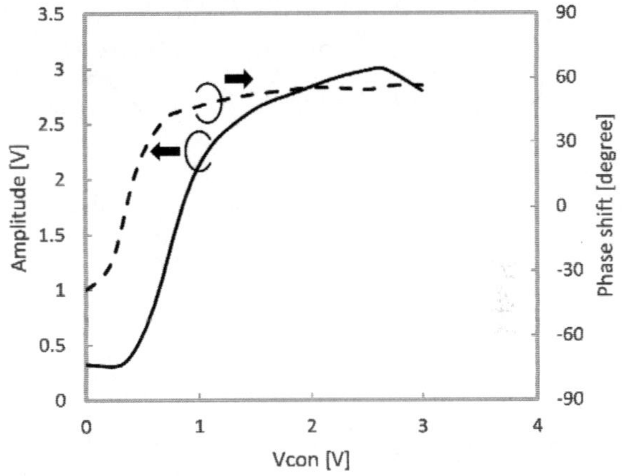

Figure 4. Output power and phase shift curves in cascade PA.

III. PERFORMANCE EVALUATION

We compare conventional OFDM system and proposed system combined CAZAC-OFDM and polar modulation PA. We show the setup of the simulation in section A and the result in section B.

A. Setup

We compare conventional OFDM system and proposed system combined CAZAC-OFDM and polar modulation PA. We have simulated the proposed system by the Advanced Design System 2016.01(ADS) and MATLAB 2014 α. In proposed system, we use MATLAB to generate text files of data set of CAZAC-OFDM IQ signals which are input to polar modulation PA designed by ADS and output signal of PA in ADS is demodulated in MATLAB.We use ADS pallet's OFDM signal source "WLAN IEEE 802.11" in 2.4 GHz and "SpectrumAnalyzerResBW" to measure spectrums.

Table I summarizes the simulation specifications. As carrier frequency, we use 2.4 GHz, which is industrial, scientific and medical (ISM) radio bands. Since we don't evaluate bit error rate performance, we apply no encoding to transmission signal. If the coding rate is 1/2, data rate of proposed system is 24 Mbps in IEEE 802.11g. CAZAC-OFDM system don't have null subcarriers. Therefore, we extend symbol time of CAZAC-OFDM to meet spectral mask in IEEE 802.11.

B. Simulation results

Figure 5 plots simulated Error Vector Magnitude (EVM)

TABLE I. SIMULATION SPECIFICATION

Modulation	OFDM	CAZAC-OFDM
Mapping	16QAM	16QAM
Symbol time	4 usec	5 usec
Guard interval rate	1/4	1/4
Data rate	48 Mbps	48 Mbps
Carrier frequency	2.4 GHz	2.4 GHz
Number of data subcarriers	48	60

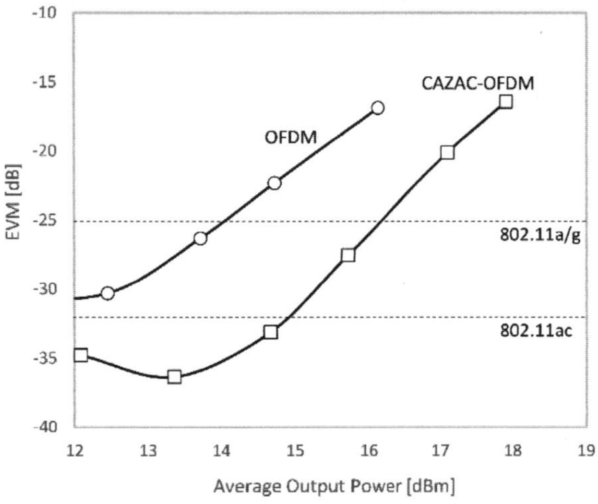

Figure 5. Simulated EVM versus average output power.

versus average output power. EVM represents demodulator performance in wireless communication system. In IEEE 802.11 a/g specifications, EVM of transmitter system must be less than -25 dB. As shown from Figure 5, simulated EVM is deteriorating with increasing average output power, which is caused by non-linear characteristic at polar modulation PA. CAZAC-OFDM system has superiority of about 2 dB in EVM as compared with the conventional OFDM system, which is caused by improving PAPR performance by CAZAC equalization (Figure 1).

The overall efficiency is shown in Figure 6. In the case of -25 dB or less of EVM, the efficiency of OFDM system is about 42 %. On the other hand, the efficiency of CAZAC-OFDM system is about 48 % in IEEE a/g specifications. Moreover, IEEE 802.11 ac specification requires the EVM of transmission signal ≤ 32 dB. The efficiency of proposed system is about 42 % at EVM of -32 dB in IEEE 802.11 ac specification, which is due to improve PAPR performance by CAZAC equalization. Efficiency means drain efficiency in this paper.

Figure 7 shows power spectral density of proposed system with CAZAC-OFDM and OFDM system. CAZAC equalization improves a roughly 5 dB in adjacent channel power ratio (ACPR). To sustain high efficiency at PA, IBO is required to be small. In the case of using high PAPR signal, small IBO causes nonlinear distortion. Since CAZAC equalization improves PAPR performance, ACPR of proposed system is suppressed.

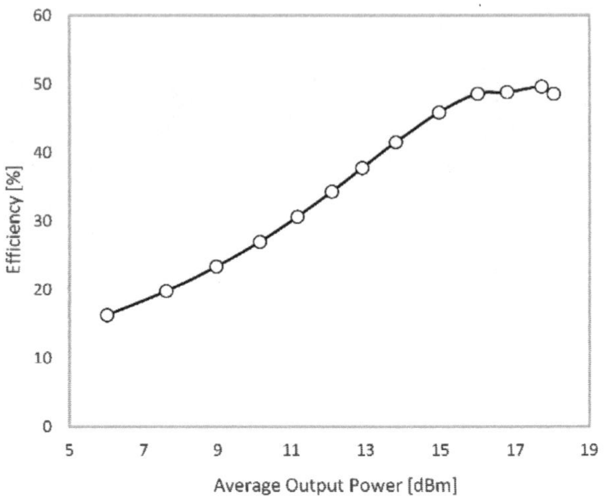

Figure 6. Simulated efficiency of cascade PA

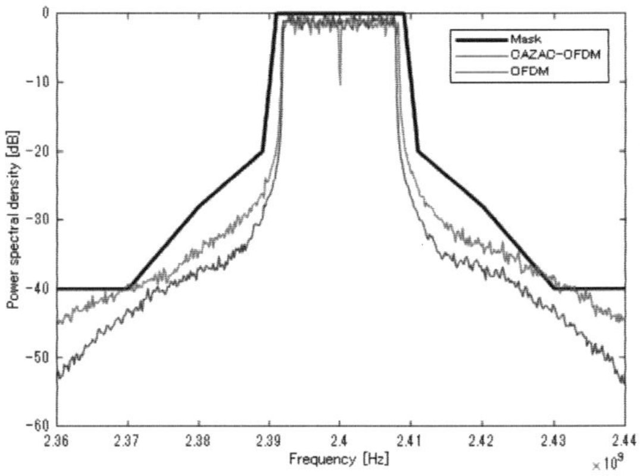

Figure 7. Simulated power spectral density of proposed system.

IV. PROPOSAL OF FURTHER IMPROVEMENT OF OFDM-PAS

In addition to conventional amplifiers, we would like to propose a class B biased wireless amplifier which we could not realize until now. There is still a problem and class B behavior is not realized, but I would like to show a prototype circuit with reference to SEPP. We show the circuit topology in section A, the setup of the simulation in section B and the result in section C.

A. Circuit topology

Since the OFDM exhibit large PAPR and wide bandwidth, the PAs should deliver high efficiency and linearity over wide bandwidth and input dynamic range. Generally, a class-A PA has preferred for good linearity, but lowered efficiency under the condition of small input range. The polar modulation PA mentioned previously, exhibits good efficiency over wide input dynamic range as well as linearity. However, it requires additional signal processing circuits and order-made look-up tables for specific devices.On the other hand, instead of class-A, a PA operated at a deep class-AB or class-B achieves a

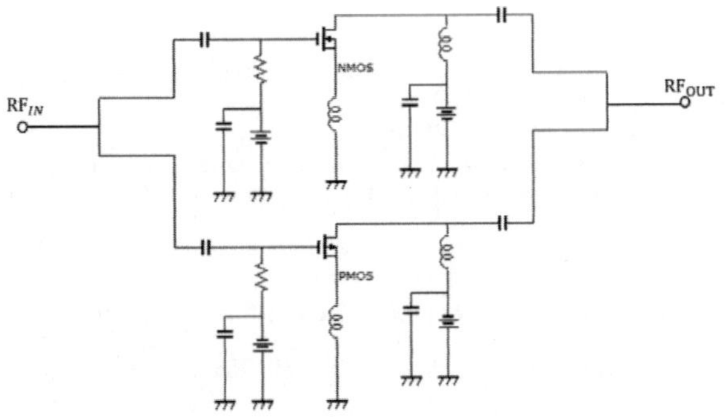

Figure 8. Circuit schematic of a prototype SEPP AMP.

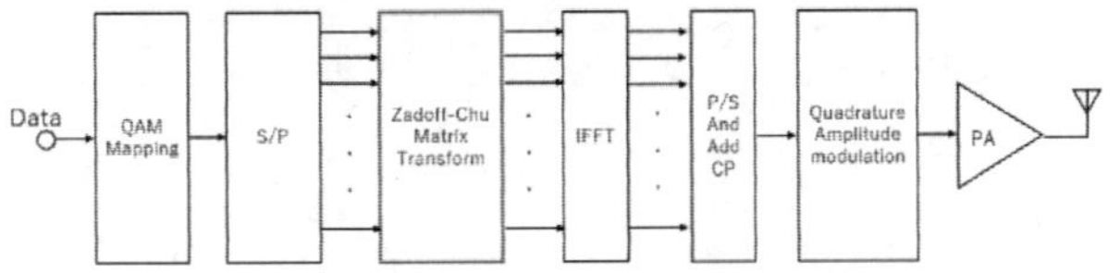

Figure 9. Block diagram of the transmitter with CAZAC-OFDM scheme for the SEPP AMP.

high efficiency in wide input dynamic range, although it has a large gain deviation and degradation of linearity performance. Here, to overcome the problems of class-B PAs, it is considered that push-pull amplifier scheme is one of dominant candidates.

Our proposal is a certain kind of single ended push-pull amplifier, or SEPP AMP, using a complementary MOSFET technology, as in shown in Figure 8. The circuit topology is suitable for monolithic circuit configuration and easily applied commercially available process of CMOS foundries. As shown in Figure 8, the output may be direct-coupled to the load connected through a dc blocking capacitor. Where both positive and negative power supplies are used, the load can be returned to the midpoint (ground) of the power supplies. The NMOS and the PMOS amplify only half the sinusoidal waveform and is cut off during the opposite half. In a deep class-AB or class-B operation, the amplifier has favorable features, i.e., low idle current and small quiescent current. The features provide improved efficiency over wide input dynamic range. Moreover, symmetrical construction of the two sides of the circuit means that even-order harmonics are cancelled, which can reduce distortion and improve linearity

Figure 9 shows the block diagram of transmitter with CAZAC-OFDM scheme for the SEPP AMP.

B. Setup

In ADS, both gate length of the NMOS and the PMOS is 0.18 μm. The transconductance gm of the NMOS and the PMOS is 513mS/mm and 253mS/mm, respectively. Ideal Class B operation requires complimentary devices are used to deliver the power instead of one. Each device conducts for alternate half cycles. To make good complementary pair, the gm of the PMOS must increase to those of the NMOS.

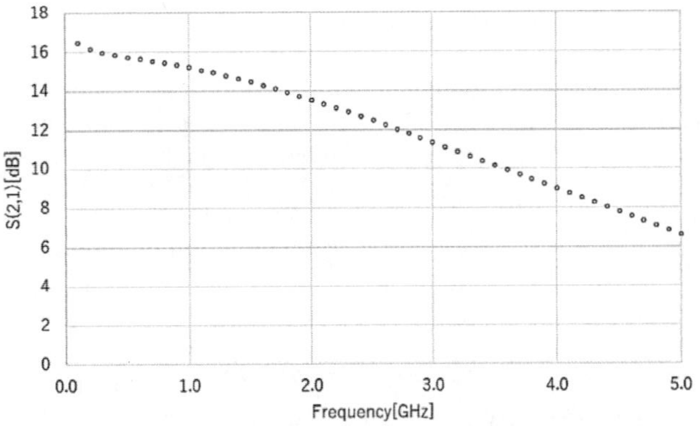

Figure 10. The S21 versus frequency characteristics of the prototype SEPP AMP with no input and output matching circuits.

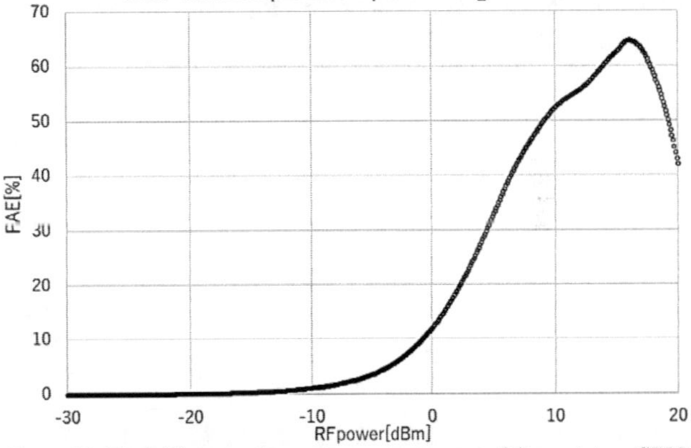

Figure 11. The PAE versus the average output power of the prototype SEPP AMP with no input and output matching circuits.

Since the ratio of the gm of the NMOS and the PMOS is approximately 2: 1, the total gate width of the PMOS is set to twice width of the NMOS. Therefore, the total gate width of NMOS and PMOS is set to 900 μm and 1800 μm, respectively. In the S21 of S parameters, "Simulation-Sparam" is used. In the PAE uses the "P_Probe" of "ads_rflib", subtracts the input power from the output power, divides the DC power and corrects it to a percentage.

C. Simulation results

Figure 10 shows the gain versus frequency characteristics of the prototype SEPP AMP. It exhibits power gain of 15dB over 100MHz to 1GHz. This flat gain performances are from no input and output matching circuits.

Figure 11 shows the efficiency versus the average output power of the SEPP AMP. The maximum efficiency of 65% has been obtained. Higher efficiency is expected if proper band-pass design of input and output matching circuits would be applied.

V. CONCLUSIONS

A new power saving technique for wireless terminals has been proposed. It is the combination of a polar modulation technique and CAZAC equalizing technique.

The CAZAC equalization scheme makes the PAPR of M-QAM OFDM signals into the PAPR of M-QAM single-carrier signals. By using CAZAC-OFDM signal, proposed polar modulation PA exhibits overall efficiency of 40% at EVM of -32dB. Furthermore, a breakthrough technique which transcends barrier of 50% efficiency has been proposed. A prototype of SEPP AMP exhibits power gain of 15dB over 100MHz to 1GHz and the maximum efficiency of 65% with no use of the polar modulation scheme.

ACKNOWLEDGMENTS

This research was supported by the UNIVERSITY LICENSE PROGRAM of Keysight Technologies, Inc. The simulations have been performed by use of the Keysight EEsofEDA.

REFERENCES

[1] S. H. Han and J. H. Lee, "An overview of peak-to-average power ratio reduction techniques for multicarrier transmission," *IEEE Wireless Communications*, vol. 12, no. 2, pp. 56–65, April 2005.

[2] J. Joung, C. K. Ho, K. Adachi, and S. Sun, "A Survey on Power-Amplifier-Centric Techniques for Spectrum- and Energy-Efficient Wireless Communications," *IEEE Communications Surveys & Tutorials*, vol. 17, no. 1, pp. 315–333, Jan. 2015.

[3] R. Ishioka, T. Kimura, and M. Muraguchi, "High-Efficiency OFDM Power Amplifier System Using a New Polar Modulation Technique," in *IEEE TENCON'16*, pp. 2521–2524, 2016.

[4] R. Ishioka, T. Kimura, and M. Muraguchi, "A Proposal for a New OFDM Wireless System using a CAZAC Equalization Scheme," in *AICT'2017*, no. 1, pp. 47–51, 2017.

[5] IEEE, "Part 11: Wireless LAN Medium Access Control (MAC) and Physical Layer (PHY) Specifications," *IEEE Std 802.11-2016 (Revision of IEEE Std 802.11-2012)*, 2016.

[6] P. Asbeck and Z. Popovic, "ET Comes of Age: Envelope Tracking for Higher-Efficiency Power Amplifiers," *IEEE Microwave Magazine*, vol. 17, no. 3, pp. 16–25, Mar. 2016.

Multinomial Distribution Based Blind Interleaver Parameters Estimation

Changryoul Choi and Jechang Jeong
Dept. of Electronic and Communication Engineering Hanyang University
Seoul, Korea
e-mail: denebchoi@gmail.com & jjeong@hanyang.ac.kr

Abstract— **In this paper, we propose a blind interleaver parameters estimation algorithm. By modeling the distribution of the ranks of the random matrices as a multinomial distribution, we can easily identify the parameters of the interleavers blindly. Experimental results show that the proposed algorithm outperforms other blind interleaver parameter estimation algorithms.**

Keywords- interleaver; channel code; error-correcting codes; blind estimation

I. Introduction

Under the inherent channel impairments during communication, Error Correcting Codes (ECC) are indispensable for reliable transmission. In general, many ECCs are robust to the random errors but they are very weak to burst errors. For this reason, the interleaver which permutes the symbols (or bits) from several codewords so that any given codeword are well separated is introduced to handle this problem. Note that, for reliable communication, the receiver has to synchronize the data and deinterleave them before a channel decoder starts to operate [1].

In a non-cooperative context, an eavesdropper tries to find information without any knowledge of the communication parameters used. For a perfect recovery of data, one of the most important steps is blind estimation of the interleaver parameters using only the intercepted sequences.

Some algorithms exploiting the linearity of ECCs are proposed in the literature [2]-[11]. Algorithms using the properties of the dual codes are proposed in [2]-[4]. By finding a basis of a dual code by using the parity check relations, interleaver parameters can be blindly estimated. Algorithms using the linear dependence within a codeword were also proposed in [5]-[9]. Sicot et al. used both of the approaches and showed very good results [10]. Another approach exploiting the linear dependence among codewords and the specific distribution of the ranks of the random matrices are first proposed in [11]. Their algorithm, first, tries to identify errorless symbols by exploiting the distribution of the ranks of the random matrices and makes a rectangular matrix using the errorless symbols. If the interleaver period is not the same as the (horizontal) dimension of the rectangular matrix, it will have full rank. Otherwise, it does not have full rank [11].

In this paper, we propose a blind interleaver parameter estimation algorithm by modeling the distribution of the ranks of the random matrices as a multinomial distribution. By this modeling, we can transform the problem of estimating interleaver parameters into that of the probability matching. Using this probabilistic setup, we can efficiently determine interleaver parameters in a non-cooperative context.

The rest of this paper is organized as follows. Section II gives a review of some previous algorithms. In Section III, we explain our proposed algorithm. Simulation results and analyses are in Section IV, and we conclude in Section V.

II. Previous Works

In this section, we describe the system setup. And we explain in detail the property of linear dependence among codewords and the distribution of the ranks of the random matrices since the proposed algorithm is heavily dependent upon these properties.

A. System Setup

Let C be an (n, k, d) linear code over $GF(2)$, where n is the codeword length, k is the code dimension, d is the minimum Hamming weight of the codewords, and $GF(2)$ represents the Galois field of order 2. By linearity, we can represent any codeword $\mathbf{c} \in C$ as follows:

$$\mathbf{c} = \mathbf{m}G \tag{1}$$

where $\mathbf{c}$ is a $1 \times n$ row vector, $\mathbf{m}$ is a $1 \times k$ row vector, and G is a $k \times n$ matrix having full rank.

Since in almost all the communication systems, the interleaver size S is a multiple of the codeword size, we can represent $S = \beta n$, where β is the number of codewords within an interleaver. We assume that the channel is a Binary Symmetric Channel (BSC) with transition probability of P_e. Let l be a predicted interleaver period.

Note that the most fundamental and frequent operations of the proposed algorithm are the calculations of the ranks of the matrices. In this case, the matrix is of size $l \times (l + q)$ ($q \geq 0$). When making a sequence into a matrix of size $l \times (l + q)$, we pile up the received symbols from leftmost top to rightmost bottom in raster scanning order.

B. Linear Dependence among Codewords

The (n, k, d) linear code C over $GF(2)$ is a k-dimensional subspace in an n-dimensional vector space. Due to this, there are k basis vectors in the n-dimensional vector space. If there are $k + 1$ codewords, at least one of the codewords can be described by the linear combination of k basis vectors. This property of linear dependence among codewords can elucidate the rank behavior better than the property of linear dependence within codewords [11].

C. Distribution of the Ranks of the Random Matrices

Let the probability P_s be the probability that the rank of the $l \times l$ square matrix is $l - s$ ($s \neq 0$) when $l \to \infty$. In this case, we assume that the entries in an $l \times l$ square random matrix take the values in $GF(2)$ with equal probability. In [12], P_s is given by

$$P_s = 2^{-s^2} \left(\prod_{i=s+1}^{\infty} (1-2^{-i})\right)\left(\prod_{i=1}^{s} (1-2^{-i})^{-1}\right) \tag{2}$$

and when $s = 0$, P_0 is given by

$$P_0 = \prod_{i=1}^{\infty} (1-2^{-i}) . \tag{3}$$

Table I shows the values of P_s for some values of s. Note that as l increases, the calculated P_s rapidly converges to theoretical values. From Table I, we can see that an $l \times l$ square binary random matrix would very rarely have a rank as low as $l - s$ ($s \geq 3$).

TABLE I. P_S FOR SMALL VALUES OF S

s	P_s
0	0.288788
1	0.577576
2	0.128350
3	0.005238
4	4.65669×10^{-5}
5	9.69136×10^{-8}

If the rank of an $l \times l$ square binary matrix A happens to be ($s \geq 3$), we can assume that there are some structures in this matrix A. That is, we can presume that the matrix has $l - s - m$ ($m \geq 1$) basis vectors and m distinct errors [11]. If we plug such ideas into the blind interleaver parameters estimation algorithm, when $l = S$, low ranks can happen frequently. When $l \neq S$, the rank of matrix A follows the distribution in Table I.

III. PROPOSED ALGORITHM

As is pointed out in Section II-C, when $l = S$, the $l \times l$ square matrices would have low ranks frequently. Otherwise, i.e., when $l \neq S$, the ranks of the $l \times l$ square matrices follow the distribution in Table I. Therefore, we can consider the problem of finding the interleaver parameters as that of the probability matching. That is, when $l \neq S$, the distribution of the ranks of the $l \times l$ square matrices would be very close to the distribution in Table I. If the distribution of the ranks of the $l \times l$ square matrices is very different from the distribution in Table I, we can assume that $l = S$.

To assess the closeness between the distribution of the ranks of the $l \times l$ square matrices and the distribution in Table I, we consider the distribution in Table I as a multinomial distribution [13]. For brevity, we partition the events into 4 categories: EVENT_0 (whose rank is 0), EVENT _1 (whose rank is 1), EVENT _2 (whose rank is 2), EVENT_3 (whose rank is no less than 3). Then, we have the following table of cell probabilities in Table II.

TABLE II. PROBABILITY OF MULTINOMIAL DISTRIBUTION

$EVENT\_I$	P_{EVENT_I}
0	0.288788
1	0.577576
2	0.128350
3	0.005286

Assume that the number of trials is N and the numbers of events are (x_0, x_1, x_2, x_3) in N. Note that $N = x_0+x_1+x_2+x_3$. We assume that the random vector (x_0, x_1, x_2, x_3) follows the multinomial distribution. We also assume that the dimension of the matrices are $l \times l$. Then, the probability P_l of this random vector is calculated as follows [13]:

$$P_l = \frac{N!}{x_0!x_1!x_2!x_3!} P_{event\_0}^{x_0} P_{event\_1}^{x_1} P_{event\_2}^{x_2} P_{event\_3}^{x_3} . \tag{4}$$

Note that when the random vector follows the distribution in Table II, the probability P_m would be 1. Otherwise, its probability would be very small.

The proposed algorithm can be summarized as follows:

1) Randomly select l vectors and construct an $l \times l$ square matrix.
2) Calculate the rank s of the matrix.
3) Count the number of EVENT_i.
4) Repeat steps from 1) to 3) N times.
5) Calculate (4). If P_l is less than a predetermined threshold. Go to 7).
6) Increment l as $l + 1$ and go to 1).
7) Declare that the interleaver period is l.

Note that a predetermined threshold is calculated according to the false alarm probability.

IV. EXPERIMENTAL RESULTS

We carry out some experiments to validate the proposed algorithm. In all the experiments, we use (7, 4) binary Hamming code and random interleavers. In this case, when the interleaver period is S, the search range of the interleaver period is set from 7 to S + 1, and the delay parameter is chosen randomly from 0 to S – 1. We set the threshold (which is related to a false alarm probability) as 10^{-10}. For each Bit Error Rate (BER) the number of iterations is set to

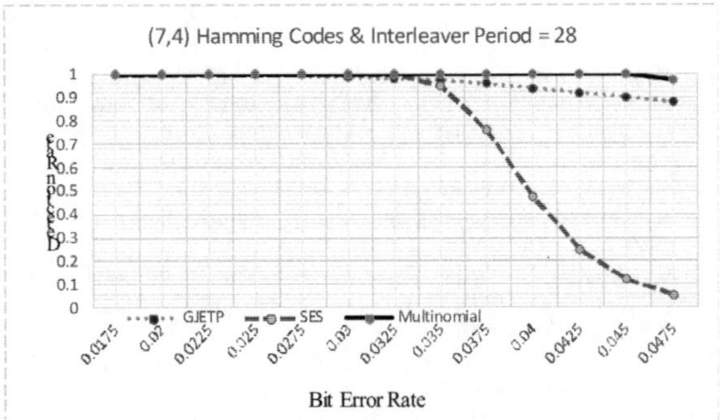

Figure 1. Detection probability for the algorithms when the interleaver size is 28.

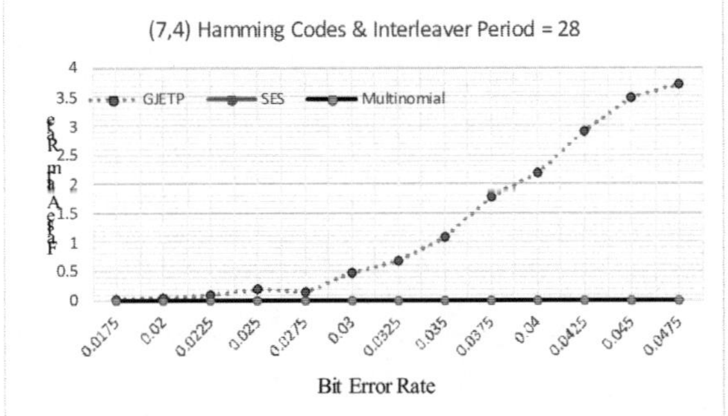

Figure 2. False alarm probability (%) for the algorithms when the interleaver size is 28.

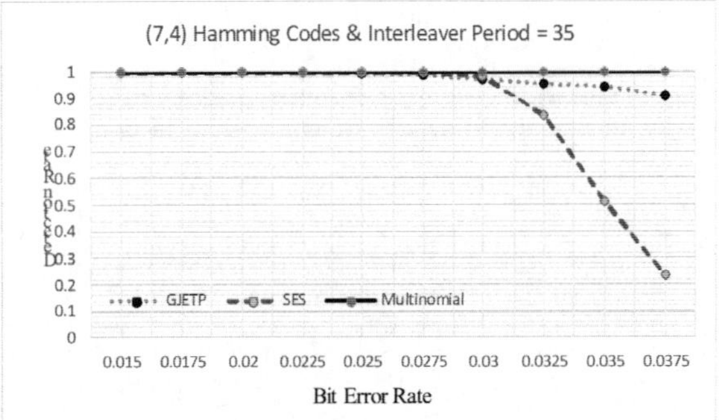

Figure 3. Detection probability for the algorithms when the interleaver size is 35.

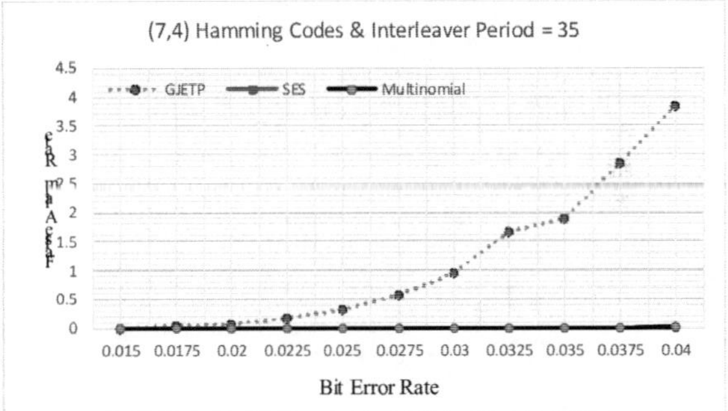

Figure 4. False alarm probability (%) for the algorithms when the interleaver size is 35.

10,000. The number of intercepted samples available is 50,000. We compared the performance of the proposed algorithm with that of Gauss-Jordan Elimination Through Pivoting (GJETP) algorithm [10] and that of the Selecting the Errorless Symbols (SES) based interleaver parameter estimation algorithm [11].

Figure 1 shows the detection performance of algorithms when the interleaver period is 28. As can be seen from the figure, the proposed algorithm outperforms the other algorithms. The false alarm probability of the proposed algorithm and the SES based algorithm is 0 over the BER range [0.0175, 0.0475] from the figure 2. On the contrary, the false alarm probability of the GJETP is relatively high and when BER is 0.0475, its false alarm probability is 3.72%.

Figure 3 shows the detection performance of algorithms when the interleaver period is 35. As with the figure 1, the proposed algorithm almost perfectly estimates the interleaver period and outperforms the other algorithms. Figure 4 shows the false alarm probabilities of the algorithms. To be specific, the false alarm events did not occur for the SES based algorithm. For the proposed algorithm, the false alarm events occurred only when BER = 0.04. In this case, the false alarm probability is 0.02%. As with the figure 2, the false alarm probability of the GJETP is relatively very high.

V. Conclusions

In this paper, we proposed an interleaver parameters estimation algorithm based on the probabilistic matching. By modeling the ranks of the random square matrices as a multinomial distribution, we can easily estimate the interleaver parameters. Experimental results show that the proposed algorithm outperforms other algorithms in terms of detection performance and the reliability.

Acknowledgment

This work was supported by the ICT R&D program of MSIP/IITP. [2014-0-00670, Software Platform for ICT Equipment]

References

[1] S. B. Wicker, Error control systems for digital communications and storage, Englewood Cliffs, NJ, USA: Prentice-Hall, 1995.

[2] A. Valembois, "Detection and recognition of a binary linear code," Discrete Applied Mathematics, vol. 111, no. 1-2, pp. 199-218, July 2001.

[3] M. Cluzeau, "Block code reconstruction using iterative decoding techniques," in Proc. of ISIT06, Seattle, WA, USA, July 2006, pp. 2269-2273.

[4] M. Marazin, R. Gautier, and G. Burel, “Some interesting dual-code properties of convolutional encoder for standards for self-recognition,” IET Commun., vol. 6, no. 8, pp. 931-935, May 2012.

[5] G. Burel and R. Gautier, “Blind estimation of encoder and interleaver characteristics in a non cooperative context,” in Proc. of IASTED, Scottsdale, AZ, USA, Nov. 2003, pp. 275-280.

[6] L. Lu, K. H. Li, and Y. L. Guan, "Blind detection of interleaver parameters for non-binary coded data streams," in Proc. of ICC, Dresden, Germany, June 2009, pp.1–4.

[7] R Swaminathan, A. S. Madhukumar, N. W. Teck, and C. M. S. See, “Parameter estimation of convolutional and helical interleavers in a noisy environment,” IEEE Access, vol. 5, pp. 6151-6167, May 2017.

[8] R Swaminathan, A. S. Madhukumar, N. W. Teck, and S. C. M. Samson, “Parameter estimation of block and helical scan interleavers in the presence of bit errors,” Digit. Signal Process., vol. 60, pp. 20–32, January 2017.

[9] R Swaminathan and A. S. Madhukumar, “Classification of error correction codes and estimation of interleaver parameters in a robust environment,” IEEE Trans. on Broadcast., vol. 63, no. 3, pp. 463-478, September 2017.

[10] G. Sicot, S. Houcke, and J. Barbier, “Blind detection of interleaver parameters,” Signal Processing, vol. 89, pp. 450-462, April 2009.

[11] C. Choi and D. Yoon, “Enhanced blind interleaver parameters estimation algorithm for noisy environment,” IEEE Access, vol. 6, pp. 5910-5915, 2018.

[12] V. F. Kolchin, Random Graphs, New York: Cambridge University Press, 1999.

[13] G. Casella and R. Berger, Statistical Inference, Duxbury Press, 2001.

Actor4j: A Software Framework for the Actor Model Focusing on the Optimization of Message Passing

David Alessandro Bauer, Juho Mäkiö
Department of Informatics and Electronics
University of Applied Sciences Emden/Leer
Emden, Germany
Email: david.bauer@hs-emden-leer.de, juho.maekioe@hs-emden-leer.de

***Abstract*—Common actor implementations often use standardized thread pools without special optimization for the message passing. For that, a high-performance solution was worked out. The actor-oriented software framework Akka uses internally a ForkJoinPool that is intended for a MapReduce approach. However, the MapReduce approach is not relevant for message passing, as it may lead to significant performance losses. One solution is to develop a thread pool that focuses on the message passing. In the implementation of the Actor4j framework, the message queue of the actors is placed in threads to enable an efficient message exchange. The actors are operated directly from this queue (injecting the message), without further ado. It was further enhanced by the use of multiple task-specific queues. Fairness and the responsiveness of the system have been raised. In particular, the performance measurement results show that an intra-thread communication towards an inter-thread communication is much better and has very good scaling properties.**

Keywords-actors; actor model; parallelization; reactive system; message passing; microservices; Java.

I. Introduction

The use of cloud computing systems is used more often, especially as a Platform-as-a-Service (PaaS) solutions (e.g., Microsoft Azure, Amazon Web Services, Google Cloud Platform). A step further is to design the architecture of software as microservices instead of a monolithic design [1]. In this case, Docker images can be used [2], which can be uploaded to them (Azure Container Service, Amazon Elastic Container Service, Google Kubernetes Engine). An alternative microservice approach is the service factory of Microsoft Azure, which orchestrates among other services. Microservices are arbitrary scalable and easy to change [3] and reusable. In Microsoft Azure service factory actors are also used (Virtual Actor pattern [4]) [5]. The advantage of actor-oriented services is that they can hold lightweight representatives (the actors). They can be used as a replacement of the traditional middle tier [4]. Actors can be seen as a pendant to Function-as-a-Service (FaaS), if the actors are themselves stateless. Actors and functions can be called nanoservices, as a lightweight derivative to microservices. Scalability can be obtained by high parallelism (to divide a task in subtasks, or parallel execution of a task, if the underlying code is stateless). See also the Scale Cube by Abbott [6], which describes the three dimensions of scalability.

To ensure high parallelization, its one benefit to use multi-core systems. The computer world of the last few years has been characterized by a change ("The Free Lunch Is Over" [7]) from constantly increasing computing power to multi-core systems due to technical limitations. In particular, technical progress always lags behind practical requirements (Wirth's law [8]). Up to now, Moore's law was “that the number of transistors available to semiconductor manufacturers would double approximately every 18 to 24 months” [9]. This will presumably continue through the transition to multi-core systems. Due to the issues with parallel programs [10] according to the classic model (especially error prone in programming of complex systems with semaphores and mutexes), actor-oriented frameworks are becoming increasingly popular [11].

This work contributes to achieving a higher performance in the field of message passing. This is relevant for all systems, where a lot of messages have to be exchanged (e.g., Internet of Things, Internet of Services). It is intended to develop a specially designed thread pool for message passing. The framework Akka is used as a reference implementation, but this is written in Scala. In order to achieve comparability and to provide a realistic picture (for benchmarks in Section 7), the degree of implementation of the underlying actor model (actor4j) must have some complexity. The four semantic properties [11] of the actor model have to be taken into account during implementation. In addition, the actor model as a reactive system should satisfy the four principles of the reactive manifesto [12]. In particular, the responsiveness of the reactive system has to be taken into account, since this is also important in regard to the achievement of this work. Akka is currently a widespread and popular (has a very good rating on GitHub [13] and a lot of contributors) actor implementation. The users of Akka are large companies like Intel, Samsung LinkedIn, Twitter and Zalando [14]. According to Suereth: “Akka is the most powerful performing framework available on the JVM” [15]. The long-term goal is the establishment of a Java framework for the actor model as an alternative to Akka. Akka is written in Scala (except the Java-API), this can be a hindrance for Java developers to understand the underlying architecture. There can be also an acceptance problem.

First, two important basic building blocks of this work are discussed. Accordingly, a brief introduction to the actor model and reactive systems is given. Then, a comparison between Akka and actor4j will be presented. Next, the solution approach of the novel framework actor4j is shown. Subsequently the results of testing actor4j are presented and discussed. This paper ends up with a conclusion and insight in the future works. The source code for actor4j is available under GitHub [16].

II. Actor Model

In classic concurrent programming, it goes over the concepts of shared state, mutual exclusion and semaphores. [17]. With increasing program complexity, the correctness of the program is difficult to proof or to verify. Especially, because concurrent programs are difficult to test [18]. However, the actor model, based on message passing, offers an alternative. The essential features compared to the classic concurrent programming are:

- no shared state,
- asynchronous message transfer, and
- message queue for each actor [17].

This eliminates the need to use proprietary synchronization techniques between the actors to protect the access to shared resources [17]. The data transmitted between the actors is conceptually immutable and thus does not require synchronization [17].

When a message arrives, actors can react by:

- myself send messages,
- instantiating more actors, or
- changing its own state [19].

These activities may influence the next incoming messages (possible behavioral change) [19]. The actor model was introduced in 1973 in a paper [20] by Carl Hewitt, Peter Bishop and Richard Steiger [21]. A message can contain any kind of data.

There are "four important semantic properties of actor systems: [state] encapsulation, fairness, location transparency and mobility" [11].

The *state encapsulation* ensures that no actor can directly call another actor. Secure messaging requires that messages are transmitted in the sense of call-by-value messages. However, call-by-reference is permitted in most actor frameworks. As the "deep copying is an expensive operation" [11], this criterion is not always followed in practice. Only actors can communicate with one another via messages [11].

Fairness means that all actors can be treated equally and supplied with appropriate messages. Uncooperative actors that, for example, perform active waiting, polling, or time-consuming calls are very likely to adversely affect other actors (actors are no longer operated, blocking the corresponding thread) [11].

Location transparency means that the naming is independent of its localization. The name of the actor is unambiguous and unchangeable [11].

Mobility allows the transfer of the actor to other nodes in the cluster. A distinction is made between weak and strong mobility. Weak mobility allows for the exchange of the underlying code with subsequent initialization of the context of the actor. Strong mobility includes the current context of the actor [11].

The actor model is successfully used in business, for example in WhatsApp or for RabbitMQ (implements AMQP protocol). For both you can set up publish-subscribe systems for messaging, based on the actor model. The programming language Erlang (actor-oriented programming language, see also Section 4) was used for that.

III. Reactive Systems

Nowadays, more and more data need to be processed in a shorter time. This is known under the term Big Data. Big Data is associated with very large amounts of data. It may be discrete or continuous data. These fall on particularly at very high frequented and interactive web services (e.g., Facebook, Google, IoT-Area). Especially, in data mining, data is evaluated in a targeted way to create value. A practical example of a use-case is the "Deutscher Wetterdienst" (Germany's National Meteorological Service) that uses Akka for parallel processing or evaluating the historical meteorological data [22]. A solution to this can be reactive systems. Reactive systems are reacting to requested requirements. Applications should be fail-safe and easily scalable [12] for security issues.

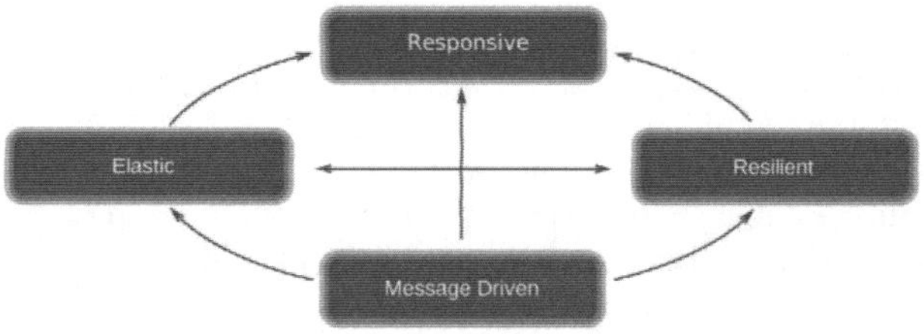

Figure 1. Presentation of the basic principles of reactive systems from the Reactive Manifesto [12]. Arrows symbolize an influence on each other.

Reactive systems are characterized by four important properties (see Figure 1):

- *Message Driven*: Messages in the reactive system are exchanged asynchronously. The components are non-transparent. [12] The actor model can serve as a basic architecture.
- *Resilient*: The reactive system is fail-safe. If errors occur, it remains responsive. Superordinate components assume the responsibility for the handling of errors (Supervision, see Erlang [23],

Akka [24]). Additional security provides the replication of functionality. [12]

- *Responsive*: The reactive system supplies time-sensitive feedback to its users and to its dependent components. This is also a prerequisite for an adequate response in the event of errors (supervision), as well as ensuring its function (task of the system). [12]
- *Elastic*: The reactive system remains adaptable even with changing requirements in regard to load capacity. If the load is changed, it can be intervened in a self-regulating manner. [12]

IV. RELATED WORKS

Akka is used as a reference implementation for Actor4j. Akka was again influenced by Erlang, in terms of fault tolerance (Supervision). The actor-oriented software framework ActorFoundry implements the four semantic properties of the actor model.

A. Erlang

Erlang is influenced by the actor model [21] and uses this directly for their language. In Erlang, so-called light-weight processes (no system processes) are used, corresponding to the actors. According to [23], the only way of communication between the processes is asynchronous message passing. Processes have a "message queue" [25] and "Processes share no Resources" [23], to eliminate the need for synchronization between the processes. The location transparency (see Section 2, Actor Model) is given by a unique process identifier (PID).

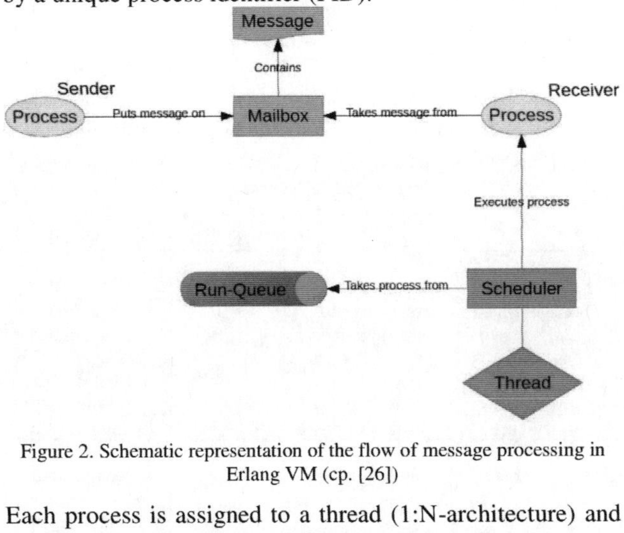

Figure 2. Schematic representation of the flow of message processing in Erlang VM (cp. [26])

Each process is assigned to a thread (1:N-architecture) and is placed in the corresponding run-queue. Processes are executed by the scheduler, that takes processes out from the run-queue (Figure 2). The process itself takes a received message out of the mailbox and processes them. Erlang can be run with one scheduler or multiple schedulers (SMP support, SMP stands for Symmetric Multiprocessing). With one scheduler synchronization is not necessary, because only one thread is interacting. The first solution for SMP was to use the schedulers with one run-queue, but this was a bottleneck. There were too much "lock conflicts" [26]. This was resolved by using one run-queue per scheduler. [26]

Characteristics of Erlang [23]:

- *Scalability*: The Erlang VM "automatically distributes the execution of processes over the available CPUs" [23]
- *Fault tolerance*: To respond adequately to faults in the processes, it is important to take precautions (see Supervision). The processes are shielded from one another so that no chain reaction occurs in the event of a failure of a process.
- *Clarity*: Processes are the representatives of a parallel reactive system. The execution of the processes runs within sequentially. Asynchronously, the exchange between the processes takes place. This structuring leads to more clarity in programming and has more reference to our real world of life.
- *Performance*: It is indisputable to see the possible performance gains when parallelizing a sequential program when this is feasible. Distributing the work to several processes can lead to success.

Supervision:

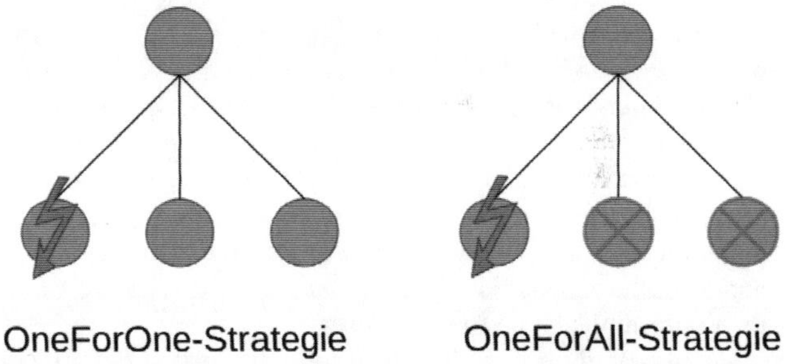

Figure 3. One-for-one supervision tree and One-for-all supervision tree [23].

The supervisor process monitors his worker processes, and in the event of an error, they are restarted. Two strategies are foreseen (see Figure 3). The OneForOne-Strategy restarts only the affected process. In the OneForAll-Strategy, on the other hand, not only the affected process is restarted, but also the neighboring processes (above the supervisor process). [23]

B. *Scala – Akka*

Scala is an object-functional programming language that runs on the JVM (is translated into bytecode). Since version 2.10.0, Akka is used as the default actor implementation [27]. Akka was influenced by the actor model, Erlang and Scala Actors [21]. By default, to forward messages to the actors Akka internally uses a "ForkJoinPool" from Java as a thread pool. An 1:N-architecture is used here. This means, each thread is responsible for the message delivery to its assigned actors (message is injected). The message exchange takes place via the queues of the actors.

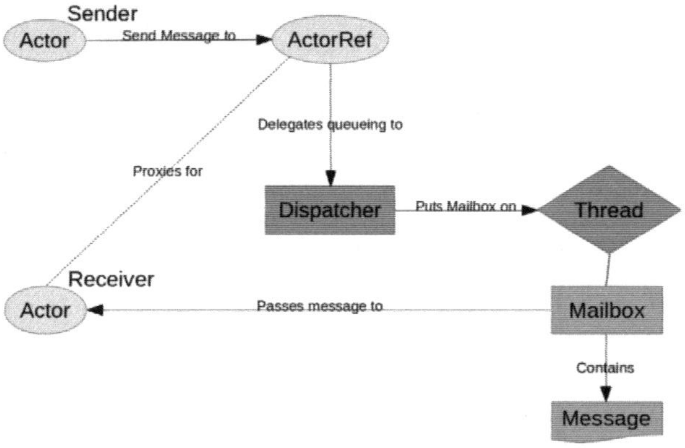

Figure 4. Schematic representation of the flow of message processing in Akka [28].

Now follows a brief explanation of the message processing in Akka. Each actor has its own mailbox (queue). The dispatcher ensures that another message is processed (Figure 4). For this purpose, a new message is taken from the mailbox of the associated actor. The message processing is executed via a thread, where a new message is injected to the actor and the message is then processed by the actor. In addition, the dispatcher ensures that no actor is called more than once at the same time.

As a thread pool, a "ForkJoinPool" is used by default. In Java 7, the "ForkJoinPool" used a central input queue for new tasks to be executed, but it was viewed as a bottleneck. With Java 8 this was improved. Instead of using a central input queue, the new task to be executed is now randomly added in one of the worker queues. „The idea is to treat external submitters in a similar way as workers - using randomized queuing and stealing" [29]. Unlike Akka, actor4j does not need these worker queues because messages are processed directly there via the message queues, belonging to the corresponding thread (see Chapter 6).

C. *ActorFoundry*

Previously, an actor was mapped to a separate thread (strict encapsulation, 1: 1-architecture). However, this led to performance problems (thread context switching). Therefore, it was switched to an 1:N-architecture. "ActorFoundry" implements the four semantic properties of the actor model adequately. Messages are transmitted by default using a "deep copy". "ActorFoundry" supports both the weak and the strong mobility. A further worker thread is provided, if uncooperative actors are recogized. This ensures system responsiveness. [11]

V. COMPARISON BETWEEN AKKA AND ACTOR4J IN TABULAR FORM

In the following section, Akka is compared with actor4j. First, the semantic properties are compared (see TABLE I). State encapsulation, fairness and location transparency were covered by both frameworks. Currently, actor4j only partly supports the mobility.

TABLE I. COMPARISON OF SEMATIC PROPERTIES BETWEEN AKKA AND ACTOR4J.

	Akka	**actor4j**
Semantic properties		
State encapsulation	Other actors cannot be referenced directly (ActorRef)	Other actors cannot be referenced directly (Universal Unique Identifier, UUID)
Fairness	Definition of a throughput	Definition of a throughput, additionally queues for different purposes
Location transparency	Actor has its unique ActorRef	Actor has its unique UUID
Mobility	Actors can be created remotely, ?	Currently partially implemented, only load balancing at creation time (related to threads)

In following, the reactiveness is compared with the reactive manifesto. Both frameworks are designed as message driven, resilient and responsive (see TABLE II). The elastic approach is currently not supported by actor4j.

TABLE II. COMPARISON OF REACTIVENESS BETWEEN AKKA AND ACTOR4J.

	Akka		**actor4j**
Reactive system			
Message driven	Asynchronous message transfer, every actor has its own message queue		Asynchronous message transfer, message queue is located at the threads
Resilient	Supervision		Supervision
Responsive	Usage of additionally thread pools		Usage of ResourceActor's for heavy computations (additionally thread pool)
Elastic	?		Currently not implemented

Both frameworks implement the following features: pattern matching, persistence, the publish-subscribe pattern, and well reactive streams (see TABLE III). Additionally, actor4j supports an anti-flooding strategy using ring buffered queues. For enhanced performance grouping of actors is also available. Caching with actors is also supported by actor4j (volatile and persistent caching over a database).

TABLE III. COMPARISON OF ADDITIONAL FEATURES BETWEEN AKKA AND ACTOR4J.

	Akka	actor4j
Features		
	-	Anti-flooding strategy, important queues are ring buffered
	-	Grouping of actors
	Pattern matching	Pattern matching
	Persistence	Persistence
	Publish-Subscribe (see Event Bus, Event Stream)	Publish-Subscribe
	Reactive Streams	Reactive Streams
	-	Caching

For the implementation of the remote communication between actors, both frameworks use different approaches (see TABLE IV). For actor4j, applications are provided that can include several actors, which can be deployed separately into the actor system. This can ensure a domain specific separation of concerns. Akka supports failure detector, sharing and a kind of distributed publish-subscribe.

TABLE IV. COMPARISON OF CLUSTER FEATURES BETWEEN AKKA AND ACTOR4J.

	Akka	actor4j
Cluster		
	TCP, UDP, Apache Camel	REST-API, Websocket, gRPC
	-	ActorApplication planned, running in the context of an actor system
	Failure Detector	Failure Detector planned
	Sharding	Sharding planned
	Distributed Publish-Subscribe	?

For testing Akka supports (see TABLE V) behavior testing and integration testing. Actor4j supports behavior testing and a verification method, integration testing is planned.

TABLE V. COMPARISON OF TESTING FEATURES BETWEEN AKKA AND ACTOR4J.

	Akka	actor4j
Testing		
	Behaviour Testing for an actor	Behaviour Testing for an actor
	Integration Testing with JavaTestKit	Integration Testing planned
	-	Verification

VI. ACTOR4J – FINAL DESIGN

In this Section the novel thread pool architecture (see Figure 5) for actor4j is presented. Actor4j uses mainly data structures that are lock-free ("synchronized by using a lock-free technique" [30]). Therefore, in contrast to classical synchronization techniques, performance loses are avoided. With the use of lock-free programming, performance loses are possible, too. This is the case especially if multiple threads are frequently accessing the same resource (e.g., compare-and-swap conflicts).

The actor-oriented implementations presented in related works use a sort of worker-queue for the thread pooling and every actor has its own queue. The first idea was to avoid this double queuing. Now the actors belonging to the thread, will be operated directly from the thread message queue. One advantage is that actor-context switches are avoided, that would happen in the classical approach, where an access to the actors queue is needed (pushing a new message to the queue). Instead new messages are pushed to the thread message queue, avoiding the actor context at first. The disadvantage is that concurrent access (mainly inbound) conflicts are raised on the thread message queue, caused by other threads. The second idea is that actors belonging to the same thread can communicate or share resources without synchronization techniques (also absence of lock-free programming). For this, a normal (not thread-safe) queue has been set up. The third idea is to use two-level queues, one that is thread safe and one that is not. This should reduce concurrent access conflicts, from the belonging working thread. The queue to the outside is protected, the inner queues enables a higher performance in the absence of additional protecting mechanism. The two-level queues where inspired by the CPU cache levels. There was taken for the overall design the same strategy as mentioned in [26]: "First make it work, then measure, then optimize". Further explanations follow in the sub-sections below.

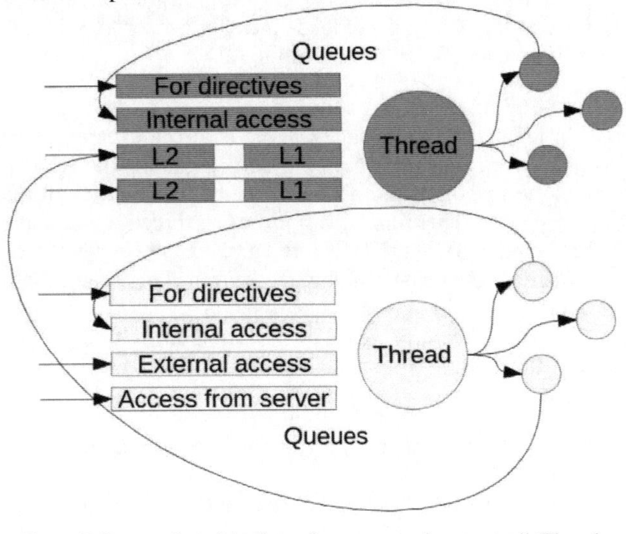

Figure 5. Presentation of the flow of message passing at actor4j (Thread pool architecture of actor4j).

A. 1:N-architecture

All actors are permanently assigned to one thread (1:N-architecture). The Thread is, in case of message delivery, responsible for injection the message and the execution of its associated actors. Actors can send messages to other actors. These messages are stored in the respective thread that is responsible for the receiving actor (see Figure 5 and Figure 6). For clarification, actors don't have their own queue, as in the classic approach.

B. Queues

The division into different queues ensures a fair message flow. This ensures that other queues are processed (whenever the thread gets a time quantum), even when the input queue is used intensively. In each round (loop within the thread) of all queues, a fixed number of messages is processed if available. This is similar to the definition of throughput in Akka [31]. So, the reactive system remains responsive.

C. Three different ways of access

All queues use a ring buffer (also an effective block for an anti-flooding strategy). If both or more corresponding actors are assigned to the same thread, the internal queue can be accessed. This is implemented as a "CircularFifoQueue" [32] because no synchronization is required in this case. If accessed from another thread, the message is placed in the external queue. This must be thread-safe now(non-blocking programming). For external access and access from the server the queue is divided into two stages.

D. Two stage division

L2 (Level 2) corresponds to a "MpscArrayQueue" [33] and L1 (Level 1) of an "ArrayDeque". This approach is intended to achieve a performance enhancement when a higher load of messages occur. The responsible thread then works mainly with L1 and loads messages accordingly. This concurrent access can be avoided to L2.

E. Directives queue

In regard to failure safety, there is also a special queue which directives are processed by the respective thread with the highest priority in order to ensure the consistency of the actor system. There are stop and restart directives that can affect single or multiple actors. If there are currently no messages at the respective thread, the thread either goes into the idle state for a short time interval or signals a yield ("Thread voluntarily releases its computing time" [34], translation).

F. Source code examples

Now follow some excerpts of the source code for clarification:

- Processing a maximum specified number of messages (throughput) per loop pass on the example of the internal queue.

```
for (; hasNextInner<system.throughput &&
    poll(innerQueue);
    hasNextInner++);
```

- For the external queue first tried L1 is to be processed. If there are no messages in L1, it will be loaded accordingly from L2.

```
for (; hasNextOuter<system.throughput &&
    poll(outerQueueL1);
    hasNextOuter++);

if (hasNextOuter<system.throughput &&
    outerQueueL2.peek()!=null) {
    ActorMessage<?> message = null;
    for (int j=0;
       j<system.getBufferQueueSize() &&
       (message=outerQueueL2.poll())!=null; j++)
          outerQueueL1.offer(message);

       for (; hasNextOuter<system.throughput &&
          poll(outerQueueL1);
          hasNextOuter++);
}
```

A complete implementation of the class ActorThread is given by default by the class DefaultActorThread [35].

G. Message processing in actor4j

Internally, message processing takes place in actor4j (see Figure 6), similar to Akka. An actor wants to send a message to another actor. This is first redirected to the corresponding ActorCell. The ActorCell class contains the actual background implementation of an actor. Each ActorCell is assigned an actor. The message is then forwarded to the dispatcher. This inserts the message according to the selected recipient into the corresponding queue of the thread (applied access options see Figure 5). As soon as the message can be processed by the thread, it is injected into the receiver actor for processing.

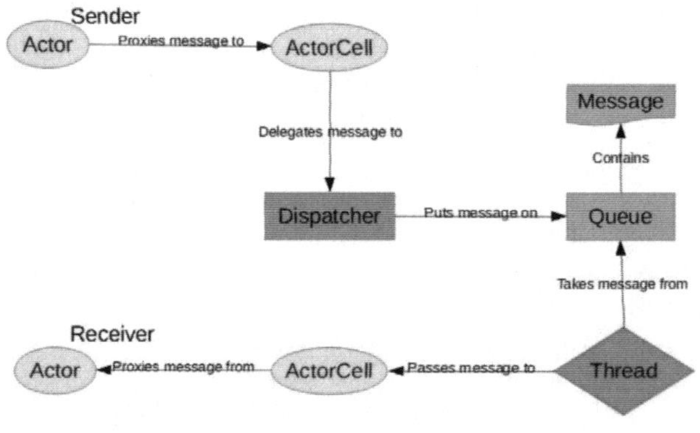

Figure 6. Schematic representation of the flow of message processing in actor4j (cp. [28] of Akka).

VII. ACTOR4J– RESULTS

The performance of message passing was tested with a DELL OptiPlex 7040, Intel® Core™ i7-6700 CPU (Skylake)

@3,40 GHz, 32 GB RAM and 8 MB L3 Cache. As the JVM Oracle JDK 9.0.4 was used under Windows 10, 64 Bit. Three benchmark scenarios are presented to get a picture of the performance of actor4j's message throughput.

1. In the first case, only the internal queue is claimed. The exchange of messages takes place on the same thread (best performance is awaited).
2. In the second case, if only the external queue is claimed. The exchange of messages takes place on different threads (worst performance is awaited).
3. As a third case, if the internal and external queue of the threads are used quasi evenly (bulk version). The exchange of messages takes place on the same or on a different thread (average performance is awaited).

Additionally, in this paper the skynet [36] benchmark as fourth benchmark is included, that shows message passing in combination of massively dynamic creating and stopping actors. In [37] this is done for "revealing the overhead for actor creation" (similar approach).

The legend "...actor4j_100" or "...akka_100" in the benchmark results means that a throughput of maximum 100 was set (cp. legends of Figure 7, Figure 8 and Figure 9). Accordingly, maximal one hundred messages per queue will be processed at once.

A. *N-fold ring benchmark*

The first is the N-fold ring benchmark. Ring or multi-ring benchmarks for actors can be found also in [11] and [37]. The idea is to bundle actors into groups, where they are guaranteed to run on the same thread and therefore no synchronization is required. For this purpose, an eightfold ring (see Figure 7) was generated for the benchmark, i.e., one ring per thread in the parallel version. Thus, no message exchange is needed between the threads at actor4j. In Akka this possibility does not exist. In the case of actor4j, only the internal queue (CircularFifoQueue) is used, since the members of the ring groups remain together on a thread. All actors are derived here from the ActorGroupMember class. In this case, Akka has no chance to equal actor4j.

In part, actor4j has a factor seven higher throughput compared to Akka. With ongoing number of actors deployed, the actor-context switches are increased in the corresponding thread. This results in less throughput. It also must be considered, that with enabled Hyper-Threading (HT), additional logical kernels through HT do not correspond to fully-fledged pure physical cores (only 30% increase in performance is expected) [9]. But with pure physical cores the result of this benchmark for actor4j should scale nearly linear, with an increased amount of cores (by less deployed actors).

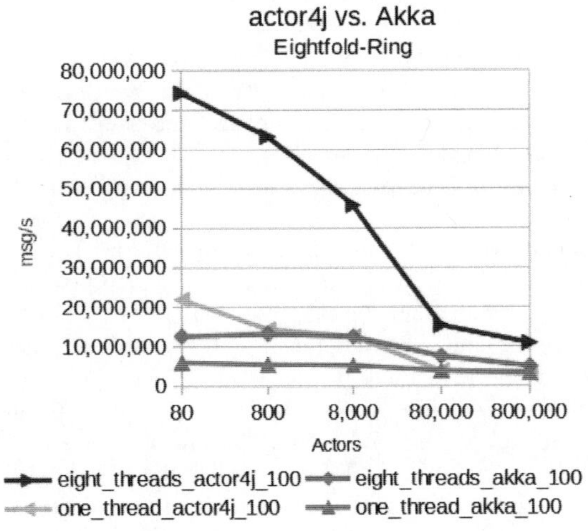

Figure 7. Results for the Eightfold-Ring benchmark. actor4j vs. Akka.

B. *Ping-Pong-Grouped benchmark*

Next, the pairs were distributed over the threads so that both partners are on a different thread. This ensures that only the external queues of the threads are used. This is only possible with actor4j in such differentiated manner. The results in Figure 8 demonstrate that actor4j has lost in performance through the intercommunication between the threads. Akka stays nearly unchanged in throughput, what was also the case in the benchmark before. Hand in hand with more actors deployed, actor-context switches reduce the message throughput. As mentioned before Akka does double queuing on the thread pool and on the actors, which is also a possible performance obstacle (see Section 4). When multithreaded and with less actors deployed, actor4j has a possible break-in in throughput, due to less work for the corresponding threads, resulting in a blocking state.

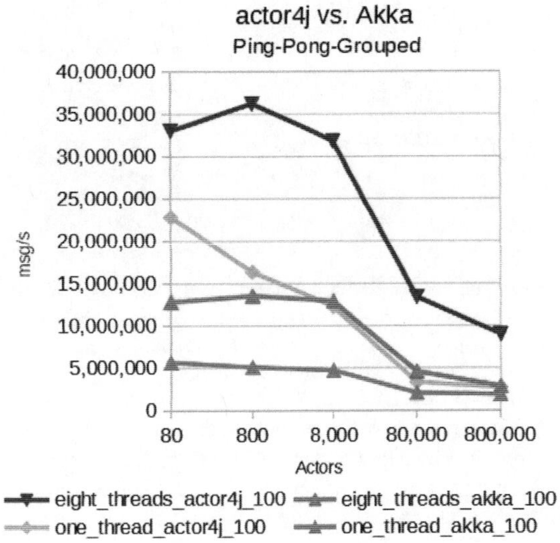

Figure 8. Results for the Ping-Pong-Grouped benchmark. actor4j vs. Akka.

C. Ping-Pong-Bulk benchmark

In the third benchmark (see Figure 9), the actors communicate with each other in pairs (ping-pong). In actor4j, the actors are randomly distributed over the threads. This means that both the internal faster queue (Circular FifoQueue) and the external queue (MpscArrayQueue) are used (see also Chapter 4, Actor4j-Final Design). However, the results should be interpreted with caution. Due to the random distribution of the actors, fluctuations can be expected when the benchmark is repeated. The same message is sent several times (in this case one hundred times) to the respective partner of the pairing (ping-pong), which starts the ping-pong scheme. As a result, a hundred messages are exchanged within the pairings each time the game is interchanged. This was also the benchmark for Akka or Akka.NET, with the advertising (50 million msg / s) over the resulting message throughput has been made [38].

It should be noted that Akka performs much better in bulk operations, with respect to message throughput. Both frameworks perform nearly constantly with the same throughput, for each data series. The reason for this is, that there are less actor-context switches, because a bulk operation is performed. Akka has at the last measuring point, problems to handle the massive amount of receiving messages, and struggles on that. Actor4j instead is protected by established ring buffer queues to the outside, this protects effectively against message flooding. The disadvantage of that is possibly losing messages (counteract by increasing the [buffer] queue size).

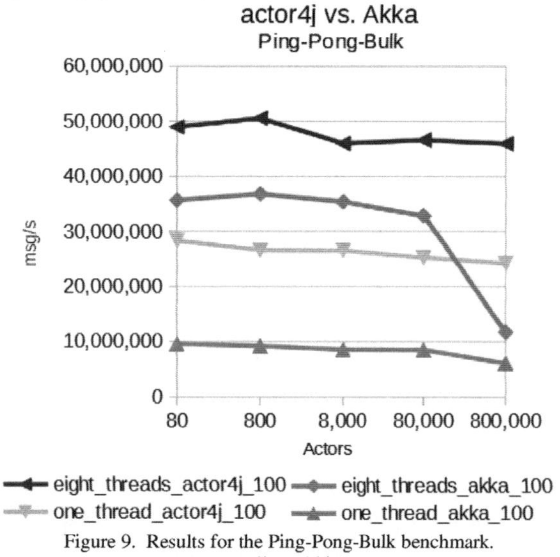

Figure 9. Results for the Ping-Pong-Bulk benchmark. actor4j vs. Akka.

Which stands out in the three benchmarks discussed before, that actor4j with one active thread reaches minimum the same (or nearly the same) message throughput as the active multi-threaded variant of Akka. At some points it has even higher message throughput.

D. Skynet benchmark

At the last benchmark [36][39], slightly over one million actors are created (exactly 1,111,111 actors), by spawning for every actor recursively tens of them. The actors are sending their ordinal number back to the parent, which are then summed up (by one million actors is this 0.5M *(1M+1)-1M), with the result of 499,999,500,000. Every branch of an actor has one child actor with the same ordinal number as his parent (so that the overall sum is correct). In Figure 10, there is an example representation of the resulting actor system structure. This benchmark can be used as a stress test, for creating and optionally stopping actors, as well that the framework is correctly implemented.

The results in TABLE VI are showing that the Akka implementation for creating and stopping actors has a better performance. For inclusively stopping actors, the Akka implementation needs three times longer than for creating them only. The reason for that is that Akka needs much more time for message passing as actor4j, as seen in the equivalent ping-pong grouped benchmark. With one thread the actor4j implementation is slightly better in performance, because of the usage of a non-synchronized queue (only in the case of non-stopping the actors). For the case "without stopping the actors", the actors will be stopped nevertheless after that, because otherwise the memory usage is going to grow constantly (is not included for calculation of the needed time).

TABLE VI. COMPARISON OF THE SKYNET BENCHMARK RESULTS.

	without stopping the actors	**without stopping the actors (only one active thread)**	**with stopping the actors**	**with stopping the actors (only one active thread)**
actor4j	5,911 ms (s=133)	4,901 ms (s=97)	8,226 ms (s=223)	9,011 ms (s=238)
Akka	2,808 ms (s=213)	3,538 ms (s=112)	7,236 ms (s=274)	8,208 ms (s=185)

Figure 10. Structure of the actor system (Skynet benchmark with 111 actors created)

VIII. Conclusion

The results show that actor4j makes a more powerful impression than Akka. The final design (see Section 4) has proved to be elastic, responsive, and resilient. Actor4j was always convincing, no matter what the actor constellation (N-fold ring, ping-pong grouped, ping-pong bulk) was. These benchmarks can be used to determine the performance of inter- and intra-communication between the threads. It has been found that even with the use of lock-free queues these counter against a good scaling (see the ping-pong benchmark). On the other hand, a very good scaling is obtained with intra-communication, i.e., within a thread.

A. Advice

It is advisable to keep communication-active actors together in one and on the same thread, especially if they have a bounded context (see Domain Driven Design). By bounded context is meant that an assignment to a together interacting actor system is possible. With the actor model, agent-based systems can be implemented well. For example, it is useful to keep the ant grouped together as an actor system (sensors, actuators, control unit) in an ant simulation. An own basic ant simulation was built with Akka. An ant is built up by a composition of systems which are describing a comparable SDA-cycle (sense-decide-act) [40]. It is expected that more interaction will occur within the ant system than the environment. In addition, scaling is easier to implement as additional actors are distributed to more threads (when more processors are used).

B. Concept of the new architecture

In the classic design, one message queue is assigned to each actor. This was relocated as already presented to the competent actors thread. In theory, that makes sense. In the real world there is a medium, the surrounding world, between two actors. In particular, the air, which transmits speech through the sound and can be recorded by an actor by its sensors. This can be transferred to the actor model. This means, it makes sense that there is a kind of network layer between the actors, which temporarily stores messages for the actors. Actor4j is also oriented on the four semantic properties of the actor model (see Section 2). With actor4j it is possible to replace very easily the default thread and dispatcher implementation. Therefore, the framework is very flexible, for changing or different providing requirements.

C. Compliance of the four semantic properties

Communication partners are awarded in actor4j via their UUID. Direct access to another actor is so avoided (*encapsulation*). By default, a "deep copy" is carried out for the message transmission, if the prerequisites are fulfilled (interface Copyable implemented for the payload). The payload contains the actual message. The header (sender, recipient, tag) of the message is copied. A new instance of ActorMessage is generated that contains the header and the payload. Senders and receivers are represented by a UUID. The UUIDs do not change (final). It is also possible to transfer the payload as call-by-reference (without "deep copy"). This remains in the responsibility of the developer.

By alternately processing the queues in the actor threads, *fairness* is given. By adjusting the value of throughput, the degree of fairness can be adjusted. A throughput of one would be absolutely fair [31], but the message processing would then be more inefficient (reduction of the message throughput). The order in which messages are transmitted within an actor thread is given (intra-communication). In inter-threading communication, the sequence is only observed between two interacting actors [41]. Otherwise, message communication is not deterministic [19].

The *location transparency* is ensured by the unique UUID for actors. In actor4j, the assignment of an alias is also possible for the simple identification of an actor. A transfer of actors within the actor system (here: relocation to other threads) is currently not implemented (also not in the cluster).

The first purpose of *mobility* is load balancing. Another reason is the displacement of actors to a different location.

D. Future work

One problem is that as the number of actors increases, the throughput drops further and further. This is caused by the constant actor-context switching. Probably this cannot be avoided unless the computing power is increased (higher clock frequency or more physical cores). One useful enhancement could be a special priority queue (belongs to the thread), for prioritized tasks, which can be added by the actors. It is planned to test the actor4j framework under the EU project STIMEY.

Acknowledgment

This project has received funding from the European Union's Horizon 2020 Research and Innovation Program under Grant Agreement N° 709515 — STIMEY

References

[1] Microsoft Azure, "Why a microservices approach to building applications," 2016, [Online]. Available from: https://azure.microsoft.com/engb/documentation/articles/service-fabric-overview microservices/ [retrieved: October, 2016].

[2] M. Jansen and B. Wenzel, "Microservice-Architektur mit Docker und Kubernetes," in Java mit Integrations-SPEKTRUM, Issue 1, February/March 16, pp. 8-14, 2016.

[3] Microsoft Azure, "Overview of Service Fabric," 2016, [Online]. Available from: https://azure.microsoft.com/engb/documentation/articles/service-fabric-overview/ [retrieved: October, 2016].

[4] Microsoft, "Orleans - Virtual Actors," 2010, [Online]. Available from: https://www.microsoft.com/en-us/research/project/orleans-virtual-actors/ [retrieved: June, 2018]

[5] Microsoft Azure, "Introduction to Service Fabric Reliable Actors," 2016, [Online]. Available from: https://azure.microsoft.com/en-gb/documentation/articles/service-fabric-reliable-actors-introduction/ [retrieved: June, 2018]

[6] M. Abbott, "Art of Scalability, The: Scalable Web Architecture, Processes, and Organizations for the Modern Enterprise," Addison-Wesley, p. 340, 2015.

[7] H. Sutter, "The Free Lunch Is Over. A Fundamental Turn Toward Concurrency in Software," In: Dr. Dobb's Journal 30(3), 2015, [Online]. Available from: http://www.gotw.ca /publications/concurrency-ddj.htm [retrieved: June, 2018]

[8] N. Wirth, "A plea for lean software," in *Computer*, vol. 28, no. 2, pp. 64-68, Feb 1995.

[9] S. Akhter and J. Roberts, "Multi-Core Programming: Increasing Performance through Software Multi-threading," Intel Corporation, p. 7, 2006.

[10] E. Westbrook, J. Zhao, Z. Budimlić, and V. Sarkar, "Permission Regions for Race-Free Parallelism", in Khurshid S., Sen K. (eds) Runtime Verification, RV 2011. Lecture Notes in Computer Science, vol. 7186, Springer, Berlin, Heidelberg, 2012.

[11] R. K. Karmani, A. Shali, and G. Agha, "Actor frameworks for the JVM platform: a comparative analysis," in PPPJ, ACM, 2009, [Online]. Available from: http://osl.cs.illinois.edu /media/papers/karmani-2009-pppj-actor_frameworks_for_the _jvm_platform.pdf [retrieved: June, 2018]

[12] J. Bonér, D. Farley, R. Kuhn, M. Thompson, and Community, "The Reactive Manifesto," 2014, [Online]. Available from: http://www.reactivemanifesto.org/ [retrieved: June, 2018].

[13] Lightbend Inc, "Akka," 2018, [Online]. Available from: https://github.com/akka/akka [retrieved: June, 2018].

[14] Lightbend Inc. "Akka: Case studies," 2018, [Online]. Available from: https://www.lightbend.com/case-studies [retrieved: June, 2018]

[15] J. D. Suereth, "Scala in Depth," p. 229, Manning, 2012.

[16] D. A. Bauer, "Actor4j an actor implementation," 2017, [Online]. Available from: https://github.com/relvaner/actor4j-core [retrieved: June, 2018]

[17] A. Miller, "Understanding actor concurrency, Part 1: Actors in Erlang," in JavaWorld, [Online]. Available from: https://www.javaworld.com/article/2077999/java-concurrency/understanding-actor-concurrency--part-1--actors-in-erlang.html [retrieved: June, 2018]

[18] B. Goetz, T. Peierls, J. Bloch, J. Bowbeer, D. Holmes, and D. Lea, "Java Concurrency in Practice," p. 273, 2006.

[19] R. K. Karmani and G. Agha. "Actors," in Encyclopedia of Parallel Computing, Springer, 2011, [Online]. Available from: http://osl.cs.illinois.edu/media/papers/karmani-2011-actors.pdf [retrieved: June, 2018]

[20] C. Hewitt, P. Bishop, and R. Steiger, "A universal modular Actor formalism for artificial intelligence," in 3rd International Joint Conference on Artificial Intelligence (IJCAI), pp. 235-245, 1973.

[21] Lightbend Inc, "Akka: Actors," 2016, [Online]. Available from: http://doc.akka.io/docs/akka/2.4.0/java/untyped-actors.html [retrieved: June, 2018]

[22] M. Lehmann and M. Werner, "Gut Wetter machen! Java, Play und Akka für meteorologische Anwendungen beim Deutschen Wetterdienst," in JavaSPEKTRUM 3/2016, 2016

[23] J. Armstrong, "Programming Erlang: Software for a Concurrent World (Pragmatic Programmers)," Pragmatic Bookshelf, 2013.

[24] Lightbend Inc, "Akka: Supervision and Monitoring," 2018, [Online]. Available from: https://doc.akka.io/docs/akka /2.5/general/supervision.html [retrieved: June, 2018]

[25] J. Barklund and R. Virding, "The Erlang 4.7.3 Reference Manual," p. 133, 1999.

[26] K. Lundin, "Inside the Erlang VM," Ericsson AB, 2008, [Online]. Available from: http://www.erlang.se/euc/08/euc _smp.pdf [retrieved: June, 2018]

[27] V. Jovanovic and P. Haller, "The Scala Actors Migration Guide," EPFL, [Online]. Available from: https://docs.scala-lang.org/overviews/core/actors-migration-guide.html [retrieved: June, 2018]

[28] D. Wyatt, "AKKA Concurrency," Artima Inc, p. 72, 2013.

[29] D. Lea, "ForkJoin updates," 2012, [Online]. Available from: http://cs.oswego.edu/pipermail/concurrency-interest/2012-January/008987.html [retrieved: June, 2018]

[30] M. Botincan and D. Runje, "Lock-Free Stack and Queue. Java vs .NET," 29th International Conference on Information Technology Interfaces, Cavtat, pp. 741-746, 2007

[31] Lightbend Inc, "Akka: Dispatchers," 2016, [Online]. Available from: https://doc.akka.io/docs/akka/snapshot /dispatchers.html?language=scala [retrieved: June, 2018]

[32] The Apache Software Foundation, "Apache Commons Collections," 2014, [Online]. Available from: https://commons.apache.org/proper/commons-collections/ [retrieved: June, 2018]

[33] N. Wakart, "JCTools," 2015, [Online]. Available from: https://github.com/JCTools/JCTools [retrieved: June, 2018]

[34] C. Ullenboom, "Java ist auch eine Insel: Das umfassende Handbuch," Kapitel 14.3.5, Galileo Computing, 2010, [Online]. Available from: http://openbook.rheinwerk-verlag.de/javainsel9/ [retrieved: June, 2018]

[35] D. A. Bauer, "Actor4j: DefaultActorThread," 2017, [Online]. Available from: https://github.com/relvaner/actor4j-core/blob/master/src/main/java/actor4j/core/DefaultActorThre ad.java [retrieved: June, 2018]

[36] A. Temerev, "Skynet 1M concurrency microbenchmark," 2016, [Online]. Available from: https://github.com/atemerev /skynet [retrieved: June, 2018]

[37] D. Charousset, R. Hiesgen, and T. C. Schmidt, "Revisiting actor programming in C++," in Computer Languages, Systems & Structures 45, pp. 105-131, 2016, [Online]. Available from: https://actor-framework.org/pdf/chs-rapc-16.pdf [retrieved: June, 2018]

[38] Lightbend Inc, "Akka: TellThroughputPerformanceSpec .scala", 2014, [Online]. Available from: https://github.com/akka/akka/blob/release-2.3/akka-actor-tests/src/test/scala/akka/performance/microbench/TellThrough putPerformanceSpec.scala [retrieved: June, 2018]

[39] R. Pressler, "Go and Quasar: A Comparison of Style and Performance," in DZone, 2016, [Online]. Available from: https://dzone.com/articles/go-and-quasar-a-comparison-of-style-and-performanc [retrievd: June, 2018].

[40] M. Wooldrige, "An Inroduction to MultiAgent Systems," John Wiley & Sons Ltd, p. 22, 2009.

[41] Lightbend Inc, "Akka: Message Delivery Reliability. Discussion: Message Ordering," 2015, [Online]. Available from: http://doc.akka.io/docs/akka/2.4.1/general/message-delivery-reliability.html# message-ordering [retrieved: June, 2018]

Stochastic Modeling for Self-evolving Botnets in Infection Control Environments

Koki Hongyo*, Tomotaka Kimura†, Takanori Kudo‡, Yoshiaki Inoue§, and Kouji Hirata*
* Faculty of Engineering, Kansai University, Osaka 564-8680, Japan, Email: {k896955, hirata}@kansai-u.ac.jp
† Faculty of Science and Engineering, Doshisha University, Kyoto 610-0321, Japan, Email: tomkimur@mail.doshisha.ac.jp
‡ Faculty of Science and Engineering, Setsunan University, Osaka 572-8508, Japan, Email: t-kudo@ele.setsunan.ac.jp
§ Graduate School of Engineering, Osaka University, Osaka 565-0871, Japan, Email: yoshiaki@comm.eng.osaka-u.ac.jp

***Abstract*—The concept of self-evolving botnets, where computing resources of infected hosts are exploited to discover unknown vulnerabilities and the botnets evolve autonomously, has been introduced and their threats have been shown in the literature. In order to protect networks from the self-evolving botnets, this paper provides an epidemic model taking into account the infection routes in infection control environments to which countermeasures against the self-evolving botnets are applied. We show the behaviors of the epidemic model through simulation experiments.**

Keywords–Botnet; machine learning; epidemic model; continuous-time Markov chain.

I. INTRODUCTION

Recently, machine learning techniques have been widely used and achieved significant results in various research areas. In addition, some researchers have proposed vulnerability discovery methods that discover bugs and vulnerabilities with machine learning techniques [5][6]. Although the main purpose of these methods is to protect software, they can be used for discovering unknown security holes and exploited for illegal attacks by malicious attackers. To perform illegal attacks, malicious attackers often control botnets, which consist of many infected hosts named zombie computers. The malicious attackers can discover unknown vulnerabilities with distributed machine learning using the computing resources of the zombie computers.

Based on these facts, in [4], Kudo et al. have introduced a new concept named self-evolving botnets. Self-evolving botnets discover vulnerabilities by performing distributed machine learning with computing resources of zombie computers and evolve autonomously based on the vulnerabilities. Accordingly, they infect other hosts and make themselves bigger. The authors have shown that the infectivity of self-evolving botnets is very high, compared with conventional botnets. In response, in [2], Hongyo et al. have proposed some epidemic models that consider countermeasures against self-evolving botnets and shown their effectiveness.

In this paper, we propose an epidemic model for self-evolving botnets taking into account the infection routes of the botnets in infection control environments to which some countermeasure methods are applied. Because the infectivity of the botnets often depends on infection routes, the proposed epidemic model expresses the infection routes by overlay networks that are constructed according to relationships among hosts. The proposed epidemic model makes continuous-time Markov chains with the overlay networks and show the behavior of the self-evolving botnets in infection control environments. The rest of this paper is organized as follows. Section II explains our proposed epidemic model. We then evaluate it in Section III.

II. EPIDEMIC MODEL FOR SELF-EVOLVING BOTNETS

We use an Susceptible-Infected-Recovered-Susceptible (SIRS) model to represent the state of each host in a network. In the SIRS model, "S" means that the host has vulnerabilities, "I" means that the host is infected, and "R" means that the host has no known vulnerabilities. Each host belongs to one of the states. We assume that hosts in the state R can get infected by unknown vulnerabilities which are discovered by a self-evolving botnet. Hosts in the state S move to the state I when they get infected by attacks of a botnet. Then, the hosts are embedded in the botnet. Hosts in the state S and the state I move to the state R when known vulnerabilities and the botnet malware, respectively, are removed from the hosts by suitable means, such as OS updates and anti-virus software. Note that we assume that all vulnerabilities are simultaneously removed in these cases. When the botnet discovers a new vulnerability, all hosts in the state R move to the state S because the botnet can infect the hosts by using the discovered vulnerability.

The proposed epidemic model considers relationships among hosts in the above SIRS model because infection routes of the self-evolving botnets depend on the relationships, e.g., their friendships, frequently accessed web sites, and physical network environments. To express the relationships, we use an overlay network consisting of hosts. Hosts in state I can infect only adjacent susceptible hosts on the overlay network. Under this assumption, the proposed epidemic model formulates the infection process of the self-evolving botnet as a continuous-time Markov chain, where the occurrence of each event a)-d) described below in the SIRS model follows a Poisson process.

(a) A new vulnerability is discovered by the self-evolving botnet according to a Poisson process with the discovery rate $\eta(v+1)$, where v denotes the number of infected hosts and η denotes the discovery rate of a new vulnerability by each infected host. The discovery rate is proportional to the number of infected hosts, which means that the self-evolving botnet performs distributed machine learning with the computing resources of the infected hosts. When this event occurs, all the hosts in the state R moves to the state S.

(b) Each host in the state S removes its own vulnerabilities according to a Poisson process with the recovery rate δ_S, and then moves to the state R.

(c) Each host in the state I infects an adjacent host in the state S on the overlay network according to a Poisson process with the infection rate α. In this case, the adjacent host moves to the state I.

(d) Each host in the state I removes the botnet malware according to a Poisson process with the removal rate δ_{I}, and then moves to the state R.

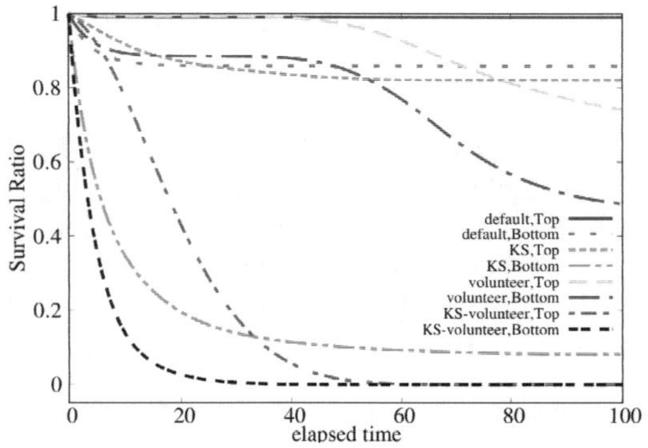

Figure 1. Botnet survival ratio.

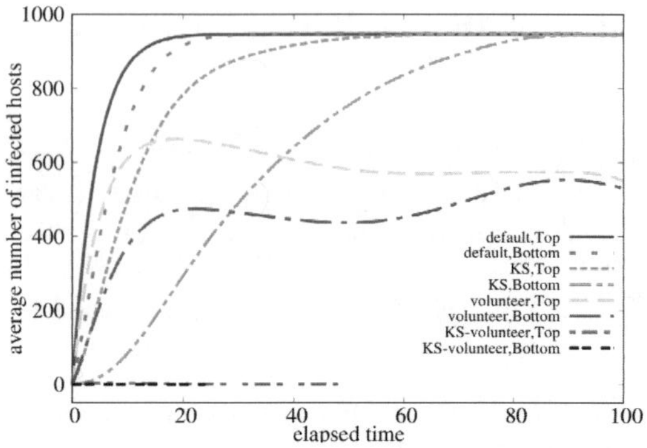

Figure 2. Average number of infected hosts.

We then consider countermeasures against the self-evolving botnet. As the countermeasures, we adopt a Kill-Signal (KS) model and a volunteer model. The KS model proposed in [3] uses a warning signal called Kill-Signal having information on known vulnerabilities. In the KS model, the hosts in the state R send a Kill-Signal to susceptible hosts. The hosts receiving the Kill-Signal can know their vulnerabilities due to the Kill-Signal and repair them. The volunteer model aims to discover and repair unknown vulnerabilities with computing resources of volunteer hosts before the self-evolving botnet discover the vulnerabilities, so that it suppresses the evolution of the self-evolving botnet. In this paper, for simplicity, we assume that all uninfected hosts (i.e., hosts in the states S or R) belong to a volunteer group and a network administrator can use their computing resources to discover vulnerabilities. The information on discovered vulnerabilities are shared by all uninfected hosts. These models add or replace the events in the Markov chain as follows.

(e) Each host in the state R sends a Kill-Signal to an adjacent susceptible host on the overlay network according to a Poisson process with the sending rate β_S. In this case, the adjacent host moves to the state R.

(f) A new vulnerability is discovered by the volunteer group according to a Poisson process. Accordingly, the infectivity of the self-evolving botnet is weakened. To represent this behavior, the volunteer model replaces the discovery rate of the self-evolving botnet described in event (a) with $\eta(v+1)/(\sigma(N-v)+1)$, where σ denotes the vulnerability discovery rate of a volunteer host.

III. EVALUATION

To examine the behavior of the proposed epidemic model, we conduct simulation experiments. We assume that there are $N = 1,000$ hosts in a network and the overlay network is constructed based on the Barabasi-Albert model [1], where the average degree of hosts is 20. One host is infected and all the other hosts are in the susceptible state at time $t = 0$. We refer to the infected host at time $t = 0$ as the initial infected host. The parameters are set to be $\eta = 0.05$, $\delta_S = \beta_S = 0.1$, $\delta_I = 0.1$, $\alpha = 0.1$, and $\sigma = 0.3$.

Figure 1 shows the botnet survival ratio as a function of the elapsed time. The botnet survival ratio means the ratio of the number of samples in which one or more infected hosts still exist at time t to the total number of samples. In this figure, "Top" (resp. "Bottom") indicates the result in the case where a host with the maximum (resp. minimum) closeness centrality is selected as the initial infected host. Furthermore, "default" represents the result of the self-evolving botnets without countermeasures, "KS" represents the result of the KS model, "volunteer" represents the result of the volunteer model, and "KS-volunteer" represents the result of the mixed model of the KS and volunteer models. As we can see from this figure, the botnet survival ratio is large when selecting a host with the maximum closeness centrality as the initial infected host. We also observe that the botnet survival ratio of "default" is very high. "KS" decreases the botnet survival ratio at early stage, but does not decrease with the time elapsed. On the other hand, "volunteer" first does not decrease the botnet survival ratio, but gradually decreases it. This result implies that the volunteer model can weaken the capability of the self-evolving botnet even though the self-evolving botnet spreads. Furthermore, "KS-volunteer" eliminates the self-evolving botnet early in all samples.

Figure 2 shows the average number of infected hosts of samples in which there exist infected hosts at time t as a function of the elapsed time t. As shown in this figure, the average numbers of infected hosts of "default" and "KS" increase and converge to a high value, regardless of the closeness centrality of the initial infected hosts. On the other hand, "volunteer" can reduce the the average number of infected hosts constantly. Furthermore, "KS-volunteer" can eliminate completely the self-evolving botnet.

REFERENCES

[1] A. Barabasi and R. Albert, "Emergence of scaling in random networks," *Science*, vol. 286, pp.509–512, 1999.

[2] K. Hongyo et al., "Modeling of countermeasure against self-evolving botnets," in *Proc. ICCE-TW 2017*, Taipei, Taiwan, Jun. 2017, pp. 1–2.

[3] J. O. Kephart and S. R. White, "Measuring and modeling computer virus prevalence," in *Proc. the 1993 IEEE Computer Society Symposium on Research in Security and Privacy*, Oakland, CA, May. 1993.

[4] T. Kudo et al., "Behavior analysis of self-evolving botnets," in *Proc. CITS 2016*, Kunming, China, Jul. 2016.

[5] R. Scandariato, J. Walden, A. Hovsepyan, and W. Joosen, "Predicting vulnerable software components via text mining," *IEEE Transactions on Software Engineering*, vol. 40, no. 10, pp. 993–1006, 2014.

[6] F. Yamaguchi, F. Lindner, and K. Rieck, "Vulnerability extrapolation: assisted discovery of vulnerabilities using machine learning," in *Proc. USENIX conference on Offensive Technologies*, San Francisco, CA, Aug. 2011.

Web Programming, Cloud Services and Quality of Experience (QoE) for Mobile Computing

Ustijana Rechkoska-Shikoska
University for Information Science & Technology UIST "St. Paul the Apostle"
Faculty for Computer Science and Engineering CSE
Ohrid, Republic of Macedonia
e-mail: ustijana.r.shikoska@uist.edu.mk

***Abstract*— A multi-platform application and its evaluation is presented in this work. It refers to the business process management software that allows organizations, institutions and companies, to use a system of integrated applications to manage the business and automate many back office functions related to technologies, services and human resources. The app is used for administration data, reviewing orders, creating invoices and adding new employees' records. The app is also implemented in Azure, which is used as a platform for the cloud. A Web API and an Android application would significantly increase the Quality of Experience (QoE) of numerous mobile users, which can be implemented using the cloud services. It facilitates user's work in terms of memory usage, hardware load, and responsiveness. QoE evaluation is done, as well. We managed to, not just create a reliable app, but also we made sure that it can expand and reach every user. Our approach improves the QoE, providing the users all necessary resources and performances, referring to Security, Easy to use concept, Time saving, and QR Code.**

Keywords- Web App development; Cloud services; QoE; Web application; Mobile computing

I. Introduction

Information and Communications Technology (ICT) leads the world of modern technologies, more and more platforms come up every day, so software developers have serious challenges choosing the right tools in order to complete their tasks. This paper gives the feedback on some tools usage and helps in further understanding the main concepts in creating a multi-platform application, giving evaluation sense as well.

The concepts of maintaining a database using SQL are presented in [14]. The procedures can help a developer in creating scalable databases and they are explained here as well. The cloud implementation is done, so the multi-platform applications can easily communicate in-between. Also, functions and procedures from [15] and [16] are implemented.

Section 2 of the paper presents the Related work in the area, Section 3 gives a general overview of an app. In the first subsection, we talk about SQL databases, ER diagram explaining the details. In addition, we talk about some of the developed functions and how they can help developers towards the maintaining the data constraints. In addition, we give a little demonstration of the power of stored procedure, and a particular procedure. Moreover, the application is deployed on the cloud. In the second subsection, a presentation of the user interface of the application and some of the core features are introduced. Sections 4 and 5 speak about testing and results, as well as QoE. Sections 6 and 7 give the reader conclusions and future work ideas.

II. Related Work

In [1], precise details on the importance of databases creation and implementation are presented. Authors give a comparison on several database management systems and their differences, which can contribute in choosing the right one. On the other hand, in [2] a web based data-driven application, and all its concepts, which give a great representation how today's applications work, is presented. The applications in [2] are developed in Java, and the concepts can be used almost in every C style language.

Authors in [4], [5] present a great result for building data driven Web App. In [3], authors talk about the basics of SQL, [5] gives an advanced look into the language and go through some of the specific individual operations that each of the most known database management systems offer. In [6], [11], [12] great examples on both developing Windows and Web applications, using the C# language are given. It takes one of the concepts and breaks it apart thoroughly, from the bottom of the Class Library to converging it with other technologies, which gives a great concept on making easy and useful steps on creating excellent applications. The authors in [7][8] give the background of the language itself, representing the Common Language Runtime (CLR), giving concise explanation how it is transformed to byte-code and more.

In [9], an introductory overview of Cloud computing, several distinctions of different Cloud platforms such as Google Web Service, Amazon web service and Windows Azure, Cloud infrastructure are presented. The authors present Mobile Cloud, a review into services and applications. The authors in [10] give an in-depth analysis into cloud design patterns, the security flaws of each setup, the stability of architecture.

Referring the related work mentioned, the App presented in this work improves the security, easy to use, time saving concepts, and QR Code.

III. Developing Windows Application

Windows applications, as well as mobile applications, are forms of application program, and are designed to perform specific tasks directly for the user or, in some cases, for another application program. Web development implementation, as a process of building the web according to its design, enhances web specification, its implementation process, and presentation.

A. App's architecture

Application architecture is built in such a way to provide efficient application and implementation. The Application itself is consisted of Web API, Web App, Employee panel, Admin Panel, connected to the Database, also connected to the PCs, Mobiles, iPads etc.

The decision to use cloud architecture is made for the simple reason of scalability and accessibility - the Web Application, its' APIs, and Database, resides in the cloud. With this decision we have managed to cover all devices on the market and in the future target each one with a separate native application. The application itself is a dot.net core application which, by the .net core standards, can be developed on any machine. This is also a positive outcome, meaning that the application is optimized to use only the APIs that it needs, and also with additional requirement easily adding new ones. Whit this, concepts of scalability and meeting clients' needs are satisfied. Another feature that can come out with the cloud is using social networks, also we can optimize the virtual machines' performance by our needs, automatic jobs, have a multi-tenant, cloud-based directory, and identity management service (such as Azure Active Directory).

The database on the Cloud has its own server, instead of being an in app database, and a link to it resides in the app, which is a web application. There is a deployment of both the application and database as well. The database has its own server, instead of being an in app database, and a link to it resides in the app, which is a web application. There is an admin panel within the application, the implementation of employee panel and several other features will be included to improve the functionality. The application can be accessed from both mobile devices and PCs or laptops via Web browsers of any choice. A Web API and an Android App would significantly increase the Quality of experience of numerous mobile users, which can be implemented using the cloud services.

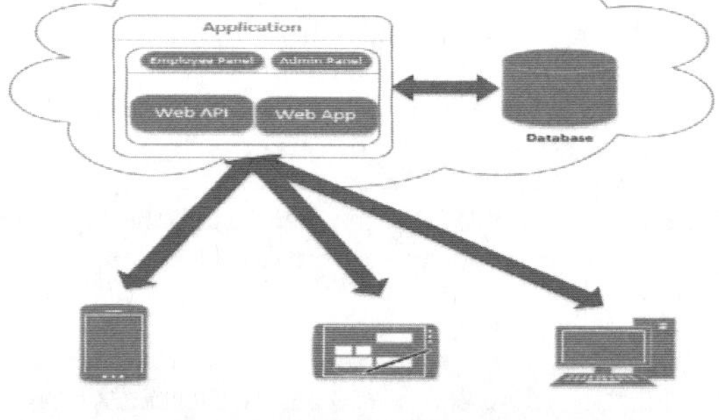

Figure 1. Application architecture

Figure 1 presents the application architecture.

B. App's Database and SQL

Each table in the database has its unique primary key and the specialized data in order to represent one entity. Some of the tables have composite keys, of two or more fields, with which we prevent concurrent data appearing in the database. In addition, there are unique keys on some of the table to strengthen the previous claim. The tables have constraints that are based on custom-made functions to help prevent inaccurate information being entered into the tables.

C. Functions Developed

Functions here serve as check constraints helpers, others as helpers to stored procedures so that large code will not be repeated, and some are used into views. One of the function checks the country calling code and the length of the phone number entered in the phone field of the Employee, Client and Supplier table. With this, we are preventing to have entries of any other country except chosen ones.

The function presented within next code lines, takes three parameters date, number of months that we want to add and the number of days that we want to add. Then, the difference between the months from zero until today are calculated, zero being 01.01.1900, and a number of month is added. After that, we add the number of day. The main key here is because the DATEDIFF function returns an integer we cannot use it as a standalone function because we a date type not an integer. That's why we have to add the DATEADD function.

```
CREATE FUNCTION [dbo].[MonthYear]
(
        @date date,
        @monthPlus int,
        @dayPlus int
)
RETURNS date
AS
BEGIN
        DECLARE @MonthYear date

        SET @MonthYear = (DATEADD(MONTH,
DATEDIFF(MONTH, 0, @date)+@monthPlus, @dayPlus))

        RETURN @MonthYear
END
```

Figure 2. Create Function

D. Stored procedure

There are many stored procedures for the database and they all serve for a different purpose. For instance, there are procedures for creating invoices both purchase invoices and regular, other server for updating the stock and so on. The procedure presented in the code snippet first checks if the date is later than the 20th of the current month and if the most recent generated pay is at least one month old. If that is true, the procedure calculates the sum of the total of working hours and inserts it into the pay table. Finally, it returns the generated pay. If it is false, it returns the most recent pay.

```
PROCEDURE [dbo].[CreatePay]
        @employeeID int
AS
BEGIN
        SET NOCOUNT ON;
        DECLARE @grossTotal money;
        IF(GETDATE() > dbo.MonthYear(GETDATE(),0,19) AND (SELECT TOP 1 dbo.MonthYear(Date,1,0)
        FROM Pay WHERE EmployeeID = @employeeID ORDER BY Date DESC) = dbo.MonthYear(GETDATE(),0,0))
        BEGIN
        SET @grossTotal = (SELECT SUM(Total) AS Total FROM LogEmployeeHoursTotal WHERE EmployeeID = @employeeID AND Date BETWEEN dbo.MonthYear(GETDATE(),-1,19) AND dbo.MonthYear(GETDATE(),0,19));
                INSERT INTO Pay(EmployeeID, Date, GrossPay)
                VALUES (@employeeID,GETDATE(),@grossTotal);
        END
        SELECT * FROM PayView WHERE EmployeeID = @employeeID AND Printed = 0;
END
```

Figure 3. Procedure listing

The developed application is a small enterprise resource planning software. It has a login screen, which every admin has its own username and password to log in, also log entry page where each employee checks in when comes or leaves the working place. In addition, with the app being implemented on the cloud, instead of a typical login you can also do an external one. This provides us with the opportunity to use social networking services, like Facebook, Google, or Twitter, to login or register into the app.

When the user logs in a tree menu, a window on the left appears in order the user can choose in which segment he/she wants to work in, and the dynamic content appears on the right. The menu is scrollable if it is expanded and out of screen but the dynamic con-tent stays fixed. If user goes deeper into the tree menu, he/she would get a specific operation for each node.

Here the user can see that there are textboxes where the required data can be written. The little three icons in the bottom represent the operations that users can perform, save, delete and edit previously generated pay. When the user clicks the generate pay button a popup appears showing the latest payment generated and there it can be either printed or updated.

The application has some good features like generating monthly wages automatically every 20th of the following month.

It shows all the required info for each sub-section (e.g., Employees name, address, when they took their last payment, how much was it, client specific invoices, etc.).

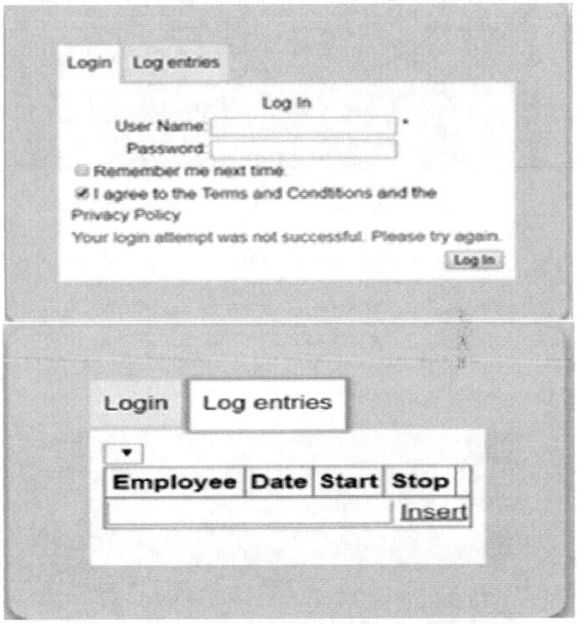

Figure 4. Login and Employee log screens

As it can be noticed in Figure 4, this is an user friendly App. In Figure 5, an example for the employee node is shown:

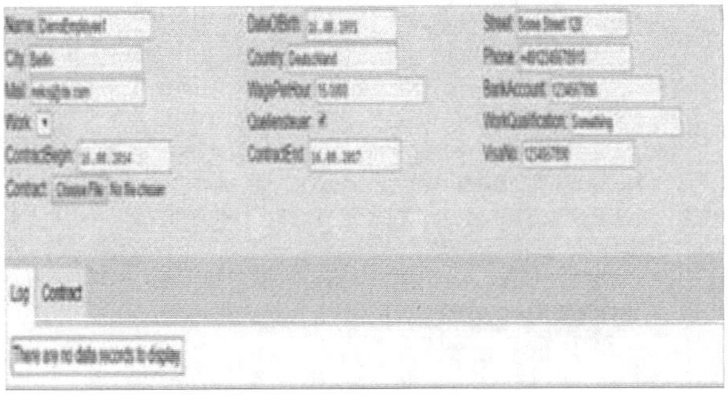

Figure 5. Employee node

It updates stocks frequently, keeps track of every out-going or incoming invoices, and all of that can be done with just a simple push of a button.

IV. TESTING AND RESULTS

Several tests were performed for the application. One scenario is about performing a test in order to follow the hardware load when the application runs.

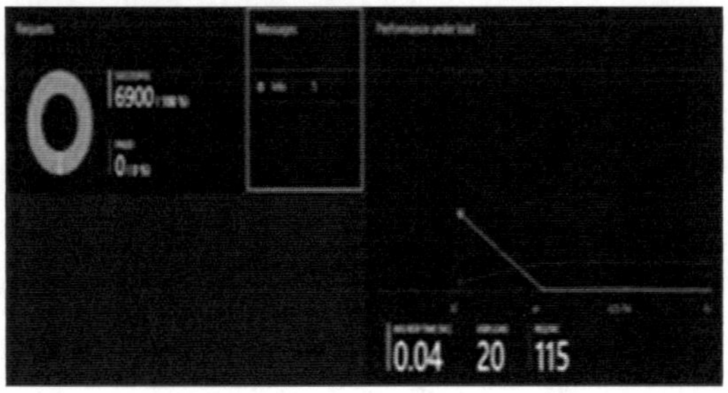

Figure 6. Testing results for performance of the application

As in Figure 6, and Figure 7 respectively, the application did astonishingly well with a 100% success. Moreover, it can be noticed that the response time is fast, meaning fast delivery of service. In addition, in the next figure it can be seen that the application does not really take much CPU time and memory while running.

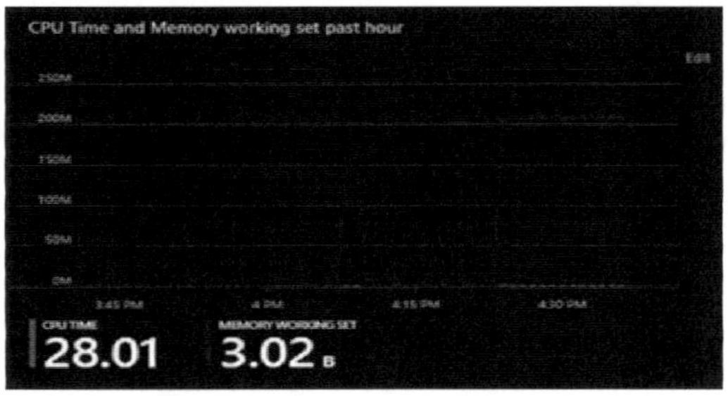

Figure 7. CPU load and Memory usage test for the app

Figure 8 is presenting the Pen testing process.

The Web Application's security was put to the test through several penetration testing tools from the Kali OS, such as Vega, OWASP ZAP, sqlmap and w3af.

There are some minor issues like low priority security, but as far as SQL injection and XSS security are concerned, the app outdone its self.

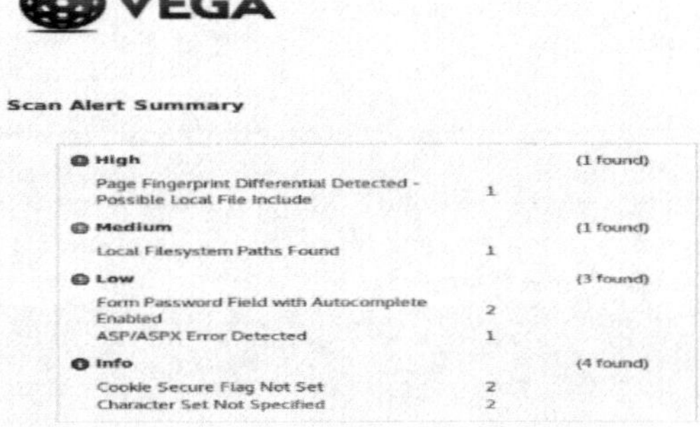

(a)

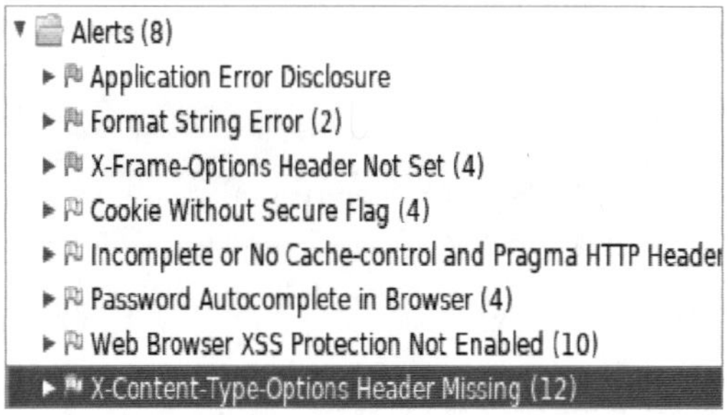

(b)

Figure 8 (a) Pen testing process – testing results from Vega (b) Pen testing process – testing tool results exposing the vulnerabilities

While Vega and OWASP ZAP found some minor security concerns, which can be easily fixed, sqlmap and w3af, which are more SQL Injection prone, found no problems regarding the previously mentioned argument.

V. QUALITY OF EXPERIENCE FOR MOBILE COMPUTING

Quality of experience (QoE) measures the difference between the user expectation and what the user received. This is beneficial to estimate the users' perception of the quality of the service and it depends users' satisfaction [12]. It represents how a service is accepted by the end-users. Using the QoE is beneficial to estimate the perception of the user about the quality of a particular service and it depends on the customer's satisfaction in terms of usability, accessibility, retaining ability and integrity of using specific service [13]. The results presented in the following chart were obtained according to the Quality of Experience evaluation performed on a group of representatives consisted of col-leagues from both Computer Science and Engineering, and Communications Net-work and Security Faculty, and one group consisted of professionals working in finances departments. They were given to run the application and a survey to rate the application's UI design, responsiveness, and user-friendly aspect of the app. The survey is based on the Mean opinion score (MOS). The MOS is calculated as the arithmetic mean over single ratings performed by human subjects for a given stimulus in a subjective quality evaluation test. Thus in (1):

$$MOS = \frac{\sum_{n=0}^{N} R_n}{N} \tag{1}$$

R is the individual ratings for a given stimulus by N subjects. The results for each of the questioners are presented in Figure 9.

Referring our scenarios, 100 subjects were questioned, and the application were tested referring the timing of approximately ten minutes.

With the previous tests done, the users felt more secure handling the application, as almost 37% replied excellent to the survey question. Referring the QR code 35.5% were shown as excellent. The time saving factor was mixed and needs further assessment. The ease to use concept didn't do so poor, with almost 30% as excellent and 28.4 as very good, improvements would surely be beneficial here.

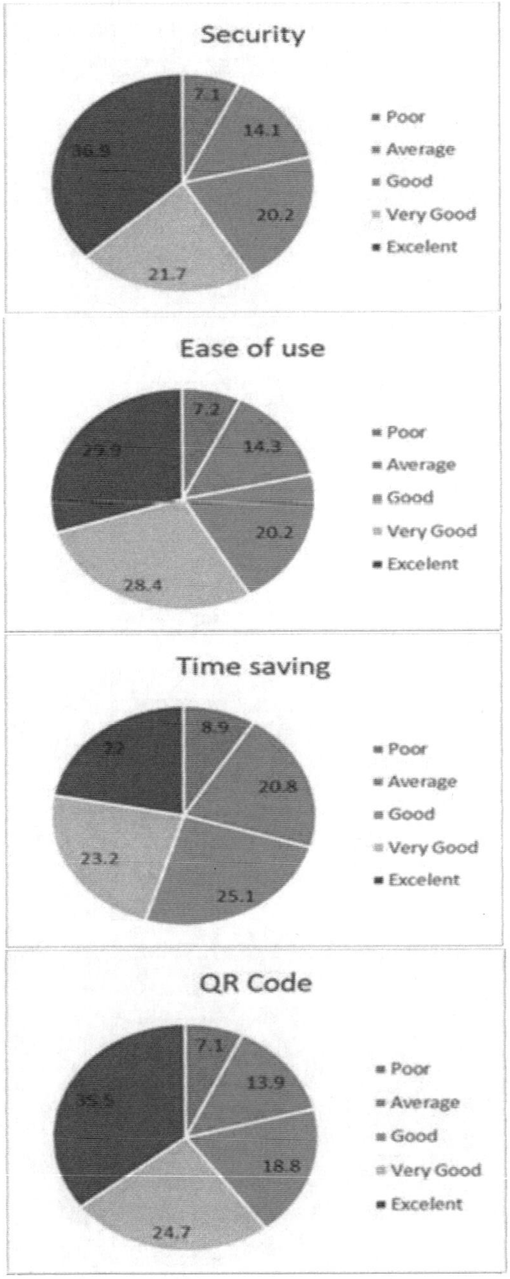

Figure 9. Survey results for the App

Easy to use: 29,9% replied as excellent, 28,4% as very good, 20,2% as good, 14,3% as average.

When it is up to time saving, 22% replied as excellent, 23,2% as very good, 25,1% as good and 20,8% as average.

For the Security concept, 36,9% replied as excellent, 21,7% as very good, 20,2% as good, 14.1% as average, which is satisfactory, since the security concept is demanded, especially speaking about web apps and cloud services, concerning database security, attacks and intrusions into the system.

About the survey results referring the QR Code, 35,5% considered as excellent, 24,7% as very good, 18,8% as good, 13,9% as average.

As it is presented in the charts, the users' satisfaction is positive. In terms of UI design and security (after presenting the test) the majority users gave an excellent review, while other thinks there can be improvements.

As for the responsiveness and ease of use the reviews were mixed, and therefore further improvement will be done.

The QoE and survey analyses show that satisfactory results are presented, of course there is always place for improvement, which is considered as future work.

VI. Conclusion and Future Work

As ICT technology goes forward, the App developing grows ever so rapidly, the developers need to adapt as well. In this work, we gave a glimpse of the tools that can help apps grow forward, and even with a simple change to readjust to the current technologies, we evaluate, as well, the App in order to show the advantages and send some recommendations to future developers. Moreover, the toolset can be expanded further thanks to the implementation of the Cloud Service. Some of the techniques and concepts that are presented can even increase the apps responsiveness, as well as the Quality of Experience that the users have. Automated some of the day-to-day tasks and made financial life easier. In a few words we managed to make sure that it can expand and reach every user.

For the future work, we will extend our work using several platforms, each one having their own app, and strengthen the current features furthermore. We will modify the web application using the Model-View-Controller pattern and the Entity Framework. A web API would greatly simplify the distribution of data on hand held devices more easily using the RESTful APIs. An Android application could to generate QR codes for employee log entries to substitute the current feature on the web app, even replace old systems and integrate IoT technologies. Furthermore, since the application will contain sensitive user data, security precautions that would be improved. In spite of that, further research in hybrid cloud will be performed, with having one private cloud and one public communicating with each other to prevent data loss, as well as further studies on how to improve current database security and web API security.

References

[1] Silberschatz, A., Korth, H and Sudarshan, S.: Database System Concepts. 6th edn. McGraw-Hill Education, 2010.

[2] Ramakrishnan, R. and Gehrke, J.: Database Management Systems. 3rd edn. McGraw-Hill Edu-cation, 2002.

[3] Elmasri, R. and Navathe, S.: Fundamentals of Database Systems. 7th edn. Pearson, 2015.

[4] Beaulieu, A.: Learning SQL: Master SQL Fundamentals. 2nd edn. O'Reilly Media, 2009.

[5] Molinaro, A.: SQL Cookbook: Query Solutions and Techniques for Database Developers. 1st edn. O'Reilly Media, 2005.

[6] Troelsen, A. and Japikse, P.: C# 6.0 and the .NET 4.6 Framework. 7th edn. Apress, 2015.

[7] Skeet, J.: C# in Depth. 3rd edn. Manning Publications, 2013.

[8] Albahari, J. and Albahari, B.: C# 6.0 in a Nutshell: The Definitive Reference. 6th edn. O'Reilly Media, 2015.

[9] Sosinsky, B.: Cloud Computing Bible. 1st edn. Wiley, 2011.

[10] Erl, T., Cope, R. and Naserpour, A.: Cloud Computing Design Patterns. 1st edn. Prentice Hall, 2011.

[11] Moon, Y.: Enterprise Resource Planning (ERP): a review of the literature. Mechanical and Aerospace Engineering, pp. 4., 2007.

[12] Fosser, E., Leister, O., Moe, C. and Newman, M.: Organisations and Vanilla Software: What Do We Know About ERP Systems and Competitive Advantage?. ECIS 2008 Proceedings. 132., 2008.

[13] W. Wu, et.al., "Quality of Experience in Distributed Interactive Multimedia Environments: Toward a Theoretical Framework," MM '09 Proceedings of the 17th ACM international conference on Multimedia, October, 2009, pp. 481-490, DOI: 10.1145/1631272.1631338.

[14] MySQL Official Site (n.d.) Retrieved from http://www.mysql.com/, Retrieved: June 7, 2018.

[15] JSON Official Site (n.d.) Retrieved from http://json.org/, Retrieved: June, 2018.

[16] PhP Official Site (n.d.) Retrieved from http://www.php.net/, Retrieved: June, 2018.